LOCAL OWNERSHIP,
GLOBAL CHANGE

LOCAL OWNERSHIP, GLOBAL CHANGE

WILL CIVIL SOCIETY SAVE THE WORLD?

───────◆───────

Edited by

Roland Hoksbergen

&

Lowell Ewert

World Vision

Printed in the United States of America.

11 10 09 08 07 06 05 04 03 02   5 4 3 2 1

MARC books are published by World Vision International, 800 West Chestnut Avenue, Monrovia, California 91016–3198, U.S.A.

Library of Congress Cataloging-in-Publication Data
ISBN 1–887983–37–6

All Scripture quotations, unless otherwise indicated, are from the New Revised Standard Version of the Bible, copyright © 1989 by the Division of Christian Education of the National Council of the Churches of Christ in the USA. Used by permission. All rights reserved.

Every effort has been made to ensure that Internet references in this book are accurate and up to date. With the rapid changes that occur in the World Wide Web, pages or other resources frequently are changed, moved, or removed, and some content modified or reorganized. The publisher, therefore, has chosen to give only general references to organisations' websites and recommends that readers use one of the numerous search engines available on the Internet to locate the specific information they seek.

Editor in Chief: Edna Valdez. Senior editor: Rebecca Russell. Copyediting and typesetting: Joan Weber Laflamme/jml ediset. Cover design: Susie Collingsood/Tobias Marketing.

 This book is printed on acid-free recycled paper.

CONTENTS

PART 3
IMPACT, INFLUENCE, AND POTENTIAL

CONTRIBUTORS

Dr. Kathleen Braden is the Associate Vice President/Dean of Student Life and a Professor of Geography at Seattle Pacific University. She is also an Affiliate Professor of Geography at the University of Washington.

Abu Brima is a Sierra Leonean currently working towards a Masters in Education with an emphasis in development at Pacific Western University in the United States. He has been active in the Sierra Leone peace process and is the National Coordinating Secretary of the National Non-Governmental Organisations Forum.

David Bronkema, currently finishing up his doctorate in anthropology, is Program Coordinator for the Latin America and Caribbean Region for the American Friends Service Committee.

Heather Eggen is a recent graduate of Seattle Pacific University, where she was an English and philosophy major, and a University Scholar.

Dr. Samuel Escobar, a native of Peru, is the Thornley B. Wood Professor of missiology and Hispanic studies at Eastern Baptist Theological Seminary and Adjunct Professor at Eastern University in Pennsylvania. He also teaches at the Seminary of the Evangelical Baptist Union of Spain in Madrid. He is President emeritus of the Latin American Theological Fraternity, has held a number of positions in the International Fellowship of Evangelical Students (IFES), and is President of the United Bible Societies.

Lowell Ewert, J.D., is the Director of the Peace and Conflict Studies Program and the Institute for Peace and Conflict Studies at Conrad Grebel College. He worked with both the Mennonite Central Committee and Mercy Corps International, initiated several civil society projects and wrote one ofthe first Rapid Assessment surveys for civil society ever prepared by an NGO.

Dr. Kenneth Martens Friesen is Professor of political science at Fresno Pacific University. He previously worked with the Mennonite Central Committee as Country Co-representative in Vietnam and as Acting Director/Legislative Associate for International Affairs in Washington, D.C.

Dr. Denis Goulet is O'Neill Professor in Education for Justice at the University of Notre Dame. He holds concurrent appointments in the Department of Economics, the Helen Kellogg Institute for International Studies, and the Joan B. Kroc Institute for International Peace Studies. He has published eleven books and over 150 articles and monographs.

Wyva Hasselblad, M.S., is a Country Consultant in Senegal for the Christian Reformed World Relief Committee in the areas of health, justice, literacy, and community development. She previously worked for the World Health Organization throughout Africa, Asia, and Europe.

Dr. Roland Hoksbergen is Professor of Economics and Director of the Third World Studies Program at Calvin College. He previously was the Program Director for the Christian Reformed World Relief Committee in Nicaragua and the Director of the Latin American Studies Program of the Council for Christian Colleges and Universities.

Dr. Terrence L. Jantzi is Assistant Professor in the Department of Sociology and Social Work at Eastern Mennonite University. He previously worked for the Mennonite Central Committee in Nicaragua, Somalia, Lesotho, and Bolivia.

Dr. Vernon E. Jantzi is the Director of the Graduate Program in Conflict Transformation, a Professor of Sociology, and the Director of the Orie Miller Global Village Center at Eastern Mennonite University.

Robert Jawara is a Team Leader with Christian Extension Services (CES) of Sierra Leone. He has worked with CES in community development since 1985 and has pursued development studies in Sierra Leone, England, and Cameroon.

Dr. Kabiru Kinyanjui is the Senior Programme Specialist for the International Development Research Centre (IDRC) in Kenya. He previously worked as a Senior Research Fellow and as Director of the Institute for Development Studies (IDS) for the University of Nairobi.

Sheku Dickson Koroma is a Development Training Officer in Sierra Leone with the African Development Education Network (ADEN). He has worked for Christian Extension Services (CES) in a variety of capacities, most recently as the Community Development Program Supervisor.

Paul Kortenhoven, M.A., has been a missionary and development trainer in Sierra Leone since 1980. He was an international NGO delegate to the United Nations conference on Sierra Leone in 1996, and participated in the Lome Peace Accord in 1997.

Dr. Paul J. Nelson is an Assistant Professor and Director of the International Development Program at the Graduate School of Public and International Affairs at the University of Pittsburgh. He has worked for Bread for the World, Church World Service, Lutheran World Relief, and serves as a consultant to nonprofit relief and development organisations.

Raymond C. Offenheiser Jr., M.A., is the President of Oxfam America. He has worked in grassroots organising the world over and has worked for or consulted with the Ford Foundation, Inter-American Foundation, Save the Children Federation, and the Grameen Bank.

Rebecca Samuel Shah, M.Sc., is a Research Analyst in the Human Development Network of the World Bank. She previously worked as a Consultant in Micro-Enterprise Development for Opportunity International, for the Oxford Center for Mission Studies, and for the Ethnic Health Unit of the British National Health Service.

Dr. James W. Skillen is the President at the Center for Public Justice in Washington, D.C. He has previously taught political science at Dordt College, Gordon College, and Messiah College.

Dr. Koenraad Verhagen is a Consultant on Microfinance and Co-operative Economy and works for the NGO "North-South Dialogue"; the International Co-operative Alliance and its Regional Office for East, Central and Southern Africa; and the Investment Company for International Development. He previously worked as a field worker, team leader and researcher in Africa, Asia, and Brazil, and as Secretary General of the alliance of Catholic Development Organizations.

Alan Whaites, M.Sc., is the Director of Policy and Advocacy for World Vision International, the world's largest privately funded NGO. He previously worked as a Manager in Policy and Research and Project Officer in Asia, both for World Vision UK.

Dr. Howard J. Wiarda is Professor of Political Science and the Leonard J. Horwitz Professor of Iberian and Latin American Studies at the University of Massachusetts/Amherst, and Senior Associate at the Center for Strategic and International Studies (CSIS) in Washington. He has published extensively on Latin America, international relations, development policy, Southern Europe, the Third World, Asia, Russia and Eastern Europe, and United States foreign policy.

Acknowledgements

For their sponsorship of this project, we would like to thank the Calvin Center for Christian Scholarship (CCCS) of Calvin College for providing funding, encouragement, and support at all stages. CCCS director James Bratt and the governing board offered important suggestions as the project got under way, and James was always helpful when we turned to him for advice and direction. Donna Romanowski and Amy Bergsma, project coordinators for CCCS, provided cheerful and always excellent planning and logistical support both in preparation for and in carrying out the November 2000 conference at Calvin College. Gary Lepsch deserves a word of thanks for his work on the graphics and layout of the promotional material.

A special word of thanks to senior Calvin College student Jennie Fennema-Hengeveld, now a graduate, who laboured for two months in the summer of 2001, at student wages, to check and revise notes and references, put the chapters in consistent format, and decipher scrawled marginal notes to type in edits. Any graduate school in economics or development will be fortunate to get her as a student.

It was embarrassing that the U.S. Consulate summarily denied visas to Sierra Leonean authors Abu Brima, Robert Jawara, and Sheku Dickson Koroma, after first requiring them to go to great expense and hardship to make their applications. These three participants in Sierra Leone's peace process could thus not join us for the conference, and their absence left a hole that was only partially filled by their participation via conference call in the presentation of their chapter. We are thankful for the technologies that allowed them to participate to that degree in the conference and that now allow them to speak with us through the pages of this book. We thank them for telling their story, and we pray with them for peaceful development in their nation.

Thanks as well to the one hundred or so people who attended the fall conference. Their comments, questions, and general enthusiasm for the topic contributed in important ways to the development of the ideas that made their way into this book.

Of course an edited book is the product of many authors. Hence, a collective thanks to the authors of this volume, who worked together to understand the significance of civil society for the development of God's people. The conversations have always been respectful and illuminating, modelling the sort of dialogue necessary for growing in understanding and learning to think straight.

As editors of this book, we would like to recognise the important roles others have played in forming our own ideas about civil society and in bringing this book to completion.

To begin, both of us were nurtured in our development backgrounds by NGOs that gave us opportunities to serve and to learn. Lowell would especially like to recognise the visionary leadership of Ells Culver and Neal Keny Guyer, both of Mercy Corps International. Ells gave Lowell the opportunity to explore the connection between human rights and development before it was popular to do so, and Neal enthusiastically supported a civil society approach to development before others fully understood its powerful appeal. Roland would like to acknowledge the relationship he has had with the Christian Reformed World Relief Committee going back to the mid-seventies, when he got his first taste of development work. Many people within the CRWRC organization and its partner networks throughout the world have contributed to his understanding of development, as well as to his appreciation of true commitment to justice and the well-being of our neighbours.

We would also like to express our appreciation to the editorial staff at World Vision Publications. Special thanks to editor in chief Edna Valdez for her encouragement and flexibility through the entire process, to senior editor Rebecca Russell for her insightful observations about content, and to copy editor Joan Laflamme for her fine attention to detail and for improving the flow and readability of the text.

Finally, we would like to thank our wives and children (Jeannette, Matthew, Maya, and Jacob; Lisseth, Laura Maria, and John-David) for providing loving homes and havens that are a joy to return to when our work for the day is done.

Introduction

CIVIL SOCIETY
AND HUMAN DEVELOPMENT

Why Christianity Matters

Roland Hoksbergen

Humanity will achieve sustainability, just as we have achieved a seemingly impossible, and nearly global, transition to democracy. The field of possible futures also includes collapse, transformation, and most likely, some mix of the two. Civil society will be the critical actor, in any event. When collapses of any kind occur, civil society will be there to pick up the pieces and rebuild. When transformation occurs, civil society will undoubtedly have hatched it. It's all but inevitable: democracy will give birth to sustainability, and civil society will save the world.

—ALAN ATKISSON, "WHY CIVIL SOCIETY WILL SAVE THE WORLD"

For God so loved the world that he gave his only Son, so that everyone who believes in him may not perish but may have eternal life. Indeed, God did not send the Son into the world to condemn the world, but in order that the world might be saved through him.

—JOHN 3:16–17

The planes of September 11, 2001, slammed into their targets and in the space of a few moments changed our world. The height of incivility, such terrorist attacks provide horrific evidence of the dangers lurking in our globalising world, but they also underscore how vital it is that we intentionally work to promote human development in all corners of the world. As Alan AtKisson says above, collapses (such as the terrorist attacks) will occur, but civil society will help us cope, get back on our feet, and work together to construct a better future. Is AtKisson right? This is among the fundamental questions the Christian authors of this book explore, and the attacks of September 11 make the analysis and assessment of the following pages all the more pressing and timely.

FROM MANY PERSPECTIVES

In addressing the issues surrounding the connection between civil society and development, we need to be aware of the array of disciplinary, regional, cultural, and theological traditions that come to bear. To that end, contributors to this volume represent a variety of national, ethnic, scholarly, and practical groups. And though there is a common denominator in underlying Christian faith of the authors, there is also a diversity of faith traditions, including evangelical, mainline Protestant, Mennonite, Reformed, and Roman Catholic traditions. What brings unity of purpose and commitment to this study is our common desire to work for the well-being and development of God's people everywhere and our willingness to work towards that purpose as followers of Jesus Christ. As the following pages attest, our varied backgrounds serve not to divide, but to provide different and valuable insights into the basic questions and practices of civil society, development, and NGOs. In the contemporary fields of civil society and development, there is much ripe grain, and Christians need to listen to and learn from each other if there is to be a rich harvest.

There are two main, and closely interrelated, purposes to this volume, one theoretical and the other highly practical. On the theoretical side, Christians need to better understand the relationship between civil society and development, to step back and evaluate the very idea of civil society in its different formulations in order to assess its intellectual integrity. Whether Christian NGOs should join networks of human rights movements, women's groups, or environmental action groups, for example, depends much on how one understands the role of civil society in development. To illuminate our theoretical understanding of civil society, some of the contributors are professional academics who come to this study as philosophers, political scientists, geographers, sociologists, theologians, anthropologists, and economists.

As we know, however, the issues of civil society and development are also highly practical and relate directly to the work of Christian development organisations. Theory is important, but learning about civil society oriented activities "on the ground" is equally important. This leads to the second main purpose of the book, which is to assess the practical relevance of civil society related work in developing nations and to reflect on the effectiveness of different strategies undertaken by NGOs. For example, this book will address how Christian NGOs can work in centrally controlled nations like Vietnam (Chapter 15), how different NGO strategies contribute to the formation of social capital in Bolivia (Chapter 14), and how to determine the appropriate mix of traditional community development work and civil society oriented initiatives in Honduras (Chapter 11). Such questions can be adequately addressed only on the basis of field experience, which is why this book includes the insights of experienced development practitioners as well as academic theorists. Disciplinary lines and the theoretical/practical divide should not be taken too strictly, however, for in the chapters that follow they are frequently blurred and crossed, generally to positive effect. A quick review of the "Contributors" section reveals the rich theoretical and experiential backgrounds of the contributors.

It is important to note that there is some tension and even disagreement among the authors as they develop their chapters. This book grew out of their dialogue, and the chapters were not edited to "agree."

UNDERLYING THEMES

Interwoven with the theoretical and practical purposes are two themes that appear in every article: why Christianity matters to the discussion and the character of effective human development. First, as we talk about development in its myriad dimensions and its holistic character, we cannot help but encounter the integral relationship between human development and our most basic beliefs about life and the world. We try to reflect on the implications of Christian faith for our understanding of development and for our assessment of the role of civil society in the larger picture of development. In the "developed" West one is often tempted to think that development is something that we already have and that others, especially poor people, need. We try to avoid this mistake as we search to define development in a way that includes all humanity in relationship, Jews and Greeks, slave and free, male and female. We attempt not so much to take our own development for granted and share its secrets with others as to participate in the process of discovering the meaning of our own development even as we talk about development of people around the world. A vibrant civil society, both local and transnational, contributes immensely to this process of discovery.

Why Christianity Matters

The conversation about civil society and development has taken place almost exclusively in secular arenas. This is somewhat natural in a pluralistic society that claims to respect all religious viewpoints without privileging any one of them. It was a hallmark of the modern era that we tried to supersede our religious differences by relying increasingly on science, which many hoped would be an objective arbiter of our disputes. In our efforts to find common truths and common ground apart from our various religious foundations, faith commitments were ruled out of bounds. In the field of development, however, the practice of keeping religion out of the discussion seems rather strange when it was religious motivation that actually played a huge role in erecting the whole development assistance enterprise. Indeed, Christians have been among the most influential supporters of relief and development aid. Moreover, many of the West's largest NGOs have self-professed Christian roots, and many work deliberately to maintain their Christian character.

The mindset of the modern age is still strong. Christians in both the academy and in the development world know the pressure to speak and act on secular terms. Bronkema identifies this pressure on both communities in his discussion of Protestant missions to Latin America in the early part of the twentieth century. In keeping with intellectual currents of the times, mission organisations attempted to be "scientific" in hopes of improving mission success, and Bronkema shows how ideas about missions and development work were secularised in the process. And this is precisely what has happened, not only in Latin America, but the world over. Christian scholars turn to modern scientific views of their disciplines, and Christian development agencies employ generalised strategies that are not linked to overtly religious principles or purposes. Consequently, Save the Children and Christian NGOs end up employing the same strategies, benefitting similarly from the financial support of the government, and becoming very difficult for the outside observer to distinguish in terms of who they are and what they do.

In many circles today, however, science, though still valued, no longer holds the same mystique and power, for its claim to objectivity was not able to withstand careful scrutiny. As a result, we live now in what some call the *postmodern* era, bringing mixed blessings for Christians as some barriers are razed and others are raised. On the one hand, foundational beliefs and values have been permitted back into the analysis, especially in realms dealing with interpreting human affairs and searching for meaning. Christians thus have an entry and can again bring the religious dimension into the conversations about development. On the other hand, postmodern thinkers, in spite of professing respect for such beliefs and values, offer no means by which one set of beliefs and values can be evaluated against any other. Anything goes, so to speak. In Western culture, traditional Christian values are still held in low regard, associated by many with centuries of dominance, oppression, and ecological destruction. At the same time, the beliefs and values of oppressed peoples enjoy higher profiles and, in some eyes, more respect.

How should Christians navigate in such a world? Or more to the point at hand, how should Christian development scholars and practitioners face the question of whether civil society actually contributes to development? Important insights to the first question are provided by Christian philosophers and mission theorists like Lesslie Newbigin, who suggests that Christians need to walk in both secular and Christian worlds, "to live so fully within both traditions that the debate between them is internalized" (1989, 65). Christians need to be fully aware of what is going on in the broad circles of their disciplines, for just being Christian does not make one's theoretical reflections correct. Nor are the ideas of non-Christians necessarily wrong, and we can certainly learn from theorists of non-Christian traditions. Even so, we must also be intentionally and constantly connected with a community of Christians to reflect on the same important issues from an explicitly Christian perspective. John Stott argues that Christians need to be involved in this world because God cares about this world and wants us to care about it too. In order to act in this world as God would want, Stott asks Christians to use the minds God gave them to step back and "think straight" about the issues before them. To do this well, he says, we need to put on a "Christian mind" (Stott 1984).

Christian thinkers and development practitioners, including many NGOs in their official documents, have worked for many years to think straight about development. The ideas of holistic development approaches that wed word evangelism with deed ministries are products of these efforts. The recent book by Bryant Myers, *Walking with the Poor,* is a wonderful example of walking in two traditions. Myers interacts with the helpful contributions of secular theorists like David Korten and

Robert Chambers and then engages in a Christian critique and works toward fash-
ioning a theoretical approach to development work that is consistent with Christian faith. He also provides many helpful working tools to the development practitioner. Similar to what Myers has achieved, we propose to engage in that sort of
Christian reflection on the specific topic of civil society.

The intersection of Christianity with our study of civil society is presented in a
variety of ways. As with the theme of civil society and development, the conversation that unfolds on the following pages is enhanced by the perspectives that people
from different traditions bring to the table. Roman Catholics and Reformed Christians come to the discussion as members of far-reaching scholarly traditions that
have well-developed theologies that carefully integrate Christian foundations into
their analysis. Denis Goulet and Koenraad Verhagen, for example, both ground
their analyses in the Catholic social teaching that has developed especially over
the last century. Well-studied principles of social order (for example, the preferential option for the poor, subsidiarity, common good) are used to measure the conduct of civil society organisations and their activities. Rebecca Samuel Shah too,
though an evangelical, employs key concepts from Catholic social teaching to evaluate the work of The Bridge Foundation, a micro-enterprise organisation in India.
James Skillen, coming out of the Reformed tradition, evaluates civil society on the
basis of a similar sort of philosophical/theological body of belief based on such
principles as differentiation, public justice, and calling. Mennonite participants
bring a peace tradition and a strong focus on community. Contributions by Terrence
and Vernon Jantzi and Kenneth Friesen both speak of the importance of building
community and the development of trusting relationships. Evangelicals like David
Bronkema, Samuel Escobar, Paul Nelson, and Alan Whaites ask how the prophetic
values of Christianity are being achieved through civil society work. They raise to
the forefront the biblical principles of justice for the poor, the importance of
emphasising spirituality in development work, and the need to understand the role
of the institutional church in promoting social, economic, and political development.

Throughout this book one can discern five levels of integration of faith in the
analysis of civil society, development, and the role of NGOs. At the most basic
level is an approach whose primary purpose is to bring into the discussion important ideas and events that inspire similar conversations from secular circles. We
need to pay attention to these discussions, for we have much to learn from them.
Lowell Ewert and Howard Wiarda are especially tuned in to these discussions as
they occur in the human rights and political science communities, and they raise
important questions and arguments to the attention of Christians working in development.

At the second level is a study of the role church-based institutions play within
civil society. To consider the question at this level does not necessarily require a
"Christian mind," for non-Christian observers can also see the relevance and influence of church-based institutions in broader society. One can see in the chapters by
Abu Brima et al. and Kabiru Kinyanjui, for example, how churches and para-
church institutions have played important roles in the peace process in Sierra Leone

and in gradually opening up the political process in Kenya. One can also see this in Escobar's treatment of how people and society have been influenced in Latin America by changes in the church, especially as regards the liberation theology movement, the rise of Protestantism, and, more recently, Pentecostalism. But one needs Christian minds like those of these authors to understand and grapple with the motivating theologies behind these movements, to see these churches as responding to God's call on their lives rather than as merely sociological, political, or economic phenomenon to be empirically accounted for.

A third level of integration is to consider how underlying values and principles in the Christian faith influence and differentiate Christian organisations from secular ones. Brima et al. and Kinyanjui both integrate these deeper values into their studies of church institutions in Africa as they analyse the motivations and actions of the church community. Bronkema, Goulet, Samuel Shah, and Verhagen each evaluate the work of NGOs against values and principles that are explicitly derived from Christian foundations. What is it, for example, that distinguishes the work of Christian NGOs in Honduras from non-Christian ones (Bronkema)? Or how is the work of Catholic Relief Services affected by the values of Catholic social teaching (Goulet)? What makes The Bridge Foundation different from secular micro-enterprise organisations (Samuel Shah)? A similar values-based orientation is evident in the chapters by Jantzi and Jantzi and by Friesen. Traditional Mennonite values of humble service, building relationships in community, reconciliation, and trust-building are shown not only to inspire the work of the Mennonite Central Committee (MCC) but are also used to evaluate the results of MCC's interventions.

At a fourth level, Christians use Christian analytical categories and concepts to evaluate large trends in society. Raymond Offenheiser, Alan Whaites, and Paul Nelson, for example, evaluate world development patterns against a Christian conception of justice, and they call for the church to exercise its voice and influence to build a more just world. Bronkema and Nelson employ the Christian understanding of sin to highlight the need for different actors in society to hold one another accountable. Kathleen Braden considers Christian understandings of charity and community in the West and in Eastern Orthodox traditions to do a cross-cultural, cross-theological comparison of how civil society is understood in two highly different theological/cultural traditions. Escobar assesses how different theologies, associated with different understandings of social order, affect the political orientations of both church institutions and individual church members. He shows how Protestant ideas and culture, then liberation theology in both Roman Catholic and Protestant churches, and finally the Pentecostal movements have had major impacts on how Latin Americans understand their own society. Escobar also shows how the shape of civil society in a nation is closely linked with prevailing theological orientations.

Finally, at the fifth level there are attempts to reconstruct a vision of how society ought to be structured if we begin with a biblical interpretation and vision of what God intended for people in society. Skillen takes on this task and attempts to build an understanding of society on biblical foundations. Skillen is uncomfortable with easily accepting terms like *civil society* and evaluating them on the basis of secular understandings. Instead, he seeks out new meanings for how society should be structured and finds that civil society as a category of thought doesn't provide a sufficiently encompassing umbrella under which to group the diverse organisations that make up modern society. Where, for example, does a school fit? Or the media? These spheres of life, as well as all others in society, like art, music, athletics, science, architecture, and health, to mention a few, must respond to God's call on them, and their responsibilities and rewards in each case are different. Envisioning a good society as a broad set of differentiated institutions or spheres, Skillen understands development as

> the unfolding, diversifying, and complexifying exercise of all the responsibilities that belong to the generations of the image of God, and this occurs in a healthy fashion only when humans steward the earth creatively with all of their talents in obedience to and in fellowship with the One who has called them into service toward the destiny of face to face fellowship with God.

In Skillen's view the idea of civil society is simply not big enough to capture this level of differentiation and subtlety.

No claim is made here that any of these levels or ways of integrating the Christian faith with an evaluation of NGOs, civil society, and development is the right one, or even that any one is better than the others. Humility requires that Christians listen to one another and engage in purposeful dialogue as we jointly seek God's will for our lives in the present world. The contributions presented here are intended to promote that dialogue.

Civil Society and Human Development

One of the central issues in understanding development is whether it is essentially about *having* or *being*. The focus on having, a natural response to the reality of poverty and hunger, inclines one towards seeing economic growth as the key objective of development. Certainly this has been the dominant theme in development economics, and most national and international aid organisations operate with economic growth as their stated goal. But if economic growth is the end of development, then one must also recognise that all other aspects of life become means to that end. Technology, finance, education, and skill training are all strategies that can be employed to increase production in order to solve the problem of poverty. Areas of our lives less directly related to production, such as religion and political organisation, are often valued in terms of how they contribute to growth too. The ease with which questions about Protestantism turn toward its impact on creativity and production illustrates the pervasiveness of such thinking. Whether democracy is necessary for economic growth or naturally follows economic growth (think South Korea, Chile, and China) is a discussion that likewise presumes the priority of having.

In spite of the overwhelming orientation of aid to economic growth, not everyone accepts economic growth as synonymous with development. Scattered dissenting voices have sought to broaden, as well as deepen, our understanding of development, including for example much of Denis Goulet's work of the last forty years. But the "development as having" paradigm remains very powerful, and if growth remains the goal of development, then civil society is just another strategy, worth considering only because it might be the formula to achieve solid performance in economic growth. Whether civil society, and NGOs as part of civil society, should play this role is addressed in this volume by Goulet, Samuel Shah, Bronkema, Offenheiser, and Skillen. Not surprisingly, all argue that true human development is much broader than economic growth and that civil society should not be thought of as merely a means to an end.

In addressing the true character of development, both Skillen and Samuel Shah interact with the ideas of Nobel Prize winning economist Amartya Sen, who argues that development should focus more on rights and capabilities than on income levels or economic growth (Sen 1999). Both appreciate Sen's focus on development as more than just economic growth, and they are encouraged that Sen recognises that development has something to do with being as well as having. Skillen notes particularly that some aspects of human development actually occur within the institutions of civil society themselves, regardless of what happens to income. The same can be said of political and economic institutions. What happens in civil society, as well as what happens in all other spheres of our lives, says Skillen, should be understood as valid ends of development, not simply as means. But Sen does not go far enough, for he is not able to identify in any adequate way what people actually should be or what they should strive to become, opting instead to say that each person ought to be able to lead the life that he or she values. Ultimately, then, Sen provides little direction, for reasons that likely have much to do with the constraints of the prevailing secular mindset that forbids the entry of religious orientations into the conversation. While Sen shies away from giving a complete picture of development, he nevertheless makes an important contribution by showing that development is much broader than the traditional focus on income and the economic would allow. Development is about having, yes, but it is also more primarily about being, which affects having, for better or for worse. Sen has given us the freedom to paint a new picture of development, which is what the authors in this volume try to do. What that picture looks like, in all its multicolored hues, is revealed in this volume as a composite of the insights of each of the different authors.

In the end, the picture presented is compelling. Individuals are central figures, but these individuals are not isolated beings; they are pictured in relationship with others in structural/institutional ways. Neither individuals nor institutions can be appreciated and understood independently of each other. Individuals become who they are – they discover and create their identities – in relationships and through institutions. Such nurturing, identity-forming institutions are essential to a good society, and they create what Robert Putnam has referred to as "bonding capital" (1993). Whaites refers to these environments as "havens." Indeed, civil society's functions include creating and strengthening such havens in which individuals find a home and also learn what Bronkema calls the values and principles necessary for true development. One such value is human dignity, which, as Ewert points out, means that each person's right to voice and participation must be respected, even as each individual is responsible to respect the rights of others. Nelson emphasises not only the rights and responsibilities of each individual, but more specifically the need for individuals to be in relationship with others, with human solidarity and justice being criteria for right relationships. Isolation and separation are representative of today's "maldevelopment," a situation in which the poor do not eat and the rich, out of fear and guilt, do not sleep. To form right relationships, civil society must go beyond the formation of bonding capital, which if over emphasised tends to foster exclusive and conflictive groups, to the formation of "bridging capital," which brings people together in associations that bridge the divides among our ethnic, national, and cultural identities. In the absence of bridging capital, our need for bonding tempts us to exclude and discriminate, starting with school cliques and extending all the way to modern-day ethnically based warfare.

Development thus necessarily encompasses the structures of society. Our political and economic institutions, for example, should be shaped to promote the true development of all. How is that to be done? How are we to form institutions that are fundamentally just, that care for the poor and needy, and that encourage all people to develop their own gifts and talents while rejoicing in the development of gifts and talents in others? Offenheiser opens this book by challenging civil society organisations, through which people are empowered to participate in the broader institutions of society, to take on the role of influencing global development by seeking justice, bearing witness, giving voice, modelling stewardship, and championing hope, all with the purpose of generating a global development in which none is excluded. In his discussion of the human rights foundations of civil society, Ewert emphasises how civil society plays the role of intermediary between individuals and the broader institutions of society. He argues that "the fundamental rights of 'dignity,' 'participation,' 'holding power accountable,' and the freedom to work for 'peaceable change' are based on the belief that every person is valuable and potentially has something meaningful to contribute."

Civil society thus nurtures individuals, prepares them to be involved constructively in the broader institutions of society, and provides a platform for influencing a society's overall development. Some contributors caution us not to expect too much of civil society. Nelson, Skillen, Whaites, and Wiarda all argue that civil society is not enough. The state and business institutions must also carry within them the desire and calling to govern and work for just societies. Civil society organisations interact with these broader institutions, but they do not, cannot, and should not try to supplant them.

In the give and take of the theoretical discussion, other cautionary notes about civil society are raised by various contributors. In spite of the generally positive evaluation of the promise of civil society, there is no call in this book to go forth and support civil society indiscriminately, whenever and wherever it may be found.

Probably the book's most pronounced critic of the contemporary focus on civil society is Howard Wiarda, who brings up twenty reasons to be sceptical about civil society. Among Wiarda's major concerns is the cultural imperialism of the current emphasis in the West, especially in the United States, to build up civil society around the world. Wiarda fears that the brand of civil society being promoted is simply too American or too Western for other cultures. Braden's study of civil society in Russia and Friesen's study of NGO work in Vietnam provide evidence that we definitely need to take the issues of cultural difference seriously. As they point out, civil society in different cultures may look very different, and the best way to promote it may be different too. Fully aware of the cross-cultural issues, Ewert nevertheless counters these warnings by arguing that the Universal Declaration of Human Rights provides a grounding for civil society that spans all the world's nations and cultures.

Closely related to the question of the cross-cultural validity of civil society is the role of foreigners in promoting it. In his study of micro-finance institutions, Verhagen points out that many global or Western-based micro-finance institutions are not sufficiently sensitive to local needs and patterns of work. Instead, they behave as if they already know what's best for the poor and implement their micro-finance programmes with little regard to local cultures and local input into programme design. In a study of the Mennonite Central Committee in Bolivia, Jantzi and Jantzi discover that foreigners who expect to contribute to development one way (for example, agricultural development) may actually have more of a long-term impact through the way they influence the formation of local social capital. Both the Jantzi and Jantzi and the Friesen chapters point out the importance of building trust through the development of long-term relationships. Foreigners, however, as explicitly stated by Bronkema, are tempted to focus more on the technical, scientific, causal relationships rather than on human relationships, even in their explicit efforts to promote civil society.

Theoretically, one of civil society's important roles is to hold government and business accountable to act in the best interests of society. In the real world, however, it is possible for organisations to be "bought off." Wiarda suggests this possibility, and both Kinyanjui and Brima et al. point out how the governments of Kenya and Sierra Leone have tried to co-opt civil society organisations, in some cases succeeding, by bringing them into their patronage networks. In quite a different cultural setting Friesen analyses the range of freedom within which Vietnamese organisations can function in a centrally planned, communist environment. In a country where mass organisations are dependent on the government and independent organisations are either proscribed or highly restricted, how can the people hold their government accountable? Goulet raises a similar issue for a Western Christian NGO, Catholic Relief Services (CRS), which receives substantial funding from the U.S. government. Can CRS withstand government pressures to make it a tool of foreign policy? Goulet says that it can, if it stays true to its mission and founding principles.

Verhagen points out that the expressed mission of civil society organisations may be compromised when they receive outside funding, say from government or international sources, for they may be tempted to put their own internal objectives ahead of development objectives. This issue is also raised by Wiarda, who is concerned that the civil society movement may be little more than the latest development fad, evidenced by the way NGOs too readily switch their missions, giving the appearance of being opportunists who chase after the easy development aid dollar. Once an organisation is created, vested interests are formed, and these may lead civil society organisations to worry more about feeding their own bureaucracies than about staying true to their missions.

One of the temptations in the promotion of civil society is to think that civil society is some manageable entity, and that any organisation in civil society is worthy of support. Nelson is wary of multilateral organisations like the World Bank that have programmes that support civil society in general, as if civil society is some congenial, co-operative agent for just development. In reality, says Nelson, civil society is a highly diverse cacophony of voices, and some organisations are created solely to serve private interests and to discredit the interests of others (for example, El Salvadoran coffee growers). Christian NGOs must be careful, he says, to work with partners in civil society whose values are sound and who really work to promote justice. In a similar vein, Ewert answers the question about which groups belong in civil society by referring to the human rights criterion. Those groups that respect the rights and the voices of others deserve recognition as legitimate members of civil society. Others, like al Queda and other terrorist organisations, do not.

Finally, Whaites points out that civil society organisations, partly because they are small and partly because their voices are inevitably muted by the voices of other civil society actors in the public square, are necessarily limited to have only small, incremental impacts. How then do we address society's very big problems, like poverty, pollution, and war? He argues that we must not expect civil society to take over for the state, which is what has happened somewhat in Africa, where disgust over the performance of the state has led some in the West to engage in actions to overtly weaken the state. Such actions are more likely to lead to the chaos of Somalia and Liberia than to development.

CIVIL SOCIETY AS SAVIOUR?

If development organisations were to implement a civil society approach to the work they do in the Third World, the practical implications would be enormous. Instead of thinking about development solely in terms of health indicators, income and production levels, agricultural output, and the like, development organisations and theorists would become increasingly conscious of the processes through which development action was taken and of the ways in which all stakeholders in development were involved both in the creative process of programme design and in the task of holding each other accountable. There would be a greater focus on building true partnerships oriented towards building organisational effectiveness and towards working in concert for common purposes. There would be an increasing emphasis on education and advocacy for justice and human rights, as well as on programmes to strengthen institutions necessary for democratic governance. Development organisations would intentionally work to build local and transnational social capital through the strengthening of cross-cultural and transnational relationships, especially in the areas of conflict resolution and reconciliation. They would increasingly focus their attention on organising people for action rather than on mobilising resources for purposes of provision. Are development organisations, often referred to as NGOs, especially Christian ones, ready to make these sorts of changes?

Some authors, like AtKisson, are more than ready. It is hard to imagine a more ringing endorsement of civil society, one that already envisions civil society not only saving humanity from evil, but also bringing us into a glorious new future. AtKisson's triumphalistic claims are certainly intriguing, and so provocative that one is inclined to excuse what appears to be obvious hyperbole. AtKisson is not alone in his high hopes for civil society. In the last ten to fifteen years the stock of civil society in the world development community has soared much as tech stocks did when they were on the upswing. People the world over profess confidence in the power of civil society to shake evil governments to their foundations, to address root causes of terrorism, to bring about democratic transitions, and to initiate and ensure progress on all fronts. In the aftermath of the Cold War, large and small development organisations are taking notice, and in the world of international development the promotion of civil society continues to attract much attention and increasing amounts of funding.

Just what is this magic elixir that AtKisson claims will save the world? Unfortunately, there is no broad consensus of exactly what *civil society* means, though such ambiguity and disagreement do not diminish its importance (Howell and Pearce 2001). Much like other vital ideas, such as justice, freedom, democracy, and love, the importance of civil society is not in dispute. Instead, the importance of these vital ideas is positively correlated with ongoing efforts to discern precise meanings and applications. Ambiguity and disagreement do not diminish the importance of these concepts; they only heighten our need to be discerning. Still, the basic ideas about civil society do comprise a relatively firm core, which starts to soften only as one moves away from the centre. At its heart, in all formulations civil society is about the voluntary actions of citizens who organise themselves to achieve some collective purpose. In most formulations, civil society is understood as being, and occurring, in a sphere of activity separate from both the state (government) and the market (private business). International development scholar Alan Fowler tries to capture the main features of civil society by defining it as a set of organisations in which people gather and through which they act. For Fowler, civil society is

the array of people's organisations, voluntary associations, clubs, self-help or interest groups, religious bodies, representative organs, NGDOs (Non-Governmental Development Organisations), foundations and social movements which may be formal or informal in nature, and which are not part of government or political parties, and are not established to make profits for their owners (Fowler 1997, 8).

Fowler says this is the definition generally accepted by people and organisations working in third-world development, which for our purposes makes it a reasonable place to begin. Ambiguity and potential conflicts of interest are immediately apparent, however, and many questions arise. Is a voluntary organisation that promotes micro-enterprise a legitimate member of civil society? How about private organisations that receive funding from the state? Why are political parties excluded? What is the proper way for civil society to engage and to interact with state and business sectors? As friends, foes, charities, lobbyists, clients? How do different cultures affect the formation and role of civil society? Does, and should, civil society look the same in the United States, Russia, Peru, Kenya? Where do churches and religion fit into this picture? Do religion and religiously oriented institutions form a legitimate part of civil society, or do these form yet a fourth, transcendent sector? In our post–September 11 world, everyone has become aware of a voluntary organisation known as al Queda, which at first glance seems to fit Fowler's definition. This is hardly a happy prospect. Would civil society really include organisations dedicated to terror and destruction? These questions and more will be addressed by various authors in this volume as we seek to discover more about civil society.

For Christians, however, there is something blatantly wrong with AtKisson's proposition about the potential of civil society, for it asks of humanity more than we, on our own, could ever deliver. We need look no further behind us than the century from which we have just escaped – the most violent century in human history – to be confronted with the folly and terror of depending solely on human plans to build a better world. In contrast with secular scholars and thinkers, whether modern or postmodern, Christians carry deep within their souls and minds the knowledge that we cannot save ourselves, and that Jesus Christ is God's provision for our salvation, in both the present world and the world beyond. No, Christians are not likely to seriously entertain the notion that civil society will, or even can, save the world, but we are right to ask the question of what contributing role civil society can and should play in God's salvation plan.

AtKisson is certainly correct that civil society is powerful and important, an assertion to which events around the world amply testify. But Christians will naturally want to assess current claims for civil society against our understandings in such basic areas as human character and purpose; social, political, and economic principles; cultural difference and cross-cultural understanding; moral responsibility; the sources of human hope and the causes of despair; proper human relationships with God, with other humans, and with the environment; the reality and consequences of sin; the movement of history; and, ultimately, the story of salvation. We will want to reflect on civil society and its possibilities so that we learn to harness this force for purposes consistent with God's plan for God's people.

ORGANISATION OF THE BOOK

Local Ownership, Global Change is divided into three parts. Part 1 opens with some enthusiastic portrayals of the power of civil society. Part 2 is populated with the book's most theoretically oriented chapters. Is it really a good idea? Is it well founded? Is it cross-culturally robust? Is our understanding of civil society sufficiently complex? Is the idea of civil society Christian? Part 3 then moves on to examine more practical questions through the down-to-earth experiences of different organisations.

In the final analysis, whether Christian NGOs should reorient their development interventions to civil society building and strengthening activities is not definitively answered. Some authors are highly supportive while others are supportive but more cautious. If the discussion herein contributes to improved understanding, sparks interest among Christian NGOs to raise the profile of civil society oriented work in their organisations, provides some ideas of how to organise such work, helps NGOs avoid some pitfalls and potential errors, and generates a commitment among development theorists and practitioners to continue the conversation about civil society and how best to achieve sustainable development, then the purposes of this book will have been achieved.

References

AtKisson, Alan. 1997. "Why Civil Society Will Save the World." In *Beyond Prince and Merchant*, edited by J. Burbidge. Brussels: Institute of Cultural Affairs.

Fowler, Alan. 1997. *Striking a Balance: A Guide to Enhancing the Effectiveness of Non-Governmental Organisations in International Development.* London: Earthscan Publications.

Howell, Jude, and Jenny Pearce. 2001. *Civil Society and Development: A Critical Exploration.* Boulder, Colo.: Lynne Rienner Publishers.

Myers, Bryant L. 2000. *Walking with the Poor: Principles and Practices of Transformational Development.* Maryknoll, N.Y.: Orbis Books.

Newbigin, Lesslie. 1989. *The Gospel in a Pluralist Society.* Grand Rapids, Mich.: Eerdmans.

Putnam, Robert. 1993. *Making Democracy Work: Civil Traditions in Modern Italy.* Princeton, N.J.: Princeton University Press.

Sen, Amartya. 1999. *Development as Freedom.* New York: Anchor Books.

Stott, John. 1984. *Decisive Issues Facing Christians Today.* Old Tappan, N.J.: Fleming H. Revell.

Part 1

THE POWER
OF CIVIL SOCIETY

———◆———

1

BEARING WITNESS FOR JUSTICE THROUGH DEVELOPMENT

Challenges for Faith-based NGOs in an Era of Globalisation

Raymond C. Offenheiser Jr.

With the initiatives being taken by President Bush to promote the work of faith-based organisations both nationally and internationally and to secure increases in federal funding for their programmes, the central questions about civil society are made all the more salient. Should faith-based organisations be given the same leadership roles and prominence internationally as President Bush would like to offer them domestically? Do they have something unique to contribute in the international civil society arena? Are they ready for the major challenges that await them in assuming this role? How might they have to change to adjust to a rapidly evolving world? What should be their voice and identity? In the end, how can they best make a difference for the poor? How should North American society relate to the rest of the world? There are serious questions as well about the relationships and understandings among faith-based communities of Christians, Muslims, Jews, and Hindus.

Samuel Huntington, the distinguished professor of political science at Harvard, warned us a decade ago about the potential clash of civilisations that might mark the post–Cold War period, a conflict defined largely along religious and ethnic lines (Huntington 1993). In the events of September 11 one can identify certain actors for whom this scenario is a desired and preferred outcome, and who would advocate violence as a means of creating opportunities for advancing their own narrow parochial agenda in the name of religious faith and practice. For people of faith around the world, this is a wake-up call to re-examine not only the pillars of our faith, but also our vision of the world, our notions of tolerance and inclusion, and our role in shaping a world that negates the possibility of the kind of clash of civilisations posited by Dr. Huntington. This has become the challenge of our time for men and women of faith everywhere. The test of our commitment and success will be our ability to construct the kinds of institutions and societies that build and sustain peace in a multi-cultural, multi-ethnic, and multi-religious world.

This chapter seeks to address those challenges at both the intellectual and practical levels by considering some broad questions and concerns facing NGOs in civil society today as they seek to advance international development and social justice. More particularly, we seek to identify the challenges facing faith-based NGOs in this era of globalisation.

The fiercely contested election of President Bush in 2000 left politicians and advocates with a great deal of time to wonder about the shape of foreign and development policy during the next administration. Behind the scenes in Washington, D.C., wheels had been turning for months to churn out recommendations to the new president for priorities in the areas of foreign policy and foreign aid. Some argued for more of the same with more robust funding. Others proposed stronger emphasis on working through global institutions such as the United Nations and World Bank and continuing to shrink bilateral foreign aid. Still others posited an emphasis on the market and on limiting aid to those actions that link countries and people to globalisation and the market. The role of civil society figured prominently in all of these proposals.

These proposals provide the initial framework for understanding how American policy will be shaped. Most important, they determine what, if any, significance the voice of civil society will have within the U.S. government during the coming decades. Unfortunately, it is rare that these proposals ever find their way into the public domain.

For this reason, it is vital that discussions on these topics also occur outside Washington and involve a broader and different constituency of American stakeholders. It is particularly important not only to take ideas back to Washington, but also to educate and mobilise students, church communities, and academic colleagues to care passionately about international issues and the role of the United States in the world. As the global village grows smaller, Americans need a redoubled commitment to internationalist values – a sense of global citizenship – if, as members of civil society, we are to shape a responsible role for the United States in the world today.

GETTING THE STRATEGIC ANALYSIS RIGHT

If civil society will make a meaningful contribution to saving the world, the first step in achieving success will require getting the strategic analysis right. In fighting for a more just world for the poor, civil society leaders will need to clarify their vision of the world, know what they are up against, and identify their adversaries and those who are on their side.

Once these issues are defined, we will derive some sense of the challenges that confront us and determine the best way to respond. It is as important for Northern development NGOs to clarify these issues as it is for those in developing countries, and for faith-based as well as secular organisations.

We will begin with a strategic overview of the context in which the interest in civil society has emerged, suggest what appear to be broad challenges confronting civil society in both the North and the South, and conclude with some observations about the more particular challenges for faith-based organisations. The perspective is that of a development practitioner who is an unabashed believer in the importance of civil society voices and actions in the process of development. This belief is the product of watching, up close, the role civil society organisations played in nurturing and pressuring for dramatic democratic transitions in Brazil, Chile, and Bangladesh. In each of these cases I have observed civic and religious groups working closely together to push non-violently but persistently for the return of democratic governance. Upon achieving such a transition, each country experienced an explosion of civic energy devoted to advancing democratic practice and social development. Living these moments alongside the leaders of NGOs and other civic actors, and seeing the fundamental changes they have brought to the practice of development, provided persuasive evidence of the essential role of civil society for achieving sustainable development.

EVALUATING THE NEW STRATEGIC CONTEXT

So why have we all become so passionate about civil society as a concept? Is it really new? Does it add to our understanding of history or social change? Or is it nothing more than another development fad that will attract millions of dollars of funding one year and be killed off the next?

Alan AtKisson, a writer, international consultant and community organiser, writes:

> In the beginning, there was civil society. Long before there were corporations or governments or even a market economy, there were self-organised groups of people committed to the betterment of human life. . . . In the final analysis "civil society" is nothing more and nothing less than a fancy name for "us." *We*, the people, are civil society, and all the ways we come together . . . are an expression of this (AtKisson 1997, 285).

If we accept AtKisson's historical interpretation, we can agree that while civil society itself may not be new, what *is* new is our recognition of its existence and its importance as a force for change in society. In the past we assumed that governments would take care of most of the business of addressing societal needs. Today we assume that governments either can't do it all or perhaps should not be trusted to do it all. Rather, it would be better if civil society could ensure that governments get it right *and* do it honestly and democratically; that is, governments need to be accountable to the "us" in every society. By linking civil society to the governing process, we acknowledge that civil society is a political actor and that development, of necessity, is in part a political process.

Therefore, we find ourselves celebrating the virtues of civil society, NGOs, and social capital as centrepieces and indispensable elements in any real effort towards sustainable development. But why is this so? Why now? What are the contextual drivers of this newfound fascination with civic participation and civic voice? Let me offer several basic hypotheses.

First, the Cold War is over. During the Cold War, foreign policy goals were focused on building an alignment of client states on either side of the East/West divide. In those years popular participation was deemed acceptable at the community level primarily as a means to foster local buy-in on community-development and service-delivery projects. But the idea of building strong, independent local or national institutions with a voice in shaping the national policy agenda was seen as too much of a political opening for left-wing opportunists.

In contrast, after the end of the Cold War, the United States and Europe no longer worried about pandering to corrupt autocrats like Mobutu, Marcos, and Suharto, whose allegiance they had had to buy on a routine basis. With the demise of the Soviet bloc, civil society was no longer seen as a potential threat to the political stability of states or as an opportunity for communist infiltration. Instead, civil society was seen as a resource advancing the broader agenda of trade and economic growth and, let us not forget, democracy.

Second, there has been a democratic revolution during the last 20 years. Somoza, Stroessner, Pinochet, Marcos, Duvalier, Giesel, Amin, and even Suharto have all disappeared and their forms of government are entirely discredited as well. The wave of democratic governance that is washing over the world has brought with it an intense desire among both governments and citizen groups to protect and defend these democratic transitions. Critical to such an effort is the need to build democratic practices and institutions. As a consequence, massive amounts of funding in foreign aid budgets have been shifted from more traditional aid lines towards supporting democratic transitions and the consolidation of democratic practice at both civil society and state levels.

Third, over the last 30 years global social movements have achieved considerable success and notoriety. The human rights, women's, and environmental movements have developed globally integrated structures and have figured out how to use the media and other institutional levers to challenge state hegemony over public policy at national and international levels.

Such social movements have been forcefully represented at UN summits, World Bank and International Monetary Fund (IMF) meetings, and at a variety of other international forums. They have been successful at applying agreed-upon international standards to these international bodies and to assessing the performance of governments across a whole range of areas. Suddenly, these institutions and states, accustomed to acting with a minimum amount of public scrutiny or accountability, are routinely being subjected to in-depth exposure of their policies and practices through the global media.

By way of example, the president of the World Bank admitted in a small meeting with Oxfam representatives that the "Fifty Years Is Enough Campaign" effectively closed down a year's worth of events to celebrate the first 50 years of the World Bank. The World Bank staff concluded that to continue with such celebrations against the backdrop of an aggressive counter-campaign challenging the bank's success in alleviating poverty would have been tantamount to committing institutional suicide. As a consequence, the events schedule was shelved, glossy history books were distributed in quiet receptions among friends, and the World Bank began to evaluate critically how it had to change.

A fourth factor stimulating greater interest in civil society has been donor frustration with the heavy transactional costs, corruption, and inefficiency of delivering aid exclusively through state agencies. This frustration, combined with interest in promoting more transparent and accountable government practice, led to a significant redirection of aid away from governments and towards NGOs.

With little more than anecdotal evidence, the donors argued that NGOs were more professional, efficient, and transparent, and that their programmes delivered more impact and funding directly to the poor. In Europe, some governments were required to re-programme their (entire country) aid budgets to assure that at least 10 per cent of their funding was being channelled through NGOs or civil society organisations.

The increased funding to NGOs in the 1980s and 1990s resulted in a great interest among NGOs to tap into these funds to further their respective mandates as well as a substantial increase in the number, density, and capacity of NGOs. NGOs can lay claim to some significant successes in fostering democratic change, in complementing the state in providing quality social services, in assuming responsibility for organising credit programmes for the rural poor, in leveraging policy reforms in a wide range of key policy areas, in supporting free and fair electoral processes, and in assisting in the processes of building decentralised governmental structures. Southern NGOs are now more capable of formulating and voicing their own visions for their societies. These developments raise serious questions of what the mission and role of Northern development NGOs, both secular and faith based, should be in the future.

Finally, since the 1980s there has been growing pressure to direct aid towards the private sector. During the Reagan years much foreign aid was overhauled to support business development. This effort to link aid to the interests of the private sector connected neatly with the interests of those who preferred to see aid channelled away from the governments and towards market-led development. NGOs and civil society became the darlings of policy-makers interested in shrinking the state and leaving development to the private sector.

The five factors described above have brought civil society into the mainstream. A peculiar convergence of social, economic, and political agendas, they offer something for everyone: liberals and conservatives, free marketers and social activists. The big winners have been NGOs and the private sector. The big loser has been the state, whose traditional role is being questioned and scaled back, and whose funding is being reduced.

There is presently great interest in civil society as a key actor in development and democracy. But will NGOs be able to maintain their new role in a rapidly changing world? I will now examine some additional strategic aspects of the new era that are likely to shape the potential of civil society for promoting sustainable development. These important strategic aspects centre around the new types of post–Cold War diplomacy and the rise of globalisation as the default development.

GRAPPLING WITH TODAY'S DYNAMIC CONTEXT

At first glance the new order appears dominated by what it is not. More than anything else, the absence of the East/West conflict has ended a bipolar world that in some ways was easier to understand. The multi-dimensional complexity of today's world has left our leaders unable to define a coherent foreign policy for this new era because a clear "enemy" is missing. Further, the end of the Cold War era un-corked all kinds of long-repressed ethnic conflicts and nationalist aspirations. It has also created opportunities for the manipulation of weak states by powerful and corrupt rulers, warlords, and religious fundamentalists. In the absence of a sup-portable geo-political rationale, the international political community has failed to formulate an effective way of dealing with these conflicts and rogue states. As a consequence, a long list of emergency situations has developed. International hu-manitarian organisations have had to step up their efforts to save lives and have found themselves subject to increased criticism and scrutiny as their work is being seen, in some cases, as aiding and abetting conflict.

Not surprisingly, foreign aid is at an all time low and continues to decline de-spite unprecedented federal budget surpluses. It is at an embarrassing one-tenth of one per cent of our annual federal budget, a budgetary and policy orphan that mer-ited no mention during either the Democratic or Republican Conventions of 2000.

This decline in foreign aid reflects a serious erosion in internationalist values in the American public. Paradoxically, as a recent *Foreign Affairs* article points out, two-thirds of the American public favours U.S. support of the United Nations and even payment of U.S. arrears (Lindsey 2000, 2). Yet Congressional leadership is reluctant to strengthen support for this global body. Why? Lindsey argues that Americans believe in internationalism in the same way they believe in exercise. While they think it is important to be engaged with world affairs, they do not necessarily do it or lobby for it. In Washington the squeaky wheel gets the grease, and foreign aid and enlightened internationalism have a small and ineffectual con-stituency.

At the same time, the so-called Washington Consensus still prevails as the domi-nant logic governing development planning and priority setting. This consensus, formed in the late 1980s, and holding even in spite of the challenge of the Asian crisis of 1997, argues that countries can only develop if they drop all tariff barriers and other impediments and participate fully in the global free market economy, irrespective of the destabilising effects this may have on their economy and social and political fabric.

The paradox of the historical moment we find ourselves in today is that absent any clearly defined foreign policy agenda, we are left with globalisation as the default development paradigm. To the world's financial leaders, globalisation is about the integration of markets. It is about creating the conditions that will optimise economic growth and profits. Their long-held assumption is that development is economic growth and nothing more. Development is thus defined rather simply by a gross national product that is high and growing.

It is opposition to the economic growth paradigm that led to the widespread participation of individuals and civil society organisations in protests at World Bank and IMF meetings in Seattle and Prague. Economic leaders are trying desperately to preserve the frameworks that drive this dynamic growth-centred model, paying much less attention to its long-run sustainability on social, political, and environmental grounds. In contrast, the model's critics hold a broader view of globalisation that sees it as the accelerated movement not only of money, but also of people, images, ideas, technology, and instant global news. There are both dangers and opportunities inherent in this new age of globalisation.

Critics of the economic growth paradigm are not all against globalisation, per se; many see aspects that would benefit poor and marginal populations. They are, however, concerned about a one-sided form of globalisation that biases the rules of the game against the poor and applies one set of free market rules to developing economies (developing countries must open their markets fully and drop all constraints to participation in global markets as quickly as possible or suffer sanctions from the international financial community, led by the IMF).

Meanwhile, poor nations being pressured to change their policies believe they are being subjected to a mean-spirited double standard. The message they hear from wealthy industrialised nations goes something like this: We are not obligated either to drop subsidies to our agricultural producers or to open our markets to developing-world products because we must protect jobs and salaries at home; and we can't be sanctioned because we control the IMF.

Part of the current globalisation process involves a power shift from the state to private capital. Considerable pressure has been exerted on governments around the world over the last two decades to reduce expenditures and balance budgets. This pressure has led governments to sell off state enterprises, turning over large sectors of the economy to private parties. As the state backs out of economic management and as nations are forced to generate the funds to pay back outstanding debts, one of the most troubling consequences has been the slashing of expenditures for social programmes.

The elimination of funding for education and health has had dire consequences for millions of children in Africa and Asia. Several generations of young people already have grown up lacking a basic education, and the government's ability to redress this situation is being undercut. Reversing this trend, reinvigorating social expenditure, and rethinking the size, scope, and role of the state are issues that both international agencies and civil society actors must address in the coming years.

One characteristic of the global transformation that we are undergoing is the transition from an industrial era to an information era. We can communicate instantly with colleagues around the world. There is a quiet social revolution under way as societies around the world find ways to hook up to the Internet. Civil society organisations have made great use of this tool to maintain contact with their allies and funders all over the world. The democratic nature of this technology has some real implications for governance and accountability of states.

To cite an example, I recall an incident in the early 1990s when I was visiting a friend in his office at the University of California, Berkeley. As we were talking, his computer was registering e-mails he was receiving from Thailand, pouring out eyewitness accounts of police attacks on demonstrators in the streets of Bangkok. More recently, I have received e-mails of political tracts from Comandante Marcos, head of the Zapatista Rebel Group, sent from the jungles of Chiapas.

In summary, the process of globalisation will be at the centre of the really important discussions about resource allocation and development for the next several decades. It is the most important social process of our generation. While many of its core characteristics are not new, tethering globalisation to the information revolution has created a fundamentally new social process capable of rapidly transforming whole societies. For policy-makers and civil society actors, this historical moment presents some unprecedented challenges that require imagination, courage, and skill. Traditional NGOs will need to become much more conscious of their global role as members of civil society; more than organisations that carry out small marginal missions, they need also to be intentional civil society organisations (CSOs) that see themselves as global players. Perhaps most important for faith-based CSOs, the era of globalisation will require a firm grounding in ethics and morals. Along with the expansion of the global markets are many opportunities but also many threats; the market is no more than a social construct which is morally neutral at best. At the heart, therefore, of the globalisation challenge is the question of which groups and institutions will have the courage and capacity to stand up to the moral indifference and potentially destructive effects of the globalisation process, all the while steering this process to positive ends.

CHALLENGES TO CIVIL SOCIETY ORGANISATIONS

Given these developments in the strategic context in which civil society operates today, there are a number of major challenges that CSOs must face in the near future. To deal with these challenges, they must rethink their fundamental approaches to development work and embrace new concepts and ideas. The following eight themes are likely to be the most significant organisational challenges for CSOs in the coming decade.

Globalisation

In an address to Oxfam staff in 2000, Michael Edwards, author and current director of the Civil Society Unit of the Ford Foundation, proposed that "harnessing the forces of globalisation to a vision of social justice is THE political project of the 21st century."

He went on to say:

Unlike the great political projects of the 19th and 20th centuries (empire, Christianity, Marxism, Fascism, and Neo-Liberalism), this one is both driven by non-governmental actors as well as by governments, and is dependent on civil society for its fulfillment. This is historic – the first time that human beings might actually agree to co-determine their future on the world stage. And that provides the NGO movement with an unparalleled opportunity to share in the mainstream of social change. . . . There has never been a more exciting time to be part of civil society, to share in these debates, and to work for [non-governmental organisations].

How civil society responds to this challenge will determine its character, relevance, and competency to shape a more just world. We have seen evidence of one type of response in the protests at the World Bank and World Trade Organization meetings in Seattle and Washington, D.C. But it is still early.

Welfare *vs.* Rights-based Approach to Development

Critical to challenging the globalisation paradigm will be the need for CSOs to move from a welfare to a rights-based approach to development. There is a growing consensus that welfare approaches to development are futile. CSOs will never have sufficient resources to address pressing social needs. Moreover, focusing only on what people have leads to poor, unsustainable development practice, particularly in terms of creating dependency. By focusing instead on people's rights, the people themselves are seen as the creative energy behind their own development,

To address issues of poverty and injustice effectively requires building global social movements focused on a broad-based human rights agenda that includes not only civil and political rights, but also social, economic, and cultural rights. The human rights and women's movements have proven the value of utilising civil and political rights frameworks to advance their agendas.

During the Cold War, geo-political fears led the West to label public support for social and economic rights as socialist or communist. With the end of the Cold War, however, there is an effort afoot to return to the intent of the original UN documents that take a comprehensive and integrated approach to the rights issue. Groups like CARE, Save the Children, World Vision, and Oxfam are increasingly moving towards a rights-based approach in the belief that this is more consistent with the frameworks used by their partners in developing countries. This approach provides a unified vision and framework for building a global social movement to address issues of equity and social justice.

Rethinking the Role of the State

CSOs that take on a rights agenda must necessarily rethink their perspective on the role of the state. Rights are guaranteed by states. The implementation of social, economic, and cultural rights (such as the right to food, health care, an adequate standard of living) will require that governments make significant investments in meeting the basic needs of their populations. As a result, government will need to become more, not less, active.

The dilemma for many CSOs is that they came into being in opposition to governments headed by authoritarian leaders and have come to equate a strong state with authoritarian practice. For these CSOs, a radical reconceptualisation of their role and the role of the state will be required. Moreover, these CSOs have often benefitted from the weakening of the state in the face of globalisation. In fact, pressure from donors on governments to democratise and liberalise their economies has created political and social space for CSOs to flourish, and it will be difficult for CSOs to risk these gains.

On the other hand, the state has become so weak in many countries that it is ill prepared to regulate the effects of globalisation within its borders or offer even minimal social guarantees to its citizenry. What is needed is a vigorous rethinking of the role of the state, and its relationship to civil society and the corporate sector, that is attuned to contemporary circumstances. CSOs, rather than avoiding such a process, should be actively leading it.

Redefining the Concept of Programme

As a rights-based approach takes root, it will be necessary for CSOs in the North and South to rethink their definition of programmes. In many organisations, *programme* is defined as what is done directly for and with the poor. Advocacy, policy research, evaluation, and public education are seen as outside the programme envelope.

In the future organisations may need to broaden their definition of *programme* to include some of these other areas and radically redistribute of funding as well. From the point of view of Southern partners, it may be far more valuable to have their Northern counterparts advocating on their behalf for changes in harsh IMF policies than having them fund several new village schools. Northern CSOs will have to find ways to explain the value of this kind of policy leveraging to their traditional donors, who are accustomed to their contributions being used to fund "pigs and shovels."

Managing the Accountability Challenge

Accountability and transparency have served as two of the moral rallying cries for CSOs. Undoubtedly, the role of CSOs in holding public officials and institutions accountable to their citizenry is a primary reason for their success. Now, however, those who have felt the scrutiny of CSOs are swinging the accountability sword in the other direction.

Increasingly, CSOs are being challenged to be more transparent about their own operations, to be accountable to performance standards, and to be open to questions about their effectiveness. Some of these challenges are coming from donor governments demanding better evidence of the value of their diminishing foreign aid funds, others are coming from recipient governments eager to undermine the support of CSOs from donors, and still others are coming from an increasingly demanding private donor public wanting to know more about how their contributions benefit the poor.

There are several dangers for CSOs in these challenges. On the one hand, donor governments are seeking measurable results, often calculated in quantitative terms, such as how many children were vaccinated or how many girls were enroled in school. The pressure to create tight systems of evaluation tends to reassert the welfare approach to development that many groups have moved away from and to force CSOs into the role of state sub-contractors. It devalues the less measurable importance of the role of CSOs in policy formulation and programme development.

At the national level, governments faced with decreasing levels of foreign aid are trying to recapture the share that has been allocated to CSOs for their own budgets by eliminating tax-exempt status, insisting on state-led sectoral planning exercises, and implementing other means of limiting the independence of CSOs. It is clear that CSOs are going to have to respond to the accountability challenge if they are to survive as critical, innovative, and independent forces for change.

Rethinking Partnership

As foreign aid funding declines, a trend not likely to reverse itself significantly, it will be necessary for Northern CSOs to rethink their tendency to "go it alone." While funding will continue to be important, it will also be critical that organisations increasingly work in complementary partner relationships and think more broadly about the kinds of assets they can mobilise to support such relationships.

There will be less acceptance of paternalistic relationships. Southern organisations have come to feel that such paternalism on the part of their funders and supporters is unjustified and actually harmful. Northern partners will be required to revise their traditional practices and begin to work towards partnerships in which Southern partners play the lead role in defining the agenda in their own countries.

Retooling for the Information Age

As policy advocacy becomes more central in CSOs, it will become increasingly apparent that information may be as important as funding in sustaining future partnerships with Southern CSOs. If this is indeed the case, Northern agencies will be required to become learning organisations in which information and information technology become major dimensions of their programme work.

As knowledge brokers, Northern CSOs can supply their Southern partners with information about advocacy issues, networking and influencing opportunities, technology, and best practices. Northern CSOs can play a major role in assisting Southern partners to manage the inequities created by the so-called digital divide.

Living Our Humanitarian Values

In the post–Cold War era the international community has retreated from many regions of the world, closing embassies, and cutting back on aid budgets.

Meanwhile, sectarian and ethnic bloodletting threatens whole groups of people. In many of these situations CSOs, both Southern and Northern, have been left with the responsibility of acting as surrogates for the international community.

In some places civil society has become not only uncivil but downright predatory. Somalia, Sierra Leone, Sudan, and Colombia are obvious examples, but they are not alone. We are not likely to see the end of such sectarian violence and humanitarian crises in the near future.

For CSOs it will become important to learn new skills for living their humanitarian values in such trying contexts. It will be important to engage actively in preventive peacemaking and conflict resolution and to know how to pressure the international community to stay aware of the many crises that are continually erupting around the globe.

Implications for Northern Faith-based Organisations

What does all this mean for faith-based organisations? Let me pose some questions that are especially important for Christian CSOs to answer in ways consistent with their basic beliefs and values.

- As faith-based institutions, are we acknowledging that globalisation is the default development paradigm, and have we considered how this framework affects the fundamental nature of our work and that of our partners? Do we, as faith-based institutions, have a point of view on globalisation? Should we not strive to develop a credible alternative to the attractive and dominant ideology of free markets, global trade, and economic growth?
- Have we considered what it would mean for us to adopt a rights-based approach to our development programming? Can we find the means to reconcile a rights-based approach with our faith-based vision and its scriptural base? Are we ready to confront the kind of neo-liberal thinking and attitudes that defend processes of exclusion as the unintended but unavoidable price to be paid for modernisation? How might such an approach strengthen our programmes, enhance our impact, and improve our relations with partners? How would this reshape our strategic focus, our programme priorities, and our funding allocations?
- Are we ready to complement our traditional deep commitment to charity and compassion with an equally fervent commitment to solidarity and justice? Are we willing to live our faith and speak truth to power alongside our Southern partners? Are we ready to embrace a vision that holds global structures responsible for local injustice and speaks about local injustice to global leadership?
- Are we connecting with the dynamic opportunities for social change that are driven by visionary CSOs in the countries where we work? Do we even have relations with such groups, or do we think the divide between their secular institutional culture and our faith-based culture is too wide to overcome? Have we become institutional anachronisms that continue reproducing outmoded

and perhaps trivial programming approaches which are focused on saving a few lives at the expense of a whole society?
• Have we considered what the relative importance of advocacy and public education may be within our institution, relative to our traditional programme outreach to poor and disenfranchised communities? Could we better serve our partners and the poor through a strengthened emphasis on advocacy and public education, and what this might leverage, than through our conventional approaches to programming?
• Do we need to re-examine our notions of partnership and how we practise it? What kinds of partnerships are consistent with our Christian values?
• Have we recognised the new levels of competency and capacity in our Southern NGO partners and given them greater leadership roles? Or are we fearful of ceding authority and responsibility to our sisters and brothers in the South and thus sustain traditional patriarchal and patronizing partner relations? Do we have the humility to give up the power that goes with being a donor in favour of the more humble position of being a co-strategist in building social movements for justice and equity?
• Are we preparing for the Information Age? Have we evaluated the importance of information in our work relative to our traditional provision of funds and goods? How would shifting our emphasis towards information as a key ingredient of our programming change who we are and what we are able to achieve? How might it improve our relations with partners?
• Have we examined the implications of the effectiveness thrust on the core character of our work? Is the effectiveness argument really intended to produce better programmes, or is it an effort to reassert state control over dwindling foreign aid resources and promote more traditional service-delivery models and measurement practices? Are we giving in to this effectiveness argument because of our dependence on government funding?
• And finally, have we, as faith-based organisations, adequately linked our values, commitments, and beliefs to our work, or have we fallen into chasing project funding? Is there a need for us to revisit our core values, reinvigorate our mission, and bring our values-based voice more forcefully into debates about resource allocation, peacemaking, and global economic justice?

FORMATIVE CHRISTIAN VALUES

There are no easy answers to these questions, yet the role of religion can be a powerful force in giving vitality and vision to CSOs. Koenraad Verhagen, former secretary general of International Cooperation for Development and Solidarity (CIDSE), a confederation of 17 Catholic development organisations, argues that to do this it will be necessary to overcome the artificial separation that has been created between the notions of believing and acting imposed by the kind of secular thinking that has championed rationalism and economism as the dominant forces shaping modern society at the expense of religion and religiously inspired practice.

The civil society agenda demands concerted action at community, national, and international levels to solve global issues. Can this agenda materialise if citizens themselves are not filled with an irrational faith, belief, and hope; a spiritual vision which recognises that poverty and injustice can be overcome; a belief that conflicts can be prevented and peace will prevail; a recognition that each person is unique and deserves respect for his/her own sake and which sees human beings as belonging to a wider interdependent universe? Who will feed that irrational optimism and spirituality at the personal, community, and higher levels? In other words, can the aspirations of a value-driven, civil society movement be realised without due recognition of religious inspiration and motivation as underlying forces?

The third sector [CSOs] cannot transform society alone. It has to build up alliances with other sectors. For this, it has to appreciate and understand the close relationship that often exists between aspirations of people and their religious convictions. Organised religions and their institutions bring . . . many of these people together and can provide a strong moral and ethical basis to any human undertaking (Verhagen 1997, 266, 273).

In that spirit I would like to argue that faith-based institutions embrace five basic values, discussed below, that are at the heart of the Christian tradition. They should strive to make these values central to how they evolve as Northern faith-based international development organisations. These values, if put into action in faith-based institutions, will serve to draw on the best of their distinct Christian traditions, on the one hand, but also enable them to reposition their assets to be better aligned and attuned to contemporary realities and expectations in developing countries, as well as with civil society movements around the world.

Seeking Justice

A commitment to justice – real substantial justice, not just formal justice; real opportunity as opposed to the promise of opportunity – can provide real power towards the goal of ending poverty in our lifetimes. Faith communities must come to distinguish between believing in justice and acting to seek justice.

Bearing Witness

Faith-based communities bring a prophetic voice to social movements that carries farther and reaches deeper than any message secular CSOs can muster. Faith-based CSOs must find the courage to bear witness to the realities of injustice, inequities, and social exclusion and do so with their own powerful prophetic voice.

Giving Voice

The poor lack the opportunity, first and foremost, to be heard and to share their reality. When the voices of the poor are brought to the corridors of power, they belie the falsehoods that are often paraded before decision-makers to mask sad and harsh realities. Our willingness to open the closed doors and stand in solidarity alongside the poor as they define their reality gives both power and legitimacy to our mission.

Modelling Stewardship

The challenge of accountability charges us with living our values both in our institutional and our personal lives. People of faith understand what it means to live the gospel. Today, living the gospel is more than just living a personally virtuous life; it is also challenging unjust policies and offering instead more reasonable and just alternatives.

Championing Hope

Perhaps the most important role for faith-based institutions is championing hope. We live in a world starved for hopeful messages and hopeful visionaries. More than anything else, the message of hope lifts the spirit, nurtures, encourages, and motivates action. We have too few hopeful messengers. We need messengers of hope with sharp minds, a fierce commitment to justice, and a passion for public policy.

CONCLUSION

The following story illustrates how these five principles might be applied and why irrational faith is so essential to the success of CSOs.

During the presidential election of 2000, there was a news story that got buried beneath mountains of reporting about the contested final results. In early November, President Clinton invited the leaders of major denominations and development and environmental groups to the White House for the signing of a bill that provides US$435 million in debt relief for developing countries. This amount represents half of what is needed to meet the commitment of the United States to debt relief.

Some 70 persons gathered for this occasion, which for many was the culmination of half a decade of work. Many of those present commented that they could not believe they were witnessing this event. It was, for many, the modern-day equivalent of a miracle.

Yet here was the president of the United States congratulating faith communities from all over the U.S. for championing this issue and building a coalition that included the pope, Pat Robertson, Billy Graham, and the Irish rock star Bono. The work of this ecumenical Jubilee campaign brought together an unimaginable bipartisan group of Congressmen and women that spanned the political spectrum from the very liberal Maxine Waters, Democrat from California, to the very conservative Spencer Bachus, Republican and evangelical Christian from Mobile, Alabama. It won the support of the leadership of both the World Bank and the IMF, as well as finance ministers from around the world.

The debt relief provided by the United States will serve to leverage some US$60 billion in funding from other countries towards the debt relief initiative and ensure that some 33 of the world's poorest countries will be able to get out of the debt trap. As a result, millions of children will be able to return to school, health services will reopen in rural areas throughout Africa, and much needed funding for AIDS education will become available.

Five years ago, when I first started working on debt relief for desperately poor nations, I attended a meeting with the president of the World Bank, who told us this kind of proposal was reckless and would bankrupt the international financial system. The secretary of the treasury at the time told us that the U.S. Congress would never approve a bill that called for increased funding for something as ludicrous as debt relief for irresponsible third-world debtor nations. Initial proposals to Congressional committees were simply dumped in the wastebasket. Yet on that November day in 2000, the bill was signed, the monies approved and budgeted.

This miracle happened because men and women of faith took it up, bore witness to the injustice of debt in letters and in public, gave voice to the reality of the poor in the halls of Congress, modelled stewardship by offering creative alternative policy proposals, and kept faith and hope alive that this kind of victory was possible.

In congratulating this diverse coalition, President Clinton expressed the hope that this idea would become a priority in our foreign policy for years to come because, "as religious leaders around the world have told us, . . . it will be good for our souls, because global poverty is a moral affront and confronting the challenge is simply the right thing to do."

He went on to say, "When we get the pope and the pop stars all singing from the same sheet of music, our voices do carry to the heavens."

Here faith and civil society came together in a profound way to move mountains and part the seas. This is a victory that all church people should celebrate, learn from, and seek to repeat in large and small ways year after year. We can indeed make other miracles happen in our lifetime. As we look beyond September 11, we need to look for similar miracles, but we also need to work even harder to build the kind of just, equitable, and peaceful world that can serve to protect all world citizens from falling victim to similar assaults on civilised values and behaviours in the future.

References

AtKisson, Alan. 1997. "Why Civil Society Will Save the World." In *Beyond Prince and Merchant*, ed. J. Burbridge. Brussels: Institute of Cultural Affairs International.

Edwards, Michael. 2000. Speech given at Oxfam America's 30th Anniversary Celebration, 6 October.

Huntington, Samuel. 1993. "The Clash of Civilizations." *Foreign Affairs* 72:3 (summer).

Lindsey, James. 2000. The New Apathy. *Foreign Affairs* 79:5 (September/October): 2–8.

Verhagen, Koenraad. 1997. "Organized Religion: The Forgotten Dimension." In *Beyond Prince and Merchant*, edited by J. Burbridge. Brussels: Institute of Cultural Affairs International.

2

THE NEW AFRICAN LIBERATION MOVEMENT

*A Case Study of the Implications of Civil Society
in the Sierra Leone Peace Process*

Abu Brima, Wyva Hasselblad, Robert Jawara, Sheku Dickson Koroma, and Paul Kortenhoven

In July 1999, in the fading and musty luxury of the twenty-five story Deux Fevrier Hotel rising in the middle of the dusty streets of Lomé, Togo, an historic event quietly unfolded. It wasn't the United Nations–hosted Sierra Leone peace talks that were taking place in the hotel, nor was it the presence of high-level delegations from the United Nations, key Northern powers, international non-governmental organisations, the Sierra Leone government, or the rebel RUF (the Revolutionary United Front) that was so historic.

Rather, it was the presence and participation in the talks of a delegation from Sierra Leone civil society that was so "grassroots" it couldn't even pay its hotel bill. Several days into the peace talks this group had established itself as so important to the outcome that other delegations agreed to cover its costs.

INTRODUCTION

Leading up to this event was the monumental inability, during the thirty years following independence in 1961, of successive Sierra Leone government regimes to ensure peace, justice, and economic viability. Either beleaguered beyond their

This chapter evolved in conversations with Peter Vander Meulen, Christian Reformed Church, whose vision and perceptions were the original inspiration, and Jan Disselkoen, CRWRC, long-time resident of Sierra Leone whose wise understanding of people and communities helped immeasurably in understanding the events. We are grateful to the following for sharing their valuable knowledge, insights, critiques, and points of view to this paper: Mohammed Bangoura, Sierra Leone Canada Watch; Abdoulai Bayraytay, Campaign for Good Governance, Sierra Leone; Sister Lois-Anne Borowitz, the Faithful Companions of Jesus, Canada; Trevor Cook, Development & Peace, Canada; Bernard Taylor, Partnership Africa Canada, Canada.

capacity to cope or frankly despotic and corrupt, the will and ability of the government to act decisively for the good of the country had long been undermined by the gradual implosion of the state as a viable structure. Finally, in the 1990s, the country erupted into violent and multifaceted conflict.

During these same thirty years, church- and community-based organisations, as well as civic, professional, and student associations, gradually developed their capacity to speak for the people. Though unsuccessful in preventing the outbreak of violence, they came to play a leading role as the only genuine advocates for the people during peace negotiations at the Lomé Conference of July 1999, and they became important contributors in the long, slow, ongoing process of constructing the peace.

Of particular interest in this chapter is how the Sierra Leone Church found its public voice and became a vital part of a constituency that would force both the government and the RUF to the negotiating table. Four key dimensions of the church's role can be identified as critical to effective citizen involvement:

- Developing a leadership able to work with and advocate for the poor, the oppressed, the dispossessed, and the violated
- Moving the locus of action from local to national scope
- Working in solidarity across religions, ethnic groups, and regions
- Encouraging and engaging all sectors of civil society in the national debate regarding the future of the country, both before and after the Lomé peace accords

Andrew Walls, a leading scholar on Christianity in Africa, has stressed the central role played by the church in the formation of African civil society. "Time after time," he writes, "the churches of Africa preserved a viable form of civil society when other forms had collapsed or had been suppressed" (Walls 2000, 106).

The purpose of this chapter is to examine two primary questions:

1. Was the church more than an island of refuge and social interaction for Christians, more than a *sanctuary* that served only the membership? If it was, did the church in Sierra Leone serve as a framework for action, as the conscience of a people rising up to act against unbearable oppression and violence? Has the church acted as *servant*, in the true sense of the word – serving the cause of kingdom justice, committed to constructing a culture of peace? As part of this examination, we will be looking at the historical origins of the church in Sierra Leone. In the process, we will uncover those aspects of the church that gave it a unique role in the search for peace in the country.

2. What are the roots of what has become known as the civil society movement – the coming together in common cause of the church and other community-based and civic organisations to build peace out of the fragments of a shattered country? How did this civil society movement, growing in maturity as the war deepened, arise and come to be recognised nationally as well as internationally as the legitimate voice of the people of Sierra Leone?

By the turn of the century civil society had indeed become a key player in Sierra Leone's peace process, and the church, as one part of civil society, also played a key role. Both the church and other civil society organisations were recognised as legitimate representatives of the voices of the people. According to Thomas Turray, a Sierra Leonean and former director of Caritas, an international Catholic relief and development assistance organisation, in Makeni (Sierra Leone):

> Among the numerous players involved in shaping the Lomé Agreement (July 1999), the Inter-Religious Council of Sierra Leone (IRCSL) stands out as the most highly visible and effective non-governmental bridge builder between the warring factions of a population devastated and divided by more than eight years of violence (Turray 2000).

Our case study will tell how this happened.

ORIGINS OF THE CHURCH IN SIERRA LEONE

"The real founding fathers of the Sierra Leone colony were 1,100 men and women, Africans or of African descent, who arrived from Nova Scotia in 1792, and marched from the shore singing *Awake and sing the song of Moses and the Lamb*" (Elliott 1851).

Though they came from Nova Scotia, these founders of Freetown, now the capital of Sierra Leone, were people of African origin who had been sold as slaves and ended up in the Americas. They were a well-educated and self-reliant people with churches (primarily Methodist), leadership, community structures, and organisations. Recruited in the Americas to fight for the British during the American War of Independence, they were promised freedom and land as a reward. At the cessation of hostilities, Britain offered their erstwhile soldiers land in Nova Scotia, but the promise of land evaporated. After years of patient waiting, the former soldiers sent a representative to England to negotiate another settlement and were presented with a new offer – land on the coast of West Africa. After accepting the proposal, they returned to Africa in 1792 to found the settlement of Freetown. "They were entering their promised land, and celebrated the crossing of the Red Sea with an appropriate song of Miriam" (Walls 1970, 108).

When Freetown was founded, the majority of the population of that part of West Africa practised African traditional religions or followed Muslim traditions. Although there were a few mission agencies operating in parts of West Africa, the churches founded in Freetown were not of missionary origin. Instead, they were established by a people whose birthplace or roots were African, which makes them "the first modern [reformation] church of tropical Africa with a continuous history to the present day" (Walls 1970, 107). These origins distinguish it from those churches that originated directly from the ancient churches of Egypt and Ethiopia as well as from chaplaincies that catered to European residents in the forts and factories founded by the colonists. The importance of these Christians in the subsequent history of Sierra Leone cannot be underestimated.

Though the original settlers of Freetown were of African origin, the settlement was governed by a British company under the authority of the British Crown. It was set up in the fervent expectation that the settlement would yield financial benefits for its financial backers in Britain as well as for the settlers. From the start, however, the economics of the settlement did not work out as expected. The amount of land available was far less than promised, and the company began imposing taxes and rents that the settlers considered to be a breach of promise. While the Christian settlers continued to pray and worship, their grievances evolved into distrust fuelled by the perception that, once again, they had been betrayed by European authority. Opposition to the company's rule arose, centred in the Nova Scotia Methodist Society (Walls 1970). A rebellion in 1800, eight years after the founding of the settlement, points to the depth of the disillusionment and frustration as well as to the vigorous refusal to accept injustice.

Twenty years after the arrival of the settlers from Nova Scotia, the British Methodist Conference sent out a superintendent whose task it was to work with established African churches. The bishop, however, shared the perspective of the Methodists among the British civil servants in the settlement who were anxious to proclaim their loyalty to the king. The tension between the two competing strains of Methodism (the settlers from Nova Scotia and the white loyalists) continued for years, though the degree to which ecumenical Christianity transcended the differences is perhaps the more remarkable story. In 1861 the successors to the former divisions made their peace and reunited.

The church council formed in 1861 was the precursor of today's Council of Churches in Sierra Leone (CCSL). It gave members a far greater role in running their churches than the government allowed them in running the colony. In addition, the responsibility for schools was largely left to the churches and to the missions that were increasingly coming into Sierra Leone. Consequently, though the school system is no longer purely an affair of the church, a large proportion of Sierra Leoneans, Christian and Muslim alike, have been educated in Christian schools that to this day continue to play a leading role in formal instruction.

Notable in the subsequent development of the church in Sierra Leone is a spirit of ecumenical co-operation. By the late 1800s a number of mission agencies were operating outside Freetown. In some areas of the country, no matter which mission agency established the first church – Catholic, Protestant, Evangelical, or Pentecostal – successive seedling church groups established by other missions would use the same building until they were secure enough to build their own. Often, structures would be used by all groups, sometimes for ecumenical activities, other times for the activities of each distinct group. In these churches, on any given Sunday, the congregation was denominationally mixed, and the person leading the service might be the local Catholic priest or a Protestant/evangelical pastor or lay leader. Andrew Walls's comment that "God's purpose [is] to transform this whole Church into the likeness of Christ, creating a great multitude out of all the tribes and nations and kindreds and tongues a new kith and kin in Christ which transcends all the old loyalties" aptly describes this tradition of tolerant acceptance (Walls 1976, 188).

Today, Christians make up an estimated 15 to 20 per cent of Sierra Leone's population of 4.5 million (the majority of whom live in Freetown); Muslims account for 60 per cent, and the remainder practice African traditional religions (Turray 2000). Interfaith co-operation and forbearance have been hallmarks of religious practice in Sierra Leone. The Inter-Religious Council of Sierra Leone, established in 1997, is composed of the Council of Churches in Sierra Leone (with a current membership of 18 Protestant denominations), the Pentecostal Church Council, the Roman Catholic Church, the Supreme Islamic Council, the Sierra Leone Muslim Congress, the Federation of Muslim Women Associations in Sierra Leone, the Council of Imams, and the Sierra Leone Islamic Missionary Union. This body became a crucial actor in the search for peace.

CIVIL SOCIETY IN SIERRA LEONE

The Roots of Civil Society in Social Organisation in Sierra Leone

A Lockean analysis of civil society as an expression of the sovereignty that ultimately resides in the people gives us some insight into how civil society is understood by Sierra Leoneans. According to John Locke, although the state originates in society as an instrument to restrain conflict, the rights of the people have to be safeguarded in this process through two types of contracts: social contracts between and among people, and contracts between people and their elected governments. Locke's thesis was that these contracts balance the manifold divergent interests of differing groups, structures, and relationships.

Looking back in Sierra Leonean history to the time when small states were ruled by noble families, one can find the roots of active civil society in the social structures and associations that have always been a key factor in organising society. Sierra Leonean society still rests on a vast network of meaningful relationships that inhabit the public space between the state and individual citizens. This network also acts as a cultural nursery in which values, norms, meanings, and social identities are formulated and transmitted. To the extent that it is dynamic and creative, this network is the locus of expressing new concerns and articulating new actions, as well as generating civic autonomy. Prior to the modern state of Sierra Leone, social associations like the Poro, Sande, Wende, Gbamgbani, Kofo, Bondo, and Tamaboros had cultural, educational, and religious functions. These were not so much tribes as social organisations that extended over a number of social domains. The Poro and Wende, for example, preserved law and order, became pressure groups against the tyranny of individual chiefs or tribes, and provided input into the ways in which Sierra Leoneans governed their own affairs. Such associations were also the space in which people met, interacted, and worked out how human relationships and contracts were to be defined, confirmed, and honoured. Although they are often referred to as secret societies, perhaps because of their association with initiation ceremonies and rituals introducing adolescents to the transmitted wisdom of the community, it is not so much secrecy as knowledge of community ethics that gives these groups their unique influence. Bound by moral codes and contracts, these social organisations have undergone changes both in meaning and in function – but they continue to exert a powerful influence. Jan Disselkoen, a Christian Reformed World Relief Committee (CRWRC) development worker who has lived for more than twelve years in villages in the northern part of Sierra Leone, recounts an experience revealing how community control is exercised through this mechanism.

The Kuranko women's secret society concerns itself for the most part with "women's business" – education of adolescent girls at bush school, pregnancy and childbirth, and preparing women for burial. During the twelve years I lived in a Kuranko village, however, I witnessed many occasions when the women's society acted beyond this orbit of concerns to address community-wide problems.

One example occurred in 1994 when the RUF attacked our village. Most people (including myself) ran into the bush when they heard of the rebel advance, but there were a number of men who stayed close to the village until the rebels left – and then seized the opportunity to steal goods that remained in abandoned or burned houses.

When I returned a month later, I found our CES [Christian Extension Service] staff discouraged about the fact that villagers with whom they were working had stolen our household possessions. We went to the chief, explaining that it would be difficult for us to take up our work again in such a climate of suspicion. He called a town meeting.

For what seemed like hours, the men debated how to solve the problem. First the chief thought he should bring in someone from the outside with the power to discover thieves in a trial by fire. Then other townspeople became furious with the chief when he suggested that it was up to us – myself and the CES staff living in the village – to solve the problem. The meeting seemed to be going nowhere.

Then the mamy queen,[1] the spokeswoman for the women in the town, spoke up. "You talk as if there are no women in this town. If you give this case to us, we will solve it." A sigh of relief went through the audience and the meeting broke up with the women given the authority to right the situation.

In the middle of the night I heard the women walking past my window to the forest, their traditional place of power, singing a hauntingly beautiful song. Every one of the villagers knew the meaning of the song. The threat of the women's censure (in whatever form they would deem it to take) coming down on their heads had its effect on the men, just as I had seen it have its effect on other occasions. The next morning my veranda was covered with our missing possessions.[2]

Traditional societies formed out of such networks are sometimes called stateless societies. In his classic analysis of West African pre-colonial society, Robin Horton suggests that stateless societies have the following features:

1. There is little concentration of authority. It is difficult to point to any individual or limited group of people as the ruler or rulers of the society.
2. Such authority roles as exist act upon a rather limited sector of the lives of those subject to them.
3. The wielding of authority as a specialised, full-time occupation is virtually unknown.
4. The unit within which people feel an obligation to settle their disputes according to agreed rules and without resort to force tends to be relatively small (Horton 1972, 78).

Operating at a largely local level and with no fixed patterns of centralised government, Sierra Leonean society employed traditional mechanisms for combining into larger confederations as the situation demanded. Chiefs, elders, and other leaders would meet as needed, for example, to make arrangements for mutual defence or some mutually advantageous commercial venture. For the most part, traditional rulers were born rather than elected or appointed, so civil society rarely played an active role in the choice of leaders. Still, over time, seemingly apolitical people's organisations became crucial for the expression of political demands (Makumbe 1998, 306–7), especially against unjust colonial practices and policies. Examples of early mobilisation of organised groups against injustice include opposition on the part of the Bai Bureh to the imposition of the Hut Tax by the British, the Hydara Rebellion in 1930 in the Kambia District, and the resistance of Pitherr Kamama of Rofainkeu in the Port Loko District to the Hut Tax. As elements of democratic forms of governance were haltingly put in place by the colonial authorities in Sierra Leone, traditional organisations were able to leverage the space for discourse into organised action.

Evolution of Civil Society in Sierra Leone

A discussion of civil society in Sierra Leone must acknowledge the tendency demonstrated by both the state and some factions of the population to be tyrannical, murderous, and lawless, operating outside the understanding of mutually respected contracts. In this environment civil society organisations provided an associative bulwark against both the power of the state and the tyranny of the majority. A civil society playing a mediating role between the individual and the state is clearly needed in Sierra Leone because the state has shown no interest in defending the rights of the citizens. According to this view, to the extent that individuals live and function locally, they can expect protection from the community network. One lesson of the 1990s, however, is that this is a fragile protection, and if the state is unable or unwilling to protect its citizens, the individual will remain vulnerable to future rebel RUFs. To the extent that it can, civil society must find a way to fill this gap left by the state. It must engage in concerted action, stand in the breach, and provide a safety net. Otherwise, Sierra Leone's experience shows that the rights of individuals will be sacrificed.

Although the response of civil society was often vacillating and weak, it none-theless gained legitimacy and relevance throughout the 1990s as events forced greater involvement. The civil society sector became a dynamic, innovative source for raising new concerns, articulating new directions, and generating an analysis of values as new collective identities took shape.

Civil society in Sierra Leone today is composed of church-based and religious organisations; trade unions; associations and forums of farmers and workers; hu-man rights groups; NGOs; community-based organisations (CBOs); and organisations of students, traders, lawyers, truck drivers, teachers, youth, miners, and other activists. These organisations include women and men from every part of the country, with traditional groups often standing alongside more modern types of organisations. Formed into self-governing associations, these groups provide a means to educate the citizenry, scrutinise state actions, redistribute power, and encourage direct citizen participation in public affairs.

Major Influences

As civil society developed maturity and effectiveness in Sierra Leone, evolving from local forms into a nationally influential force, three main types of organisations emerged: local, regional/national, and international. First, structures for action at a local level evolved; they include local churches, traditional societies, civil tradi-tional defence forces made up of hunters, village committees and structures, local market networks, and schools. Second, regional or national alliances were created which include trade unions, alliances of women's groups, student movements, and associations of churches and other religious groups. Finally, the influence of the DELTA (Development Education and Leadership Training for Action) leadership development movement, an organisation spread across Africa, engaged the civil populace across national borders in genuine participation in its journey toward the radical transformation of society.

Weaknesses of Sierra Leone's Civil Society Regarding the State

From the time of independence in 1961 until the 1990s, civil society was not a co-ordinated movement and suffered from several fundamental weaknesses. Some civil society organisations tolerated or even supported oppressive state power. In a nation where the government had never enjoyed a strong sense of legitimacy, the consequence was successive coups and manipulations of the nation's constitution to consolidate authoritarian power. One result was the gradual "depoliticisation" and withdrawal of popular participation from the political process. This was espe-cially evident as each regime used its powers to suppress all opposition. Political life came to be seen as a farce. People saw that their trust in the government was betrayed as "the ants of the savannah"[3] carried off all the resources of the country for personal enrichment (Nyong'o 1992).

Kabiru Kinyanjui points out in his case study of Kenya in Chapter 3 that a "method used to control dissent was to incorporate the offending organisation into the political party and thereby manage its activities." So it was in Sierra Leone as civil society organisations were created by a succession of national governments in an attempt to create a facade of legitimacy. But of course these organisations lacked autonomy, credibility, and neutrality. Only occasionally did they openly pursue the national good. The lack of true independence meant that the activities of civil society, with some organisations demoralised and others controlled by the government, for many years did not significantly influence the socio-economic and political spheres of the country or alter the terms of national discourse.

And yet, when the war in Sierra Leone expanded from a local cross-border skirmish into a conflict that engulfed the nation, civil society found its voice – both in actions for justice and in redefining the terms of engagement by which people came together in common cause. This common cause was compelled by the conflict which, erupting in the early 1990s, was primarily a war by the rebels against civilians, against communities, against families, against the ethos of a people that still wanted to believe that neighbours could trust neighbours. It was a war in which a rebel group intentionally worked at systematically destroying trust by turning children against parents, neighbour against neighbour, stoking hatred and hostility through a strategy it called "disrupt civil life."

THE CONFLICT IN SIERRA LEONE IN THE 1990S

Key Dates Marking the Civil War

The world hardly took notice when the war in Liberia, a neighbouring West African state, began to spread to Sierra Leone. Although it is not our purpose here to analyse the history of that war, the following time line provides a sense of the chaotic context in which Sierra Leone was living in the 1990s.

March 1991   An attack in the East of the country by a little-known group, the RUF, led by Foday Sankoh, is a harbinger of the waves of violence and brutality to come.

1992   The APC (All People's Congress) government that has ruled Sierra Leone as a one-party government for twenty-four years is overthrown in a military coup. A military regime, the NPRC (National Provisional Ruling Council) takes power and presides over a gradually deteriorating situation marked by the continuing RUF-initiated war against civilians.

1996   Church and CBOs and associations as well as local NGOs allied with the international community force the NPRC military regime to return power to elected civilians. The NPRC is compelled to hold national elections that bring an elected government into power with Ahmed Tejan Kabbah as president.

May 1997	These democratic gains are again reversed by the military. The AFRC (Armed Forces Revolutionary Council) junta[4] takes power by force. Incredibly, the AFRC and the RUF join forces to pursue a campaign of murder, torture, rape, looting, and the shutdown of all licit banking and commerce, bringing the country to a virtual standstill.
February 1998	The AFRC/RUF is driven out of Freetown by a coalition of West African forces (ECOMOG) under Nigerian leadership; President Ahmed Kabbah returns from his safe haven in neighbouring Guinea to resume his presidency in Freetown.
January 1999	AFRC/RUF elements attack Freetown. During two weeks of arson, terror, murder, and rape, over 6,000 civilians are killed and 2,000 children are reported missing. Again, ECOMOG forces (primarily Nigerian) push the AFRC/RUF out of Freetown.
June 1999	After many failed attempts at negotiating a return to civilian rule, peace talks are organised in Lomé, the capital of Togo, between the government elected in 1996 and the RUF.
May 2000	Foday Sankoh, the RUF commander, having refused to carry out the terms of the peace agreement, remains in Freetown and surrounds himself with armed guards. The civil society movement, by now an increasing force in Sierra Leone, organises a march on his house to demand that he abide by the peace agreement. Frightened, he jumps over the back wall to hide in the surrounding hills. His guards open fire on the crowd of 20,000 peaceful marchers and more than 20 are killed. Two weeks later, Foday Sankoh emerges, is arrested, and is remanded into custody.
September 2001	A formal end to the 10-year civil war is declared following disarmament of warring factions by the United Nations Mission to Sierre Leone.
May 2002	Ahmed Tejan Kabbah is elected president in an internationally supervised election, while Foday Sankoh awaits trial on charges of murder.

These dates give a deceptively linear, sequential, almost methodical profile to what was in fact a bewildering aggression operating at myriad levels of mercenary self-interest.

Between 1991 and 1999, violence took a minimum of 75,000 predominantly civilian lives, caused half a million Sierra Leoneans to become refugees outside their own country, and internally displaced another half of the country's 4.5 million population, more than the entire population of Kosovo.

In the Grip of Civil War

The war in Sierra Leone was not an ideological struggle, a crisis of modernity resulting from three decades of inept post-colonial government, or even a rebellion on the part of disillusioned youth. In fact, the few ideologists of radical intellectual roots as may have attached themselves to the RUF "were extinguished in murderous internal purges during the RUF's first year of operation" (Smillie, Gberie, and Hazleton 2000, 10). While there is no doubt about widespread public disenchantment with the failing state, corruption, and lack of opportunity in Sierra Leone in the late 1980s and early 1990s, these were not the impetus that led to years of brutality by forces devoid of ideology, political support, and community identity. Instead, the best explanation for the war and its incredibly brutal violence is the economic opportunity presented by the breakdown in governance.

Ibrahim Elbadawi and Nicholas Sambanis, World Bank economists who have written widely concerning the economics of war in Africa, argue that deep political and economic development failures – not tribalism or ethnic hatred – are the root causes of Africa's conflicts. Their conclusion, based on an analysis of the likelihood of civil war in 161 countries, is that Africa's ethnic diversity, contrary to popular stereotypes, actually helps the emergence of stable development because it encourages the establishment of intergroup contracts through a bargaining process. They argue that "Africa's ethnic diversity is a deterrent rather than a cause of civil war" (Elbadawi and Sambanis 2000, 10). Diversity and the relationships among groups can be peaceful if ethnic groups feel adequately represented by their national political institutions and if the economy provides opportunity for productive activity.

On the other hand, good predictors of civil wars are a country's heavy dependence on resource-based primary exports (which are easy to loot, and thus an easy source of reward for rebel recruits) and, especially, failed political institutions. "Rebellions are often financed by natural resource depredation, such as alluvial diamonds in West Africa. . . . Natural resources are . . . lootable . . . and they may be the sole source of rebel finance" (Collier and Hoeffler 2000, 3). This analysis finds a textbook corroboration in Sierra Leone, where the diamond mines provided the easily lootable resource that generated the profit to sustain the war throughout the 1990s.

Diamonds Are at the Heart of the Matter

What has been abundantly clear in Sierra Leone is that the use of violence for economic gain was anything but random. Mercenaries, mining companies, military forces, intelligence agencies, governments, banks, and commercial interests were often involved in supporting one or another warring faction, often in sequence. Meticulously researched documents, reports, and publications have provided names and affiliations of those causing conflict for economic reasons.[5] None is new to the business of looting a country, for this, in fact, was their objective. A destabilised country was merely an aid to the end of profiting as quickly as possible from the rich diamond mines.

Clausewitz's formula that "war is the pursuit of politics by other means" was replaced in Sierra Leone by David Keen's assertion that "war is the pursuit of economics by other means" (in Smillie, Gbere, and Hazleton 2000, 12). One could go further and say that the war in Sierra Leone has been the pursuit of profit by other means. Looking at those with interests in Sierra Leone – diamond companies, mining interests, arms dealers, mercenaries, security firms, PR companies, and big-name attorneys representing rebel leaders – one is not surprised at the estimations of mind-boggling profits accruing to all these. And all the while the world seems to prefer believing that the war is an intertribal conflict in a small West African state.

In 1960 Sierra Leone officially produced one-third of the world's diamonds, and taxes on the industry were the government's primary source of income, providing about 70 per cent of the country's foreign exchange reserves (Smillie, Gberie, and Hazleton 2000, 42). By 1957, there were an estimated 75,000 illicit miners in just one area, Kono, and smuggling was entrenched. The mining areas were fast moving out of the control of the government, which tried with little success to control the trafficking by issuing mining permits. After the peak in 1960, the system in place continued evolving according to its own logic, which encouraged a lack of authority or mechanisms for control. As private illicit commercial interests profited from instability, opportunism was rewarded and, along with the illegal diamond industry, the arms trade also thrived.

By the 1990s only 8,500 carats of diamonds were legally exported from Sierra Leone annually. Antwerp diamond dealers, on the other hand, report receiving 80,000 carats from Sierra Leone. Other sources report even wider discrepancies; estimates are that 85 per cent of the production was smuggled out of Sierra Leone (Smillie, Gberie, and Hazleton 2000, 17). During the same period the Belgian Diamond High Council (the organisation that monitors diamond dealing in Antwerp – the world's centre for the diamond business) reports receiving 2.6 million carats per year from Liberia – a country whose diamond mines were closed down in the 1980s for lack of production. Liberia shares a border with Sierra Leone and has been a backer of the RUF (Revolutionary United Front) throughout the war. According to the UN news agency IRIN, on 5 October 2000 a team of UN experts finally visited Liberia to investigate charges that the government of President Charles Taylor has been the major channel of smuggled diamonds from Sierra Leone in exchange for providing weapons to the RUF. What had been an open secret for years had finally been officially recognised. Since then, the evidence has mounted of the involvement of many other West African countries in the diamonds-for-arms smuggling that kept the RUF rebellion supplied with unprecedented quantities of arms and enriched a vast network from heads of governments to rebel recruits.

With an already weak, post-colonial state, governing the nation and controlling the diamond industry proved to be beyond the government's ability. Contributing to the problem, the government gave over security in the mining areas in 1960 to the various mining companies, which imported mercenaries advertising themselves as "security firms." These "security firms" enabled competing outside interests to gain operational control of the mines. The heads of state of successive Sierra

Leonean governments made sure, however, that they received their cut from the system. Several Lebanese families, resident in Sierra Leone since the turn of the century, were positioned as middlemen who ensured that the pay-offs needed to keep the system running were made. These operations were only slightly disguised, for many of the players had legitimate headquarters in financial capitals of the world; they hired law firms linked with governments and government agencies; and they mingled with the rich and famous in many legitimate enterprises. Their ability to plunder the diamond mines of Sierra Leone depended not only on financial backing but also on their links with legitimate governments and corporate interests.

Operating with near impunity in the context of a failed political system, rebels and their outside "investors" pursued their goal of profitable crime under the cover of warfare (Smillie, Gberie, and Hazleton 2000, 12). Criminal interests competed, bought off, manipulated, and preyed on the self-interest of successive in-country power merchants. William Reno described this "shadow state" as being ruled "by fiat through a patronage network, manipulating factions and tensions, and weakening any formal institution – army, police, universities, central bank, the civil service" (in Smillie, Gberie, and Hazleton 2000, 14). Under President Siaka Stevens and his successor, Joseph Momoh, state kleptocracy and the general disintegration of government control continued through the 1970s and 1980s, allowing organised crime and diamond smuggling to become entrenched, along with their close allies, weapons and drug trafficking, all of which helped lay the groundwork for the chaos of the 1990s.

Civil Society – Beginnings of the Resistance

Organisation for Action – Local Level

In the face of the seemingly intractable conflict, civil society initiatives in the 1990s began to influence and mobilise public opinion in favour of working for peace, and an end to the conflict began to take shape. Early initiatives have been well documented (*Accord* 2000). For example, in 1994 a group of community leaders walked, singing, into an RUF camp on the Sierra Leone–Liberia border, bearing banners with peace messages. After delivering their requests, as community representatives, for the cessation of the offensive against civilians, several of the group volunteered to remain as hostages in the hands of the RUF, whose leaders were afraid of being attacked during the subsequent days of talks. They were to remain captives for two years. There were no discernible results directly linked to their initiative, but their example was a highly public message for peace to the nation.

Other organisations adopted an approach called "strengthening local peace constituencies," which attempted to support local groups in their resistance to rebel attempts to divide and fragment communities.

Still other attempts by civil society groupings were made to mediate between the various governments (military or civilian) and the rebels. Some of these initiatives were characterised by extreme efforts to meet whatever demands were made by the RUF (for example, to call the RUF "fighters" rather than "bandits" in national and international publications, or to deliver food and tools to villages under RUF control). Occasionally the leaders of the initiatives were jailed by the government, suspected of collaboration with the RUF. The RUF, on the other hand, rarely responded to overtures for mediation and negotiation. Some of the efforts gave more legitimacy to the RUF than intended, and the initiators became identified as RUF sympathizers or even spokespersons (Lord 2000). A number of these initiatives came from organisations based in the Sierra Leone diaspora rather than in grassroots CBOs. For example, the efforts of two prominent Sierra Leoneans living in London, Omrie Golley and Ambrose Ganda, were taken as apologia for the RUF or as self-serving efforts to develop political leverage, and had little impact on the search for peace.

Organisation for Action – National Level

More credible were the actions of women's groups that encouraged wide debate in the public domain rather than attempting to position themselves as mediators or spokespersons. These women's groups were instrumental in the national Bintumani Consultative Conference called in 1996, a national consultation which was called to make one decision – whether to seek peace with the rebels first (a decision which would allow the military regime, the NPRC, to remain in office indefinitely), or rather, to first seek national elections to return a civilian government to office. The NPRC, having stacked the conference with selected delegates, expected that there would be an easy decision allowing them to continue in power. In the middle of the meeting, however, one of the women present stood up and insisted that the people wanted elections to be held first. In frequent retellings of this powerful moment, the woman is regarded as one who was willing to stand up and tell the simple truth. When she did this, other co-opted delegates were moved to join her, which led to a massive defection of the carefully selected "appointed representatives." The result was a decision to call for elections. To the NPRC's credit, it bowed to the pressure, and Ahmed Tejan Kabbah was elected as the country's president, replacing the military government. In an impressive demonstration of the desire for peace, civilians literally protected the ballot boxes with their bodies as they were transported to counting centres in order to prevent the rebels from taking and destroying the ballots.

Yet for all the efforts made in 1996 to produce a civilian government, it led neither to a participatory peace process nor to sustainable peace. The mercenaries stayed on. "According to the Sierra Leone bi-weekly New Citizen, the only action Kabbah's government took was to cut the payment to the mercenaries from US$3 million a month to US$1.2 million" (Madsen 1999, 381).

Nonetheless, the experience of influencing national decision-making encouraged civil society actors to take increasingly effective action on a larger, national scale. The attempt by the military regime (the NPRC) to remain in power had been strongly rejected by the IRCSL, many women's organisations, the students, the Labour Congress, and many others. The collaboration of these groups was a turning point for civil society in recognising its shared potential to be the legitimate voice of the people and to steer the country in a transition toward a peace process and eventual democratic governance.

Organisation for Action – Leadership Development

One of the commonalities of these strong civil society groups is that many of their leaders graduated from the DELTA programme started by the Catholic National Pastoral and Social Development Centre in Kenema in 1983. Using the Training for Transformation paradigm, it embraced parish communities, youth groups, women's groups, trade unions, student movements, NGOs, community-based organisations, and natural leaders of many different denominations (Anglican, Wesleyan, Apostolic, Catholic, and others). Based on biblical understandings of community and justice, participants learned to see themselves and their communities not as passive victims of social forces, but as agents for social change and transformation (Mihevic 1995, 246). DELTA worked under the assumption that overcoming fear and lack of confidence among people at the grassroots is one of its most important contributions to a strong civil society movement.

At the heart of the training is the quest for the radical transformation of society through the genuine participation of those hitherto disenfranchised, exploited, alienated, suppressed, and relegated to the periphery of society. The principles of the transformation paradigm emphasise that

- All learning and development are meant to bring about radical transformation of the self, community, the environment, and society at large.
- Liberating education and development can take place only in an atmosphere of trust and dialogue where no one claims either to have all the answers or to be totally ignorant – each person is both learner and trainer.
- For learning and development to be transformative, it must create critical consciousness through the use of the question posing approach where the participants are challenged to actively describe their situation, critically analyse the factors/causes/consequences, and decide upon and plan for action to effect change.
- Learners must determine the subject of their own learning. "Generative themes" that arise out of their own lives and experience are the issues that will move them to action for transformation.
- The action/reflection/action praxis becomes the organizing principle that allows people to constantly reflect critically in order to move further and avoid getting locked into "solutions" (Mihevic 1995, 246).

Learning how to mobilise people for action; analysing situational, structural, and social problems; developing solidarity teams; and organising work and activities from within Sierra Leonean cultural and religious traditions have allowed DELTA graduates to build community leadership. They have been deliberate about constructing social capital, and they have translated the DELTA training into local languages and abstractions, thus providing people with tools for leadership, communication, and action.

Jonah Katoneene, director of the Association of Christian Lay Centres in Africa (ACLCA), regards the Training for Transformation model as the lifeblood of the churches in Africa in the 1990s (Mihevic 1995, 246). As powerful as the techniques of social analysis and building civil society movements are, even more potent has been the development of local and national networks of people sharing a common vision and using a common language of biblically understood transformation. "The renewed goal of the lay centres is to transform those educated into 'prophet/teachers' who realize that their role in society is not only a matter of speaking out against evils in society but, more significantly, a question of seeking to transform the present oppressive structures into humane and just relations among the children of God" (ibid.).

Beginning in 1985, in the Kuranko area, CES sent its entire staff, village animators[6] and church workers alike, through the DELTA training programme. These staff members in turn enabled village committees, associations, and churches to define and construct their own development using transformational social analysis and community-building tools adapted to their particular circumstances. With the complete collapse of governmental services in that area of the country during the latter half of the 1990s, the village-based programme continued providing a network for food distribution, health care, services for displaced people, and church ministry. The Sierra Leonean staff members, evacuated to Freetown when the programme infrastructure was totally looted and/or destroyed by the RUF, carried with them skills which they continued to use in the vast camps for the displaced population, collaborating with other organisations that shared the approach.

CIVIL SOCIETY AND THE PEACE PROCESS

The June-July 1999 agreement that was finally signed between the Sierra Leone government and the RUF reflected the "visible hand" of the civil society movement. The Lomé Agreement, as a conflict management and resolution document, aimed at bringing peace as well as social and economic development to Sierra Leone. Controversially, it gave respect and status to the RUF, despite the years of suffering to which the RUF had subjected the civilian population.

In preparation for the peace conference in Lomé, the Network Movement for Justice and Development (NMJD), an organisation with its roots in DELTA, organised countrywide consultations. Bringing together people across the social spectrum, these consultations wrestled with the pragmatic issues of a peace process. How should disarmament take place? Should the RUF rebels be given a place in the government? How could space be created for the continued involvement of civil society in the peace implementation phase? How could the plundering of national resources and the proliferation of weapons be stopped? Skilled in enabling communities to use social analysis to define their own vision, the NMJD also enabled the consultations to come up with recommendations based on this grassroots input. Although no civil society organisation was included in the official roster of participants at the Lomé peace talks, civil society representatives never-theless constituted their own delegation and showed up uninvited, recommenda-tions in hand. This delegation included representatives from across the spectrum of civil society, and their views carried the moral impact of legitimacy as the genu-ine voice of the people, for they represented society as a whole rather than some limited special interests.

During the talks the position of the civil society delegation as legitimate broker became apparent. Among the leaders of this delegation was the IRCSL. Prior to the talks, the IRCSL had opened channels of communication with Foday Sankoh, leader of the RUF, with little effect. Indeed, when RUF attacks increased in late 1998, they seemed to target religious establishments, churches, hospitals, and mosques. Nevertheless, because of its genuine representation of the claims of civil society as well as its reputation for steadfast probity, the IRCSL remained the most credible organisation for continuing to initiate contacts and build trust between Sankoh and the government.

During the peace talks the IRCSL consistently argued that peace in Sierra Leone depended on a fair hearing for everyone, including the RUF rebels who had un-sparingly violated Sierra Leoneans through raping, killing, abducting civilians (in-cluding children), chopping off people's limbs, indiscriminately burning and loot-ing, and causing massive displacement of terrified villagers. Understandably disturbed that the talks would include the RUF, other civil society groups were sharply critical of the IRCSL perspective. Nevertheless, through persistent pres-sure and constant dialogue, this position eventually became a keystone for the talks. It allowed the IRCSL to maintain its strategy of confidence building, thereby providing neutral support for the mediation process. In moments when the negoti-ating parties failed to see eye to eye on burning issues such as power sharing and the removal of regional military forces from Sierra Leone, IRCSL members turned to preaching and praying to break the deadlock (Turray 2000).

In a subsequent analysis of weaknesses and strengths of the peace talks and their follow-up, the director of the NMJD, Abu Brima, wrote:

> We wondered if indeed the negotiation approach presented the parties with adequately defined guidelines that [would] assist them [to] determine their positions in the light of a genuine and thorough analysis of the context [and] identification of the strategic needs and interests of the general populace of Sierra Leone, who are the victims of the situation. Most of the time was spent playing the game of politics with no sense of urgency and very little regard for the ongoing suffering of the ordinary people (Brima 1999, 4).

The divide between the legitimacy of civil society representing the demands of the people and the agenda of the RUF and the government of retaining and gaining prize pieces of power and economic gain demonstrates the seemingly impossible task before civil society. By definition, the power of civil society lies in its legiti-macy. But when the state cares little about its own legitimacy and rules instead on the basis of power stemming from its control of resources, how should civil society respond? One thing it must do is ensure its own legitimacy and integrity. This need is recognised in the same report:

> There·is the danger that the civil society movement [and other non-govern-mental institutions] may run afoul of the government, especially a govern-ment like ours that is strapped for cash – which might become suspicious of [our] motives and see [us] as challenging its authority and undermining its governance. International donors should help to ensure accountability of these [civil society] institutions, while at the same time putting pressure on the government to allow these institutions to operate under a set of mutually agreed upon rules for the benefit of the country, without compromising their independence and impartiality (Brima 1999, 9).

This is a key point about a well-functioning civil society. As Robert Putnam says, "Citizens in a civic community, though not selfless saints, regard the public domain as more than a battleground for pursuing personal interest" (Putnam, Leonardi, and Nanetti 1993). At the Lomé peace talks, while the government and its opponents sought to establish claims on the resources and means of power for the future, only civil society could claim to be the genuine and honest advocate for justice for the people of Sierra Leone.

THE WAY AHEAD

The Task of the Future

The task ahead for civil society in Sierra Leone can be summarised as follows:

- to strengthen the determination, self-confidence, and ability of civil society to resist violence
- to create alliances internally and externally with churches and organisations willing to stand for justice
- to establish and carry out a comprehensive plan to construct a culture of peace

Weighing the chances for peace in Sierra Leone, Dr. James Obita observes that "a durable settlement will have to be built on the strong foundations of democracy and popular participation and not on the shifting sands of buying off interests" (Obita 2000). Overcoming this legacy will not be easy, but it can be done. The challenge facing civil society in Sierra Leone is the pressing need for norms and networks of civic engagement. Without those, the outlook for collective action is sombre. Norms of collaboration and reciprocity, along with networks, provide the foundation for effective civic action. In the absence of democracy and a strong culture of popular participation, however, clientelism, lawlessness, ineffective gov-ernment, and economic stagnation will continue to nurture a climate of aggression and violence as colliding interests contend for power and resources. The RUF sought to destroy the norms and the ethic of community life, and the country was left with a legacy of families destroyed, trust destroyed, children destroyed. Women have been violated beyond comprehension and men compromised by brutality. It is ironic that, though enormous profits have been made from diamonds throughout the conflict, the only impact of these obscene profits on the citizens of the country where they are mined has been terror, murder, rape, abduction, dismemberment, and unprecedented poverty (Smillie, Gberie, and Hazleton 2000).

What role will the church play in restoring peace and justice? If the church in Sierra Leone has not been as forceful or courageous in confronting tyranny during the past thirty years as could be hoped, it nevertheless has a history of engagement in *pursuing justice and raising its voice against tyranny.* There are, of course, some church groups who opted for the role of *sanctuary* rather than *servant* during the years of breakdown of nationhood and destruction of human life. Even now some churches adopt quietism, though they may hope that others will go to the bar for them. Nevertheless, another large group of churches was engaged and active, and they were instrumental in leveraging those voices finally raised in condemnation of the pillaging of the country by the RUF and its supporters.

Célestin Monga writes that the struggle for liberation from oppression and exploitation is a process that includes renewing a sense of civic responsibility when a people have been exploited over decades.

> Despite apathy from opposition parties and unions, African societies [are] able to generate their own networks of communication and forums for discussion within which it [is] possible to express collective fears and dreams. For me, the term "civil society" refers to those birthplaces where the ambitions of social groups create the means of generating freedom and justice (Monga 1996, 148).

Creating the means to generate freedom and justice is an arduous process that includes building networks of trust that provide the context for action. Some churches in Sierra Leone have sought to be those birthplaces, those places of trust, where freedom and justice can be generated and dreams are translated into reality. Just as the Sierra Leone church was built by Africans for Africans, so too civil society must rise from the foundations of freedom, justice, and trust found in the Sierra Leoneans themselves. As Andrew Walls says: "Christianity in Africa will come bringing no gifts – except the gospel. . . . It will be the religion of the (comparatively) poor people, and of the (comparatively) poor world. On the other hand, it will manifestly come from the peoples of Africa to the peoples of Africa" (Walls 1976, 186). In its best moments, the church continues to act, as did those early Methodists, against injustice and betrayal, and civil society must do the same.

The Strengths of the Church in Building Peace

While organisations such as the Council of Churches and the IRCSL were strongly influential in bringing the warring parties to the negotiating table, there is still a long way to go. The ongoing effort to construct a viable peace and to bring

Sierra Leone to the path of long-term development for all the people is daunting. Yet recent developments and recent actions of the church give some reason for hope. Our experience with the churches in this terrible moment of Sierra Leone's history, leads us to the following hopeful observations:

1. The churches have acted *in response to the demands of their members* and not as hierarchies intent on their own business, giving hope that the churches can continue to be active participants and provide valuable leadership.
2. Sierra Leone has a strong history of *civic engagement* by the churches, and many churches see civil engagement as a natural part of their mission.
3. The IRCSL, itself a broad-based coalition, has continued to be active *in collaboration with other groups* such as the NMJD in efforts to disarm the rebels, to mediate the many incidents of continuing hostility, and to keep the impetus going for constructing a durable peace. The pervasive lack of trust brought on by the decade of terror is a primary impediment to collaboration, but the IRCSL is building bridges across groups to rebuild that trust.
4. The church has been committed to a deliberate process of *developing leaders* who are trained to listen to the voice of the people and to facilitate their reasoned and knowledgeable engagement in their own development. Sister Lois Anne Bordowitz, who was among the founders of the DELTA training centre, reports, "The leaders who came out of DELTA have a strong commitment to justice and the skills to empower people for organised action."[7]
5. The church has been instrumental in developing an *educated citizenry,* encouraging the outspoken and lively press which has often bluntly disclosed facts that those in power would rather keep under wraps. Numerous journalists have been jailed, but the struggle for truthfulness continues. In 2000, two Sierra Leonean journalists were recognised for their courage by receiving the Press Club award of the year in New York.
6. The church remains the *voice of conscience* and is respected by the people as a legitimate moral authority.

The Lomé Agreement carves out a specific space for civil society in Articles VI, VII, and VIII. The IRCSL is given a role in Article VIII. A meeting called in March 2000 by the Council of Churches of Sierra Leone brought together representatives of key implementers of Sierra Leone's peace accord: the IRCSL; the Civil Society Movement, which encompasses many civil society organisations; the government of President Ahmed Kabbah; and the RUF. The theme of the discussion was the prospect for justice and reconciliation and the potential impact of the Truth and Reconciliation Commission (TRC) envisaged in the Lomé Agreement. There was broad divergence among the participants, with a much greater emphasis on reconciliation (coupled with forgiveness) than on truth.

Bishop George Biguzzi, a member of the IRCSL, believes the truth must also come out. He highlighted the dilemma in noting that people might assume that the TRC would act like "a sponge – to clean up the whole thing and go forward." He insisted on the need for "religious amnesty from God, which implies that it touches my soul, my inner being. I have to understand what I have done, accept, repent if I'm the perpetrator, so that I can be healed. I will receive eventual amnesty from God and that will bring me to a point where I can be healed and my brother or sister can accept me."[8]

Calling to account, with love but with insistence, is unpopular in an environment where "forget the past – let's move on" is the predominant theme. The experience in South Africa has brought to the conscience of the world the fact that moving on must be based on truth. Those who suffered cannot be brushed aside as an unfortunate side issue. Their condition must be centre stage in the reconstruction of trust and the ethics of justice.

Civil Society and Peace Building

John Makumbe states that "African civil society (is) largely focused on the people's struggle against despotic rulers, repressive regimes and governments that violated both their individual and their collective rights" (1998, 305). With little to oppose the RUF from the various national governmental regimes that came and went in the 1990s, the only real opposition came from the people themselves. Little wonder that the RUF set about destroying the ethical basis of society in its attempt to open the way to unopposed plunder of the country. The challenge now is to bring an end to the political arbitrariness of the modern state of Sierra Leone and construct an era of accountability and justice. Is civil society up to this monumental task?

Though the process of developing democracy in Sierra Leone has only begun, civil society can nevertheless point to a steady growth and nurturing of what David Korten identifies as fundamental to a strong and an active civic engagement: "rich networks of nonmarket relationships [that build] a generalised sense of trust and reciprocity – 'social capital' [and] that increase the efficiency of human relationships in both market and governmental affairs" (Korten 1998, 55). Even in a decade marked by violence, conflict, and the deliberate destruction of trust, civil society has taken root in the continuing desire of people to work with and for each other.

The consequent network of civil society organisations in Sierra Leone demonstrates the characteristics that J. O. Ihonvbere identifies as indicators of change at a deeper level: It has grown in number (of organisations); challenged the state and its custodians; mobilised popular forces for political action; presented Sierra Leoneans with an alternative agenda for recovery, growth, accountability, and respect for human rights; and strengthened civic engagement through the steady empowerment of the people, their organisations, and communities (Ihonvbere 1998, 16).

Issues Which Confront the Peace-Building Process

A major tension in any society is the proper balance between individual rights and community responsibilities. This tension expresses itself in the discourse that questions the extent to which the individual has rights or freedoms that are "natural" and go beyond the right of the state to "manage" its citizens. If the government is considered to be the only legitimate expression of community and abrogates all power to manage its citizens, human rights have little meaning, for the government can always claim to represent the wider good in its actions to suppress individual rights. In countries based on Western liberal tradition founded on the rule of law, human rights are understood to be a legitimising force for the government. Whether or not a society searching to define its own political and social traditions apart from "Western" influences can exclude human rights from its power calculations is the question facing Sierra Leone (Marks 1998, 29). (In Chapter 5 Lowell Ewert argues that the principles of human rights are universal, not Western, and provide the most persuasive and legitimate basis for civil society.)

Still, civil society in Sierra Leone has historically focused primarily on rules for living in local community, and not on developing a blueprint for the just organisation of national power. Clientelist politics filled the vacuum, contributing to the eventual disarray and breakdown of governance. In the aftermath of the war the challenge for civil society is to advocate and act for the judicious division and use of power that puts the rights of the individual citizen first.

The experience during the 1990s has been a rich source for learning, for analysis, and for planning next steps. During the decade of war, civil society in Sierra Leone made two types of transitions: First, the focus of action moved from development to advocacy, and skills in critical thinking and structural analysis shifted the paradigm of engagement. Through DELTA training and other consciousness-raising experiences, civil society is well placed to work effectively to lay the groundwork for liberty. At the community level this work includes identifying, validating, and advocating for "non-conventional resources" of local organisations (community organisations, popular economic organisations, grassroots Christian communities, women's movements, and so forth) in which the underlying structures of liberty are embedded. Among these non-conventional resources are social awareness, organisational know-how and managerial ability, popular creativity, solidarity, and the ability to provide mutual aid, expertise, and training provided by supporting agencies, and dedication and commitment from internal and external agents (Max-Neef 1991, 79).

Second, the locus of action moved from the local to the national arena. In mid-2000, as mentioned earlier, the peace process was stalled due to the intransigence of RUF leader Foday Sankoh and his failure to carry out the terms of the peace agreement that he had signed. A coalition of women went to his house in an effort to meet with him and remonstrate. He refused to see them, but their action led to a massive "walk" by thousands of civilians saying "we have to talk with Sankoh – he has to understand that he cannot go on holding the country in crisis." This event was indicative of the growing recognition among civil society leaders that they needed to be active at the national level.

Success in creating a new "space" in which democracy can grow and be sustained through popular participation at the national level will be a benchmark of the maturing of civil society. An example is the two-day national consultative conference on Sierra Leone's mining industry organised by the NMJD in October 2000. The conference, bringing together representatives of government departments, civil society groups, and international NGOs aimed at generating information regarding the relationship among mining, security, and politics. Information of this kind, generally the property of the inner recesses of political manoeuvring, can be liberated in the civil society arena for decision-making that reflects the interests and rights of all citizens.

Conclusion

One question posed at the beginning of this chapter was whether the church in Sierra Leone has served as a catalyst for action and as the conscience of a people rising up to act against unbearable oppression and violence. This case study has illustrated that the church in Sierra Leone has learned and is learning to "do justice."

But the question is wider than that.

Not only Sierra Leone but all of us are caught up in the contemporary discourse about human rights and the nature of the interweaving of religious, economic, social, and cultural rights with political rights. Debates rage over formal versus real rights, liberty versus equality, social development versus market-based globalisation. In Sierra Leone, we, the authors, have seen first-hand the results of the distortion of rights. The initial timidity and caution of the churches in Sierra Leone are only reflections of the timidity and caution of churches in general, especially those who have not had to live with the terror and violence of a brutalising civil war. It is a timidity and caution we must overcome if we wish to forestall the forces of darkness that overtook Sierra Leone.

The church of Christ stands in the midst of the human suffering brought about by our failure to understand that the story continues, and we are all accountable.

Notes

[1] This is a Sierra Leonean term of respect and honour for women who head women's societies.

[2] Personal communication with Wyva Hasselblad, September, 2000. For this and previous information about traditional civil society organisation, the authors are grateful to Jan Disselkoen.

[3] This is a reference to Chinua Achebe's book, *Anthills of the Savannah* (London: William Heinemann, 1987).

[4] Among the various military coups and regimes, only the AFRC is known as the junta in Sierra Leone.

[5] See, for example, Jean-Francois Bayart, Stephen Ellis, and Beatrice Hibou, *The Criminalisation of the State in Africa* (Bloomington, Ind.: Indiana University Press, 1999); Smith Hempstone, *Rogue Ambassador* (Sewannee, Tenn.: University of the South Press. 1997); Wayne Madsen, *Genocide and Covert Operations in Africa 1993–1999* (New York: Edwin Mellen Press, 1999); Ian Smillie, Lansana Gberie, and Ralph Hazleton, *The Heart of the Matter: Sierra Leone, Diamonds and Human Security (Complete Report),* edited by

Bernard Taylor (Ontario: Partnership Africa Canada, 2000); William Reno, *Warlord Politics and African States* (Boulder, Colo.: Lynne Reinner Publishers, 1998); Ibrahim Abdullah, *Bush Path to Destruction: The Origin and Character of the Revolutionary United Front*, *Journal of Modern African Studies* 36/2 (1998); Yusuf Bangura, "Understanding the Political and Cultural Dynamics of the Sierra Leone War: A Critique of Paul Richards' *Fighting for the Rainforest*," *African Development* 22/3–4 (1997); Ibrahim Abdullah, et al., "Lumpen Youth Culture and Political Violence: Sierra Leoneans Debate the RUF and the Civil War," *Africa Development* 22:3/4; Global Witness, "A Rough Trade: The Role of Companies and Governments in the Angola Conflict" (London: Global Witness, 1999).

[6] Village animators play a key role in community-managed development. They are community members chosen by the community to be trained as facilitators of participatory community discussion, analysis, and organisation for action.

[7] Sister Lois Anne Bordowitz, personal communication with Wyva Hasselblad, September 2000.

[8] Dialogue on justice and reconciliation facilitated by Florella Hazely, Council of Churches in Sierra Leone, March 2000. Available online at <http://www.c-r.org/accord/accord9/dialogue.htm>.

REFERENCES

Accord. 2000 (September). A publication of Conciliation Resources

Brima, Abu. 1999. *Report of Civil Society in the Sierra Leone Peace Talks in Lomé, Togo, May/June 1999*. Submitted by civil society delegates to the peace talks in Lomé, Togo, 24 June 1999.

Collier, Paul, and Anke Hoeffler. 2000. "On the Incidence of Civil War in Africa." First draft for the World Bank. Online at the World Bank website.

Elbadawi, Ibrahim, and Nicholas Sambanis. 2000. "Why Are there So Many Civil Wars in Africa? Understanding and Preventing Violent Conflict." *Journal of African Economies*.

Elliott, J. B. 1851. *Lady Huntingdon's Connexion in Sierra Leone: A Narrative of Its History and Present State*. London.

Hope, Anne, and Sally Timmel. 1992. *Training for Transformation: Handbook for Community Workers*. Zimbabwe: Mambo Press.

Horton, Robin. 1972. "Stateless Societies in the History of West Africa." In *History of West Africa*, edited by A. Ajayi and M. Crowder. New York: Columbia University Press.

Ihonvbere, J. O. 1998. *Africa and the New World Order*. New York: Peter Lang.

Keen, David. 1995. *War as a Source of Losses and Gains*. Oxford: Queen Elizabeth House.

Korten, David C. 1998. *Globalizing Civil Society: Reclaiming Our Right to Power*. New York: Seven Stories Press.

Lord, David. 2000. "Early Civil Society Peace Initiatives." *Accord: An International Review of Peace Initiatives* (September).

Madsen, Wayne. 1999. *Genocide and Covert Operations in Africa 1993–1999*. New York: Edwin Mellen Press.

Makumbe, J. M. 1998. "Is There Civil Society in Africa?" *International Affairs* (April).

Marke, C. 1913. *Origins of Wesleyan Methodism in Sierra Leone*. London.

Marks, Stephen, P. 1998. "'From the Single Confused Page' to the 'Decalogue for Six Billion Persons': The Roots of the Universal Declaration of Human Rights in the French Revolution." *Human Rights Quarterly* 20:3. Also available online.

Max-Neef, Manfred A. 1991. *Human Scale Development: Conception, Application and Further Reflections*. New York: The Apex Press.

Mihevic, John. 1995. *The Market Tells Them So: The World Bank and Economic Fundamentalism in Africa*. London: Zed Books.

Monga, Célestin. 1996. *The Anthropology of Anger: Civil Society and Democracy in Africa*. Translated by L. Fleck and C. Monga. Boulder, Colo.: Lynne Rienner Publishers.

Nyong'o, Peter Anyang. 1992. "Africa: The Failure of One-Party Rule." *Journal of Democracy* 3/1 (January): 90–96.

Obita, James. 2000. "Paying the Price: The Sierra Leone Peace Process." *Accord: An International Review of Peace Initiatives* (September).

Putnam, Robert, Robert Leonardi, and Raffaella Nanetti. 1993. *Making Democracy Work: Civic Traditions in Modern Italy*. Princeton, N.J.: Princeton University Press.

Smillie, Ian, Lansana Gberie, and Ralph Hazleton. 2000. *The Heart of the Matter: Sierra Leone, Diamonds and Human Security (Complete Report)*, edited by Bernard Taylor. Ontario: Partnership Africa Canada.

Turray, Thomas. 2000. "Civil Society and Peacebuilding: The Role of the Inter-Religious Council of Sierra Leone." *Accord: An International Review of Peace Initiatives* (September). Online at the Conciliation Resources website.

Walls, Andrew F. 1970. "A Christian Experiment: The Early Sierra Leone Colony." In *The Mission of the Church and the Propagation of the Faith: Papers Read at the Seventh Summer Meeting and the Eighth Winter Meeting of the Ecclesiastical History Society* edited by G. J. Cuming. Cambridge: Cambridge University Press.

———. 1976. "Towards Understanding Africa's Place in Christian History." In *Religion in a Pluralistic Society*, edited by J. S. Pobee. Leiden: Brill.

———. 2000. "Eusebius Tries Again: Reconceiving the Study of Christian History." *International Bulletin of Missionary Research* (July).

3

THE CHRISTIAN CHURCHES
AND CIVIL SOCIETY IN KENYA

Kabiru Kinyanjui

The cry of the African – of the African human being – ought to
move the churches to question themselves as to what they are,
what they are saying and what they are doing in Africa.
—JEAN-MARC ELA (1986)

The mainline Christian churches have played a role in widening the space for the emergence, development, and operation of civil society in Kenya. [1] By "space" we mean freedom to form an organisation or pressure group, to hold meetings, articulate ideas, plan, and mobilise citizens towards realisation of objectives without hindrance, threat, or harassment. The churches themselves are part and parcel of the "associational life," or civil society, in Kenya. After President Moi assumed power in 1978 the development of an authoritarian state, through the consolidation and concentration of power in the executive and a dominant political party, led to the weakening of the legislature, the judiciary, and the civil service. The way power was consolidated and maintained in the 1980s spurred the churches to fill the vacuum caused by the banning of political parties and other civil society institutions.

At an historical conjuncture in the late 1980s, the churches played a critical role in civil society by contributing significantly to the process of democratisation, by opening and/or widening a space for the emergence, development, and operation of other civil society organisations. This analysis underlines the factors and the circumstances that made it possible for churches to play such a critical role in the process of democratisation at a time when the state stifled, controlled, or suppressed civil society organisations (trade unions, women's and students' organisations, university staff union, and so on). It is important to understand how some churches assumed a civil society role and became significant players in the struggle for greater political, social, and economic citizen involvement. The history, theological outlook, organisational capacity, resources, ethnicity, leadership, and international character of the churches shaped the prominent role that the churches played in the agitation for change (Ndegwa 1996; Kassimir 1998). These struggles also changed the churches themselves, in particular the way they viewed their roles as civil society actors. Finally, we discuss how this legacy of civil participation in the churches can be strengthened for the future.

CIVIL SOCIETY IN KENYA: THE PLACE OF THE CHURCHES

How does civil society in Africa fit with the organisation, operation, and existence of the church in society? How does the concept of a prophetic church precondition churches to play certain roles in society that correspond to secular understanding of civil society? The ascendancy of the notion of civil society in the discourse on the African situation is related to wide disillusionment with the performance of the post-colonial state, which critics argue has failed to safeguard citizens' rights and freedom, to provide for the basic needs of the poor, and to spur economic development (Commonwealth Foundation 1999). These weaknesses of the state have led to the emergence of strong forces for democratic governance and liberalization of the economy, which have contributed to the building and strengthening of civil society institutions, even as they created an enabling environment for private investments. While the nature of the state required in emerging African nations is still a matter of debate and struggle, there is a marked tendency to be optimistic about the potential for civil society institutions and actors to act both as a force against an authoritarian and "retreating" state and as a source of hope for democratisation (Mwengo and All Africa Conference of Churches 1993; Chabal and Daloz 1999). Civil society articulates and safeguards the interests of groups in the society whose freedom and basic needs are threatened, encroached upon, or denied either by the state or by powerful economic players. In this way these groups are interconnected with the state, even as they stand apart from it.

The churches have always justified their role in the process of democratisation as that of pursuing a prophetic mission. How does this relate to their role as civil society agents? In both theoretical and practical terms, church involvement in political, social, and economic issues is essentially what defines it as an institution of the civil society (Gifford 1998). Precisely how the church acts, whether in collaboration or conflict with the state, depends on how its prophetic mission is understood and translated into practice. The theological stance taken by mainline churches in Kenya has been a major bone of contention with the state and a subject of acrimonious debate between politicians and progressive church leadership. It has also been a matter of sharp division, both theologically and politically, between the progressive segments of the churches and conservative evangelicals. This division has been prevalent for a long time and continues to be a main obstacle in the churches' involvement with democratic governance and constitutional change. The state apparatus benefits from theological thinking that reduces the role of the churches to that of the "praying department" of the state and denies them a role in changing the status quo. Some churches in Kenya, as we shall note, have accepted this role.

Although interaction between church and state in Kenya has received much attention (Gifford 1995; Ngunyi 1999; Throup 1995; Abuom 1996; Assefa and Wachira 1996; and Mugambi 1997), there have been fewer attempts to provide a critical assessment of the churches' contributions to the struggle for democratic space and to the building and strengthening of civil society.

THE POLITICAL AND HISTORICAL CONTEXT

The emergence of the churches in the late 1980s must be understood in the context of how President Moi consolidated power, attempted to establish his social and political legitimacy, and built his own social base of support apart from the old regime. Although he portrayed himself as following the footsteps *(Nyayo)* of Jomo Kenyatta, he instead built power structures that he could control and from which he could command total allegiance. In the process, the country witnessed systematic destruction of institutions and mechanisms by which power relations between the state and society had been mediated in the Kenyatta era. Similarly, civil society institutions were stifled, controlled, or co-opted to the extent that they lost their independence to act or to express views different from those in power. While some churches were also co-opted by the regime, mainline churches frequently resisted, though not without suffering the bruises of state animosity and internal division. Even so, the events of this period provoked intense discussion among key church leaders and theologians on the prophetic role of the churches in the processes of democratisation, constitution making, and peacebuilding. As it turned out, the struggles of the 1980s widened the scope of religious organisations in the society.

Moi embarked on a systematic process of building his own social bases of political support, which he thought required the destruction of institutions, processes, and individuals that exhibited any measure of independence (*Weekly Review,* 9 December 1988). Moi also enacted administrative and legislative changes to anchor and legitimise his political ambition. Notably, the government changed the constitution in 1982, 1986, and 1988 and changed election procedures in 1986. These changes made KANU (Kenya African Nation Union) the sole political party in the country, weakened the parliament, and removed the tenure of the office of the attorney general, the auditor general, and the judges of the High Court and the Court of Appeal. Consequently, power was concentrated in the executive. These steps added to the enormous power the executive already possessed through its control of state institutions such as the provincial administration, police, intelligence, armed forces, prisons, and monopoly of the broadcast media. A few remaining civil society institutions, such as the churches and the university staff and student organisations not under his patronage, remained a thorny and persistent problem for the Moi regime.

Kenya became a de facto one-party state in 1969, when the Kenya People's Union led by Jaramogi Oginga Odinga was banned, and it became a de jure one-party state in 1982, even though political parties were legally permitted. In response to the lack of political pluralism, two politicians, Oginga Odinga and George Anyona, who were denied participation in politics through KANU, tried to register a new party, the Kenya African Socialist Alliance (KASA). Moi was already too powerful, however, and KASA was unsuccessful. As Kiraitu Murungi points out, the ruling party in the first decade of Moi's rule became a formidable organ for the control and exercise of political power. It not only blurs the distinctions of government organs sought to be maintained under doctrine of separation of powers, but also asserts its superiority and primacy over them. It also permeates all sectors of the social, economic and political life of the nation by directly intervening in private economic activities: *matatu* business, trade unions, women organisations as well performing judicial and police functions (Murungi 1992).

From the time Moi ascended to power, the relationship between the government and civil society became increasingly problematic and strained. Those organisations with which he disagreed, or which he perceived to be a threat to his hold on power were outlawed, dissolved, or co-opted. Individuals perceived to be posing a threat were detained, silenced, or forced into exile. As one example, immediately upon his accession to power, Moi banned ethnic welfare associations (Gikuyu, Embu and Meru Association [GEMA], Luo Union, and Abaluhya Union being the most prominent). Ethnic names for football clubs were no longer permitted. In 1982 two trade unions, the Kenya Union of Civil Servants and the University Academic Staff Union, were banned. In December 1988 Moi banned three transport organisations: the Kenya Country Bus Owners Association (KCBOA), the Matatu Vehicle Owners Association (MVOA), and the Matatu Association of Kenya (MAK). This was followed by control and surveillance of dissent, especially at the universities. Professional organisations were soon affected; registration was denied to the Medical Practitioners and Dentist Union, the Universities Academic Staff Union (UASU), and the Bank Workers Union. Leading intellectuals, lecturers, and lawyers critical of the regime were imprisoned, detained, or forced into exile. The intensified repression and the discontent during this period precipitated a situation that led to an attempted military coup on August 1, 1982, which in turn resulted in further crackdowns on dissent, especially among university staff and students. The process of co-optation also continued as a leading organisation for women's development (Maendeleo ya Wanawake) and the Central Organization of Trade Unions (COTU) were incorporated into the ruling party.

Moi's response to the attempted coup was to accelerate the purge of individuals in all state institutions who were perceived to be opposed to his regime and who came from ethnic groups perceived to be hostile to his rule. The most dramatic example was that of Charles Njonjo, a powerful attorney general during Kenyatta's rule, who stage-managed the transition of power from Kenyatta to Moi. Njonjo was accused of being a traitor and found guilty of attempting to overthrow the government with foreign support (he was later pardoned). Moi's willingness to allow this to happen to a person who was a close lieutenant in his ascension to power indicated how far he was willing to go. Njonjo's public humiliation was followed by a purge of those in state institutions and KANU deemed to be Njonjo's allies. The Njonjo affair was a watershed in the consolidation of Moi's presidency. The national general election held in 1983, immediately after the Njonjo humiliation, led to further consolidation of power and to the erosion of the parliament as an independent institution. Total control of parliament was not fully achieved, however, until five years later, when election procedures for party nomination and election of members of parliament, initially proposed in 1986, were implemented during the general elections of 1988.

These electoral changes ushered in new procedures for selecting the party's candidates for local and parliamentary elections. Among these were new procedures for nomination and selection of KANU civic and parliamentary candidates, popularly known as the "queuing system" (as opposed to secret ballot), and a rule stipulating that a candidate gaining 70 per cent of the votes cast during the party's primary elections automatically became an elected member of parliament. Such rules, of course, allowed manipulation of the election process in favour of those who were loyal to the regime. They also disenfranchised citizens who were not members of the ruling party or wanted to queue behind their preferred candidate.

These procedures were highly controversial and became the first major source of conflict and confrontation between the church and the state. A resolution passed at a pastors' conference organised by the National Council of Churches in Kenya (NCCK) raised concern about the implications and consequences of these changes, thus opening a new confrontational chapter in the relationship between the state and the main churches in Kenya. Before this, the relationship between the churches and the regime was rather cosy. President Moi had attended church services of various denominations every Sunday, and he had appointed numerous church leaders to state, parastatals, and party positions. Rev. Lawi Imathiu, the former presiding bishop of the Methodist church in Kenya was nominated as a member of Parliament (MP) by Moi. Politicians often raised funds for church buildings and development work, which also tended to compromise their independence. Such practices endeared Moi to the churches and helped him to legitimatise his rule during his first five years. By 1986, however, this relationship was starting to turn sour.

The state employed three methods to manage dissent emanating from civil society. First, organisations or institutions that posed any perceived challenge to the emerging authoritarian order were banned. The enactment of a one-party state essentially outlawed political organising in any form. Other civil society institutions, such as trade unions, farmers' organisations, and business organisations, were outlawed by presidential decree. Second, offending organisations were incorporated into the political party, which thereby managed their activities. This eliminated organisational autonomy and fostered sycophancy. In other instances the state controlled who was selected to take leadership of local community based organisations that managed school, water, or health projects. Party branches were established within public institutions, like the universities, to monitor and contain dissent. The third mode of control was confrontation, destruction, or the use of "divide and rule" tactics. This was the primary method used to deal with the churches. Divisions were created across denominational lines – for example, between the mainline churches and the evangelicals – as well as within particular churches that were opposing repression. In addition, individual church leaders were threatened and harassed.

Moi's efforts to control, manipulate, or dismantle independent institutions extended to economic organisations. Some indigenous banks owned by ethnic groups and viewed as hostile by the regime were subjected to conditions and manipulations that led to their collapse. Major farmers' commodity-marketing organisations such as the Kenya Farmers Association (KFA), the Kenya Tea Development Authority (KTDA), and the Kenya Cooperatives Creameries (KCC) were reorganised and controlled by installing state appointees in senior management. With these changes came corruption and misappropriation of public funds and resources, leading some of these institutions to collapse or become ineffective or highly indebted. Economic institutions that still enjoyed autonomy and resources were viewed as suspect and subject to possible control or dismantling. The whole education system was also changed. A new system of eight years of primary, four years of secondary, and four years of university education, popularly known as the 8–4–4 system, was established to enable less privileged areas to catch up with regions from which past political leaders had come.

As a consequence of these changes, tactics, and machinations of the state, most of the independent civil society and economic institutions were silenced, disabled, or controlled. Fortunately, some churches and their leadership emerged to fill the vacated space. In some instances these efforts went further and widened the space that allowed other civil society players to emerge, especially in the 1990s (Ngunyi 1999; Mutunga 1999). On the whole, as argued by Kanyinga, "The Nyayo one party state, once it consolidated, was marked by the further narrowing of the space for civil society activism, increased political repression that bordered on tyranny, the severe constriction of popular participation in the political process, and intensified corruption" (Kanyinga 1998, 55).

In the meantime, the churches were informed and encouraged by prevailing thinking and trends in other parts of the world, as well as specific events in Latin America, the Philippines, the former Soviet Union, and indeed elsewhere in Africa.[2] Widespread calls to respect human rights, the convening of national conventions to resolve governance issues, and the exposure of how state repression was justified in the name of state security influenced the thinking of Kenyan church leadership.

CHURCHES AS CRITICAL PLAYERS IN STRUGGLES FOR DEMOCRATIC SPACE (1986–93)

Three aspects of the work of mainline churches in the expansion of democratic space and the emergence of a vibrant civil society in Kenya are especially important: contributions of church leaders to the debates on major concerns of the day; the practice of the churches as part of civil society; and the willingness of the churches to collaborate with others in building and strengthening the capacities, leadership, and outlook of nascent civil society organisations. The latter was especially notable in 1992, when the repeal of section 2A of the Kenya Constitution (which had sanctioned one-party rule) provided space for multiparty democracy. KANU was still in a dominant position, as it controlled state institutions and had enormous organisational and financial resources. Though the NCCK recognised this, it nevertheless provided neutral space to new political parties for discussion. KANU was invited but boycotted these opportunities.

The contribution of the churches to the democratisation process in Kenya resulted from the unique position they occupied in the society between 1985 and 1993. First, in the social, economic, and political context outlined above, they retained autonomy, which other institutions had lost. As David Throup wrote: "The CPK [Church Province of Kenya – the Anglican church], Presbyterian, and Roman Catholic churches have occupied the ground emptied by the silencing of serious political opposition since the attempted coup and Njonjo's downfall" (Throup 1995). Second, the resistance of the churches to the emerging repression contributed to their rise to prominence in the political and governance arena and was in stark contrast to the colonial and the early years of independence when their stance was more supportive of the political status quo and their social involvement focused more on the provision of social services, education, health, rural and urban development, and so forth (NCCK 1984). During the colonial era the churches' main purpose was in the spiritual domain. What then were the internal factors that led the mainline churches and their leaders to respond differently in the 1980s and 1990s? Why did other Christians remain silent or openly support the authoritarian state?

Change in the Electoral Process

In 1986 KANU proposed to change the electoral process and procedures for electing party leaders at all levels, but especially in the primary selection of candidates who thereafter would be elected to parliament. Instead of the secret ballot, the new system required voters to queue behind their candidate or the candidate's agent. This proposal was immediately rejected by clergy from Protestant churches and Christian groups attending a seminar in August 1986 organised by NCCK and funded by World Vision, a conservative international Christian NGO (Kobia 1995 and Okullu 1997). The pastors' conference passed a mild resolution against the proposed changes, which still generated a great deal of criticism from the party and the government.

For the clergy to accept the queue voting system would have meant compromising their commitment to serving people in the local communities impartially, for everyone's political loyalties would be public information and thus subject to misuse. From this time on, the leadership of the CPK, the NCCK, and the Catholics[3] stood in the forefront of the intense debate on the implications of queuing system of voting (Kobia 1993 and 1995; Okullu 1997; Mejia 1995). KANU and the government did not give in and rescind the proposed changes, although the clergy, the army, and other professional groups were exempted from voting in this way. As no alternative voting procedures were provided, however, some members of society who valued secrecy and confidentiality in voting were disenfranchised. The whole situation raised widespread doubt as to whether the elections were free and fair.

Discontent grew among the political elites who lost through alleged rigging of elections, as well as among the voters, who felt they were denied freedom of choice.

The new electoral 70 per cent rule, which provided that those who received 70 per cent of the votes in primary elections through the queuing system were automatically elected to parliament, also allowed KANU to consolidate its control of all aspects of public life. The consequences of this new rule were evident in 1988 when 64 KANU members of Parliament (MPs) were elected unopposed, an event unprecedented since independence. Leaders deemed disloyal to the party or the president were blocked from participating in the elections. The parliament that resulted from this system was not only loyal to Moi but also silent on many critical issues.

The implementation of these election procedures and the hardening position of the party in dealing with dissent spurred the churches to take a more confrontational stance. The NCCK was condemned by government ministers as political. At the urging of the state, three "loyal" member churches and organisations withdrew from the NCCK. Church-based dissent to this point had largely been respectful rather than confrontational. The pastoral letters issued by the Catholics in November 1986 and December 1988, for example, began by reaffirming the loyalty and deep gratitude of the church to the president. The letters continued, however, by expressing concern over the emerging supremacy of the party even over the parliament, a trend which the bishops argued posed a danger of totalitarianism.[4]

The change in the electoral procedures and the emerging dominance of the party not only spurred the churches to make their voices heard, but also provided an opportunity for new church leadership to emerge. Among the new torch bearers were Henry Okullu, David Gitari, Samuel Kobia, Alexander Muge, and Timothy Njoya, and, collectively, the Catholic bishops of Kenya. These well-educated and internationally well-connected individuals eventually became the voice for those alienated from the ruling party and for those who had no other channels for expressing themselves.

Mainline churches found valuable support and a strong ally in the Law Society of Kenya, which brought its knowledge of law and legal procedures, prestige, and members to the cause that the churches had already taken up. As with the churches, the participation of the Law Society in these struggles transformed its role and character in society. It became a champion of human rights and the rule of law, fending off various attempts by the state to control its leadership and direction. In addition to the Law Society, some segments of the mass media also played a supportive role. The development of alternative mass media during this period, in particular, complemented what the churches were doing in the pulpit, forming a subtle alliance that continues today. Sermon topics on Sundays became issues of national debate all over the country through the coverage provided by newspapers and magazines. The state reacted by harassing journalists most active in this respect and banned some of the magazines.

As part of its new more confrontational role, the NCCK in 1988 furthered the process of democratisation by taking up the role of monitoring elections. In response, the *Beyond Magazine* of the NCCK was banned and its staff harassed for highlighting the "rigging" which occurred during the general elections of 1988.

By involvement in the controversies related to elections, the churches moved from merely providing social services to being critical agents of change in the governance realm. They thus became a new voice for the voiceless and at the same time opened doors for other civil society organisations to join the struggle for social justice and human rights (Ndegwa 1996).

Agitation for Constitutional Change (1989–92)

Another critical concern for churches during this period was constitutional change. Initially, their concern was the manner in which the constitution was changed to serve the narrow interests of the executive arm of the state. These changes were quickly passed, one by one, without consultation or meaningful debates (Gitari 1988; Okullu 1990; NCCK 1990; KEC 1986; KEC 1988a; KEC 1988b). Subsequently, especially in 1990, churches started agitating for constitutional changes that would allow for political pluralism. This was a radical departure from their previously meek appeals to the political leadership to take into consideration the views of the churches. No longer content to beg the state for change, church leadership exhibited a new confidence and began *demanding* change.

A number of factors led to the change in approach and strategy: the abuse of the electoral process in 1988; the assassination of Robert Ouko, a respected minister for foreign affairs in February 1990; and the call for multiparty democracy by former cabinet ministers Kenneth Matiba and Charles Rubia, and by Raila Odinga, son of the radical nationalist Oginga Odinga. Following the events in Eastern Europe, which resulted in greater citizen influence, a 1990 New Year sermon by a Presbyterian clergyman Rev. Timothy Njoya which called for dismantling the one-party rule in Kenya, emboldened church leadership. The riots of 7 July, popularly known as Saba Saba, brought public anger into the open and left scores dead. International pressure emerged as international agencies tied donor aid to respect for human rights and practise of multiparty politics. These external and internal forces coalesced to give the churches courage to call for constitutional reforms. A 23 April 1990 press statement by one of the leading church leaders and a champion for democracy, Bishop Henry Okullu, depicts the prophetic agenda of the church with regard to the constitutional reforms at that time:

> Let me throw up some points in the air which I believe may begin to demonstrate what I hear people talking about.
> The first one is that it was a mistake to make Kenya a de jure one-party government and that this decision should be reversed. This will allow a freer atmosphere for discussion.
> Secondly, I wish to suggest that if the Party insists on the system of lining up behind candidates, the provision which allows a person to be declared elected after receiving seventy per cent of the votes should be removed immediately. The Party could use this method to limit the number of those to proceed to secret ballot to three or two.

Thirdly, I should like to suggest an amendment to the Constitution to limit the term of office of the future Presidents to not more than two terms. Power corrupts a person with even the best of wills in the world. Therefore, power must be limited by clearly acceptable checks and balances.

Lastly, there is harboured a strong conviction among some of us that a free society is one that is in constant debate with itself. I believe that this is what I am attempting to do, but I believe that one of the ways in which we could debate this is to appoint a widely representative commission to thoroughly help us to discover what political and economic systems are relevant to Kenya today. This is my second time of calling. It may include some "foreign" elements, for we are living in a global village, but it should be a "home made" system and can even be envied and adapted or adopted by other African countries.

What I am trying to put forward is a suggestion to rise above purely academic argument as to whether to have one or more political parties as our solution to political and economic issues.

Let us accept change or change will change us (Okullu 1997, 172).

In June 1990, as a result of the ongoing agitation in the country, KANU appointed a review committee under chairmanship of the country's vice president, George Saitoti, to look into nomination and election procedures and the code of conduct within the party. This became a venue for the churches and the ordinary people to make their views known on many issues that were not covered under the mandate of the committee. The churches were critical of the review process because it tended to concentrate on narrow interests of the ruling elite. An NCCK statement issued on 21 May 1991 observed:

As soon as the KANU Review Committee embarked on its task, it became increasingly clear that its mandate was too narrow *vis a vis* the prevailing interests of the Kenyan people. Freely and openly the people presented their views to the KANU Review Committee both verbally and in writing. This exercise was certainly a landmark in the socio-political history of the country. It reflected a national agenda set by the people of Kenya (NCCK 1991).

This process was a good example of how to expand a limited window of opportunity to become a channel for democratic expression and agitation. Attempts to limit what was presented to the committee failed. The churches also made presentations to the committee and covered many of the burning issues in the country. Memoranda by the NCCK, the Catholic Diocese of Murang'a, the CPK Diocese of Eldoret, the Catholic Justice and Peace Commission, and the Rev. Njoya, then a rural priest at Tumutumu Parish, were notable for their frankness and their ability to articulate a wide range of sensitive issues. Although a few other civil society organisations made equally strong presentations to the committee, the presence of church-related organisations and individuals was overwhelming (*Nairobi Law Monthly* 1990).

As their confidence grew, the churches went beyond calling for change in electoral rules to advocating broad and radical reforms in the governance of the country, including the repeal of the 1982 amendment making the country a one-party state, limiting presidential terms to two terms of five years each, and holding a national convention on constitutional changes. They called also for the separation of powers among the executive, the judiciary, and the legislature, respect for freedom of expression, and abolition of detention without trial, among other issues.

In the meantime, as 1990 came to an end the pace of democratic change quickened. By this time other actors were entering the arena, evidenced by the number of organisations and individuals that made their views known to the KANU review committee (*Nairobi Law Monthly* 1990). By the end of 1991 KANU had no alternative but to yield to popular pressure and repeal section 2A of the Constitution. This was implemented in 1992, and multiparty politics became the law (NCCK 1991; *Nairobi Law Monthly* 1990–91; KEC 1990–92 [multiple pastoral letters]).

The involvement of the churches in the search for a constitutional order that would serve the majority of Kenyans persisted beyond the first and second multiparty elections of 1992 and 1997. After 1992, however, the mantle of spearheading constitutional reform was taken up for a brief period by secular organisations. This process is well documented by Willy Mutunga in *Constitution Making from the Middle.* Currently, the churches are critical players in the religious-led initiative known as the Peoples Constitution Review Commission, which is opposed to the parliamentary-led process under the control of the executive.[5] Notwithstanding the existence of many political parties for several years, the churches continue to have the confidence and trust of the ordinary people and are still perceived as representing their true interests.

Multiparty Elections

The change to multiparty politics in 1992 confronted mainline churches with new challenges. The first was preparing the electorate to participate effectively in multiparty elections by initiating and conducting voter education. The NCCK was in the forefront, followed by the Catholics, who eventually became fully engaged and ardent implementers of what was to become the civic education programmes, later to be taken up by secular and other religious NGOs. The pioneering and innovative work of the churches in this field has remained one of the strong areas of ecumenical co-operation between the NCCK and the Catholic church.

Second, in 1988 the Protestant churches, through the NCCK, took the initiative of monitoring the conduct of the elections in the country. In 1992 this evolved into a national effort professionally organised and co-ordinated under the auspices of the National Election Monitoring Unit (NEMU). This became an umbrella body comprising the National Ecumenical Civic Education Program (NECEP) of the NCCK, the Catholic church, the Kenya chapter of the International Federation of Women Lawyers (FIDA), the Kenya chapter of the International Commission of Jurists (ICJ), and the Professional Committee for Democratic Change. The unit was chaired by the General Secretary of the NCCK and attracted wide attention of the public, the media, and had international donor funding that strengthened its role and credibility.

The work of the churches in preparing for the first multiparty elections went well beyond the activities reviewed above. It included monitoring and calling for a free and fair voter registration process and ensuring that the composition of electoral commission and its operations embraced all interests in the country. The church also tried to prepare political parties to face up to the challenges the national issues posed, while at the same time alerting them to the rapidly changing governance concerns in the country. The NCCK organised two symposiums for all political parties in 1991, in which a wide range of civil society organisations and pressure groups participated (*Weekly Review,* 19 June 1992; Mutunga 1999).

Ethnic Clashes: A Prophetic Role

Besides the first multiparty elections since the first decade of independence, in the early 1990s the politically motivated ethnic clashes in the Rift Valley, Western, and Nyanza provinces were of deep concern as well. The clashes challenged the core theological and ethical understanding of the churches' role in the affected communities and challenged them to go beyond the provision of services to dealing with the difficult and painful issues of conflict resolution and reconciliation.

Churches put their credibility on the line by providing organisational capacity for service provision, defending and sheltering victims of violence, and caring for displaced persons. The churches became the voice of the victims to the state, to their society, and to the international community. They were clear and fearless in their stand, a fact that was fundamentally and indelibly to shape the profile of the churches in the politics of governance in Kenya. The role they played in calling the state to be accountable and responsible, and to play its constitutional role in ensuring the security of all its citizens was not only courageous but also prophetic.

In a joint message of the Kenya Catholic bishops and the NCCK to the president, 30 April 1992, the churches wrote:

> Your Excellency, the very short notice in requesting to see you, by this joint delegation of Church Leaders of the NCCK and the Kenya Episcopal Conference, must mean that there is a very important matter to bring to your notice.
>
> What brings us here is nothing less than the life or death of Kenya, the question of the lives and future of hundreds of families who have been treated inhumanely, butchered, slaughtered. The scenes are truly heartbreaking. No human being can be left unmoved. Anyone who carries responsibility before the nation even more before our God and Father, must be forced to stop this bloodshed and human misery at once.
>
> As religious leaders who have walked among hungry and crying women and children, who have seen corpses, wounds, blood, homes burnt to the ground, empty food stores, thousands of people trekking for safety to our church compounds, who have buried hundreds. . . . We have to tell you plainly

that you are wrong in your assessment of the situation. Unless you change the present policies, Kenya will not be KANU but a cemetery for thousands of its sons and daughters.

We have seen with our own eyes warriors in their hundreds, well organised and trained. How can anyone deny that they exist? Why do you not commit your administration officers, your police and army to capture these young men? It is irrelevant whether they were trained in Libya or by any group or party. There is only one thing necessary as an immediate step – to apprehend and disarm these warriors at once and to bring them to justice. . . .

At this last hour, we ask you *in God's name* to change your heart, to change your policy. Even Parliament has shown that they *[sic]* cannot stand the present situation. Your officers are assuring everyone that there is peace and security, but burning, looting, fear and hopelessness continue.

How can we continue to ask innocent people to be patient and non-violent when they are being disarmed by the police and later attacked by the warriors? These warriors are suspected of being led by highly-trained personnel. Your Excellency, your people are hopelessly demoralised. This situation could never be believed to be possible. Your duty is not to any party; it is to all the people, ALL; every citizen has a right to live in any part of Kenya and dwell in peace and security. At present you seem to be securing the interest of a small clique of rich powerful men who are surviving at the cost of life-blood and misery of thousands of small people.

Your Excellency, we as Church Leaders, know we must speak out. God wants a Kenya which is a good country to live in for all. We believe God wants you to forget yourself, your party and your personal interests. You have to think of Kenya and its people.

We believe that there is still time to save the situation if you take the appropriate steps *now without delay.* We assure you of our prayers and full support in stopping this bloodshed.

This prophetic advocacy and risk taking not only expanded the churches' activities and programmes in service to the victims of internal conflicts and violence, but also opened up new avenues for other civil society institutions and international organisations (such as Action Aid – Kenya, Dutch Interchurch Aid, Muslims for Human Rights, Oxfam, UNDP, World Vision) to work in the field of peacemaking and reconciliation in Kenya.

OBSERVATIONS ON THE WORK OF CHURCHES DURING THIS PERIOD

The churches were ill prepared for the events that unfolded, but its resilience was evident as it mobilised local and international resources to assist the victims of the clashes. In many respects the vitality, creativity, and vision of the churches was rediscovered in these very trying circumstances. By accompanying the victims through times of violence, the churches earned their trust and that of many

Kenyans, who supported the initiative to have churches lead the popular review of the Kenya.

Two additional factors explain why the mainline churches acted the way they did in this period. First, internal factors such as the theology and church social teachings provided a greater rationale for involvement in national political life. Statements of the Kenya Catholic bishops, the NCCK, CPK Bishops Gitari and Okullu, and PCEA (Presbyterian Church of East Africa) pastor Njoya are replete with theological justifications and references to teachings of the church on the need to be in solidarity with the oppressed and to be involved in all aspects of human development. The churches increasingly acted on such socially concerned theologies despite the many appeals made by the politicians for them to stay out of politics. This more activist role of the churches in Kenya was developed and articulated by a well-educated young clergy who were assuming leadership positions. These new leaders had not only a wide knowledge of what was happening in their country but they were also aware of events elsewhere in the world. They travelled and had many international connections. Moreover, church leaders could share their views weekly with members who gathered in places of worship, and as a result, their influence spread rapidly all over the country. Sermons and pastoral letters had a ready audience even when the state controlled most of the mass media and broadcasting.

Second, the churches' experience in relief and development work exposed church leaders to the theories and practices of development, which were moving in the direction of empowering the poor and challenging the power structures and institutions of governance. Mainline churches and many Christian NGOs were not dependent on the state and thus were more secure than NGOs that received state funds.

The new ideas spreading among church leadership combined with grassroots networks of local resources to make the churches powerful agents for change. Churches stood alone as institutions that had not succumbed to co-optation by the government, and they benefitted from courageous, committed, and well-connected leadership. As a result, their activities attracted the attention of both the local and international press as they fed and protected internally displaced people in church compounds, mobilised local community support for relief and international humanitarian aid, and provided an alternative source for news and information. Finally, they supported not only their own church members but *all* Kenyans. These factors combined to make the churches a formidable agent for democratisation.

SOME CONSTRAINTS ON THE CHURCHES' ROLE IN DEMOCRATISATION

Not surprisingly, the churches also faced constraints and risks at both institutional and individual levels in their efforts to expand democratic space and fight against encroachment by the state and the dominant party. Most obviously, attacks and threats to ban institutions like the NCCK came from the political elites in the party and the government. It is a credit to the churches and the energy of the clergy and bishops that they held their ground in these trying circumstances. The struggles for democratic change and constitutional reforms continued unabated despite many threats and personal attacks.

A number of more subtle constraints on the operation and practice of the churches, however, were also in evidence. To begin with, the churches represent a diversity of theological understanding and leadership styles, which naturally impinged on the way they responded to issues and situations. For example, while the mainline churches' theological position made no distinction between spiritual mission and socio-political engagement, evangelical and Pentecostal groups saw such a coupling as anathema to their beliefs. Evangelical and Pentecostal churches are theologically conservative and generally interpret their duty to the state as being supportive, irrespective of the state's performance. A second constraint revolved around the inconsistency between the churches' own governance structures and the democratic principles they advocated for the nation. The hierarchical and male leadership that existed in some of the churches tended to contrast with the democratic principles and participatory values they ardently proposed for the wider society.[6] Such diversity of theology and institutional practice, though at times a source of creativity, often impinged on the effectiveness of the churches in the process of democratisation. The differences tended to undercut concerted efforts, collaboration, and consensus building. Duplication of efforts, mixed messages, and spreading available resources thinly made the churches less effective than they might have been, and at times the ordinary citizens were confused by the churches' actions and pronouncements.

Stemming from their theological differences, the churches also lacked unity and coherence in their overall strategies. The withdrawal of three churches (the African Inland Church, the Church of God in East Africa, and the Pentecostal Assemblies of God) from the membership of NCCK immediately after it expressed criticism of the queue voting system clearly indicated theological differences coupled with political manipulation and ethnic considerations (Okullu 1997). The emergence of the Evangelical Fellowship of Kenya (FEK) was intended to counter the NCCK, which some viewed as too political. The state, of course, appreciated church organisations that emphasised a more spiritual role for the churches and that would support the state and the status quo. "Loyalty" was rewarded financially and by the allocation of public plots to churches and individual leaders. The pronouncements of the leadership of the African Independent Pentecostal Church of Africa (AIPCA) and the Baptist Church of Kenya, for example, were often supportive of the state and KANU positions.[7]

Denominational differences were compounded by internal conflicts that resulted from leadership wrangles, theological conflicts, individual leadership style and ethnic differences, and these also weakened the effectiveness of the churches in building a strong civic culture. Such internal divisions were evident in CPK and the PCEA. The prophetic mission was often carried out by only a few church leaders (Archbishop Manases Kuria and Bishops Gitari, Muge, Njuguna, and Okullu of CPK; Rev. Timothy Njoya and the Right Rev. George Wanjau of the PCEA; Methodist Rev. Dr. Samuel Kobia of the NCCK), giving the impression that a whole church was in the forefront of democratisation struggles. These few leaders were crucial, however. Their differences were often exploited by the political establishment to weaken the churches' work in the democratic arena.

Another significant constraint was the lack of a systematic and well-co-ordinated ecumenical co-operation, especially between the Protestant churches and the Catholic church. When co-operation did occur (as in April 1992, when the NEMU was formed), the results were impressive. Co-operation, however, was limited to the election monitoring process and was not intended to lay down a general strategy to consolidate democratisation in the country.

As the churches struggled to find their role in an unfamiliar arena, it also became clear that they lacked the capacity and knowledge to promote political and constitutional change. Although they were able to draw upon the experience and expertise of the laity, their lack of depth and political understanding often showed in the pronouncements of some church leaders. The churches failed to see a need to strengthen their capacity as change agents. This has continued to constrain their involvement in the political arena today.

On the other hand, it must also be said that the churches compensated for their lack of theoretical knowledge in the political-economic arena by the direct interaction they had with the people at the community level. Their knowledge of local situations was a source of strength, especially when it was necessary to challenge state propaganda. At this level, information that churches possessed was well grounded, and it helped in their advocacy work and in confronting injustices. For instance, when the churches confronted the state during the ethnic clashes, their knowledge of the reality was an important factor in being effective and credible in what they said and did. This information needed, however, to be supported by sound political analysis, documentation, and quality research which they lacked.

A final constraint was the churches' inherent ambivalence about taking up political causes, which frustrated their secular allies and congregations who failed to understand why the leaders were unable to tap the enormous strength in the churches for sustained mass action. The popular expectation that they would take political leadership in the second liberation in Kenya has been misplaced. It is common for the churches to make radical pronouncements but then be unwilling to organise people to go into the streets and confront the state or its institutions. The churches' reluctance to be prominent political actors may stem from their desire to avoid confrontation, fear of the consequences of such actions (for example, outbreaks of violence or divisions among their members), or a view that activism is not their primary mission. All the same, there is need to recognise the important implication of what Gifford calls "organic linkages" between the state and the church – with both having the common interest to maintain stability and consensus in the society. The churches in Kenya had to go the extent they did as a result of the excesses of the state in the late 1980s and especially during the ethnic clashes. The breakdown in 1992 of the unwritten consensus which existed between the state and the church created a distance between the mainline churches and the state and has kept them apart since then, especially in regard to constitutional review and critical issues of governance (see Mejia 1995, 141–43; KEC 1988b, 77–81).

Outcomes

Events in the 1980s and 1990s cried out for church involvement, and the churches responded; they were propelled into the movement to create political change, and they were transformed along the way. The churches could not ignore the need for transparent, free, and fair elections; the need for changes in the Constitution to allow for a multiparty political system; the need for means by which citizens could fairly influence political leaders; and the need to speak up against the violence and ethnic clashes that were believed to have been sanctioned, condoned, and perpetrated by agents of the state. This led to the transformation of the churches from organisations merely dispensing spiritual and social welfare to vibrant civil society advocates for social, economic, and political change. Mainline churches thus were able to break away from the spiritual "ghettos" in which the state wanted to contain them and become not only critics of the status quo but also strong proponents of constitutional review, political reforms, and a peace agenda for the country.

The change in outlook and attitudes was not limited to church leaders; it also found expression in local communities where issues of social justice, peace, and citizen rights were taken up by the people (Ngondi-Houghton and Wanjala 2000; MUHURI 1998). Churches gradually restructured themselves to take account of their new space and roles in the socio-political situation. The Catholic bishops of Kenya established the Justice and Peace Commission in 1988, a structure which now operates in all the dioceses (Mejia 1995). Protestant churches have established similar institutions in their churches. The NCCK established the Justice, Peace, and Reconciliation Commission, which was chaired at different times by some of the most vocal Protestant church leaders. Its work with victims of ethnic clashes in the early 1990s has evolved into a community and regional peace programme, leading to the articulation of a National Peace Agenda for the whole country rather than simply the two provinces, the Rift Valley and the Coast, that were the main theatres of ethnic clashes (NCCK 2001). The National Ecumenical Civic Education Program (NECEP), with a mandate to educate people on issues of reforms and participation in elections, also emerged during this period. Apart from the church-related organisations, secular organisations were developed to carry forward the struggle for constitution reform and democratisation of the society. These organisations came to the forefront in the period after 1992 and dominated the reform agenda in the following seven years (Mutunga 1999). New local institutions took up local issues of peacemaking, conflict resolution, workers' and citizens' rights, land issues, and marketing and pricing of agricultural commodities. These local organisations have kept state institutions and functionaries accountable.

At the national level churches provided leadership and guidance to the political parties (*Weekly Review*, 19 June 1992), especially immediately after the constitutional change allowing multiple parties (Kobia 1993). They challenged oppositional political parties to engage in dialogue and to break away from the tendency to focus on parochial issues and ethnicity. They also opposed opportunistic tendencies to access power and instead urged political parties to embrace issues of national concern rather than narrow interests. This led to convening Symposiums I and II, which were presided over by the church leaders associated with the NCCK (Kobia 1993). This formative role has diminished as political parties have become more confident and started to form and pursue their own platforms.

The Roman Catholic Church in Kenya in this period was transformed into a consistent and persistent champion for social, economic, and political change. An analysis of pastoral letters issued from 1982 to 1995 attests to this transformation:

> [They departed] from their traditionally reticent pastoral letters on the political situation issued twice a year, [and they] began issuing tougher and more frequent letters. . . . Since return to political pluralism . . . Catholic bishops seem to have undergone a transformation, and their pastoral letters this year have been far harder towards the government than any of the NCCK statements (*Weekly Review*, 19 June 1992).

Most of the pastoral letters issued during this period dealt with socio-political issues and were critical of the state and the president. They were read in all Catholic congregations in the country and published in the major newspapers and magazines, making their messages widely available to ordinary people in both urban and rural areas.

The churches also assumed other new roles in the society that were beyond their traditional purview. They started undertaking civic education (see Kobia 1993; Mejia 1995), monitoring general elections (1988, 1992, and 1997) through the NEMU, and leading the process of constitutional reform, initially calling for a national convention but now taking the role of key players in the Peoples' Constitutional Commission.

Ecumenical co-operation has emerged in various areas of the struggle. Catholics and Protestant churches have co-operated in election monitoring, agitation for change, dealing with ethnic clashes and violence in various regions of Kenya, and in fostering constitutional reform. This co-operation has been extended to secular civil society organisations, especially in the period after elections of 1992. The churches have produced new leadership, both clergy and lay, which has taken up the cause of the democratisation in Kenya. The new leadership has not remained in the churches but has often moved into other spheres – NGOs, the mass media, and universities.

The churches have provided space and at times encouragement to new organisations and pressure groups. The CPK provided space for Release Political Prisoners (RPP) and Mothers in Action to operate and articulate their agenda. These two groups were allowed to camp at the All Saints Cathedral, which became the focus for struggle for human rights and change. The NCCK and KEC have provided Ufungamano House (the Christian Student Leadership Centre) as a meeting place for pro-democracy and reform groups in the country. Ufungamano has come to symbolise religious defiance against the state and has been a beacon of hope for the people. The symposia which NCCK organised in that venue in May and June of 1992 brought together not only the opposition political parties but also a wide range of nascent civic organisations with broad interests in democratisation (Mutunga 1999; *Weekly Review,* 19 June 1992; Kobia 1993). At times it was difficult to distinguish where the church role ended and that of other civil society organisations began.

Conclusion

Some democratic space has now been gained. It is up to the opposition leaders and Kenyans in general to expand that space. Let us all work together in the hope of freedom now and in the life to come (Okullu 1997, 140).

The participation of the churches in democratic struggles for free and fair elections, constitutional reforms, human rights, social and economic justice, and ending of ethnic conflicts and violence in the period from 1986 to 1993 expanded the space for Kenyans to speak out without fear of arrest, to organise political parties, and to build new organisations and processes for dealing with human rights, peace and conflict resolution. This has all been to the good, but the struggle continues. Efforts so far have been unable to dislodge the ruling party from power or dismantle all structures of domination and authoritarianism in the country. There were gains in terms of representation obtained in Parliament, but ethnic divisions as well as parochial and individual interests hindered parliamentary effectiveness as well as that of opposition parties. Although the country achieved a high level of political awareness and participation in the general elections, this did not translate into control of the excesses of the regime. Corruption deepened and ethnic tension and conflict spread widely in spite of these changes, while accountability and transparency in the use of public resources remained minimal in the governance process. More work in the reform of institutions and processes of governance is still needed. The World Bank and the IMF and other donors also took up some of these issues with the government with limited success, despite their financial clout.

To deal with the realities of the struggle for democratisation the churches have had to assume new roles, creating new institutions, structures, and leadership styles to deal with the rapidly changing circumstances. This has meant new modalities of working, ecumenical collaboration, and cultivating new allies in the secular world. In the process the churches exposed their weaknesses and limitations as actors in a complex arena in which ethics and rules were not always clear. While the churches have a nationwide audience, support, structures, credibility, courage, and a prophetic vision, their intellectual base is weak; they lack the capacity and mechanisms to generate knowledge, information, and strategies for sustained involvement.

A better understanding of how state institutions change and how international donor agencies work is essential for the next stage of struggle for democratisation in Kenya. This may require building new alliances and collaboration not only with local and international NGOs but also with international donors. This has happened in the past, but it needs to be cultivated systematically and focused on limited but achievable and realistic objectives. These strategic alliances will need to go beyond donor funding to creative utilization of the available space and resources for change.

The churches also have to rethink their strategies for future involvement. In the past they relied on making pronouncements and statements but were reluctant to mobilise people. This has frustrated the social constituencies who feel that the churches abandoned them at critical times. These seeds of mistrust have to be addressed in the future if the faith the ordinary people have placed in the churches is to be justified. Kenyans have been disillusioned by the performance of political parties and could also lose trust in the churches. If this happens, the trend towards pietism and religious escapism could become even more pronounced. This would give comfort to the state and the conservative forces in the society who have always viewed a progressive church as a thorn in the flesh of their vested interests. Rethinking how the democratic space and role of civil society in this process can be consolidated is essential if the momentum for change is to be maintained. Thus the churches must reflect seriously on its future role in the democratisation process, not lose hope, and take the actions necessary to be faithful witnesses to the Lord's call.

NOTES

[1] Kenya has a population of about 28 million whose religious affiliation are 38% Protestants (comprised of mainstream churches such as the Anglicans, the Presbyterians, and the Methodists – who make the bulk of NCCK membership – as well as the Evangelical, Pentecostal, and African instituted churches), 28% Roman Catholics, 26% indigenous religions, 6% Muslims, and 2% others. Global Ministries, Fact 2000.

[2] The call for aid to be tied to democratic reforms in Africa by the United States (as Ambassador Smith Hempstone made clear in Kenya) and the UK (Douglas Hurd, Minister of Foreign Affairs, had made similar conditions for British aid). Note also the 16 November 1990 Paris Club meeting that indicated further aid to Kenya would be tied to democratic reforms.

[3] Of Kenya's 28 million people, approximately 28 per cent are Roman Catholic.

[4] The Catholic bishops also addressed the dangers of divisiveness of the queuing system and the 70 per cent nomination rule. Like their counterparts in the CPK and the NCCK, they respectfully asked for the system to be reconsidered.

[5] The parliamentary and Peoples' Constitutional Review Commission have been merged into a single process, the Constitution of Kenya Review Commission (CKRC).

[6] The Church Province of Kenya, now known as the Anglican Church of Kenya and the Kenya Episcopal Conference, as well as the Roman Catholic Church fall into this category.

[7] In personal communication with church leaders I have heard of cases where loyalty to the state was rewarded financially. Reports of the Parliamentary Public Accounts Committee have also disclosed instances of allocation of public resources such as prime pieces of land in the urban areas to church leaders who were (or are) close to the state leadership.

REFERENCES

Abuom, Agnes C. 1996. "The Churches' Involvement in the Democratization in Kenya." In *Peace Making and Democratization in Africa,* edited by H. Assefa and G. Wachira, 95–116. Nairobi, Kenya: East African Publishers.

Assefa, Hizkias, and George Wachira, eds. 1996. *Peace Making and Democratization in Africa.* Nairobi, Kenya: East African Publishers.

Chabal, Patrick, and Jean-Pascal Daloz. 1999. *Africa Works: Disorder as Political Instrument.* Oxford: James Currey.

Commonwealth Foundation/CIVICUS. 1999. *Citizens and Governance: Civil Society in the New Millennium.* Pall Mall, London: Marlborough House (September).

Ela, Jean-Marc. 1986. *African Cry.* Maryknoll, N.Y.: Orbis Books.

Gifford, Paul, ed. 1995. *The Christian Churches and the Democratization of Africa.* Leiden: E.J. Brill.

———. 1998. *African Christianity: Its Public Role.* London: Hurst and Company.

Gitari, David. 1988. *Let the Bishop Speak.* Nairobi, Kenya: Uzima Press.

Kanyinga, Karuti. 1998. "Contestation One Political Space: The State and the Demobilization of Opposition Politics in Kenya." In *The Politics of Opposition in Contemporary Africa,* edited by A. O. Olukoshi, 39–90. Uppsala: Nordiska Africainstitutet.

Kassimir, Ronald. 1998. "Social Power of Religious Organizations and Civil Society – The Catholic in Uganda." *Commonwealth and Comparative Politics* 36/2 (2 July).

KEC (Kenya Episcopal Conference). 1986. "Catholic Bishops' Open Memorandum to the President of the Republic." Africa: Paulines Publications (November).

———. 1988a. "Justice and Peace Commission Pastoral Letter." Africa: Paulines Publications (January).

———. 1988b. "Pastoral Letter of the Kenya Catholic Bishops on the Occasion of the 1988 Elections." Africa: Paulines Publications (December).

———. 1990. "On the Present Situation of Our Country Pastoral Letter." Africa: Paulines Publications (June).

———. 1991a. "Declaration of the Catholic Bishops of Kenya." Africa: Paulines Publications (April).

———. 1991b. "Catholic Bishops' Statement on Pastoral Concerns in the Present Situation." Africa: Paulines Publications (September).

———. 1992a. "Looking Towards the Future with Hope Pastoral Letter." Africa: Paulines Publications (January).

———. 1992b. "A Call to Justice, Love, and Reconciliation Pastoral Letter." Africa: Paulines Publications (March).

———. 1992c. "The Pre-Elections Concerns Pastoral Letter." Africa: Paulines Publications (August).

———. 1992d. "On the Eve of Elections Pastoral Letter." Africa: Paulines Publications (November).

Kobia, Samuel. 1993. "The Quest for Democracy in Africa NCCK." Nairobi, Kenya: NCCK.

———. 1995. "Promoting Democracy in Africa: Experiences and Future Perspectives." *Church and Society* (Presbyterian Church, USA) (March/April).

Mejia, Rodrigo, ed. 1995. *The Conscience of Society: The Social Teaching of the Catholic Bishops of Kenya 1960–1995.* Nairobi, Kenya: Pauline Publications Africa.

Mugambi, J. N. Kanyua, ed. 1997. *Democracy and Development in Africa: The Role of Churches.* Nairobi, Kenya: All Africa Conference of Churches.

Murungi, Kiraitu. 1992. "Kenya's Constitutional Theory and the Myth Africanity." 56–65 In *Law and the Administration of Justice in Kenya*, edited by Kivutha Kibwana, 56–65. Nairobi, Kenya: International Commission of Jurists (Kenya Section).

MUHURI (Muslims for Human Rights). 1998. *Banditry and the Politics of Citizenship: The Case of the Galjeel Somali of Tana River*. Mombasa, Kenya: MUHURI.

Mutunga, Willy. 1999. *Constitution Making from the Middle: Civil Society and Transition Politics in Kenya 1992–1997*. Nairobi, Kenya: SARREAT/Mwengo.

Mwengo and All Africa Conference of Churches. 1993. *Civil Society, State and African Development in the 1990s*. Mwengo.

Nairobi Law Monthly, The. 1990. No. 25, special edition (September).

Nairobi Law Monthly, The. 1990–91. Various issues.

NCCK (National Council of Churches in Kenya). 1984. "A Report on Churches Involvement in Development." Nairobi, Kenya.

———. 1990. The NCCK Memoranda to the KANU Review Committee, mimeo, and the NCCK preliminary response to the report of the KANU review committee, mimeo.

———. 1991. *Kairos for Kenya, NCCK Reflections on the KANU Review Committee Report and KANU Special Delegates' Conference Resolutions On It*. Nairobi, Kenya: NCCK Publications.

———. 1992. The Cursed Arrow: A Report on Organized Violence Against Democracy. Nairobi, Kenya: NCCK.

———. National Council of Churches in Kenya (NCCK) Press Statements, 1985–95.

———. 2001. "National Agenda for Peace Survey Report: Making Informed Choices for a Better Future." Nairobi, Kenya: NCCK.

Ndegwa, Stephen N. 1996. *The Two Faces of Civil Society: NGOs and Politics in Africa*. Bloomfield, Conn.: Kumarian Press.

Ngondi-Houghton, Connie and Smokin Wanjala. 2000. "Protection and Promotion of Rights in Kenya: The Utility of a Basic Rights Framework." Nairobi, Kenya: International Development Research Center (IDRC). Memo.

Ngunyi, Mutahi. 1999. "Civil Society and the Challenge of Multiple Transition in Kenya." In *Civil Society and Democracy in Eastern Africa*, edited by J. E. Nyang'oro, 117–37. Harare, Zimbabwe: Mwengo Publications.

Nyang'oro, Julius E. 1999. *Civil Society and Democracy in Eastern Africa*. Harare, Zimbabwe: Mwengo Publications.

Okullu, Henry. 1990. Sermon preached at St Stephen's Cathedral. 15 July (Kisumu Sunday).

———. 1997. *Quest for Justice, An Autobiography of Bishop John Henry Okullu*. Kisumu, Kenya: Shalom Publishers and Computer Training Centre.

Throup, David. 1995. "Render unto Caesar the Things that Are Caesar's: The Politics of Church-State Conflict in Kenya 1978–1990." In *Religion and Politics in East Africa*, edited by B. Hansen and M. Twaddle, 143–46. London: James Curry.

Weekly Review. Issues of 9 December 1988, 5 October 1990, 30 November 1990, 14 December 1990, 21 December 1990, 4 January 1991, 6 December 1991, 15 May 1992, 19 June 1992, and 25 September 1992.

Part 2

THINKING STRAIGHT
ABOUT CIVIL SOCIETY

———◆———

4

Civil Society
and Third-World Development

*Models, Philosophical Issues,
and Cross-Cultural Validity*

Howard J. Wiarda

Civil society is an attractive notion, particularly to scholars, foundations, policy advocates, and the NGO community. First, it has a nice ring to it: *civil society* as a term sounds lofty, nonpartisan, citizen-oriented, participatory, and democratic. Who could argue with those attributes? Second, civil society conjures up images of Madisonian, Tocquevillian pluralism, town meetings, grassroots participation, checks and balances, and countervailing yet ultimately harmonious interest-group competition and democratic public policy. The images most of us have of civil society include bowling leagues, PTAs, soccer moms, scouts, neighbourhood associations, town meetings, religious institutions, and peaceful, harmonious collective bargaining (Putnam 2000).

Third, civil society holds out the promise of taking policy-making out of the hands of often corrupt, venal bureaucracies, governments, and "evil" international organisations like the World Trade Organization (WTO) or the International Monetary Fund (IMF), and placing it directly in the hands of popular organisations or "the people." Fourth (and this by no means exhausts the list), civil society is popular because it looks "just like us" or at least what we imagine ourselves to be: democratic, grassroots-oriented, participatory, pluralist. It seems to avoid bad attributes (the influence of money on politics; gridlock between the executive and legislative branches; large, impersonal bureaucracies; and so on) and to restore an earlier, more pristine form of citizen participation, town meetings, and democracy. Civil society has thus taken on aspects of a civic renewal, the apparent rediscovery of our long-lost and better attributes, even a quasi-religious crusade and reconversion (Carothers 1999).

During the last two decades policy-makers have recognised the importance of civil society and have seized upon it as an instrument of policy. For example, in the

The support of the Aspen Institute for this research is gratefully acknowledged.

1980s and 1990s the United States government and others used emerging civil society organisations to assist in the ouster of discredited authoritarian regimes (Marcos, Duvalier, and others) as well as in the overthrow of communist regimes in Eastern Europe. Recognising the incapacity and/or corruption of central governments, civil society organisations have been used to carry out policies in the areas of health, education, environmentalism, and democratisation. Civil society has proven a means to "think globally but act locally" on a variety of policy fronts; it has also proved to be a useful conduit for US and other foreign assistance programmes. Where civil society has not existed in many third-world nations, the United States – including the government, the US Agency for International Development (USAID), foundations, and American civil society groups – has created, aided, and even invented it. So we can find several reasons to worry about the civil society approach.

Whenever a concept like civil society has so many positives, achieves widespread popularity and consensus, and seems to accomplish so many positive goals (overthrowing both authoritarianism and communism) at once, its attractiveness to politicians becomes irresistible. The concept then becomes politicised and used for purposes other than those intended. Already USAID, the State Department, the Defense Department, the CIA, the White House, Congress, and sundry others have latched onto the concept. The National Endowment for Democracy (NED), the Republican and Democratic international affairs institutes, the Ford and MacArthur foundations, the Washington-based Aspen Institute, Washington think tanks, and several human rights and religious groups also have seized on the concept. Civil society has become a growth industry, and when that happens, the concept itself and its purposes run the risk of being hopelessly distorted and of falling victim to the same policy cycle that so many other well-meaning programmes in the past – agrarian reform, community development, basic human needs – have gone through. There is initial excitement and enthusiasm, followed by politicisation and distortion, resulting in disillusionment, disappointment, and eventual petering out (but never complete *disappearance*; remember, these are *government* and *bureaucratic* programmes).

The issues are compounded once the concept travels abroad. First, as we see in more detail below, different societies and cultures mean different things by civil society than do Lockean, Tocquevillian, Madisonian Americans. Second, the *form* that civil society takes in different countries may vary greatly from the US model – and not all of these by any means are happily liberal, pluralist, and democratic. Third, there is money involved – often big money – and there are always opportunists in the United States and abroad waiting to take advantage of the largesse now going into civil society projects. Often these are the same opportunists who milked other USAID and US government panaceas – agrarian reform, community development, and so on – dry without producing much in the way of reform. And fourth, when host governments observe civil society activities, which by their nature are often oppositionist, outside of state control, and cast in a US mould, the temptation is powerful to control, regulate, co-opt, expel, or repress them. In the past, elites and national governments in Latin America, East Asia, and elsewhere used corporatism as a way to harness and control pluralist interest groups (Wiarda 1996); now, since corporatism at the national level gradually is being replaced by forms of neo-liberalism, it is being resurrected at the local level, where civil society groups are increasingly being required to register, divulge their members' names, disclose their financing, and seek recognition or "juridical personality" from local authorities, which also carries with it the possibility of non-recognition and therefore suppression if the group persists in its activities.

These preliminary comments suggest the need for caution in our enthusiasm for civil society. Other policy panaceas that began as noble and ennobling concepts went through a familiar life cycle: initial popularity and enthusiasm, widespread acceptance, then politicisation, distortion, and decline. I judge that civil society is now on the cusp of these disillusioning, downward-sloping transformations. Hence, a cautious and prudent approach to civil society rather than an excessively enthusiastic one may be called for.

These cautionary warnings are particularly directed at advocates of civil society in the Christian community. The Christian community tends to have contact with and to work through some of the best in civil society – local, honest, responsible, grassroots, religious organisations with noble intentions – and to have less acquaintance with the thieves, opportunists, and political operatives from all nations who also inhabit the civil society community. This limited experience may make Christians more positive about civil society than is warranted. In addition, it has been my experience that many Christian civil society advocates are often romantic and idealistic concerning the concept, traits that I would not want necessarily to discourage but which can also spill over into naivete. They often need to be tempered by a dose of realism.

CIVIL SOCIETY: HISTORY AND MEANING

The concept of civil society has a long and distinguished history in political science. Reviewing that history briefly helps us understand the distinct meanings the concept has had over time as well as its variations from country to country and from culture to culture (Ehrenberg 1999; Gellner 1997).

For the ancient Greeks, civil society was conceived as a commonwealth of the politically organised. The "civil" part referred to the requirements of citizenship, not necessarily proper manners. Plato's conception of good citizenship was driven by an attempt to state an inflexible ethical base for public life that would be articulated by his philosopher kings. Aristotle remained committed to an ethical concept of citizenship but also recognised that life takes place at multiple associational levels. Nevertheless, his view of civil society was based on face-to-face relations, not the large-scale associations of modern mass society, and on an elitist or aristocratic ethos that would convey the lessons of citizenship down through the social hierarchy. Rome, especially Cicero, added to this the notion of legally protected corporate bodies but, of course, not any sense of an egalitarian, participatory, or democratic polity. In Latin America's concepts of the nation as those who are politically *organised* and of the system of state-society relations based on juridically recognised corporate groups, the Greek and Roman influences are still very much alive (Wiarda 2000).

Following the fall of Rome, Christianity provided the main structural and intellectual frameworks of social and political life for a thousand years, even longer in Southern Europe and Latin America. There are, of course, subtle and not so subtle differences within Christianity regarding civil society over this millennium as we move from Augustine, who emphasised human depravity, condemned the classical tradition, and desired that human or societal effort guide moral action, to Thomas Aquinas, whose writings provided the main bases for social and political organisation in Christian/Catholic societies until at least World War II. Among other things, Aquinas emphasised the "great chain of being" by which all groups are both secure and fixed (locked) into their station in life, the corporative and hierarchical structure of society and politics, and a certain tension between absolute monarchy, on the one hand, and the rights of those same corporate social groups, on the other. The proper balance between monarchical rule and the rights of these corporate groups constituted for a long time, and still does in some quarters, the Iberian–Latin American definition of *democracy*. With the great sixteenth-century Jesuit Francisco Suárez (architect of the Spanish state [colonialism] in Latin America), the primitive contract theory of Aquinas was converted into a system of "prior consent" which gave absolute authority to the monarchy to act "on behalf of" the people and their corporate interests, which has long provided an excuse for authoritarianism and totalitarianism and which endowed the Spanish state in Latin America with near absolute authority. Aquinas helped revive Aristotelian logic and also took from Aristotle as well as the Christian tradition the idea that society required a moral, in this case God-given, base; civil society was thus constituted by religion, and only Christians could be a part of it. But such an exclusionary, hierarchical, and fixed system of civil society could not last permanently – except perhaps in Iberia and Latin America, which raises a problem for contemporary proponents of civil society (Morse 1964).

When we get to the modern age, a greater diversity of conceptions of civil society begins to emerge; remember, we are still talking only about the West. Modernity came in the form of an emerging capitalism, centralising nation states, and, in a handful of countries, greater impetus to political freedom. As John Ehrenberg notes, civil society was no longer understood as a universal Christian commonwealth, as in the Thomistic conception, but focused more on individual interest, state power, representative democracy, the rule of law, and an economic order emphasising prosperity (1999, xii–xv). The amoral *The Prince* made Machiavelli the first "modern" (secular) political scientist, but his preoccupation with power, a strong state, and the achievement of Italian unity left no room for civil society outside of central state control. The discovery of the individual was the work of the Reformation (Luther and Calvin), but over time each Protestant prince was given free reign to choose his subjects' religion and organise civil society as he saw fit. With Thomas Hobbes's *Leviathan* we have the appearance of a new, calculating individual who also had to take into account the interests of other calculating, self-interested parties.

To Hobbes, civil society was not "natural," as it was in Aristotle and Aquinas, but an artificial creation of the state. The state shaped and even created civil society as a way, in Hobbes's ruthless state of nature, of providing peace and security; civil society had no independent existence of its own. For John Locke, civil society was constituted by property, estate, production, and acquisition; it required a state governed by law to preserve order and liberty. Civil society now meant the possibility of living together in a condition of economic life and political freedom, and thus served as a precursor to the Madisonian concept of competing, counterbalanced interests with which we are all familiar. With Adam Smith, however, we see even more clearly that civil society is a market-oriented system of production and, indeed, that civil society was actually constituted by the market.

We recognise this tradition of thought from Machiavelli through Hobbes, Locke, and Smith as the beginning of the Western liberal, individualistic, and "modern" tradition. Most of us are products of this tradition. But another and less widely known though equally Western tradition, that of the Spanish-Portuguese (and other) Counter-Reformation (Soto, Molino, Vitoria, and especially Suárez), which was also the founding and often ongoing philosophy of Latin America, went in quite a different direction. It rejected the separation of morals from politics advanced by the so-called moderns and insisted that the basis of society had to be Christian "right reason." Rather than the individual, it emphasised corporate or group rights. Moreover, it rejected the notion of a state of nature, insisting that society was natural and God-given. What it meant by *democracy* and *civil society* was not Lockean or Madisonian liberalism and pluralism but close harmony and equilibrium between an emerging, centralising monarchy and the component corporate units that make up society (Wiarda and MacLeish Mott 2000).

While the structure of the Latin American colonial (and beyond) state was built on Suárez's foundations, independent Latin America found its inspiration in Rousseau. In contrast to Locke and Madison, Rousseau was little interested in the processes and institutions of politics (elections, checks and balances, and so forth); instead, he presented a great and glorious vision, a secular, updated, and Enlightenment version of the Thomistic vision. Rousseau's vision was of a spontaneous eruption of liberty, unencumbered by institutional restraints, and led by a heroic figure who knew and embodied the general will. Every subsequent dictator in history has admired Rousseau for providing justification for those who presumably know the general will unencumbered by the inconvenience of holding democratic elections. Moreover, Rousseau was manifestly hostile to civil society, seeing it as an obstacle to heroic revolution and the singular expression of the general will. Rousseau not only was the intellectual inspiration of the Latin American independence movements, but his influence even today pervades all areas of Latin American political life: constitutions, strong presidential authority, the role of the state, the limited conception of human rights, weak local government, poor checks and balances, and so on. Those who see civil society as the salvation of Latin America need to reread Rousseau to discover how civil society is viewed in Latin America.

In the nineteenth and early twentieth centuries, four major (and many minor) ideologies vied for political influence. The first was liberalism which, at least in the United States (but not in continental Europe or its colonies), evolved into the modern, pluralist, interest group–competitive, civil society–focused political system (and model that many of us now seek to export to the Third World) with which we are all familiar (Hartz 1957). The second was Marxism, which believed that civil society, as an agency of the bourgeoisie, was the problem, and that in order for the socialist society to be achieved, civil society had to be destroyed. Later Marxists like Lenin and Stalin agreed that bourgeois civil society needed to be eliminated but that, after the revolution, official, state-created and state-run monopolistic organisations, ancillary to the Communist Party, could be created for all revolutionary groups in society: workers, peasants, women, youth, and so forth.

A third tradition continued to be attracted to Rousseau's message and was particularly popular in the less developed areas of Europe (East and South) and Latin America. There, in the absence of democratic traditions or viable national institutions, hope sprang eternal, from El Cid to El Ché, that a heroic, charismatic "man on horseback" would somehow emerge out of the confusion (Rousseau's "state of nature"), seize the moment as well as power, know and personify the general will, and rule triumphantly even without the training, civil society, institutions, elections, or "prerequisites" that we more prosaic Lockeans and Madisonians know are absolutely necessary if one wants stable democracy and development and wishes to avoid totalitarianism. The history of Latin America and of Eastern and Southern Europe, at least until the mid-1970s, offers abundant evidence of the folly of those romantics and wishful thinkers who follow the Rousseau formula; Venezuela's Hugo Chávez and Peru's recently exiled Alberto Fujimori, neither great democrats by any universal standard, provide ongoing examples of Rousseau's formula (and Chávez even proclaims himself a "Rousseauian democrat") (Rosenberg 1992).

At least equally relevant to our discussion of civil society is a fourth great "ism": corporatism. Following the French Revolution of 1789, the Roman Catholic Church, which had lost a great deal in the revolution, turned reactionary for 50–60 years and sought to turn the clock back to the pre-revolutionary status quo ante. Beginning around the mid-nineteenth century, however, the church recovered its political good sense and began to adapt to the new social conditions, culminating in the promulgation of the papal encyclical *Rerum novarum* in 1891 and *Quadragesimo anno* in 1931. The philosophy elaborated was *corporatism*, the church's answer to the emerging social question. Corporatism reversed the church's earlier position of hostility to labour unions and set forth a formula not of class conflict (to distinguish it sharply from hated Marxism), but of class harmony, in which labour and employers would be organised jointly in "corporations."

Corporatism could take the form of free associability, as in Scandinavia, but most often, in the regimes of Franco, Salazar, Dolfuss, Stroessner, Batista, Trujillo, and *scores* of other European and Latin American authoritarians, it took the form of top-down, authoritarian, *state* corporatism. After largely eliminating the older, nascent civil society (parties, unions, peasant associations, and the like), these regimes created a state-structured system of associations that was generally docile in the face of encroaching dictatorship. Civil society lost its autonomy and independence and was subordinated to the state, often serving as an instrument of dictatorship. And while corporatism was most prevalent in Southern and Eastern Europe and in Latin America and in its Catholic forms, it was also present in Protestant Northern Europe (see the writings of future prime minister Abraham Kuyper in The Netherlands), where it generally took a more benign or societal (pluralist) form. In the post–World War II period, while societal corporatism was resurrected in Europe, the state form spread to many areas of the Third World, where it was used to control, co-opt, and/or repress the rising social groups that emerged with modernisation.

As we ponder these theoretical and political cultural developments, we can see that there are at least five main models of civil society and state-society relations. Each of them implies a different system of politics and governance, not all of them liberal, pluralist, and democratic. And it is only the Western tradition of thought and political system that we are talking about here. When we consider non-Western areas, the situation becomes not only more complex and confusing but also less amenable to quick, simple, one-shot ("civil society") solutions.

The five main models are: (1) *totalitarianism*, in which the state eliminates *all* civil society groups and totally controls the official societal associations it creates to replace them; (2) *authoritarianism*, in which the state controls most groups but usually allows some limited pluralism (Linz 1970); (3) *Rousseauism*, in which there is a direct, personal connection between rulers and ruled without the presence of active intermediaries; (4) *corporatism,* in which the state reorganises, regulates, controls, and absorbs civil society in order to guarantee social peace; and (5) *Lockean, Madisonian, pluralist, democratic civil society*, with which most of us are more familiar and tend to favour. Obviously in some cases the distinction can become fuzzy and the categories may overlap.

Now let us introduce some non-Western variations. Japan is the world's second-most-powerful economy, one of its richest, and is usually thought of as democratic; yet its civil society is inordinately weak, with little apparent loss to the quality and rhythms of Japanese life. China and other East Asian countries cast in the Confucian mould have achieved remarkable, even miracle economic growth rates under strong, centralised, bureaucratic governments seemingly without the presence of strong civil society. The Indian Buddhist tradition is more individualistic than the Confucian communalist one; here the dominant civil society groups may well be the caste associations, but is that what political planners have in mind when they speak of democratic, pluralist, egalitarian civil society (Wiarda 1998, 2001)?

There is a great debate as to whether Islam and democracy are compatible; while there is no express prohibition against democracy either in the Qur'an or the *Shariah*, certainly the Islamic tradition has not been supportive of democracy or of autonomous, independent civil society. Finally, in sub-Saharan Africa democracy, social structures and political systems are under severe, perhaps mortal, threat; what there is of civil society is largely found in ethnic or tribal groups and, as with caste associations in India, that parochial institution may not be the kind of civil society we want to see (Syed 2001; Woldemariam 2001).

TWENTY REASONS TO BE SCEPTICAL OF CIVIL SOCIETY

Let's shift directions away from political theory and towards empirical field work by myself and others on civil society problems and dilemmas. For as the civil society concept has been operationalised in distinct regions, culture areas, and political systems, numerous difficulties have arisen. Increasingly, the theory of civil society has diverged from its practice.

1. *Civil society as panacea.* Over the decades since we first started to pay attention to the developing world, American foreign aid and the international donor community have settled on a variety of "solutions" to third-world problems. Typically programmes begin with great hope and fanfare, are well-funded for a time, then run into the harsh realities of politics and social structure in third-world countries or the fleeting, fickle interest of the American public and Congress. They prove less successful than expected, start to run downhill, and are effectively abandoned. But they are never quite dismantled, because whole networks of bureaucratic and private interests grow up around them. Then a new panacea appears. Is civil society about to go through the same life cycle? My own sense is that it is. As a fresh, new idea, it still has cachet with the Congress, foundations, intellectuals, and activists, but the first serious studies are starting to come in with disappointing results. Thus this concept will soon begin its downward slide as have other "cure alls" in the past (Carothers 1999; Salamon and Anheir 1977).

2. *Theory vs. reality.* Civil society sounds wonderful in the abstract: democratic, pluralist, private-sector oriented, Tocquevillian, non-bureaucratic, Madisonian, *Clintonian*, participatory, like a New England town meeting full of yeoman citizens. The reality, however, is often considerably less than that.

3. *Risks and benefits.* Civil society is undoubtedly beneficial where it works. But suppose the growth of civil society weakens governmental authority and policymaking in countries where the state's ability to deliver public services is already too weak? Suppose civil society emerges as a substitute for, and therefore weakens, political parties, which most analysts believe to be absolutely essential for democracy? Suppose civil society undermines traditional but time-tested modes of interest articulation and aggregation, leaving societies with the worst of all possible worlds: old interest associations undermined before the newer civil society ones have had a chance to take root.

4. *Varieties of civil society.* Our theoretical survey has highlighted the variety of conceptions of civil society: totalitarian, authoritarian-corporatist, Rousseauian, Lockean. Only the fourth conforms to our preferred model. In the developing world the most prevalent form is still authoritarian-corporatist (state regulated, officially controlled), with some preference for the Rousseauian solution (direct rule, no intermediaries) combined (often under foreign pressure) with some usually grudging acquiescence in the Lockean-Madisonian model. The variety of outcomes should give us pause before we too precipitously pursue the civil society route.

5. *Nondemocratic civil society.* The above point is so crucial that it deserves reiteration in another framework. Civil society development will not necessarily,

inevitably, or universally lead to more democratic, or socially just outcomes. At least equally plausible are authoritarian, statist, corporatist, and Rousseauian outcomes. Even more likely are mixed or combined systems in which elites and those in power manoeuvre and manipulate to satisfy diverse constituencies, allowing just enough civil society to keep international donors and domestic social groups satisfied but not so much that the elites' own power and position are threatened.

6. *Limited pluralism.* As Latin America and other third-world areas have developed, new social and political groups have emerged, including business and commercial elements, a larger middle class, trade unions, women, peasants, indigenous elements, and others. But in most of these countries this is still often a limited, controlled, regulated pluralism, not the unfettered, free-wheeling, unregulated, virtually anarchic pluralism of US political society. Nor does most of the developing world practice the kind of pluralist interest group lobbying found in the United States. So while we applaud the ofttimes greater pluralism of these societies, we still need to recognise that there are degrees and gradations of pluralism, that some groups are better organised and more influential than others, and that some, often very large social sectors are not organised or represented at all.

7. *Biases of civil society.* There are many biases in the civil society literature and in the actions of civil society groups; here we enumerate only a few of them. First, the foreign foundations, donors, groups, and strongest apostles of civil society are overwhelmingly liberal, activist, and associated with the US Democratic Party, although Republicans may support it as well. Second, the movements abroad that these groups support tend not only to be similarly liberal, often radical, activist, and on the left, but also, almost by the definition of civil society itself, anti-government. To be identified with such anti-government activism, which may or may not be justified, is very dangerous for outside groups and may lead to suppression, suspension of programme activities, expulsion, and, overall, the over-politicisation of programme activities. Third, these outside groups, often naive and well-meaning, are sometimes destructive when they get involved in the internal affairs of other nations. A dramatic case in point is in the Mexican state of Chiapas, where many foreign NGOs have identified with and aided the revolutionary Zapatista movement. The Mexican government sought to regulate and control them in classic corporatist fashion (hard to do with foreign-based groups while undergoing democratisation and liberalisation, under constant media scrutiny) but finally threw up its hands in disgust and expelled many of the organisations from the country. This is not a forward step for civil society (Carothers 1999).

8. *Whom to include.* Most of us think of civil society as peasant groups, labour unions, women's groups, maybe political parties, neighbourhood and community groups, human rights organisations, and so on. But if we define civil society as *all* those associations that are intermediary between state and citizen, we may have to include business groups, oligarchic sectors, para-militaries, guerrillas – and certainly in Latin America, the Roman Catholic Church and the rising Pentecostal movements. Now let us complicate the issue even more by including such unlovable groups as the European skinheads and the North American militias. An even more complex issue is presented by African ethnicity and tribalism, Indian caste

associations, and Latin American patronage networks. Each of these is parochial and traditional in some ways, and we would probably prefer to confine them to the dustbins of history. Yet African tribalism often provides the only public and social services that many communities have; India's caste associations have become rather like modern interest associations and political parties; and without patronage networks much of Latin America (plus Louisiana, Arkansas, and a few other states) would disintegrate. In short, there is a large variety among civil society groups, including many that we don't particularly like politically or consider passé. But if democracy is what we want, then we must be prepared to accept the outcome of the process even if it produces abhorrent results.

9. *Weakened states?* The concept of civil society implies limits on state authority; indeed, its purpose is to develop intermediaries between the state and its citizens that rein in the potential for the exercise of dictatorial power. However, the problem in many developing countries is not excessive state power but a state that, like other groups in society and civil society itself, is weak, underdeveloped, and thus ineffective. Many third-world states, ostensibly strong and powerful, cannot make their writ felt in remote areas and are ineffective in carrying out the policies most of us would approve (Huntington 1968; Hammergren 1983). The problem in these societies may not be a state that is too strong, and therefore needs the mediating influence and checks and balances of civil society, but a state that is too weak and cannot govern or carry out effective public policies. We need both a strong and effective civil society and a strong and effective state, but with the current emphasis almost entirely on civil society, we run the risk of rendering states powerless and thus contributing to further fragmentation and ungovernability, already a major problem in many third-world nations.

10. *Ethnocentrism.* Much of the literature on civil society seems to be based on the perception that one model fits all. And that one model almost always bears a striking resemblance to the Lockean, Madisonian, Tocquevillian interest-group pluralism of the United States. But we have already seen that there are different models of civil society and state-society relations in the West; when we move out of the West the differences become even more striking. Japan, South Korea, and Taiwan are democracies and developed nations with only weak civil society. The Islamic world also has weak civil society, but almost no democracy at all. Clearly, one size does *not* fit all, especially when that one size is modeled on one nation (the United States) and its particular history and society (Somjee 1986; Wiarda 1985).

11. *Opportunists.* In both the donor countries and the developing recipient ones, opportunists await the latest panacea emanating from Washington, looking to turn it to their own private financial or political advantage. I have been following the life cycles of these various panaceas since the beginning of the Alliance for Progress in the early 1960s, and it is striking how often the same people, whether on the US end or the developing country end, are consistently involved. This cannot be sheer coincidence, nor is it simply that the same people consistently have an interest in parallel progressive policies. In the developing countries that I know best, whether the issue is agrarian reform, community development, basic

human needs, sustainable development, or (now) civil society, the same people always seem to form the local commissions and agencies that show the aid donors how and where to spend their monies. It is not merely love of public policy issues that motivates these persons; having been in quite a number of their homes, I can report that, as in political Washington, they have learned to "do well by doing good." Indeed, quite a few of these individuals are widely admired on nationalistic grounds for having, over a forty-year period, hoodwinked the (usually) American donor agencies while enriching themselves and rising to positions of prominence in the process. Of course, most of us will respond that "*my* friends and contacts would never do that and in any case there are controls in place," but my experience is that the locals are at least as practised as the donors at milking programmes for private advantage.

12. *A weak popular base?* The figures we have for all of Latin America indicate that only 13 per cent of the population are members of civil society in any form. This figure includes political parties, labour groups, peasant groups, women's groups, community groups, religious groups, and other groups of all kinds. First, this is an incredibly low number when compared with Western Europe or North America and offers scant evidence for the prospect of a mushrooming civil society in Latin America anytime in the near future. Second, people in Latin America tend to be members of one group and one group only; one does not find the webs of multiple and cross-cutting group memberships that one finds in US society and that tend to moderate citizens' position on any one issue. Rather, in Latin America one tends to go "all out" for the singular group of which one is a member, thus producing a society of almost stock types – *the* oligarch, *the* cleric, *the* military officer, *the* unionist, *the* student, and so forth – whose behaviour must conform to the stereotype. Such stereotyping and the rigidities of the categories, which probably go back to Saint Thomas, are not supportive of the moderating and stabilising tendencies that civil society is supposed to engender (Carothers 1999; Salamon and Anheir 1977; Inglehart 1990).

13. *A product of elites and intellectuals?* Civil society now has a certain cachet. But is this sentiment widespread or only the preference of elites and intellectuals? Has anyone checked with the masses in the developing world to see if they believe in civil society as much as we do? The few survey results we have indicate that, when it is explained to them, people often have a favourable view of civil society; at the same time, it remains vague, distant, and divorced from their everyday realities. At the local level people may be reluctant to get involved; traditional fatalism is still widespread; and in those many countries based on the Napoleonic Code, one waits for guidance and the direction of the central ministries. The issue may be parallel to that of *sustainable development,* a concept to which the Brazilian government with considerable reluctance eventually agreed; meanwhile, Brazilian peasants, often with that same government's approval, continue to cut, burn, and pave over the Amazon Basin, which supplies 40 per cent of the world's oxygen. So too with civil society: elites and intellectuals approve at least in the abstract, but meantime overriding material interest and self-preservation take priority.

14. *Divorced from power realities?* Civil society cannot be seen as some magic formula to save the world. Instead, civil society must be seen in a broader political and power configuration. No government is going to favour civil society if it sees its own power base eroding in the process. Instead, it will try to co-opt, control, regulate, and maybe even repress civil society, to offer carrots or sticks or maybe both at once. At the same time, civil society groups will try to mobilise international public opinion and support to maintain their autonomy and freedom of action. These are political processes that will produce a mixed bag of results.

15. *Outside sponsorship and control.* A related problem is that of foreign sponsorship, control, and manipulation of civil society groups. In the Dominican Republic, for example, the US Embassy concluded that the aging and increasingly infirm president, Joaquín Balaguer, was not only corrupt but also that his continuation in office might be destructive of democracy and stability. Hence, the embassy and USAID provided massive support to a so-called citizens' group, the Red Ciudadana (Citizens' Network) to oppose Balaguer, find alternative candidates, and rally oppositionist sentiment. It brought in the National Endowment for Democracy (NED), the National Democratic Institute (NDI), and a host of well-paid civil society, political party, and elections experts to help support this campaign. One may or may not approve such actions, but one should not confuse these embassy fronts and their political machinations with genuine, indigenous, or grassroots civil society. Moreover, once the embassy had accomplished its short-term political goal, the funds for this ostensible civil society organisation quickly dried up, leaving the Dominican groups without sufficient support in most cases to survive. Such manipulation of civil society by governments and foreign embassies happens all the time, and we need to distinguish between genuine civil society of the homegrown kind and that sponsored by states and outside powers (Sabatini 2000).

16. *Is civil society self-sustaining?* The above discussion touches on an important point: Is civil society sustainable after the foreign support and funds are gone? No one knows. The issue is important and fraught with policy implications because, if civil society is not sustainable once outside support dries up, the political system may well fragment, disintegrate, and collapse – precisely the outcome that civil society initiatives were designed to prevent. But it is just as likely that another scenario will play out and that quite a number of countries may be left with the worst of all possible worlds: traditional civil society (tribes, caste associations, patronage networks) undermined and destroyed under the impact of both modernisation and US pressures, and its fledgling modern civil society floundering because of popular indifference and a withdrawal of critical foreign funding.

17. *Civil society as a reflection of the United States.* It is striking how often, when we speak of civil society, we have in mind a society that looks just like that of the United States. When foreign funds are involved, the types of civil society supported tend to look just like their sponsoring groups. Take the case of the National Endowment for Democracy. For partisan reasons and to get the bill through Congress, NED consists of four constituent groups: the Republican and Democratic parties' international affairs branches, big labour (the AFL-CIO), and big

business (represented through the Chamber of Commerce). This structure is, of course, a reflection of internal US political power and interest-group relations. That such a structure is appropriate for all other societies, cultures, and political systems is unlikely (Wiarda 1990). Similarly with other, more narrowly focused groups. What the Worldwatch Institute, the National Wildlife Fund, and others have as their agendas may be quite appropriate in the United States, but do mirrors of these groups need to be established abroad? Civil society, it seems to me, needs to be variable and appropriate for diverse societies and cultures; patterning civil society in other countries exclusively or nearly so on the US model and society may be inappropriate, self-defeating, and ultimately lead to failure.

18. *Central vs. local controls.* As liberalisation and democratisation have expanded in recent decades, we have seen a gradual dismantling of the authoritarian corporative or regulatory controls by which states control civil society. Democracy, in short, means not just parties and elections but a freeing up of associational life in general. In most countries one cannot just go out and organise an interest group; instead, the interest group must seek recognition and "juridical personality" from the state, and there is a vast web of regulations and corporative controls used to co-opt, control, and limit such group activities. But while in many countries these corporative controls are being repealed at the national level, they are being re-enacted at the local level (where most civil society groups operate), with local authorities forcing civil society groups to register, show their membership lists and sources of financing, and gain recognition from local officialdom. Of course, the power to grant recognition to a group also implies the power *not* to grant it. So while corporatism is often in decline at national levels and democracy triumphant, at local levels corporatism often reemerges. Democracy in its formal form may thus not be incompatible with a high degree of illiberalism at both national and local levels, but then is that truly democratic?

19. *Civil society as romantic vision?* Are the focus and hopes that have come to be centred on civil society realistic? Or are they the product of unwarranted idealism and romance? Is civil society another one of those concepts that inflate expectations, provide short-term employment for thousands of consultants, and then fall to earth again? So far, the results of all civil society efforts have been disappointing: slightly over 10 percent organised in any fashion in all of Latin America. Surely civil society has done little so far to enhance democracy or development in Africa or the Islamic countries, and East Asia appears both not to want *or* need civil society. In Peru and Venezuela, under authoritarian-populist leadership, civil society has all but been destroyed; Cuba has no or minimal civil society to speak of, apart from the state; and, particularly in the small, underdeveloped, weakly institutionalized countries of Latin America, the Rousseauian model of direct identification between leader and masses, sans civil society, continues to be attractive. Is civil society, which seems to many to be an agency of hope, really a clutching at straws?

20. *Can civil society be exported?* So far, there is not a *single case* of the West being able to export its model *en toto* to other lands and cultures; that is, the model that includes the Renaissance; the Reformation, particularly its economic

and political ramifications; the Enlightenment and its rationalist way of thinking; and the revolution of democracy in its Lockean, Madisonian, Jeffersonian form. *Parts* of the model – usually easily imitated institutional arrangements such as elections or parliaments – may be exported, both because people want them and because they are pressured to accept them, but not the underlying values of democracy (tolerance, egalitarianism, mutual respect) or the vast webs of associability that Tocqueville described. Those are peculiar, particular, a part of Western history, culture, and tradition; they cannot be packed up and shipped to countries where the culture, society, and traditions are distinct. Of course, we can get thin and pale imitations of civil society and democracy ("democracy with adjectives" – limited, controlled, organic, delegative, Rousseauian, corporatist) but not the real thing. That takes two or three generations, as in Russia, not two or three years. Other than in superficial ways, it remains doubtful if civil society is transplantable from one model country to another.

Conclusions

Having said all of these sceptical things about civil society, let me also say that I tend to be in favour of the concept and what it implies in a policy sense. For most (not all) countries, a web of intermediary associations between the citizen and the state serves both to limit state power and to be a transmission belt by which citizens can make their interests known to government officials. To the degree civil society is present, it *tends* (not always) to be good for the state, for society, and for democracy.

To some, this positive conclusion may seem surprising after the barrage of criticism levelled. But my purpose has not been to disparage or destroy the concept of civil society, only to introduce some cautionary restraints in our understanding and practice. In their eagerness to advance their mission, and because the civil society groups *they* deal with most often *do* have dedicated people and undertake noble, even heroic activities, Christian civil society advocates may fall into the trap of romanticising and idealising the concept. Christians, too, need to be pragmatic and realistic about what civil society can do, and what it cannot.

Extrapolating from the list of twenty reasons, three problems are especially important. The first is the incredible variety of civil society forms; their diverse underlying philosophical, social, and cultural assumptions; the frequently "crazy quilt" patchworks that exist; and often our own inability or incapacity to appreciate, on their own terms, this diversity and pluralism. The second is the problem of ethnocentrism: our inability to comprehend and accept forms of civil society and state-society relations, let alone democracy, other than our own. The third problem is politicisation of the concept by *everyone:* local elites in third-world countries, foundations, the AFL-CIO, the Chamber of Commerce, USAID, NED, US embassies abroad, successive US governments. Once that happens, and the issue gets enmeshed in domestic politics and politicised foreign policy, it is probably hopelessly lost; we should expect the gaffes, shortsightedness, and frequent misfires that have, in fact, occurred in many countries.

Civil society cannot save the world. One is tempted to say cynically that civil society has already peaked, that it is already too late, that we should forget about the idea and wait for the next cure-all to come down the pike. But that is too negative and, in fact, ignores the political process factors that need to be taken into account. That implies acceptance or at least understanding of the compromises, mixed forms, and the frequent use and misuse of civil society in the political process. Hence, let us support and aid civil society – it is still a good idea – but do so with our eyes wide open, realistically, recognising both the opportunities and the limits that championing civil society in other people's countries offer.

REFERENCES

Carothers, Thomas. 1999. *Aiding Democracy Abroad: The Learning Curve.* Washington, D.C.: The Carnegie Endowment for International Peace.

Ehrenberg, John. 1999. *Civil Society: The Critical History of an Idea.* New York: New York University Press.

Gellner, Ernest. 1997. *Conditions of Liberty: Civil Society and Its Rivals.* New York: Penguin Press.

Hammergren, Linn. 1983. *Development and the Politics of Administrative Reform: Lessons from Latin America.* Boulder, Colo.: Westview Press.

Hartz, Louis. 1957. *The Liberal Tradition in America.* New York: Harcourt, Brace and World.

Huntington, Samuel P. 1968. *Political Order in Changing Societies.* New Haven, Conn.: Yale University Press.

Inglehart, Ronald. 1990. *Culture Change in Advanced Industrial Society.* Princeton, N.J.: Princeton University Press.

Linz, Juan. 1970. "An Authoritarian Regime: Spain." In *Mass Politics,* edited by E. Allardt and S. Rokkan, 251–83. New York: The Free Press.

Morse, Richard. 1964. "The Heritage of Latin America." In *The Founding of New Societies,* edited by L. Hartz. New York: Harcourt, Brace, Jovanovich.

Putnam, Robert. 2000. *Bowling Alone: The Collapse and Revival of American Community.* New York: Simon and Schuster.

Rosenberg, Tina. 1992. "Latin America's Magical Liberalism." *Washington Quarterly* (autumn): 58–74.

Sabatini, Christopher. 2000. "Whom Do International Donors Support in the Name of Civil Society?" Paper presented at the 2000 meeting of the Latin American Studies Association, 16–18 March, Miami.

Salamon, Lester H., and Helmut K. Anheir. 1977. *The Third World's Third Sector in Comparative Perspective.* Baltimore: Johns Hopkins University, The Johns Hopkins Comparative Nonprofit Sector Project.

Somjee, A. H. 1986. *Parallels and Actuals of Political Development.* London: Macmillan.

Syed, Answar. 2001. "Democracy and Islam: Are They Compatible?" In *Comparative Democracy and Democratization,* edited by Howard J. Wiarda, 127–43. Houston, Tex.: Harcourt Brace.

Wiarda, Howard J. 1985. *Ethnocentrism and Foreign Policy: Can We Understand the Third World?* Washington, D.C.: American Enterprise Institute for Public Policy Research.

———. 1990. *The Democratic Revolution in Latin America: History, Politics, and U.S. Policy.* New York: The Twentieth Century Fund, Holmes and Meier.

————. 1996. *Corporatism and Comparative Politics: The Other Great "Ism."* New York: M. E. Sharpe.

————. 2000. *The Soul of Latin America: The Political Culture and Tradition.* New Haven, Conn.: Yale University Press.

Wiarda, Howard J., ed. 1998. *Non-Western Theories of Development.* Houston, Tex.: Harcourt Brace.

————. 2001. *Comparative Democracy and Democratization.* Houston, Tex.: Harcourt Brace.

Wiarda, Howard J., and Margaret MacLeish Mott. 2000. *Catholic Roots and Democratic Flowers: The Political Systems of Spain and Portugal.* Westport, Conn.: Greenwood/ Praeger.

Woldemariam, Johannes. 2001. "Democracy in Africa: Does It Have a Chance?" In *Comparative Democracy and Democratization,* edited by Howard J. Wiarda, 144–61. Houston, Tex.: Harcourt Brace.

5

HUMAN RIGHTS,
THE FOUNDATION FOR CIVIL SOCIETY

Lowell Ewert

CONTEMPORARY INTEREST
IN CIVIL SOCIETY

The breakup of the former Soviet Union and the wave of citizen engagement that swept over Eastern Europe and parts of Central Asia following the Soviet collapse have demonstrated the incredible appeal of the idea of civil society and citizen engagement. It is remarkable that the emergent Russian civil society was able to stand up to the might of the Soviet army during the attempted coup in 1991, when ordinary citizens successfully protected the government from military assault by standing between them.

The fact that even the most intractable opponent of civil society, the Russian military, has acknowledged the legitimacy of some of the core values of civil society, such as transparency and accountability, is nothing short of astounding. Recently, in response to an ambush in Chechnya in which 43 Russian servicemen died, Russian Defense Minister Igor Sergeyev announced that an inquiry would be held to determine who is to blame for the ambush. Using language that could have been written by civil society enthusiasts, Minister Sergeyev said, "We are ready to expose these mistakes since if problems and mistakes are not revealed, it will be impossible to eliminate them" (Sergeyev 2000).

The more recent Kursk disaster, in which a Russian nuclear submarine carrying 118 sailors sank, is another example of how government and military officials reacted far more positively to citizen engagement than was once imagined possible. Newspaper headlines in *The Record* said it all when they proclaimed "Relatives of Lost Sailors Confront [Russian President] Putin" (23 August 2000) and "Russia's Officials React to Outrage: Authorities Respond with Meek Apologies, Confessions and Quick Offers of Resignations" (24 August 2000). These articles explain how the government, in response to public pressure, released information and took steps publicly to mitigate the impact of the disaster. Inside Russia, commentators were also reported to have "heaped ridicule" on the Russian military's version of events – illustrating a level of public debate that was unimaginable even 10 years ago.

Outside the former Soviet Union the impact of civil society and citizen action movements has been equally startling. Ordinary citizens in the Philippines, South Korea, East Germany, Poland, Romania, South Africa, and Serbia, who have long been denied the opportunity to influence their governments, have emerged as powerful political actors who caused the downfall of their autocratic rulers. The emergence of nascent civil society movements has changed the world's political landscape by demonstrating that mass "people power" is a force to be reckoned with. As the political journalist Gwynne Dyer wrote the week after Slobodan Milosevic's fall in Serbia, "The men and women who ended the Milosevic regime in Belgrade last Thursday were following a trail blazed by others in Manila and Seoul and Bangkok, in Berlin and Prague and Bucharest, in Moscow and Pretoria and Jakarta. It's no longer a trail, but a broad, well-marked route that can be taken by anybody looking for a way out of a dictatorship" (Dyer 2000).

The evidence is in. Like it or not, governments are increasingly, perhaps grudgingly, acknowledging (or at least accepting) the legitimacy and efficacy of citizen involvement. Civil society, while not without significant shortcomings, now has successful adherents practising civic engagement in countries dominated by every major religion or political philosophy and living in nations referred to as the East, West, North, South, traditional, or modern. It is no longer defensible, if it ever was, to dismiss civil society as simply the manifestation of a neo-colonial "Western" form of liberal political thought that civic enthusiasts are trying to force-feed to the rest of the world.

But if civil society is really that positive, successful, and universal, why are so many red flags being raised by critics? Even in this volume, including but not limited to Chapter 4 by Howard Wiarda, readers will notice a great deal of discomfort with the notion of universally applicable norms of civil society. While eventually expressing support for the concept of civil society, Wiarda does so only after providing 20 reasons to be sceptical about civil society and calling many civil society advocates romantic and idealistic.

It is my thesis that much of the current disquiet with the contemporary notion of civil society is based on a fundamental misunderstanding of what civil society is and where the hybrid we see today has actually come from. If civil society is what its critics say it is, and if it has come from purely Western philosophical foundations, then critics are justified in their scepticism. Viewed from their perspective, civil society cannot support the high expectations that many have for it around the world, and it is unwise to base lofty goals on its flawed foundation. Such Western foundations may be totally inappropriate for constructing well-governed societies in non-Western societies. Seligman has even argued that the original notion of civil society was inadequate for the context in which it originated. "The classic early-modern version of civil society . . . rested on a vision of human nature and of the place of reason in human action that had begun to unravel even before it was fully promulgated" (Seligman 1993, 139–40). Hence it is doubly important to understand the strength and legitimacy of the foundation of civil society before we advocate building a universally applicable political theory upon it.

My argument is that the critics are wrong for the simple reason that they are overlooking the true contemporary and universal foundation for civil society. As the old proverb states, Where you stand will determine what you see. It thus behooves us to take another look at common presuppositions and analyse whether in fact the critics have a clear view of civil society or whether their sight is obstructed by a Western historical lens that distorts rather than sharpens. My contention is that many contemporary analysts have ignored an important point of view – the powerful impact of the international human rights movement – leading critics to come to an inaccurate view of civil society's deficiencies and a distorted understanding of its possibilities.

The Origin of Civil Society as Commonly Understood

Since the early 1990s there has been an explosion of written material on the subject of civil society as scholars have rushed to define and explain its apparent universal appeal. As Whaites writes below (Chapter 7), "As late as 1989 major texts were written that were largely devoid of references to civil society." Today, discussion of civil society is virtually required.

Scholars researching the idea of civil society typically imply in their analyses that what we see today is primarily the rebirth, renaissance, or resurrection of something that has been around for a long time (Barber 1998, 7; Seligman 1993, 139; Van Rooy 1999, 6; Van Rooy 1998, 7). Events in Eastern Europe in the last decade of the twentieth century are often given credit for reinvigorating civil society. As Alexander (1998, 1) writes, "Almost single-handedly, Eastern European intellectuals reintroduced 'civil society' to contemporary social theory. Until they started talking and writing about it, it had been considered a quaint and conservative notion, thoroughly obsolete."

While some authors have cited the influence of early philosophers such as Aristotle, Cicero, and Plato for introducing civil society concepts (Van Rooy 1999, 9; Van Rooy 1998, 7; Ehrenberg 1999, 4), others have emphasised the impact of seventeenth- to nineteenth-century political events in Europe and the influence of intellectuals such as Hobbes, Rousseau, Hume, Ferguson, Marx, and Gramsci (Van Rooy 1999, 9). Others emphasise the role of the Scottish Enlightenment (Moran 2000, 62). Hyden has gone so far as to attribute honourary "founding father" status to Hegel, Locke, Paine, and de Tocqueville for their roles in defining relations between the governed and their governors (Hyden 1997, 19). Hyden emphasises that civil society emerged from a European philosophical tradition. Still others credit the underlying philosophy of Christian natural-law thinking as the intellectual basis for civil society (Seligman 1992, ix).

Given the many different views of where civil society has come from, or who has been responsible for articulating its attributes, one can be forgiven for being confused about the genesis of civil society. Consequently, the view that the current phenomenon is "nothing new but very much changed" (Van Rooy 1998, 7) seems logical and persuasive.

THE EMPHASIS ON THE HISTORICAL "ORIGINS" OF CIVIL SOCIETY IS MISPLACED

While there are useful comparisons between the contemporary experience of civil society and the Western philosophical political tradition, basing the modern-day understanding of civil society on these historic roots ignores the fact that something radically different has emerged on the political horizon. As such, it is inappropriate to dismiss the contemporary vision of civil society as something that is simply "very much changed," for it is, under better lights, profoundly new. It grew from different rootstock, and though it may have some similar characteristics with that first proposed by the ancients, it did not emerge from the same gene pool. Those who claim that the modern understanding of civil society is simply a new and improved version of the old model ignore the emergence of universal human rights, the most significant driver behind the growth of civil society today.

Since World War II human rights standards have permanently changed, and significantly elevated, the status of the individual under international law. Prior to the adoption of the Universal Declaration of Human Rights in 1948, "the individual was regarded as an object: that is to say, he enjoyed no rights and was burdened by no duties" (Daes 1990, 1). Nations were deemed to be generally free to operate within their borders as they saw fit – as long as they did not harm the interests or property of another nation state.

Seeing human beings as objects rather than subjects of international law, or essentially as property of the state where they were citizens, had three practical consequences. First, individuals who were wrongfully harmed by a country not their own were not able to maintain a claim against the offending state in their own right. Considered to be equivalent to chattel, the harmed individuals could only have their rights advanced if their own country (that is, the property owner) chose to assert those claims (Daes 1990, 1). Compensation granted by nation A for violating the rights of a citizen of nation B belonged to the party deemed to have been harmed – nation B – and not to the individual citizen who was injured.

In practical terms this principle of international law meant that individuals had great difficulty in making claims against an offending state when their only possible advocate, the country of their own citizenship, often had larger and perhaps contradictory political interests to manage with the offending nation. This conflict of interest between being an advocate for its own citizens and maintaining a relationship with the offending nation often affected the nature of the claim put forth. Injured parties, therefore, were subject to the hurdle of convincing their own government that their claim was politically worth the risk. In addition, citizens of nations demonstrating no commitment to respect for human rights had no recourse at all when another nation mistreated them.

On the other hand, a nation had the legal right to raise a claim on behalf of an individual whose interests had been harmed by an offending state even though the harmed individual did not consent. This practice of giving priority to state interests over individual interests opened the door for nations to exploit harm done to their nationals and thus advance their own political agendas. Again, by being essentially treated as property, individuals were often innocent pawns in interstate relations, with no power to navigate a way out of their dilemmas. In truth, there was little difference in how animals and humans were treated according to this now discredited juridical philosophy.

A second practical consequence, even more troubling, is that individuals were generally accorded no special status under international law vis-à-vis their own country of residence or citizenship. With some limited exceptions, nations were free to treat persons under its authority in any way that it deemed politically expedient. While some of the Minorities Treaties, peace treaties associated with the end of World War I, and the League of Nations documents placed some limits on how nations could treat minorities within their jurisdictions, these limits were very specific, narrowly defined, and only applicable if a formal treaty existed. The rights of minorities, in other words, were not inherent but contractual (Daes 1990, 2). No independent universal claim of rights, apart from that enshrined in national law and therefore subject to manipulation or abuse by powerful leaders, was applicable to citizens or residents. Stateless persons were particularly at risk prior to the development of international human rights law as "it was widely accepted . . . that injustice to a stateless person was not a violation of international law since no state was offended thereby; surely, there was no state that could invoke a remedy for the injustice" (Henkin 1990, 14).

In effect, no international restraints limited governmental mistreatment of citizens. "How a sovereign prince treated his own subjects, or later a nation state its own citizens, was entirely their own affair" (Sieghart 1991, 25). While the torture, extrajudicial killing, and discrimination against certain domestic populations may have been morally repugnant, they were not violations of international law prior to World War II. Nations not only were deemed to have a divine right to rule, but in the words of one plainspoken observer, a nation also had a "divine right to be a monster" to its citizens. "What they [nations] did to their own citizens was their own business, beyond the reach of international law, and not the legitimate business of other countries or of the international community" (Humphrey 1984, 10).

Third, because state rights trumped any notion of individual rights, the ability of individuals to act alone or in concert with others depended totally on the freedom granted by their nation of citizenship. Stateless persons were particularly vulnerable as they lacked effective mechanisms to claim rights. No independent international justification existed for individuals to speak on their own behalf or on behalf of others. This view of individuals precluded effective foreign external criticism of how a nation treated its own people or advocacy on their behalf. To criticise the actions of a foreign government, or to challenge the mistreatment or disempowerment of its citizens, was seen to be unwarranted interference in the internal affairs of a sovereign state. No recognised basis existed in international law for human rights organisations or humanitarian-minded nations to advocate for universal rights or to raise the cause of any disadvantaged group. No legal space existed even to begin talking about a notion of civil society that transcended national borders. National sovereignty was the overarching political value, not the value of the individual.

The horrific consequences of this prevailing view of human rights, especially the genocide carried out by Nazi Germany, forced the world community to rethink the centrality given to the principle of sovereignty in international relations. Revolted by knowledge that much of the genocide, "however monstrous, had never been proscribed as 'criminal' in any orthodox legal sense" and by the claims that the German defendants at Nuremberg were improperly charged with crimes that were not crimes when committed (Frankel and Saideman 1989, 36; Morsink 1999, 52), the world community responded by opening the door to a fundamentally new approach to sovereignty that would limit excesses of the abuse of power.

After World War II the world community's motivation for finding a new approach to sovereignty was clear. Drafters involved with promulgating the various provisions of the Universal Declaration of Human Rights repeatedly reaffirmed their abhorrence about what had happened to civilians during the Second World War, stating explicitly in the Preamble that "disregard and contempt for human rights have resulted in barbarous acts which have outraged the conscience of mankind." The drafters sought to establish rules that would unequivocally condemn the barbarism of World War II. This goal was evidenced by many of the internal debates on the declaration's 30 articles that frequently cited the justification for the declaration's human rights protections as being the problems inherent in Nazism. The drafters of the Declaration "made it abundantly clear that the Declaration . . . had been born out of the experience of the war just ended" (Morsink 1999, 36). "If any single thing could account for complex developments like the international human rights movement, it is Hitler's repulsive theory and the barbarities committed under the Axis Aegis" (Frankel and Saideman 1989, 37–38).

While some have claimed that the notion of state sovereignty fell with the Berlin Wall in the later part of the twentieth century (Philpott 1996, 37), the actual seeds of its destruction were planted in fertile soil when the 56 nations in attendance at the United Nations first general assembly voted 48 (in favour), 0 (opposed), and 8 (abstentions) to accept the Universal Declaration of Human Rights. With this vote the delegates inadvertently set in motion a process that to this day proceeds inexorably to dismantle the concept of national sovereignty.

The adoption of the Universal Declaration of Human Rights at approximately 3:00 A.M. on 10 December 1948 (Frankel and Saideman 1989, 41) changed everything. This act, which has been called the advent of the global human rights system (Dunne and Wheeler 1999, 1), triggered the unplanned elevation of the status of the individual in international law and also the unintentional legitimisation of civic engagement. The limitation of state sovereignty in favour of the individual has been described as "being one of the most dramatic events in the entire history of jurisprudence," which has developed more in the last "forty years than it did in the previous forty centuries" (Drinan 1987, 5, 8). The declaration is the "greatest ethical and normative achievement of the United Nations, and perhaps even the international community as a whole in the course of the past fifty years" (Alston

1998, 28). It is hard to overestimate the importance of the shift in international political thought triggered by the adoption of the Universal Declaration of Human Rights.

One must also keep in mind that the declaration was not negotiated either in a vacuum or in the ivory towers of the liberal, capitalist West. Although his count wasn't perfect, Philippe De La Chapelle estimated that among the nations engaged in the drafting process, "thirty-seven of the member nations stood in the Judaeo-Christian tradition, eleven in the Islamic, six in the Marxist, and four in the Buddhist tradition" (Morsink 1999, 21). The religious and cultural diversity represented by participating nations was unusual for its time.

The process undertaken by the Committee on Social, Cultural, and Humanitarian Questions, tasked by the United Nations to review the declaration, was comprehensive and onerous. According to John Humphrey, who has been credited with preparing the original draft of the declaration, this committee "devoted eighty-one long meetings to the Declaration and dealt with one hundred and sixty-eight resolutions containing amendments" (Humphrey 1984, 63). Susan Walz, who has written about the role of non-Western states in the development of the declaration, has debunked the myth that the declaration was simply a reflection of the Western powers. She claims that delegates who were from "small states" and made up the majority of the 250 delegates ensured that socio-economic rights were enshrined in the declaration. They also vigorously promoted women's rights, highlighted the issue of discrimination (something the United States was less enthusiastic about), ensured that every provision of the declaration was carefully considered and debated, and attempted to end colonial rule. It is evident from this history that the declaration received as much input from diverse traditions as was possible in the late 1940s. "Contrary to a belief that, ironically, has served hegemonic interests, the [declaration] was not the brainchild of the great powers. At best, it was their stepchild" (Walz 2001, 63–65, 72).

The historical record also demonstrates that the delegates of the 56 states present at the birth of the declaration had no intention of unleashing the revolutionary shift that ensued. On the contrary, delegates repeatedly assured sceptical and hesitant national representatives that the declaration was little more than a statement of moral precepts and nice platitudes. The chairperson of the Commission on Human Rights, Eleanor Roosevelt, reminded delegates just before it was adopted that the declaration "is not a treaty; it is not an international agreement. It is not and does not purport to be a statement of law or of legal obligation" (Kirgis 1977, 782). The non-binding character of the declaration was designed to allow the world community to express its revulsion at atrocities committed during the war, but not to create obligations that might affect state freedom later. It was to serve as a convenient, low-cost response to the genocide and was not intended to trigger a radical departure from unilateral state freedom.

But that is not the way it turned out. As Thomas Buergenthal writes:

The great irony here is that the Universal Declaration was drafted in hortatory language designed to emphasise its non-binding character because many member states of the United Nations did not want a binding legal document. Their governments no doubt believed that 'mere words' could do no harm, provided they did not impose legal obligations. How wrong they were! It is precisely the Declaration's language – at once eloquent, expansive and simple – that allowed it to express unequivocal universal truths in words human beings all over the world could understand and wanted to hear. No formal legal instrument could have achieved that result and had quite the same inspirational impact on the human rights movement (Buergenthal 1998, 91).

The national representatives who voted for the declaration failed to appreciate the depth of the yearning for human rights that this document would unleash. Contrary to the common perception that international agreements are only of real interest to diplomats and that they only have a direct impact on states, the declaration was seized by the world's citizenry in a way no one could have predicted. Encouraged by the United Nations, which published and circulated the declaration far and wide in multiple languages, NGOs, political and community activists, and ordinary citizens drew inspiration from its idealistic words. The declaration raised the expectations of citizens throughout the world, who increasingly began demanding a changed view of humanity under international law. They rejected the pre–World War II notion that human value was determined by the whim of one's government and that every nation could treat its citizens in any way it deemed best.

The impact of the declaration has been keenly evident elsewhere. Although the declaration itself is not a binding document and specifies no mechanism by which it can be enforced, it has inspired some 50 other international human rights instruments that *do* bind signing states and that further elaborate specific human rights protections (Morsink 1999, xi). According to Morsink, the lack of an enforcement mechanism, viewed by many as a weakness, turned out to be the strength of the declaration: "The adoption in 1948 of a Declaration that did not itself include any machinery for its own implementation has been a blessing in disguise. Because it floats above all local and regional contingencies and is a statement of more or less abstract moral rights and principles, the Declaration served as a midwife in the birth of all these other more concrete and detailed international instruments" (ibid.).

The cumulative impact of the foundational declaration, and the international human rights regime that it inspired, has been to turn international political practice on its head, completely reversing the underlying presumptions that supported the philosophy of seventeenth-century political thinkers. The result of this change, in the words of Sir Hersch Lauterpacht, has been that "the individual has acquired a status and a stature which have transformed him from an object of international compassion into a subject of international right" (Sieghart 1991, 26).

The human rights documents that grew out of the womb of the declaration affect the relationship of the state to the individual in almost every area of human activity including religion, conscience, political expression, ethnicity, gender relations, value of children, peaceful assembly and free speech, and respect for cultural and social differences. Prior to the adoption of the international human rights structure, managing all these areas of life had been in the exclusive domain of sovereign nation states. By changing the parameters within which a nation can act towards its citizens, the declaration has been more responsible for profoundly changing the relationship of a nation to its own citizenry than any other written document. It is without precedent in the history of law or jurisprudence. It has permanently altered the world's understanding of the relation of the individual to the state, creating the political conditions needed for civil society to grow. Its legitimation and affirmation of the conditions necessary for civil society have no equal. As such, the Universal Declaration of Human Rights has become the global foundation or "constitution" for contemporary articulations of civil society.

HOW HUMAN RIGHTS PRINCIPLES ARE SIMILAR TO CIVIL SOCIETY PRINCIPLES

Nowhere in the primary international human rights treaties will one find references to the term *civil society*. The link between human rights and civil society must therefore be inferred, as it is not stated explicitly.

If one figuratively puts all human rights treaties into a blender, grinding them up and mixing them so that each mingles with the others, and then distils the ensuing potion down to its core elements, one observes four closely interrelated and overarching commonalities which in my view define civil society.

First, the idea of human dignity (even though it is never defined) stands behind the human rights conventions as a coach stands behind a skilled athlete. Conceptually, human rights and dignity are so thoroughly interlinked that they are virtually indivisible. One cannot exist without the other, and each gives meaning to the other. As Kofi Annan has said, human rights create the "sacred home for human dignity" that gives human life meaning (Van der Heijden and Tahzib-Lie 1998, 18).

In some international declarations and conventions (including the Universal Declaration of Human Rights; the International Covenant on Economic, Social, and Cultural Rights; the International Covenant on Civil and Political Rights; the Declaration on the Granting of Independence to Colonial Countries and Peoples; and the United Nations Declaration on the Elimination of All Forms of Racial Discrimination), the reference to "dignity" is made explicitly and given prominence in the language of the preamble. In other documents (including the Declaration of the Rights of the Child, Principle 2; Declaration on the Promotion Among Youth of the Ideals of Peace, Mutual Respect and Understanding Between Peoples, Principle III; Declaration on Social Progress and Development, Article 1), this foundational principle of dignity is stated in the actual articles and provisions.

The breadth of the subject matter in the treaties and declarations built on a foundation of dignity is noteworthy as these documents deal with such diverse issues as women's rights, children's rights, racial discrimination, economic rights, general civil rights, torture, slavery, and banning apartheid. Moreover, the importance of dignity crosses cultural boundaries. International documents highlighting human dignity reflect indigenous African aspirations (African Charter on Human and Peoples's Rights, Article 5) as well as Latin American ones (American Convention on Human Rights, Article 5).

In addition to explicit references to dignity made in a wide variety of human rights instruments, human rights conventions share a view of humanity centred around various aspects of human dignity. Provisions guaranteeing individuals the right to be respected, valued, and protected implicitly acknowledge that individuals are worthy of respect simply because they are human beings, not because they possess some unique economic, social, or political value. Alston identifies human dignity as the "single most important principle which underpins the Universal Declaration" and its subsequent conventions and treaties (1998, 30).

A second common principle is the call to protect the political space necessary for individuals to participate in the life of their community and nation. Citizens are guaranteed rights to freedom of thought, to hold opinions without interference, to peaceful assembly, to free association, to take part in public affairs, to vote, and to equal access to public services. None of these protections limits the right of participation to the intellectual elite, religious leaders, the economically powerful, or the politically astute. Everyone, irrespective of race, intelligence, political preference, gender, physical appearance or stature, charisma, social graces, or economic status is guaranteed the right to significant participation in the political life of the community. Increasingly, these participatory principles are evolving into a right to participatory democracy.

While the right of participation is not absolute, the limitations allowed by human rights language on individual participatory space are generally restricted to those necessary to ensure the health and safety of the population or to ensure a democratic society. Still, the underlying norm is the right to participation, and the burden of proof to demonstrate compelling reasons to lawfully limit this right is on the nation that chooses to restrict it. The presumption in this new era is in favour of the individual, not the state.

A third common element is the guarantees given to citizens to hold power accountable, is variously described in language that guarantees a recourse to persons detained by national governments, the right freely to express disapproval of government policies, and the right to assemble with other like minded individuals to express political opinions. The right to vote in genuine periodic elections, guaranteed by the International Covenant on Civil and Political Rights, is perhaps the most vital tool in holding governments accountable.

The all-important principle of accountability has two distinct faces. While those in power must accept being held accountable by the citizenry, so too must the citizenry accept that power serves a legitimate function and must be respected when exercised with justice. Human rights agreements assume that strong governments or authority structures will, and should, exist. Human rights are not intended to replace these structures, but rather to define clearly the limits of power so that those who govern do so on behalf of the governed. Citizens, for their part, have the obligation to respect both power and the diverse opinions of citizens in a pluralistic society.

Fourth, human rights conventions are founded on a guiding principle that individuals must be encouraged to work for political, cultural, or social change nonviolently. Persons whose dignity and value are respected, who enjoy the freedom to participate in the life of their community and country, and who are able to hold power accountable, are entitled to work in such an environment to promote change. Barring such a peaceful climate, the only alternative is to use violence. As the Universal Declaration of Human Rights states in the Preamble, "It is essential, if man is not to be compelled to have recourse, as a last resort, to rebellion against tyranny and oppression, that human rights should be protected by the rule of law." This does not mean that every citizen will "win" his or her cause, or be happy with the outcome of a political decision. Rather, this is an acknowledgement that a political battle, fairly fought within a set of nondiscriminatory rules guided by human rights principles, must be respected.

The fundamental rights of dignity, participation, holding power accountable, and the freedom to work for peaceable change are based on the belief that every person is valuable and potentially has something meaningful to contribute. *Civil society results when these fundamental human rights are respected and guaranteed and thus empower all citizens in concert with one other to promote their interests, participate in the life of the nation, to hold power accountable, to work for change in a manner respectful of others and of the rights of others.* This definition has two parts that flow out of an understanding of human rights. First, it acknowledges that civil society is often defined to be a set of civic groups that are active in society – citizens acting in concert. However, it adds as second qualitative dimension of process – which modifies how these groups work in society – and requires that citizens acting in concert with one another do so in a way that acknowledges their duties to others.

WHY CONTEMPORARY DEFINITIONS OF CIVIL SOCIETY ARE NOT ENOUGH

In contrast, the most common definitions of civil society omit reference to one or more of these fundamental human rights principles. Some view civil society as a set of "values and norms," a state of social civility (Van Rooy 1998, 12). According to this view, civil society is present when society at large is well behaved and appears to act "civilly." The absence of violence is thus seen to be a key indicator of civil society. The problem with this version of civil society is that it can co-exist with, even benefit from, a totalitarian state that uses brute power to stifle or control social conflict. The experience of the former Yugoslavia illustrates both the benefit of this type of civil society and also its weaknesses. Through the use of power, the Tito regime was able to maintain peaceable relations among long-standing ethnic rivals to the point that some dared hope that ethnic conflict in the Balkans had been overcome. But within a few years of Tito's death, terrible violence erupted. While explanations for the outbreak of violence often lay blame at the feet of political leaders who saw it in their own political interest to fan nationalist flames, this explanation does not explain why citizens supported the policies of their leaders and took hostile steps against long-time neighbours with whom they had shared decades of apparently good relations. If a deep and underlying commitment to respect human rights has not been cultivated, "civility" alone is not a good indicator of a genuine civil society.

A second definition suggests that civil society is only a noun meaning citizen organisations (Van Rooy 1998, 15). This definition gives primary importance to the existence of institutions and citizen associations, assuming that greater citizen involvement is the key to a good society. According to this perspective, with tenuous roots in de Tocqueville,

> civil society is nothing more than a set of non-governmental institutions and processes that have the ability to act in a way that limits the power of the government or private market sector. It functions as a corrective to the actions of the government or market and gives voice and expression to the perspectives of the citizenry as it relates to these other sectors. The health of civil society can be measured by the "number and type" of civil society organizations, associations and agencies that exist (Ewert 1998, 10).

According to this view, the more civil society organisations that exist, the better. The goal of civil society enthusiasts in developing nations, therefore, should be to stimulate the creation of a more vibrant associational life. What this view fails to take into consideration, however, is the Rwanda factor. Prior to the genocide of 1994, civil society in Rwanda was considered to be one of the most advanced in Africa; there was an estimated "one farmers' organization per 35 households, one cooperative per 350 households . . . more than 12 percent of the Rwandan population belonged to peasant organizations" (Uvin 1998, 163, 166). Unfortunately for Rwanda, however, the primary achievement of this organisation in society was a highly participatory genocide that was more effective than any previously known in history. The number of associations by itself is not a sufficient condition for a well-functioning society. Something more, respect for human rights, is required.

Third, some view civil society to be a set of Western liberal democratic values and norms that critics fear are being imposed on the rest of the world by donor-driven civil society enthusiasts. According to this view, there is no such thing as an international, or universal, definition of civil society. There are only local and culturally specific manifestations of it. Therefore, these critics believe that it is inappropriate to promote a rights-based brand of civil society around the world, as it simply does not fit outside of cultures or political traditions that emphasise individualist freedoms. The shortcoming of this view of civil society is that it can be used to justify discrimination – usually against women, children, or cultural undesirables – if such discrimination is rooted in tradition or culture, as it usually is. Others respond that the emphasis on personal freedom, which is the central freedom of human rights and its progeny civil society, is not a Western value but rather a modern one (Franck 1997, 593). Human rights principles act as a corrective to those who would excuse discrimination for cultural or traditional purposes.

Fourth, some view civil society as a mechanism to confront, challenge, or oppose the state (Van Rooy 1998, 24). This Gramscian view of civil society primarily
emphasises its adversarial nature and function in protecting individuals and groups
from the dominant or potentially abusive power of the state. It assumes that the
state is inherently self-interested and that only by banding together can citizens
protect themselves. It creates an adversary in the state rather than a possible partner, thereby potentially limiting the influence that civic groups may have with the
state. It does not acknowledge the appropriate role reserved for the state by human
rights conventions and can actually at times undermine the state. This is a concern
most clearly expressed by Whaites in Chapter 7 of this volume. Advocates of this
perspective fail to understand the legitimate role of the state and the corresponding
implied duty of civil society to support it appropriately. In addition, advocates of
this adversarial perspective often do not look for ways that civil society can actively collaborate as a partner with the state as required from time to time to serve
the public good. Instead, advocates of an adversarial approach to civil society tend
to be aggressive, demanding, and self-righteous, thereby reducing the movement's
influence with the state. It reflects a focus on rights or claims against the state
without any corresponding sense of duties.

WHAT IS THE SIGNIFICANCE OF BASING THE DEFINITION OF CIVIL SOCIETY ON HUMAN RIGHTS PRINCIPLES?

As we have seen, there are profound differences in how civil society can be
viewed. While all approaches have advantages and the potential to "save the world"
to some degree, each suffers from corresponding weaknesses. Something is profoundly missing in how civil society is traditionally understood. That missing element, in my opinion, is understanding how a human rights foundation undergirds
civil society and strengthens its impact. The addition of human rights adds a corrective to many of the shortcomings of classical views of civil society and provides
an answer to many of the criticisms that have been levelled against it.

The first common criticism of civil society is its perceived Western bias, which
some argue makes it inapplicable to non-Western regions of the world. However,
this criticism fails to acknowledge that human rights documents are among the
most widely accepted political documents in history. One hundred forty-four nations, governing a vast majority of the world's people, have become parties to the
International Covenant on Civil and Political Rights (the foundational treaty breath-
ing political life into the Universal Declaration of Human Rights). One hundred
forty-two nations have become parties to the companion Covenant on Economic,
Social, and Cultural Rights. The guarantees contained within these two documents,
especially the civil and political guarantees so essential to enable civil society to
thrive, reflect international agreement on an unprecedented scale and thereby undercut the charges of Western cultural bias.

As legal scholar Rosalyn Higgins has stated, human rights are "not a set of
imposed western ideas, but are of universal application, speaking to the human
condition" (Franck 1997, 627). The declaration is a powerful affirmation that greater

value should be ascribed to human life (and indirectly to the elusive notion of human dignity) than to state sovereignty. As stated earlier, the principle of state sovereignty, as the predominant international legal value, is dead. States the world over are obligated to partner with their people – not to manipulate and dominate them. There exists, therefore, a clear international rationale, nearing international consensus, for basing the notion of civil society on the rights of each individual human being.

The fact that many nations routinely violate the same rights that they have guaranteed does not diminish the firm foundation upon which human rights rest. Blatant hypocrisy is no reason to discount the value of human rights. The hypocrisy is simply further evidence that human rights standards have forever changed the nature of how a nation relates to its own people. No state now publicly claims the right to violate human rights with impunity. When nations today are called to account for violations of human rights, they routinely respond not by claiming that they are lawfully entitled to violate human rights, but rather by denying that the violation occurred in the first place. By their denial that human rights violations have occurred, instead of contesting the underlying principle, even hypocritical nations demonstrate recognition of the legitimacy of human rights. "Even hypocrisy may sometimes deserve one cheer for it confirms the value of the idea, and limits the scope and blatancy of violations" (Henkin 1990, 28–29).

Second, some critics argue that developing nations are being pressured against their will by donors and development workers to accept Western manifestations and institutions of civil society, in effect fostering a new brand of imperialism. However, if we understand that the contemporary origin of civil society is rooted in the human rights principles that nations themselves have formally and legally accepted, we discover a rationale for civil society that is based on a nation's own consent. It strips away objections of wary governments and politicians that citizen advocacy is a form of Western imperialism, capitalism, or any other kind of other foreign domination. For how can civil society be dismissed as foreign imperialism if the nation itself has signed the basic human rights documents that underpin the formation and action of civil society? No nation has been forced to sign or become party to human rights instruments. Yet all nations that have signed these fundamental documents have by this very act implicitly committed themselves to allowing civil society an important place in the nation.

Because civil society emerges from the agreements that a nation itself has endorsed, there is no basis for the criticism that civil society is a Western form of an "ism" being crammed down the throats of unsuspecting people. Foreign efforts to promote a healthy civil society may well be fully consistent with the obligations a nation itself has assumed. This new civil society is a modern international version, not primarily a Western, democratic, Christian, politically liberal, or capitalistic one.

Third, grounding civil society in human rights principles reaffirms the notion that civil society is appropriate for a range of economic systems. It challenges the common misconception that civil society is biased in favour of capitalism and opposed to other economic systems. Strict capitalism is not at all necessary. As

Henkin argues, human rights "has no commitment to any particular economic system, and a society is free to choose between a market economy and socialism and among the various gradations and combinations of each" (Henkin 1990, 7). Human rights offers the broadest view, the biggest tent, for each nation to include unique local or cultural economic aspirations. As it does everywhere, the human rights approach ensures only that citizens will actively choose and regulate the economic structures under which they live.

Fourth, basing civil society on human rights provides a different context for understanding how civil society intersects with the state. It directly responds to the suggestion that civil society will weaken and destabilise legitimate states as much of the literature on civil society assumes. In contrast, a human rights approach presupposes a strong and effective state. It is the premise of human rights that a good and decent state will exist, for the whole orientation of human rights is to mediate and define the role of the state vis-à-vis those subject to its power. Human rights principles do not support the faulty view that the primary role of civil society is to attack the state. Rather, they call on the state to carry out its obligation to respect individual and collective action and implicitly require individuals to respect the authority of legitimate government.

Fifth, a human rights framework brings not only government but also business into its purview. Just as human rights principles have provided a useful perspective by which to view the relationship between civil society and the state, so too can it provide guidance in developing an understanding of how civil society should relate to the business sector. In one of the most dramatic shifts of economic philosophy in the last one-hundred years, the business community is increasingly expected to respect human rights too. The old Milton Friedman dictum that "the only social responsibility of business is to increase its profits" no longer persuades (Avery 2000, 10). Corporations are now finding that their human rights record is subject to scrutiny by civil society and that inaction or denial of this emergent notion of accountability is no longer tenable. Even though a corporation cannot technically violate human rights (because it is not a nation), private watchdogs are more aggressively pursuing corporations that ignore human rights and holding them publicly accountable to the same standards that apply to nations. Given that twenty-five of the world's largest thirty-eight "economies" are multinational corporations, the application of human rights standards becomes all the more important (Forsythe 2000, 192).

What remains yet unclear is how the human rights obligations of business intersect with the responsibilities of the state and civil society, but now is the time for civil society groups to be engaged in defining this emergent relationship. Initiatives are afoot to create "hard law" that is codified and more explicitly definable. In January 1999 UN Secretary General Kofi Annan called for the development of a global compact that will result in corporations implementing a set of core human rights, labour, and environmental practices. In July 2000 the United Nations convened a meeting of nearly 50 companies, labour groups, and human rights agencies to talk about labour rights, environmental standards, and especially to eliminate child labour. A human rights code of conduct for multinational corporations is currently being drafted by one UN agency that will codify the balance between the bottom line and human rights. These efforts will profoundly change how the business community relates to civil society. The human rights principles that undergird civil society will likely play a critical role in articulating this new understanding.

Sixth, human rights principles influence how post-conflict national reconstruction should be handled and counter those who assume that peacemaking is strictly the job of the state and warring factions. Whereas in the past leaders of countries who abused their authority have often been allowed to negotiate with the victors a right of passage to a safe haven for themselves and their loot, emerging human rights norms are shutting down this loophole to impunity. At a minimum, human rights standards require that an effort must be made to expose to the public the scale and extent of the violations that were carried out under the auspices of the departing regime. While there is disagreement concerning when amnesty may be appropriate, it is clearer that amnesty is never appropriate unless the human rights record of the regime is made public. The involvement of civil society groups, especially human rights organisations and civic advocacy groups, is essential for creating that public record and holding power indirectly accountable. What is not known cannot be forgiven, and social divisions cannot be healed unless past wrongs suffered by the population are revealed and acknowledged. Civil society is the key player in creating the conditions for reconciliation.

Seventh, human rights principles provide a perspective to respond to the concern that modern notions of civil society are inappropriately changing relationships within traditional and cultural groups. The rights of persons who have typically been most excluded from civil society, women and children, are explicitly and unambiguously affirmed by human rights documents. The Convention on the Elimination of all Forms of Discrimination Against Women, which has been called the "international bill of rights for women" (United Nations 2000, 24) has been signed or ratified by 165 nations. The Convention on the Rights of the Child has become the most widely ratified human rights instrument in the world with 191 nations now bound by this document. These documents affirm that women and children are to be valued, protected, and included; they require nothing less than changing cultural and social patterns in the societies that have traditionally ignored these important two groups. The practical impact of these cultural changes on civil society can profoundly affect those societies that routinely discriminate against these vulnerable groups.

Eighth, a human rights framework provides the most appropriate basis to determine who is a part of civil society. Civil society literature is replete with conflicting definitions of which groups belong in civil society and which do not. The answer to who belongs in civil society need not hinge on whether the group is a religious group, family group, clan association, and so on. Rather, all groups that respect the inherent right of other groups to enjoy their human rights (enjoying the right to dignity, participation, accountability, and working for change peaceably) are a legitimate part of civil society. Groups that do not accept these fundamental principles (such as hate groups whose sole purpose is to deny others the right to participate) do not meet this test and hence should not be considered to be part of civil society. A guideline of this nature, focusing on the underlying values of human rights, provides a better criterion then one oriented, say, to a group's profit status, its organisational structure, or its particular purpose.

CONCLUSION

The purpose of this chapter has been to demonstrate that a human rights framework provides a firm foundation upon which to build a broad, culturally inclusive notion of civil society. Human rights reflect widespread international agreement and provide a rationale for transcending destructive political practices aimed more at preserving a political leader's or party's political power than serving the public good. While civil society does not possess the ability to save the world, it does offer the best opportunity the world has to respond most effectively to the challenges it faces. To do so, however, it must be rooted in basic respect for human rights.

Democracy alone is not a sufficient remedy for the world's ills as democratic majorities can tyrannically and unfairly dominate marginal peoples. Domestic law, while useful as a check on the arbitrary use of power, can also be subverted to contribute to the oppressive marginalisation of one group by another. International human rights principles restrict domestic national law by acting as an ethical umbrella under which domestic law must fit. It has already been shown that international standards transcend national prejudices and practices and can significantly limit the abuses of national regimes. Yet human rights agreements alone cannot save a nation from itself. All human rights can accomplish alone is the creation of conditions that make it more likely for citizens acting alone or in concert to improve their lives. If the dignity of citizens is respected, if they can and do participate to hold power accountable and to bring about constructive change, then people will be able to protect themselves from some of the most dire affects of famine, natural disaster, pollution, poverty, and conflict (Ewert 1998, 10). And they will also be able to envision and implement change for the future that brings about a better life for all. Civil society may not be able to save the world, but without it there is little hope that significant improvement of the condition of persons served by Christian relief and development organisations will be sustainable.

REFERENCES

Alexander, Jeffrey C. 1998. "Introduction to Civil Society I, II, III: Constructing an Empirical Concept from Normative Controversies and Historical Transformations." In *Real Civil Societies: Dilemmas of Institutionalization*, edited by J. C. Alexander, 1–19. London: Sage Publications.

Alston, Philip. 1998. "The Universal Declaration of Human Rights in an Era of Globalization." *Reflections on the Universal Declaration of Human Rights: A Fiftieth Anniversary Anthology*, edited by B. Van Der Heijden and B. Tahzib-Lie. The Hague: Martinus Nijhoff Publishers.

Avery, Christopher L. 2000. *Business and Human Rights in a Time of Change*. London: Amnesty International.

Barber, Benjamin R. 1998. *A Place for Us: How to Make Society Civil and Democracy Strong.* New York: Hill and Wang.

Buergenthal, Thomas. 1998. "Centerpiece of the Human Rights Revolution." In *Reflections on the Universal Declaration of Human Rights: A Fiftieth Anniversary Anthology*, edited by B. Van der Heijden and B. Tahzib-Lie. The Hague: Martinus Nijhoff Publishers.

Daes, Erica-Irene A. 1990. *Freedom of the Individual Under Law: A Study on the Individual's Duties to the Community and the Limitations on Human Rights and Freedoms Under Article 29 of the Universal Declaration of Human Rights.* New York: United Nations.

Drinan, Robert F., S.J. 1987. *Cry of the Oppressed.* San Francisco: Harper & Row.

Dunne, Tim, and Nicholas J. Wheeler, eds. 1999. *Human Rights in Global Politics.* Cambridge: Cambridge University Press.

Dyer, Gwynne. 2000. "Another Tyrant Bites the Dust." *The Record* (7 October).

Ehrenberg, John. 1999. *Civil Society: The Critical History of an Idea.* New York: New York University Press.

Ewert, Lowell M. 1998. "Introduction." In *Civil Society: A Foundation for Sustainable Economic Development*, edited by M. N. Rose and L. M. Ewert, 10–12. Portland, Ore.: Mercy Corps International; Washington, D.C.: Coalition of Christian Colleges and Universities.

Forsythe, David P. 2000. *Human Rights in International Relations.* Cambridge: Press Syndicate of the University of Cambridge.

Franck, Thomas M. 1997. "Is Personal Freedom a Western Value?" *American Journal of International Law* 91/4 (October): 593–627.

Frankel, Marvin E., with Ellen Saideman. 1989. *Out of the Shadows of the Night: The Struggle for International Human Rights.* New York: Delacorte Press.

Henkin, Louis. 1990. *Age of Rights.* New York: Columbia University Press.

Humphrey, John P. 1984. *Human Rights and the United Nations: A Great Adventure.* New York: Transnational Publishers.

Hyden, Goran. 1997. "Building Civil Society at the Turn of the Millennium." In *Beyond Prince and Merchant: Citizen Participation and the Rise of Civil Society,* edited by J. Burbidge, 17–46. New York: Pact Publications.

Kirgis, Frederic L., Jr. 1977. *International Organizations in their Legal Setting: Documents, Comments and Questions.* Portland, Ore.: Book News.

Moran, Mary Catherine. 2000. "The Commerce of the Sexes." In *Paradoxes of Civil Society: New Perspectives on Modern German and British History*, edited by Frank Trentmann, 61–84. New York: Berghahn Books.

Morsink, Johannes. 1999. *The Universal Declaration of Human Rights: Origins, Drafting, and Intent.* Philadelphia: University of Pennsylvania Press.

Philpott, Daniel. 1996. "On the Cusp of Sovereignty: Lessons from the Sixteenth Century." In *Sovereignty at the Crossroads? Morality and International Politics in the Post-Cold War Era*, edited by L. E. Lugo, 37–62. New York: Rowman & Littlefield Publishers.

Seligman, Adam B. 1992. *The Idea of Civil Society.* Princeton, N.J.: Princeton University Press.

———. 1993. "The Fragile Ethical Vision of Civil Society." In *Citizenship and Social Theory*, edited by B. S. Turner, 139–61. London: Sage Publications.

Sergeyev, Igor. 2000. "Inquiry Called on Deadly Ambush." *The Record* (3 April).

Sieghart, Paul. 1991. "International Human Rights Law: Some Current Problems." In *Human Rights for the 1990s: Legal, Political and Ethical Issues*, edited by R. Blackburn and J. Taylor, 24–42. London: Mansell publishers.

United Nations. 2000 (July). *Millennium Summit Multilateral Treaty Framework: An Invitation to Universal Participation*. New York: United Nations.

Uvin, Peter. 1998. *Aiding Violence: The Development Enterprise in Rwanda*. West Hartford, Conn.: Kumarian Press.

Van der Heijden, Barend, and Bahia Tahzib-Lie, eds. 1998. *Reflections on the Universal Declaration of Human Rights: A Fiftieth Anniversary Anthology*. The Hague: Martinus Nijhoff Publishers.

Van Rooy, Alison. 1998. *Civil Society and Aid Industry*. London: Earthscan Publications.

———. 1999. "Why Civil Society?" In *Canadian Development Report: Civil Society and Social Change*, edited by Alison Van Rooy. Ottawa, Ontario: North-South Institute.

Walz, Susan. 2001. "Universalizing Human Rights: The Role of Small States in the Construction of the Universal Declaration of Human Rights." *Human Rights Quarterly* 23/1: 44–72.

6

CITIZENS, JUSTICE, ACCOUNTABILITY, AND THE PROBLEM WITH CIVIL SOCIETY

Paul J. Nelson

International networks and alliances of NGOs have developed the capacity to draw attention to humanitarian, environmental, and human rights issues, and to provoke policy responses to them. These actors can bring issues to public attention, place them on policy agendas, and at times influence the behaviour of international, national, and corporate institutions. At their most effective, they promote greater equality and freedom and express values – empowerment, dignity, personal ownership, and responsibility – that are widely praised but generally neglected by the powerful institutions of world politics.

These values echo prophetic justice themes of the Judaeo-Christian tradition, which call for societies to protect the most vulnerable, practice solidarity with the poor, treat workers justly, safeguard natural resources, protect religious and civil freedoms, and build institutions that are just and accountable. How are citizen organisations and NGOs involved in promoting such change, particularly international NGOs based in the industrial countries?

In order critically to analyse civil society, we divide the topic into five sections. The first asserts that the welfare of rich and poor people is profoundly linked, and that both suffer under present patterns of mal-development. The second and third focus on the political context of NGOs' work. Section 2 accepts the prevalent view that voluntary, non-governmental action can contribute to redressing this mal-development but insists that the contribution will require concerted political action.

Section 3 examines NGO advocacy in more detail. International development NGOs have begun to accept the need for political action, as illustrated by some important and strategically chosen advocacy successes. These successes are cause for hope, and they suggest the growing strategic importance of public institutions that are open, transparent, and accountable. The growing understanding of the demand for accountability should apply not only to governments, but also to corporations and to voluntary agencies themselves, and should be a welcome challenge to NGOs.

Section 4 argues that the concept of civil society has limited value as an analytical and political tool to further the growing demand for transparency and accountability.

Common understandings of civil society lump together social groups and economic interests so diverse that they obscure important conflicts, differences, and power relationships that must be brought to light. Its fashionability in the international development industry has made civil society subject to misuse by governments and aid agencies alike, whose agendas may coincide only partially with those of citizens' organisations and social movements. The highly political use of *civil society* calls for a careful and selective employment of the term, one that recognises the breadth and diversity of civil societies as well as the conflict inherent in them.

Civil society at its best is the social and political space in which negotiation can be carried out and trust among diverse actors can be built. But this process is only fair and effective when weaker, poorer participants can assert their positions freely and forcefully and thus gain the attention and respect of the more powerful participants. Without this sometimes conflictive process, reliance on civil society only reinforces or even masks the inequities that dominate our present patterns of mal-development.

Section 5 argues that dynamic, voluntary leadership will be required for people of faith and conscience in the rich world to act effectively. Work in progress among some NGOs provides some models that together suggest the potential for expanding the impact of voluntary agencies within the Christian churches to hold out hope, to propose radical changes, and to articulate the values and language of the Judaeo-Christian tradition. New initiatives by NGOs suggest promising ways to allow their members and constituents to express their support for just relationships not only through charity and conventional political action but also in their daily activities in the marketplace and social settings.

RICH AND POOR ALIKE SUFFER
FROM CURRENT PATTERNS OF MAL-DEVELOPMENT

Whether rich or poor, humanity is held in a state of captivity, oppression, and indignity. The materially poor suffer deprivation, have few options with respect to livelihood, and frequently have their physical, cultural, and political freedoms limited. The weak political voice of the poor in most situations perpetuates their exclusion from the wealth around them. Even while the number of people living in absolute poverty shrank slightly in the 1990s, the gap among incomes, wealth, and economic choices between countries, and between rich and poor people within countries, continued its long-term widening (UNDP 1999, 36–39).

The costs of poverty for the poor themselves are widely recognised and bemoaned, but the highly unequal pattern of mal-development enslaves the wealthy as well. Surrounded by a glut of material goods and cultures bent on selling to them, the wealthy often express their discontent with the world of work and possessions. The voluntary simplicity movement reflects this growing unease with consumption and wealth as the driving force of life in the industrial economies (Center for a New American Dream 2001). But the wealthy are not only troubled by their cluttered lives and by the noise of consumer cultures. They are also diminished as persons by the knowledge that others are suffering extreme deprivation, as Christian scholars such as John Stott makes clear (1984, 128–37). Yet the rich are often moved only to guilt or resignation by the complex of factors that separate them from the suffering they occasionally glimpse.

Tom Sine's stinging critique of the spiritual, cultural, and social impact of material culture in an era of economic and cultural globalisation suggests that in perverse ways, MTV, fast food, and the Internet are unifying youth as consumers (Sine 1999). But the profound differences are captured by Brazilian Clodomir Santos de Morais, who offers the powerful image of a world divided between "those who do not eat and those who do not sleep." The rich do not sleep for the simple reason that they "are in permanent fear of those who do not eat" (Carmen and Sobrado 2000, 11). I believe that this figurative lack of sleep can also be attributed to the deeper reason that the rich are uneasy living in a world that they sense, at some level of awareness, to be fundamentally out of order.

Economic, geographic, and social factors all conspire to drive a wedge in the relationship between the rich and the poor, a reality that has insidious impacts on everyone. To the extent that relationships across these boundaries do exist, they are typically mediated either by the market or the media. In the former, people are objectified by their function as labour, consumers, or competitors, while in the latter we are presented to one another as stereotyped caricatures. Nonetheless, the deep desire for human contact is still in evidence, as can be seen in the large number of wealthy people who sponsor children or families in poor communities. Though a vast gulf separates sponsors from beneficiaries, both treasure the photographs, letters, and reports that link them to another person and another world.

The gap between rich and poor is aggravated and perpetuated by the prevalence of a vocabulary that treats our lives and societies as different worlds. The language of development distances and objectifies the world of the poor, rendering it inaccessible to the rich, while popular culture and advertising present a fantastic and idealised world of the rich to poor people for whom it is an unattainable paradise.

Development has professionalised and objectified an enterprise that originates in a deep desire for care and relationship. Consider the submerged vocabulary of the Christian tradition, whose emotionally powerful language is replaced, in development agencies, by abstraction and jargon. Neighbours are "beneficiaries" or "target groups"; solidarity is reduced to "partnership"; stewardship becomes "sustainability." Poor countries are now "emerging economies," and supporting social movements or peasant or women's organisations are "capacity building" in civil society. Lewis observes a similar irony in the separate, parallel vocabularies for community development and nonprofits in the industrial and poor countries (1999).

DEVELOPMENT REQUIRES A POLITICAL STRUGGLE AGAINST INEQUALITY AND FOR FREEDOM AND JUSTICE

At no time in history has escaping from poverty been easy or free of conflict. The present world economy, more closely integrated than ever before, presents new opportunities but also difficult new challenges for poor people seeking an increasing share of rising global wealth. Neither growth nor charity nor small-scale self-help projects will correct the inequalities that define the present global mal-development. Instead, fundamental changes in economic and political systems are necessary, and they are also possible. To achieve such fundamental changes, sustained leadership outside of government is essential.

Neither Economic Growth nor Charity Alone Will Make Major Reductions in Poverty

Decades of research, national and cross-national, make it clear that, other things being equal, rapid economic growth is better for poverty reduction than slow or negative growth. But experience and the logic of *global* development make it equally clear that rapid growth is neither a sufficient nor a desirable solution by itself. There is little chance of generating the high levels of growth that would be required – if we accept the optimistic models – to enable the rise from poverty of most of the world's impoverished (UNDP 1996).

But even if such rates of growth were possible and economically sustainable, they may not be *desirable* from the point of view of global development. Stimulating growth in the present global economy rapidly depletes finite natural resources and depends on further accelerating North American consumption, that already super-heated engine of global growth.

But if growth alone is not enough to address poverty adequately, several decades of experience also make it clear that project-oriented action by nonprofits and governments is not sufficient either. Nonprofits and voluntary agencies created in the industrial countries to aid communities in the poor world now number in the thousands. While these NGOs are known for their charitable and community development projects, many have concluded that larger systems must change in order to accommodate development with freedom, and some NGOs have embraced a mission that includes promoting such change.

Scholars and practitioners of NGOs have noted the limitations of charity and of locally based self-help and have argued that promoting development also requires action to change systems. Korten's definitive statement of this need for systematic change posits that NGO action can be characterised by three "generations," which have developed over time, but which are not necessarily successive in time (Korten 1987). The first generation of NGO action responds to acute needs with charity. The second-generation initiatives encourage self-sufficiency through local community development projects, and these are the projects that have won NGOs their current acclaim in the development aid industry.

Korten, however, asserts that just as charity is not enough, neither is local-scale community development. Small may be beautiful, but it is still small, and NGOs need a third generation of interventions that promote change in social, political, or productive "systems." These systems are not only national (or global) economic systems or models; they can also be local. NGOs targeting and helping reshape agricultural research or extension systems through sustained and strategic co-operation with government agencies provide a good example of this approach.

From local to international, the systems that distribute knowledge, control access to decision-making, and allocate property, energy, wealth, and income are all subject to change. The rules that govern the distribution of these assets are the substance of politics, and political decisions about them are at the core of the future of development. And although the present enthusiasm for civil society and NGOs as agents of this change is sometimes coloured by the wishes and visions of scholars and participants, citizen action has shown through history that it can help to produce important changes in economic and political systems.

Struggles Can Succeed Against Apparently Overwhelming Odds

Many NGO advocacy agendas focus on incremental or reformist changes because these are "winnable." The prospect of victories helps motivate continued advocacy work. While there is often good reason for such a strategy, the historical record also suggests that sweeping changes in social or political institutions are possible even where political obstacles appear very great, and that voluntary agencies as political actors can play critical roles.

Margaret Keck and Kathryn Sikkink, for example, have sought to demonstrate the historical relevance of transnational networks, including NGOs, to international policy-making in human rights and the environment. They point out how slavery and the trans-Atlantic slave trade, pervasive, fundamental, international practices with deep links to powerful economic interests, were eliminated through the concerted efforts of a relatively small number of individuals and organisations (Keck and Sikkink 1998). Other major political changes – the liberation of colonial countries in much of the world, near-universal suffrage in several of the major liberal democracies, and the abolition of apartheid in South Africa – have been accomplished in recent history over the resistance of formidable interests and institutions.

Whether these "costly international moral choices" (Kaufmann and Pape 1999) have origins in domestic or international political movements, or in the calculations of self-interested governments, is a matter of debate. Keck and Sikkink (1998), many scholars of human rights (Risse, Ropp, and Sikkink 1999) and of environmental policy (Arts 2000) argue that international networks and institutions are fundamentally important in shaping norms or applying leverage for policy changes. Others are sceptical, emphasising national interests and domestic politics (Kaufmann and Pape 1999) or national social movements (Tarrow 1994).

The effectiveness of the particular strategy – whether national movements or international networks – is less important than the fact that citizens are participating in civil society to bring about changes in policies and institutions. In the next section both strategies are explored through the experiences of NGOs that have promoted development, defended the environment, and advocated for human rights.

Some Development NGOs Recognise and Embrace the Promotion of Systemic Change as Part of Their Mission

In the early 1980s villagers living up and down the Narmada River of Western India learned that a flood was coming. The flood was not to result from seasonal rains. Instead, it would be a deluge of biblical proportions caused by a long-planned series of dams on the river. The flood would inundate ancestral lands on which some 150,000 *adivasi* (indigenous) people, among the least politically powerful in Indian society, lived and farmed (Morse and Berger 1992). Thus began a fifteen-year tale of protest, repression, and international networking that started with the intensely local struggle of a threatened, outcast population living in what project authorities refer to as the "submergence area"; it grew into an international campaign that challenged the dam-building industry and forced reforms and institutional changes in the world's most powerful aid donor (Khagram 2000).

Whenever village leaders raised concerns with state government officials, they were rebuffed: the project couldn't be delayed or changed; it was for the greater good; it was needed to produce electricity and supply water for irrigation. The project proceeded as planned, financed by the first of several loans from the World Bank that would total US$450 million. More urgent inquiries and protests provoked violent responses from two state governments, with security policy repeatedly crushing protests by local organisations.

International NGOs became involved through the work of the Environmental Defense Fund, Cultural Survival, and others. The network of international NGOs supporting the appeals of Narmada Valley villagers grew to include several church-based organisations, but leadership came from organisations that concerned themselves with environmental impact and the cultural and civil rights of indigenous groups. Locally, the movement was grounded in decades of resistance to other dam projects in India.

Internationally, recent projects in Brazil, Thailand, and the Philippines had helped coalesce an effort by several US-based environmental NGOs to block damaging projects and force policy reforms at the World Bank. NGO demands in these cases were varied: to stop the projects, to decrease the size of dams, to investigate alternative energy sources, and to provide humane resettlement and compensation for resettled communities. Taken together, the impacts of these protests were far-reaching. They included:

- Delays on the Narmada Dam project;
- International news media attention to the plight of the Narmada Valley villages;
- New, far-reaching standards at the World Bank for consultation and treatment of populations to be resettled for World Bank–financed projects (Fox 1998);
- An unprecedented independent panel created to investigate the World Bank's role in the most notorious of the Narmada dams, Sardar Sarovar (Morse and Berger 1992);

- Cancellation of the World Bank loan by the government of India;
- Creation at the World Bank of a permanent independent inspection panel to hear and investigate certain citizen appeals;
- A rigorous internal review of involuntary resettlement for World Bank–financed projects, credited by World Bank critics with helping to reinforce the position of internal reformers. Fox argues that sustained public attention and internal leadership have forced more attention to implementing social and environmental safeguards in other projects involving resettlement (Fox 2000).
- Formation of a World Commission on Dams, involving dam-building corporations, governments, international organisations such as the World Bank, and NGOs in a two-year effort to study dam-building worldwide and arrive at shared recommendations for best practices in dam construction (Khagram 2000).

NGO Advocacy: Global Campaigns Grounded in Local Relationships

The success of civil society advocacy, illustrated by the Narmada story of international campaigning around local injustices, can be retold dozens of times the world over. Consistently, the most effective campaigns for national or international policy change begin with strong roots in the plight of particular local communities and organisations.

The international campaign to ban anti-personnel landmines, which succeeded in crafting an international treaty in the late 1990s and won the Nobel Peace Prize in 1998, had its beginnings in the concern and frustration of medical aid workers in Cambodia, Angola, and other countries who saw the repeated tragedy of civilians' lives and limbs lost to mines buried in what were once their fields and roads (Price 1998).

The Jubilee 2000 campaign to forgive the crushing debt of the world's poorest countries is grounded in calls from African church leaders for international support. It is a movement that would not have happened without the initiative of Christian activists, motivated by the Levitical call, amplified by Isaiah and Jesus, for forgiveness of debts and restoration of justice.

Human rights organisations, both secular and Christian, have worked to document abuses that deny freedom to worship or to organise in the workplace or political sphere. They have also exposed practices that systematically impoverish ethnic or other groups. Although international human rights law gives a strong principled foundation for international civil society, each human rights victory is closely linked to the suffering of particular individuals and communities who cry out not only for material aid but also for protection from arbitrary and violent abuses of power.

Agendas and Methods

In keeping with their varied agendas, NGOs have employed a variety of methods in their efforts to change political, economic or social systems by affecting the rules or institutions that govern them. The dimensions of this activity can be seen by noting the three categories of activities it includes: policy advocacy, movement building or public advocacy, and purposive co-operation. The three are often complementary and sometimes carefully co-ordinated, but they need to be understood as separate capacities of NGOs.

Policy advocacy refers to direct and explicit proposals, lobby efforts, and demonstrations of public support for policy change. Citizens advocate for public and corporate behaviour at every political level from local schools to national or international agencies and programmes.

Movement building or *public advocacy* organises and educates to create a moral and political constituency. Public advocacy appeals especially to organisations with an established membership base, such as churches and church-based agencies, trade unions, and federations, who may understand part of their mission to be informing and motivating their members. Their efforts often include exchanges of individuals or pairing of communities in wealthy and poorer countries at a municipal, parish, or union local level.

Advocacy campaigns have also taken humanitarian and development NGOs well beyond the agenda of aid itself. Recent campaigns have mobilised international support for limiting child labour, abolishing anti-personnel landmines (Meketa 2000), and forgiving international debts owed by the world's poorest countries (Keet 2000). These and others have deployed traditional lobbying of national governments and international organisations, built networks and alliances internationally, and at least occasionally encouraged mass citizen action.

Purposive co-operation is a third form of deliberate NGO action to change institutions and systems that affect the distribution of power and wealth. Development NGOs routinely co-operate with governments and major donors in implementing parts of projects, but strategic, *purposive* co-operation with the aim of influencing a larger system is less common. NGOs have more often replaced government services in the late 1990s than sought out ways to strengthen and influence them through co-operation. One notable example of purposive co-operation has been the Aga Khan Foundation Rural Support Program in Pakistan (Uvin et al. 2000).

Influencing International Financial Institutions[1]

NGO efforts to influence the World Bank and the International Monetary Fund (IMF) have targeted what might have seemed among the least accessible of public institutions. With a reputation for avoiding the "political" aspects of development, confidentiality that verged on secrecy, and reliance on technical expertise and neo-liberal economic doctrines, the Washington-based international institutions are organisations established, governed, and owned by their member governments, with most influence held by the wealthiest countries. Yet in certain issue areas, NGOs have managed to win a measure of influence. Their work illustrates the diverse methods as well as the potential and pitfalls of international civil society.

The broad NGO agenda at the World Bank has encouraged the international financial system to become more generous, egalitarian, and responsive to gender and minority concerns; more transparent and open to effective civil society participation; more sensitive to natural resource use and human rights standards; and less powerful.

NGOs have worked with the World Bank on educational policy (Oxfam International 2000), energy (Tellam 2000), forestry (Seymour and Dubash 2000), mining (Chamberlain 1997), and a variety of other resource management topics. NGOs have also been involved in World Bank policy debates over structural adjustment, debt, and governance issues. Their strategic approaches are varied, including cooperation in projects and policy discussions (Covey 1998), campaigns to block or alter particular projects (Fox and Brown 1998), attacks on the World Bank's public funding (Nelson 1997), and private-sector bond offerings (Center for Economic Justice 2000).

Resistance to many World Bank–financed infrastructure projects has forced the World Bank to pay attention to environmental and social issues involved in major dam and energy projects. A campaign demanding greater transparency and accountability in the World Bank was successful; this has the potential to transform the World Bank's relationships to societies in borrowing countries. And the World Bank became the uneasy ally of the debt relief campaign in the late 1990s, as a surprisingly powerful public movement forced responses by the major industrial countries and the World Bank and IMF.

Accountability, Transparency, and the Inspection Panel

In 1993 the World Bank substantially liberalised its information-disclosure policy and created the first independent mechanism for citizen appeals against an international governmental organisation. NGOs had succeeded in putting transparency and accountability on the agenda by participating in a long history of high-profile protests against errant projects and thus creating the perception that these new accountability measures were needed.

NGO proposals for appeals mechanisms date from a 1990 paper (Christensen), but the immediate motivation for the new disclosure policy and inspection panel came in 1992 when a US Congressional committee threatened to withhold funding until a new policy was in place. While NGOs could not control the policy response, the information-disclosure policy and inspection panel come remarkably close to implementing the NGOs' proposals, despite counterproposals within the board and from the legal counsel's office that would have created a less independent mechanism (Shihata 1994).

The independent inspection panel has received more than 20 requests for investigations, carried out four full investigations, and significantly altered several projects. The panel has come under frequent attack internally, notably in the spring of 1999; NGOs and panel members mounted a spirited defence to prevent a significant weakening of its powers.

Debt Relief

NGOs have played a role in preventing the World Bank, IMF, and G-7 governments from dismissing the possibility of debt forgiveness while moving these important players to a serious, if reluctant, grappling with the options.[2]

In the early 1990s major creditor governments gradually granted more generous terms for bilateral debt servicing. But NGOs argued for more decisive debt forgiveness, and for direct relief by the World Bank and IMF. The proposal seemed outside of the realm of possibility until World Bank president James Wolfensohn authorised an internal study of options for international financial institutions' involvement in 1995. There followed a series of negotiations between World Bank and IMF management, during which NGO advocates co-operated with the World Bank while pressing for debt relief that was generous and free of excessive conditions.

The creation of an extremely limited mechanism for relief to highly indebted poor countries (HIPC) in 1996 began a second stage of debate and policy change. While some NGOs gave close attention to implementation of relief for HIPC nations, many also backed a proposal, originating in the churches, for more dramatic debt relief at the millennium. Jubilee 2000 gained support rapidly during 1998 and 1999, and when the World Bank acknowledged that many HIPC economies required more decisive debt relief (World Bank and IMF 1999), G-7 leaders adopted debt relief measures in Cologne that went well beyond the HIPC plan, but fell far short of the campaign proposals (Pettifor 1999). In 1999 debt relief suddenly rose to the highest levels in international discussions, and NGO advocates confronted two somewhat surprising successes: a global social movement in the making, and G-7 leaders racing to adopt and publicise debt relief measures.

How did NGOs gain their present stature and legitimacy on the issue of debt relief? Persistent efforts, since the late 1980s, invoke four major sources of NGO legitimacy: representation of excluded voices, expertise, a Northern political constituency, and moral authority (Nelson 2002). Oxfam Great Britain and the Brussels-based European Network for Debt and Development (Eurodad) led the painstaking effort to reshape bilateral Paris Club terms. NGOs in Great Britain secured leadership from the Conservative government of the early 1990s, and from the present Labour government, and Oxfam built an alliance with UNICEF to link debt relief to poverty reduction strategies (Evans 1999).

What effect has all this attention had on the actual work the World Bank does to promote development? The complex political environment makes it difficult to sort out causes of policy change, but NGOs have arguably had important roles in four trends at the World Bank, both intended and unintended: (1) They have helped make greater space for innovators on staff, (2) greater openness to external scrutiny, and (3) extensive changes in formal policy, and (4) they have helped expand the World Bank's influence over many borrowing governments. Criticism from NGOs has blocked one project, provoked amendments to others, and helped to motivate the creation of an independent inspection panel to which affected communities can appeal (Umaña 1998). NGOs have also motivated the World Bank to carry out an unusually thorough and self-critical review of its role in involuntary resettlement of communities for major infrastructure projects (World Bank 1996; Fox 1998).

It is often difficult to credit NGOs for complex policy changes. On debt forgiveness, for example, Wolfensohn's willingness to open the debt issue and to confront the IMF changed the environment for multilateral debt relief: World Bank staff could devote energy to developing cautious proposals rather than to devising explanations for the increasingly implausible claim that direct multilateral debt relief was not needed. In the process, networks of NGOs, government agencies, and committed individuals have arisen that mobilise information and co-ordinate their voices.

Re-creating Relationships?

One way to assess the significance of the networks is on the basis of their policy influence. But the networks themselves – the relationships formed and the new ways of interacting and governing – are arguably as significant as the particular victories won. Among the most attractive features of international advocacy is the possibility that the shared struggle can re-create relationships among individuals and communities divided by distance and extreme inequalities. Transnational alliances among citizen organisations from widely different societies allow the possibility of co-operation that is not only strategic but also an expression of common concern and solidarity. Practitioners and scholars have been quick to recognise and encourage this potential and have more recently begun to address openly the real difficulties and failings of such networking.

Networks built among the World Bank's NGO critics help to shape the structure, orientation, and capacity of civil society organisations. Sustained NGO campaigns on involuntary resettlement and energy policy, for example, have built enduring networks, and these links can help build capacity for self-representation, an important addition to other civil society capacity-building programmes, which often focus on capacities for service delivery.

But NGO networks have no clear model for democratic decision-making, and their democratic aspirations do not negate the fact that the "partners" based in the industrial capitals have vastly greater access to funds and to the headquarters of international organisations and powerful governments. These power differences are one of the major themes among critics of the idea of a *global* civil society, a parallel global community in which might does not make right but in which relationships are founded in shared values and identities. Enthusiasts of global civil society (Lipschutz 1996; Willetts 1996) rightly point to the significance of alliances and networks of NGOs, but these networks are as tattered, flawed, and human as they are vitally important.

Mustapha Kamal Pasha and Davil L. Blaney argue that "global" civil society's agendas and activities are not global at all but can be traced to the values and interests of middle-class groups in the industrial countries. Supporters of that agenda – global environment, human rights, human security, and democracy – have been "premature" in declaring consensus around a "global common good," because the agenda is largely that of "a few transnationally active NGOs" (Pasha and Blaney 1998, 436).

Such networks will also need to meet standards of democracy and accountability if they are to be considered legitimate political actors. International NGOs figure prominently in advocacy networks and coalitions, and the World Bank's debtor governments and Southern NGOs are increasingly demanding greater clarity on agendas and on who represents whom in advocacy towards international organisations such as the World Bank (Nelson 1997).

The NGOs also wrestle with how to structure and manage these relationships to reflect their commitments to democratic participation and shared initiative, and to address the differences in power and political risk involved in political advocacy in many countries (Keet 2000; Jordan and van Tuijl 2000; Nelson 2000; Fowler 1998).

The stakes for civil society networks are high when they engage in political advocacy, not only because of the potential policy impact, but also because the advocacy efforts themselves can succeed or fail to rebuild relationships of trust and solidarity, expand mutual knowledge, and make neighbours of distant individuals. Many people involved in NGO advocacy work affirm the high value they place on these fragile and hopeful relationships (Clark 1991; Edwards and Sen 1999). If these relationships are to endure, they will require the same kind of openness and accountability that NGOs demand of public institutions. Openness and mutual accountability may indeed be even more essential for NGOs, which rely on these relationships and on voluntary support – rather than governmental or market mechanisms – to accomplish their missions.

For voluntary agencies, this openness begins with the relatively routine forms of disclosure required by law. Agencies in most countries must register with the national or local government, make financial records available, hold open public meetings of their memberships or boards, and practise other routine forms of transparency that make them at least theoretically accessible to the public.

NGOs that seek an international political voice are also being called upon to practice a measure of openness about who speaks for whom in international advocacy networks (Edwards 1998; Nelson 1996). As such openness becomes increasingly important for strategic reasons, it is also inherently important to creating the trust and solidarity that NGOs assert as a value. Alan Fowler describes this as a voluntary setting aside of privilege in order to enter into partnerships as nearly as possible as equals (Fowler 1998). For Christian organisations recognition of equality and of mutual accountability should be a fundamental objective.

THE PROBLEM WITH CIVIL SOCIETY

The term *civil society* should be used with care when discussing the advocacy work of NGOs and civil organisations. The concept tends to obscure important differences and power relationships that must be brought to light, and it is subject to misuse by actors in the international system. Development advocates need a vocabulary of social action that clarifies these power relations and that motivates, sensitises, and enables them to work effectively with poor poeple in the struggles they face. *Civil society* should be tested against this standard.

Gross inequality and lack of freedom hold captive poor and rich alike. Decisive political action to change institutions and policies is essential to achieving humane and just development. Some private development agencies and other voluntary organisations are dedicated to this kind of political action at local, national, and international levels. If we accept these agendas as an important aspect of the development effort, then does civil society (the concept) help advance this politically difficult agenda?

The answer, I believe, is a qualified no. Scholars and practitioners of development have not exercised the necessary caution in adopting civil society as the analytic approach to institutions in public life. More critical and selective use is in order. This need for care is especially relevant when discussing steps to encourage a sustained, pro-poor transformation of economic and social systems. Indeed, civil society (the concept) could be the undoing of the work of the thousands of organisations we have taken to calling civil society. This danger is in part because the concept itself confuses and blurs important distinctions. But the more serious danger lies in the political uses to which civil society is put by state, international, and corporate actors.

The popularity and contributions of civil society are unquestioned. But its broad meaning leads to a blurring of distinctions among social groups with genuinely opposing interests. Despite the importance of reconciliation and building trust and co-operation, it is also essential that poor and disenfranchised people assert their interests and power, and win the political leverage they need to elicit co-operation from other social groups. Without this assertive and sometimes conflictive strategy, building trust and co-operation in civil society sentences the powerless to subordination and poverty.

Finally, aid donors and governments make particular uses of civil society in shaping and controlling influence in societies. NGOs that support a cause such as human rights, fair labour standards, or religious freedom, and side with particular groups (the poor, homeless, landless, an ethnic or religious minority) should articulate this support specifically and directly rather than resorting to the language of "promoting civil society."

Let's look at these assertions in more detail.

The Popularity of Civil Society

Civil society as a concept has experienced a resurgence of popularity for good and important reasons. It expresses the possibility of community, suggests lively participation in public life, and asserts freedom of action apart from state and corporation. In societies undergoing transition from authoritarian, centrally planned governments, the term has come to represent the sometimes heroic efforts of groups and individuals – artists, intellectuals, trade union leaders, and religious leaders – who have worked to solidify new roles for voluntary associations in public life.

Civil society is a reality. There are organisations and patterns of association among people in every society, and they shape social and economic change. The point is not to dispute the existence of civil society, or to make fine distinctions about who belongs, but to examine critically the concept's usefulness in assessing NGOs' development agendas.

Two themes have helped win civil society its current popularity. These emphasise, first, the creation of trust and the habit of co-operation, and second, the capacity to challenge, or at least balance, the dominant role of the state. Civil society as a concept spotlights the set of common activities that builds the capacity to co-operate across traditional dividing lines of institution, class, ethnicity, and ideology. There are clearly circumstances, as the proponents of "social capital" argue, in which communication, trust, and co-operation among diverse groups are essential to reducing poverty or resolving conflict (Brown and Ashmann 1995). Moreover, it is argued that the practice of democratic participation is nurtured in civil society because citizens come to believe that they will gain by participating in common solutions to social problems.

Civil society's second great virtue is closely related to this democratic participation: Institutions in civil society can balance the power of the state and maintain independent initiatives that monitor and check government's power.

Civil society is a broad concept, more inclusive than other categories of social actors; social movements and social movement organisations, and interest groups are all more partisan. Categories based on race, ethnicity or class, political alliances, coalitions, and networks subdivide society. Civil society's power as a concept is its breadth; it includes all of these headings and other, informal associations in which people communicate, co-operate, and express their interests and beliefs.

The Danger in Civil Society

This breadth and stress on co-operation and shared interests is also civil society's greatest danger. Civil society tends to obscure important differences and to suggest the importance of co-operation where conflict is perhaps essential. In many settings civil society is another in a long series of efforts by powers outside of poor communities to define their development process for them. A concept with a long heritage in Western philosophy, civil society has inspired activists and analysts in Central and Eastern Europe, where asserting the freedom of voluntary organisation is an important aspect of the post-communist political and social transformation (Toepler and Salamon 1999).

Among the most enthusiastic global advocates of the civil society framework have been official governmental funders of development. Their embrace of civil society has helped to convert the idea from its important meaning – as an arena in which social interaction, both conflictive and co-operative, takes place – to a collection of co-operating social groups with a shared vision of common interests.

The World Bank, for example, defines civil society as "the arena in which people come together to pursue the interests they hold in common," to carry out "civic engagement" in which organisations form "constructive independent relationships with governments and others to achieve their common objectives" (World Bank 2000). The emphasis on common interests and "constructive" engagement underscores the World Bank's and other aid donors' desire to reach out to non-state social groups without taking sides and without appearing to encourage conflict.

But civil society is also the arena in which these interests contend, compete, and conflict. The co-operative ethos of civil society has become so dominant in the development profession that one might almost forget the variety of other frameworks we have for understanding social interactions, frameworks based in class, race, social movements, and interest groups. These are nearly obscured by the adoption of civil society as the primary framework for understanding social development.

Such blurring of distinctions among groups and interests makes civil society problematic. Conflict and consensus are both essential dynamics of the social and political processes that underlie the distribution of economic resources and the construction of social relationships. Does civil society expose or obscure the relationships of power that underlie gross inequality? Evidence from Africa and Central America illustrates the importance of maintaining other categories for our thinking about social realities.

Studies from East Africa that probe the most systematic exclusion of groups – ethnic minorities and women – from social choice and economic opportunity have argued that a focus on civil society obscures the fundamental issue of gender inequality (Tripp 1994). Gender issues extend from the level of the household all the way to the state, as articulated profoundly by social movements such as Kenya's Greenbelt Movement, which understands its own agenda as one of transforming gender inequalities and political institutions, and resists being folded into an imagined seamless and agreeable civil society.

Civil society is pushed to the sidelines analytically not only by social movement activists but also by eminent and established scholars such as Crawford Young, who incisively suggests that civil society is "merely a metaphor masquerading as a [political] player" (Young 1994, 43).

In Central America, aid programmes have sought to move from civil wars of the 1980s to civil society by promoting public dialogue. But it is unrealistic to expect landless people in El Salvador or Guatemala, women working to gain ownership and other economic rights in patriarchal societies, or ethnic minorities pushed aside by the dominant pattern of development, to embrace "strengthening civil society" as the strategy under which they will gain respect, protection, and economic opportunity.

Cathy McIlwaine's work on El Salvador makes two themes clear: first, civil society itself is deeply divided. Among the important divisions is that between formal civil society organisations sponsored and supported by aid donors during the civil war and post-war periods, and "popular organisations" at the village and neighbourhood levels. Second, this polarised reality is largely unacknowledged by major donors such as the US Agency for International Development (USAID), the

Inter-American Development Bank, and the World Bank, which will finance either business-related or local CSOs (civil society organisations) as long as the CSOs implement local social programmes (McIlwaine 1998).

In situations of profound inequality, in which social and political structures limit rights and freedoms, poor and disenfranchised groups must first be able to assert their interests and win a secure position before they can be effective participants in civil society. Therefore, promoting civil society indiscriminately is unlikely either to build trust and true civility in the foreseeable future or to promote the kind of change in social relations that permits greater equity and trust in the future.

The Uses of Civil Society

The issues discussed above are of more than theoretical interest because the idea of civil society is being put to political and institutional uses in three different ways by powerful governments and international agencies.

First, civil society permits aid donors to justify cutting aid levels to poor governments. David Rieff argues that although the fact that the increasing emphasis on "fostering civil society arose at exactly the moment when development aid from most major donor countries was plummeting" is no coincidence (Rieff 1999).

With government services and regulatory powers de-funded and weakened in the poorest countries across three continents, some major donors are now expressing concern about whether the legitimate roles of government have been undercut and whether civil society can effectively replace them. Reducing government bureaucracies has been an attractive and dominant theme of development funders in the last two decades. But when international donors engineer the wholesale replacement of government services, as in health provision in Kenya, with international NGO service providers (Hearn 1998), how are citizens and consumers to exercise accountability and influence over voluntary agencies?

Second, *civil society* provides aid agencies with a way to talk about and promote social institutions without taking sides among the contesting social groups. This appearance of promoting a nonpartisan civil society is sometimes vitally important to many official bilateral donors, who need to persuade governments to practise a minimum level of tolerance of social organisations in order to promote co-operation in delivering social services.

But in most circumstances the idea of impartial aid that builds civil society is an illusion; any intervention in support of organisations in another society has political implications. Van Rooy's study of the relationships between civil society and the aid industry, sums up case studies by local scholars in Hungary, Sri Lanka, Kenya, and Peru by observing the profoundly political nature of any choice to support civil society organisations (Van Rooy 1998, 209–11). Whether organisations are more radical or conciliatory, rural or urban, gender-based or not, religious or secular, has profound and different implications in each social and political setting.

Governmental aid donors may have good reasons to down-play these political implications, but NGOs should not. If NGOs are not completely deliberate and aware of the implications of their choices, they abandon and even betray the public's trust that they, unlike government aid, can reach and support those who have the greatest need and least voice.

Third, and most important, civil society conforms to the dominant development strategy of the 1980s and 1990s, grounded in neo-liberal economic theory and advocating privatisation, export oriented strategies, and sharply reduced government roles in economic policy and planning. The purpose here is not to debate the merits of the neo-liberal economic strategy. The point is rather that civil society has won popularity with influential development actors because of its utility in promoting this larger liberal agenda. The link to economic liberalisation has made development funders willing to provide significant funding for civil society programmes (Van Rooy 1998).

Civil society in the hands of the US government, European Union, IMF, and other guardians of the global economic order may be a way to help transform global economic relationships. But there is surely no widespread agreement that the transformation they envision will reduce inequalities, expand the choices of poor people, and strengthen social and political freedoms.

Implications

If there are reasons for caution about civil society, what are the implications for practitioners and advocates of development? How are we to speak, write, and strategise about NGOs, social movements, and citizen organisations without abandoning a commitment to the side of poor and under-represented people? Let me suggest two cautions.

Specificity
Civil society should not be shorthand for sets of social organisations. When an NGO discusses a programme to strengthen church leadership, provide technical assistance to co-operatives, or support organisations of women or landless people, it is best to describe those organisations on their own merits, avoiding the temptation to lapse into the easy shorthand of "civil society." Such programmes do more than building capacity in "civil society" writ large; they express solidarity with particular people and communities and strengthen particular organisations that express their interests in society.

Clarity About the Relationship Between Conflict and Co-operation
There are a variety of strategies for promoting greater civility, trust, and trust-worthiness, in society. In some situations dialogue and collaboration are the tools that build social capital and the habits of co-operation among capital and labour, international investors and local business owners, indigenous peoples and colonists, women and men. But in other situations more partisan and conflictive strategies are

needed to give credibility to the weaker parties. The history of labour, social movements, or human rights advocacy demonstrates that poor and oppressed people need strategies to assert their voices and power. Only after gaining such credible voices should poor and oppressed people be expected to engage in co-operative strategies.

Practitioners and theorists have found important uses for civil society. But in an environment in which the concept has many and diverse uses and associations, caution is required to discern its usefulness for a practitioner's personal and political mission. The temptation to adopt the phrase from donors and the academic literature because of convenience, fashion, or funding should be avoided.

NGO LEADERSHIP CAN EDUCATE, MOTIVATE, AND ENABLE EFFECTIVE POLITICAL ACTION

Many development NGOs based in North America accept the challenge of advocacy. Advocacy on behalf of aid programmes, in defence of compassionate foreign policy, or in opposition to specific economic or military policies has become common for development NGOs. They have occasionally linked with global networks in efforts that at least momentarily seem to upset the norms of national and international policy-making.

But it appears to have been more difficult for US-based NGOs to embrace the challenge of helping people of faith and of conscience to involve themselves directly in promoting these changes. Their donors, members, and the general public are rarely stirred to any form of mass action, except in moments of great humanitarian emergency. How can NGOs, including those grounded in Christian faith, create a growing movement that supports the voices of dispossessed and under-represented people?

Uphold Hope, Act Boldly

Limited, reformist agendas built around protecting development aid programmes have been a double disappointment. They have had only minimal success in defending aid spending, and they have failed in the United States to inspire widespread public interest. Despite exemplary organising and public advocacy work of Bread for the World on aid programmes, for example, its public membership has hovered between 40,000 and 50,000 for almost two decades. NGOs need to integrate their support of aid programmes into a more sweeping and prophetic vision of change. The power of the Jubilee 2000 movement to mobilise action is evidence of the potential impact of bold initiatives.

Demand Transparency

Transparency, the openness that makes information from within governments and organisations "accessible, visible, and understandable" (IMF 1998), enables others to evaluate an organisation's policies or performance (Florini 2000). Such openness is essential to sustained, effective advocacy for just institutions. NGOs have exploited the power of transparency in advocacy with the World Bank, and it has important strategic value in relating to the marketplace as well. Information has facilitated consumer, shareholder, and other political actions that have helped change corporate labour and environmental practices (Wapner 1996) and enabled consumers to make informed choices.

Access to information is central to the effectiveness of human rights standards intended to prevent systematic discrimination based on race or on political or religious views and to prevent gross individual violations. Human rights NGOs such as Amnesty International, Human Rights Watch, International Justice Mission, and the thousands of organisations with which they co-operate, obtain information from governments and corporations and give that information full and strategic exposure.

Encourage Public Advocacy Through the Routines of People's Daily Lives

It is time to end the separation between political action – voting, communicating to an elected representative – and the rhythms of daily life. While affirming the importance of political action to influence governments and international agencies, some NGOs also practise models that allow people to link their care for others with their daily choices and with their desire for simpler, more ordered lives.

In the UK, the NGO Christian Aid has motivated tens of thousands of its donors to "lobby" their supermarkets and grocery stores to stock the "fair trade" products that US consumers can buy only through small co-ops or catalogues. The campaigns have been highly successful, both in the supermarket chains and in mobilising Christian Aid supporters to act on a monthly campaign initiative, nudging their own local market towards considering the values and principles of exchange.

The model suggests a means of expanding public advocacy and of deepening the meaning of faith communities and Christian citizenship. Advocacy for justice deepens when a congregation or parish considers the source of beverages for its weekly coffee hours and regular church meetings and switches to products that express the parish's commitment to justice and fair international trade (Lutheran World Relief 1999).

Agencies that command the loyalty of their donors and constituents have profound responsibilities to those supporters. Those responsibilities include fiscal honesty and programme effectiveness, but they should grow to include enabling and challenging those individuals to express their desire for a new order not only when they write a check to the agency or a letter to a political representative, but also in the practical matters of everyday life.

Use Language of Justice, Neighbour, Stewardship, Jubilee

Consistent, unified witness to global justice motivates action for decisive policy changes in the public sphere as well. Justice-based initiatives, when expressed in the powerful language of Judaeo-Christian traditions and teaching, offer an opportunity for people of faith to lead their personal lives and the practices of their institutions into a role that is both prophetic and effective. Many Christians have already responded to a call to recognise global neighbours, to practise the politics and the spirituality of Jubilee, and to express solidarity between South and North, poor and rich.

If the churches and agencies to which North Americans look for faithful and principled leadership express that desire in the language of faith and values, it is now clear that many people will respond. In so doing they may reunite their interests and those of the world's poor majority and, in time, provoke policies and actions that go far beyond our limited political imaginations.

NOTES

[1] This subsection and the two following draw heavily on Paul Nelson, *Globalization, NGO Advocacy and International Financial Policy: Unlearning Lessons from Lobbying the World Bank*, working paper (Boston: Oxfam America, 2001).

[2] The G-7 countries are the United States, Great Britain, Germany, France, Canada, Japan, and Italy.

REFERENCES

Arts, Bas. 2000. *The Political Influence of Global NGOs: Case Studies on the Climate and Biodiversity Conventions*. Utrecht: International Books.

Brown, L. David, and Darcy Ashmann. 1995. "Participation, Social Capital, and Intersectoral Problem-Solving: African and Asian Cases." *IDR Reports* 12.

Carmen, Raff, and Miguel Sobrado. 2000. "Those Who Don't Eat and Those who Don't Sleep." In *A Future for the Excluded*, edited by R. Carmen and M. Sobrado. London: Zed Books.

Center for a New American Dream. 2001. "About Us." Online at the New Dream website. Accessed 8 April 2001.

Center for Economic Justice. 2000. "World Bank Bond Boycott Campaign." Online at the Center for Economic Justice website.

Chamberlain, Christopher. 1997. "Mining and Development: The Private Sector and the Competing Interests of the World Bank Group." Washington, D.C.: The Bank Information Center.

Christensen, Eric. 1990. "Green Appeal: A Proposal for an Environmental Commission of Enquiry at the World Bank." Washington, D.C.: Natural Resources Defense Council.

Clark, John. 1991. *Democratising Develpoment*. West Hartford, Conn.: Kumarian Press.

Covey, Jane G. 1998. "Critical Cooperation? Influencing the World Bank Through Policy Dialogue and Operational Cooperation." In *The Struggle for Accountability: NGOs, Grassroots Organizations and the World Bank*, edited by J. Fox and D. Brown, 81–120. Cambridge, Mass.: MIT Press.

Edwards, Michael. 1998. *Future Positive*. London: Earthscan.

Edwards, Michael, and Gita Sen. 1999. "NGOs, Social Change and the Transformation of Human Relationships: A Twenty-First-Century Civic Agenda." *Third World Quarterly* 21: 605–16.

Evans, Huw. 1999. "Debt Relief for the Poorest Countries: Why Did It Take So Long?" *Development Policy Review* 17: 267–79.

Florini, Ann M. 2000. "The Politics of Transparency." Paper presented at the annual meetings of the International Studies Association, 17 March 2000, in Los Angeles.

Fowler, Alan. 1998. *Striking a Balance.* London: Earthscan.

Fox, Jonathan. 1998. "When Does Reform Policy Influence Practice? Lessons from the Bankwide Resettlement Review." In *The Struggle for Accountability: NGOs, Grassroots Organizations and the World Bank*, edited by J. Fox and D. Brown, 303–44. Cambridge, Mass.: MIT Press.

———. 2000. "The World Bank Inspection Panel: Lessons of the First Five Years." *Global Governance* 6 (July-September): 3.

Fox, Jonathan, and David Brown, eds. 1998. *The Struggle for Accountability: NGOs, Grassroots Organizations and the World Bank.* Cambridge: MIT Press.

Hearn, Julie. 1998. "The 'NGO-isation' of Kenyan Society: USAID and the Restructuring of Health Care." *Review of African Political Economy* 75: 89–100.

IMF (International Monetary Fund). 1998. "Report of the Working Group on Transparency and Accountability." Washington, D.C.: International Monetary Fund.

Jordan, Lisa and Peter van Tuijl. 2000. "Political Responsibility in Transnational NGO Advocacy: Exploring Emerging Shapes of Global Democracy." *World Development* 28: 2051–65.

Kaufmann, Chaim D., and Robert A. Pape. 1999. "Explaining Costly International Moral Action: Britain's Sixty-year Campaign Against the Atlantic Slave Trade." *International Organization* 53: 631–68.

Keck, Margaret, and Kathryn Sikkink. 1998. *Activists Beyond Borders.* Ithaca, N.Y.: Cornell.

Keet, Dot. 2000. "The International Anti-debt Campaign." *Development in Practice* 10: 461–77.

Khagram, Sanjeev. 2000. "Toward Democratic Governance for Sustainable Development." In *The Third Force: The Rise of Transnational Civil Society*, edited by A. Florini, 83–114. Tokyo: Japan Center for International Exchange; Washington, D.C.: Carnegie Endowment for World Peace.

Korten, David C. 1987. "Third Generation NGO Strategies: A Key to People-Centered Development." *World Development* 15: 145–60, Supplement (autumn) entitled *Development Alternatives: The Challenge for NGOs*, edited by A. G. Drabek.

Lewis, David, ed. 1999. *International Perspectives on Voluntary Action.* London: Earthscan.

Lipschutz, Ronnie D. 1996. *Global Civil Society and Global Environmental Governance: The Politics of Nature from Place to Planet.* Albany, N.Y.: SUNY Press.

Lutheran World Relief. 1999. "Faith Meets Fair Trade." Online at the Lutheran World Relief website. Accessed 3 March 2001.

McIlwaine, Cathy. 1998. "Contesting Civil Society: Reflections from El Salvador." *Third World Quarterly* 19: 651–72.

Meketa, Motoko. 2000. "Building Partnerships Toward a Common Goal: Experiences of the International Campaign to Ban Landmines." In *The Third Force: The Rise of Transnational Civil Society,* edited by A. Florini, 143–76. Tokyo: Japan Center for International Exchange; Washington, D.C.: Carnegie Endowment for World Peace.

Morse, Bradford, and Thomas Berger. 1992. *Sardar Sarovar: The Report of the Independent Review.* Ottawa: Resource Futures International.

Nelson, Paul J. 1996. "Internationalising Economic and Environmental Policy: Transnational NGO Networks and the World Bank's Expanding Influence." *Millennium* 25: 605–33.

———. 1997. "Conflict and Effectiveness: Who Speaks for Whom in Transnational NGO Networks Lobbying the World Bank?" *Nonprofit and Voluntary Sector Quarterly* 26: 421–41.

———. 2000. "Heroism and Ambiguity: NGO Advocacy in International Policy." *Development in Practice* 10: 478–90.

———. 2002. "Agendas, Accountability, and Legitimacy Among Transnational NGO Networks." In *Restructuring World Politics: Transnational Social Movements, Networks, and Norms*, edited by Sanjeev Khagram, James V. Riker, and Kathryn Sikkink, 131–54. Minneapolis: University of Minnesota Press.

Oxfam International. 2000. "Oxfam International Education Campaign: 'Education Now! Break the Cycle of Poverty.'" Online at the Oxfam website. Accessed 7 March 2001.

Pasha, Mustapha Kamal, and David L. Blaney. 1998. "Elusive Paradise: The Promise and Peril of Global Civil Society." *Alternatives* 23: 417–50.

Pettifor, Ann. 1999. "What Does the Koln Agreement Mean for the Jubilee 2000 Campaign Worldwide?" 8 July.

Price, Richard. 1998. "Reversing the Gun Sights: Transnational Civil Society Targets Land Mines." *International Organization* 52/3 (summer): 613–44.

Rieff, David. 1999. "The False Dawn of Civil Society." Online at *The Nation* website. Accessed 7 March 2001.

Risse, Thomas, Stephen C. Ropp, and Kathryn Sikkink, eds. 1999. *The Power of Human Rights: International Norms and Domestic Change*. Cambridge: Cambridge University Press.

Seymour, Frances J., and Navroz K. Dubash. 2000. *The Right Conditions: The World Bank, Structural Adjustment, and Forest Policy Reform*. Washington, D.C.: World Resources Institute.

Shihata, Ibrahim F. I. 1994. *The World Bank Inspection Panel*. New York: Oxford.

Sine, Tom. 1999. *Mustard Seed versus McWorld: Reinventing Life and Faith for the Future*. Ada, Mich.: Baker Books.

Stott, John R. W. 1984. *Issues Facing Christians Today*. Basingstoke: Marshalls.

Tarrow, Sidney. 1994. *Power in Movement: Social Movements, Collective Action, and Mass Politics in the Modern State*. Cambridge: Cambridge University Press.

Tellam, Ian, ed. 2000. *Fuel for Change: World Bank Energy Policy, Rhetoric vs. Reality*. London: Zed Books.

Toepler, Stefan, and Lester M. Salamon. 1999. "The 'Rebirth of Civil Society' in Central and Eastern Europe." Paper presented at the annual conference of ARNOVA (Association for Research on Nonprofit Organizations and Voluntary Action), 4–6 November 1999, in Washington, D.C.

Tripp, Aili Mari. 1994. "Rethinking Civil Society: Gender Implications in Contemporary Tanzania." In *Civil Society and the State in Africa,* edited by J. W. Harbeson, D. Rothchild, and N. Chazan. Boulder, Colo.: Lynne Rienner Publishers.

Umaña, Oscar. 1998. "The World Bank Inspection Panel: The First Four Years (1994–1998)." Washington, D.C.: World Bank.

UNDP (United Nations Development Program). 1996. *Human Development Report 1996*. New York: Oxford University Press.

———. 1999. *Human Development Report 1999*. New York: Oxford University Press.

Uvin, Peter, Pankaj S. Jain, and L. David Brown. 2000. "Think Large and Act Small: Toward a New Paradigm for NGO Scaling Up." *World Development* 28: 1409–19.

Van Rooy, Alison, ed. 1998. *Civil Society and the Aid Industry: Politics and Promise*. London: Earthscan / The North-South Institute.

Wapner, Paul. 1996. *Environmental Activism and World Civic Politics*. Albany, N.Y.: SUNY Press.

Willetts, Peter. 1996. *The Conscience of the World: The Influence of NGOs in the U.N. System*. Washington, D.C.: Brookings Institution Press.

World Bank. 1996. *The Bankwide Review of Projects Involving Involuntary Resettlement*. Washington, D.C.: World Bank.

———. 2000. "Consultations with Civil Society Organizations: General Guidelines for World Bank Staff." Washington, D.C.: World Bank.

World Bank and IMF. 1999. "Heavily Indebted Poor Countries Initiatives: Progress Report by the Managing Director of the IMF and the President of the World Bank." 21 April.

Young, Crawford. 1994. "In Search of Civil Society." In *Civil Society and the State in Africa,* edited by J. W. Harbeson, D. Rothchild, and N. Chazan, 33–50. Boulder, Colo.: Lynne Rienner Publishers.

7

HEAVENS NOT HAVENS

Civil Society and Social Change

Alan Whaites

Civil society is not a static concept, and its Western origins have given rise to a lively debate concerning the applicability of the original political theory to developing contexts. The new orthodoxy of civil society that has arisen over the last two decades has also generated a complex picture involving Northern, Southern, global, donor-driven, primordial, and many other versions of civil society. Within such a diverse context, the original theory of civil society still helps to provide a useful interpretative framework. Further, the theory helps us to realise that civil society acts as both an active participant in political, social and economic life (a direct promoter of development) and also as a source of social identity.

A review of the activist role of civil society concludes that it is, to an extent, hampered by burgeoning diversity as individuals seek the security of the identity that civil society organisations (CSOs) can offer. The desire for identity has made it difficult for individual civil society groups to achieve aims that do not involve direct service provision, as advocating for broad political or social change takes place within a sea of voices all competing to be heard. The analysis of civil society's impact in development overall is mixed, creating conditions for a critical backlash. Those groups that do achieve their goals in the public arena tend to do so incrementally, although many small changes taken together can substantially alter the world at the macro level. But is this enough? Christians are perhaps also called to greater ambition for social change, which may mean going beyond civil society as a vehicle for achieving change and looking also at the direct role of government.

Michael Edwards (1998) has referred to the task of defining civil society as one akin to nailing jelly to the wall. True, the tremendous rise in usage of the phrase has rarely been accompanied by any kind of rigour in identifying its underlying intellectual foundation. Results of the exponential growth in the use of the concept are best summarised by John Keane, a political scientist who in the 1980s was himself influential in re-popularising the concept:

> Its burgeoning popularity accelerates the accumulation of inherited ambiguities, new confusions and outright contradictions. For this reason alone the

expanding talk of civil society is not immune to muddle and delirium. There are even signs that the meanings of the term "civil society" are multiplying to the point, where, like a catchy advertising slogan, it risks imploding through overuse (Keane 1998, 36).

This confusion reminds us that civil society is ultimately an intellectual concept applied to social forces, a neat pattern superimposed on a shifting and evolving mass.

A Product of Change

The definition of civil society has from its inception been an attempt by social and political theorists to keep pace with the rapidly changing nature of social organisation. The origin of the construct lies in the emergence of modern forms of political organisation at the start of the nineteenth century. The Enlightenment and the decline of absolute monarchy created processes of political transition that rapidly changed prevailing ideas of political organisation. The idea of the nation state, separation of powers, and mass suffrage were a result of the deep-seated changes in popular understanding of the world. The same period saw the gradual replacement of the idea of a providential God by Adam Smith's guiding hand. Old assumptions of political and economic life were rapidly being left behind.

Within this context of rapid intellectual, economic, and political change, traditional ideas of social organisation were swept aside. Large conurbations and the emergence of an educated middle class replaced the social order of communities centred on small families, feudal landowners, and the church.[1]

One of the founders of modern political theology, Samuel Taylor Coleridge, pointed to the potential disequilibrium that such changes brought. Society, he argued, was now at the mercy of the fast-moving pace of industrialisation, and stability brought by traditional structures was threatened. Coleridge saw in these changes a struggle between the forces of progress and permanence, which if out of balance could erode the fabric of society and create chaos (Coleridge 1975). As we shall discuss, society needs elements of permanence, sources of social affirmation, or havens.

Indeed, Coleridge advocated the institutionalisation of "permanence" safety valves, particularly a clerisy, to ground society in clear values and principles. By "clerisy" Coleridge was referring to a semi-institutionalised intelligentsia, what might be described as a zone of thoughtfulness within the hurly-burly and breakneck change of capitalism. The clerisy was to stand apart from both the greed of the market and political ambition, a reservoir for social altruism. His call for sources of identity and social stability that were to be found in the new communities, themselves based on altruism, was to re-emerge consistently as industrialisation gathered pace. Did civil society evolve to become the "new clerisy," a source of community and identity that can balance the naked drive of market-driven greed?

The Place of Theory

The period in which Coleridge wrote his most important political theology was also the era in which civil society theory was beginning to emerge in its modern form. Rather than addressing the need to balance the rapid social change brought by the market, newly conceptualised civil society was seen as the force necessary to balance the other new arrival on the scene, the modern state. This initial context for the emergence of a politically important concept of civil society is of real significance to our understanding of its strengths and weaknesses today. Civil society theory helped map changes in society that wider contextual forces were shaping.

Three figures have arguably done more to construct the modern theory of civil society than any others: Hegel, de Tocqueville, and Gramsci. Each left markedly different emphases on our understanding of its role in the process of political life. Hegel saw civil society as the rise of competitive social forces, seeking to dominate and over-run the state in order to secure their own goals. For Hegel, the strong state became the necessary evil needed to hold the ring among the forces of civil society. De Tocqueville, conversely, began with a premise of the strong, modern state. The modern state held a potential for domination and repression that would have been a dream for the despots of the Middle Ages. For de Tocqueville, it was essential that this state be balanced by social groups (or civil associations) that enabled citizens to band together for common purposes. To avoid the outright competition of the Hegelian view, these civil associations would band together around "small issues" (see Whaites 2000b). For both Hegel and de Tocqueville, civil society was a phenomenon associated with a stage of industrialisation and economic development that included the decline of primordial identities.

The third major theorist, Gramsci, articulated this same phenomenon by defining civil society as very much a middle-class aspiration, though he deliberately excluded the market from the mix (Whaites 2000a; Keane 1988). All three clearly associated civil society with a powerful and modern state, a view still shared by theorists such as Richard Jefferies who continues to argue that a strong state is a prerequisite for civil society (Jefferies 1993). In such a view the rise of civil society outside the context of an effective state (such as in much of the developing world) is the recipe for a Hegelian nightmare: competing social forces that are unrestrained.

Western Philosophers and Development in the South

The possibility of a Hegelian nightmare raises interesting questions for those who deal in contexts in which civil society can often be stronger, more vibrant, and more discernibly altruistic than the state. We must ask, for example, if overreliance on the Western philosophical origins of civil society theory equate to a kind of political "modernisation" theory in which the South has no room to find a different path? These issues have given rise to theoretical attempts to contextualise a new understanding of civil society theory, particularly with Africa in mind. The French political scientist Jean-Francois Bayart is perhaps most notable in this field (Bayart 1993).

I have argued elsewhere that practical benefit can be gained from application of the original Western theory of civil society without necessarily typecasting the experiences of the South as a rerun of countries in the North (Whaites 2000a). This benefit, whether in North or South, comes because socio-economic change tends to affect family, traditional values, traditional community leadership structures, and also social identities. Such changes may not generate the same kind of associational patterns in different parts of the world, but they are likely to require new directions in the organisational life of civil society. For example, it can be argued that historical analysis of social change in Pakistan points to the impact that urbanisation and rising income have had in increasing associational life in that country (Whaites 1995).

Accepting that the original thinking of Hegel, de Tocqueville, and Gramsci still has relevance for mapping social change does not resolve the conundrum of the state. The early theorists envisioned civil society to be a social force that existed in tension with the state while at the same time promoting "issues." From the start, civil society has been seen as securing its significance through its impact on the state. Civil society sought change that only the state could realistically deliver.

This picture of civil society as coalescing around issues, or visions of change, was encapsulated in Western experience by the rise of European and North American social movements. Not surprisingly, the development of the world's first modern Western democracy in Britain created an environment ripe for popular organisation around issues of public policy.[2] The result was the popular pressure group, including the Anti-Corn Law League,[3] the anti-slavery movement, and associations pressing for the improvement of factory conditions and prisons (de Tocqueville 1835/40). Today we might point just as strongly to the Namada Dam Movement, ECPAT International, or Casa Alianza. These associations came together to press for definable causes. The target of these calls were institutions of government, ranging from the electorate up to parliaments (and in some countries, presidents).

The interaction of civil society with institutions of government has left a question mark over the role of those groups that straddle a clear divide in the theory by serving both governmental and civic interests. A useful recent development in civil society theory has therefore come from a group of Latin American political scientists who tracked the role of civil society in the political upheaval of the 1980s. This group, led by Alfred Stepan, has called convincingly for clarity in the divide between civil society and those groups that move constitutionally in and out of the state sphere, particularly political parties. Stepan has argued for a conceptual grouping of "political society," a term that would apply to those groups outside the permanent and static structure of the state but nevertheless constitutionally essential to the operation of political process (Stepan 1988).

CIVIL SOCIETY AND SOCIAL PROVISION

The causes around which CSOs coalesce are not, however, always overtly political. The activism of civil society often initially includes direct service provision. Civil society is a means through which people can reach out to improve their own and their neighbour's lives. Even these CSO activities, however, have political consequences and causes, and many of these ultimately come back to the state. The developing world provides an illustration of the influence political context can play. The rise of civil society in the 1980s coincided with the height of the third-world debt crisis, a period during which structural adjustment programmes were stipulating wholesale shrinkage of the state in developing countries.

A central article of all structural adjustment programmes was the need for fiscal balance. In societies where much of the economy was within the informal sector and tax receipts were low, adjustment led to cuts in public services, including education and health. Retreat of the state from local communities often created a humanitarian catastrophe, and Western institutions responded by pressing civil society to take up the slack. Civil society thus took on the role of what is now known as gap filling, which is the replacement of the state (Cannon 2000; Robinson 1995).

By the mid-1990s awareness within civil society of the dangers of gap filling became acute. Developmentally, the lack of effective co-ordination affected everything from school curriculums to adequate referral systems within health provision. As states slashed budgets, many development programmes were also cut without any clear relationship to an overall development strategy. This is a problem that the World Bank and IMF (International Monetary Fund) are belatedly trying to put right through their Poverty Reduction Strategy Papers. Gap filling was also symptomatic of the erosion of the African state's ability to emulate the role of government in South East Asia in promoting development. The role of the state in economic management in Asia is well-covered ground (World Bank/OUP 1993; Leipziger and Thamas 1993; World Bank 1995), but the state also provided a central role in service provision to the poor, boosting human capital formation and helping create a virtuous cycle of growth and poverty reduction (Griffin and Ickowitz 1997; Deiniger and Squire 1998; Rodrik 1999; Milanovic 1999; Kim 1997; Islam and Chowdhury 1998, 120).

The retreat of the state, particularly in Africa, not only created problems developmentally but also had negative implications for democracy. State shrinkage reduced direct contact between citizens and their state and thus removed the main means citizens had to judge government efficiency. State shrinkage also led to internal dynamics such as the flight of talented staff, thus further draining already weak government bodies. Some political scientists now see in these dynamics the roots of what by the mid-1990s was being perceived as the collapse and criminalisation of some states, particularly in Africa. Bayart, Chabal, Clapham, and others have suggested that civil society in some instances simply became an extension of the patrimonial system. Elsewhere civil society actually worked to undermine what little state authority was left (Jones 1997; Bayart et al. 1999; Clapham 1996; Chabal and Daloz 1999). An unavoidable corollary of these changes was the declining ability of increasingly weak states to play the Hegelian role of ringmaster.

Many within civil society celebrated rather than mourned the decline of the state (Midgley 1986). The state was seen as corrupt, indifferent, and inept particularly when compared to a more responsive and locally owned civil society. Such a view, however, all too often reflected a failure on the part of critics to bridge the micro-macro gulf, resting instead on a limited view of national development policy. These views rapidly came to epitomise the arrogance and lack of legitimacy of some NGOs, which had, by the end of the 1990s, precipitated a growing backlash against CSOs. Governments might be imperfect, but they usually had some claim to constitutional legitimacy. This triumphalist attitude toward state decline failed to perceive that weaker states might not simply be inept, but could actually cause growing conflict.

The link between weak states and conflict is nothing new. The inability of weak states to mediate the ring among competing groups (Migdal 1988), however, was made more dangerous by the fact that civil society groups in some developing countries were based not around small issues so much as around primordial identity. Proliferation of conflict throughout the 1990s fed on primordial identity – that part of one's identity that is received (ethnicity, language, and so forth) rather than adopted (political affiliation) – and can become the focus for entirely selfish group competition, including manipulation by actors who are now termed conflict entrepreneurs (see Douma 1999; Peiris 1999; O'Reilly 1999; see also Migdal 1988). Groups organised according to primordial identities have been quick to adopt the guise of CSOs to access resources and acquire a cloak of respectability. Interestingly, in 2000, the VHP, a Hindu Nationalist group, applied for the ultimate status of civil society acceptance, United Nations Economic and Social Council (ECOSOC) recognition.

It would be wrong to suggest that civil society in the developing world has been predominantly negative. Research has also shown that promotion of integrative civil society – those groups that draw people together across identities, along the lines originally envisaged by de Tocqueville – have reduced tension and even prevented conflict. Civil society has also done much to promote local development and articulate the concerns of the poor. The picture is therefore neither wholly good nor wholly bad. What we see is that the rise of civil society was accompanied by a weakening of the state, a trend that prevents civil society from achieving many of its goals (because the state would be a key vehicle for achieving change). The rise of civil society also gave reign to opportunists willing to jump on the bandwagon for personal profit. The key lesson to be drawn from this analysis is that civil society is a human construct and capable of being used to achieve altruistic goals or, alternatively, to promote vested self-interests.

Necessary Ingredients: Civil Society and Democracy

The problems of gap filling and state erosion only became widely discussed at the end of the 1990s. Earlier, at the end of the 1980s, the use of civil society to help provide a "safety net" during structural adjustment was seen largely as a success. These perceived successes created the environment for something of a golden era in civil society's image. If the 1980s were a period of service provision and gap filling, even more came to be expected of civil society in the 1990s, when it came to be seen as the magic bullet, providing not only health and education but also strengthening democracy as well.

In the minds of Western policy-makers, civil society has become a prerequisite for a stable and sustainable democracy. Civil society has now come to be associated with enabling citizens to engage with the state. In the OECD (Organisation for Economic Co-operation and Development) this belief flowered with the growth of modern issue-based movements ranging from environmentalism to consumer protection. Civil society is viewed to be part of what makes a Western democracy a Western democracy, and every nation must cultivate it if it wishes to become, or remain, a true democracy.

In relation to poorer countries – characterised by low human development index scores or within the low-income bracket favoured by the World Bank – which are often either young democracies or one-party states, OECD donors saw civil society as a positive force because it fostered civic virtues (Robinson 1995; Whaites 1995; Oxfam UK 1995). The image of people banding together to improve their communities and countries was seen in bright de Tocquevillian light. It was thus hoped that new civil society groups would serve also as a source of new identity, replacing traditional social permanence with a new locus for social affirmation. Civil society would thus play two roles, both of which would benefit the polities of the South. One role would be as activist organisation, either in service provision or advocacy; the other role would be as a new source of social identity.

The image of civil society as a magic bullet capable of solving everything from poverty to repression was reinforced by the events in Europe at the end of the 1980s. During these turbulent years civil society played a seminal role in some Eastern European states, providing outlets for opposition to totalitarian governments and nurturing alternative forms of organisation that transformed Eastern Europe. It was not surprising that with the drive for global democratisation that followed the collapse of the Berlin Wall, Western governments themselves seized hold of the concept. Promotion of civil society became an article of faith for donors and global institutions, and certainly the growth of indigenous social movements in poor countries meant that there were plenty of groups to support (Robinson 1993; OECD/DAC 1995; World Bank 1991, 132).

These inclinations toward the value of civil society were reinforced by political scientists who worked to repopularise the concept, particularly authors such as John Keane. As late as 1989 major texts were largely devoid of references to civil society (the most obvious example is Migdal 1988). Within two years, however, almost no political science book, particularly relating to state-society linkages, was published without frequent reference to the concept. For donor bodies and major global institutions, the rise of the concept was perfectly timed.

Active promotion of civil society through donor programmes has been documented by political scientists who advised the process (Blair 1997; Carrothers 1999). The belief was that the nurturing of CSOs would be constructive, regardless of the purpose or nature of the CSO. The "more is better" approach led to the rise of new civil society units within donor aid ministries, which articulated their goals in formal policy documents and provided for them with generous budgets (UK Department for International Development 1997; OECD/DAC 1995). Inevitably this grab for civil society would lead to Western policy creating distortions within civil society development, serving to put Westernised, urban, and elite-led groups at something of an advantage.

It would have been surprising if some problems had not occurred, particularly given the frequent failure to take account of issues of state competence, primordialism, and elite manipulation. The experience of gap filling, the erosion of the state, the rise of primordially based civil society groups, and criticism from political scientists are all part of the picture. We must remember, however, that they are not the whole story. The gap filling of the 1980s and the promotion of civil society as a political goal during the 1990s point us to some of the problems which arise with an imperfect sector, but other actors (including the state) also have questions to answer.

Despite the potential pitfalls, it is likely that much good was done through these civil society programmes. Certainly the last two decades have seen an explosion of civil society in the developing world. Many of the CSOs that emerged have been at the forefront of campaigns for human rights and development. International NGOs learned that they could nurture Southern CSOs not simply to enhance their local developmental roles but also in the hope of encouraging participatory political change.

CIVIL SOCIETY IN THE RICH (OECD) WORLD

We have seen that civil society theory helps to place new forms of associational life within an understanding of engagement with the state, although this creates peculiar complexities in relation to the Third World. Traditional theory focuses on this dual relationship (state and society) rather than seeing civil society more widely as a product of broad political and economic change. In reality, civil society is diverse, sometimes dynamic, but also potentially divisive and even corrupt. The complexity of civil society means that while we might see in activist civil associations the attributes of Coleridge's forces of progress, we can also see attributes of permanence, particularly the new identities that civil associations can confer.

Civil society, even in its most neutral form (service provision), has sometimes had unintended negative effects. Indeed, though the rise of civil society in the Third World has come to some extent at the expense of the state and has illustrated the imperfect nature of any human endeavour, this is not unique to the South.

During the 1980s and 1990s experiments with civil society also took place in the rich world and revealed the problems of seeing the sector as some sort of cure-all for a country's ills. Recent Western experience with civil society has led to greater understanding of the possibilities and limits of civil society in any national context.

The free-market revolutions of Ronald Reagan and Margaret Thatcher promoted the idea of voluntary provision replacing the nanny, or welfare, state. Programmes to cut state provision (and with it expenditure and taxes) were coupled with the promotion of charitable activity. Large-scale state provision of social and welfare services was also deemed by political scientists such as Samuel Beer to have led to a condition of pluralistic stagnation (Beer 1982). In effect, the state had become beholden to the many groups needed to implement its vast array of duties and could consequently be held hostage by any number of interest groups. In contrast, in many developing states in the 1980s service provision was reaching an extent that seemed to compromise the autonomy of government itself.

The weakness of the nanny state had been foreseen by earlier advocates of alternative forms of social organisation. In the 1940s V. A. Demant, along with T. S. Eliot a leader of the Christendom movement of political theology, had argued that the erosion of traditional forms of social organisation resulting from the rise of the state was similar to continually extending a house on inadequate foundations (Demant 1936, chaps. 1, 2; Demant 1939, chaps. 2, 3). The eventual structural flaws would lead inevitably to the collapse of the house. In the same way, Demant saw social fragmentation as the greatest threat to the survival of capitalism. Demant, following in the tradition of Coleridge, argued that community was the essence of social stability, modelled within the Trinity itself, and that without real community, humanity would seek replacements, including the state, that would fail ultimately to satisfy.

Demant, writing at the height of Fascism and Stalinism, saw in the state the potential centre of human craving for identity and security. Before the establishment of modern welfare states, Demant predicted that reliance on the state to provide security against rapid social change would rapidly expose the weakness of the state itself. He believed that no force, including the state, could be strong enough to offset the impacts of rapid change. Instead, the whole of society would need to be rebuilt on stronger foundations. Demant's perspective, which saw a major role for the church, was underlined by Eliot, who, in *The Idea of a Christian Society*, called for institutionalisation of steps that would reinforce the cultural and social roots of Christianity, thereby embedding the values involved (Eliot 1977).

Demant's prediction that the state as a replacement for a providential God would lead to its downfall was to resonate in those industrialised states that by the end of the 1970s were affected by Beer's pluralistic stagnation. The notion that the extended state was politically weak was supported by arguments of neo-liberal economists that, even in social sectors, state provision would inevitably be inefficient compared to that brought by competitive market forces. Programmes of retrenchment and privatisation did bring market actors into a new prominence but also led to gaps that charities and communities were encouraged to fill.

Politicians appealed to rosy pictures of past community structures in which neighbours cared for local needy families. Ideas of "communitarianism" seemed to imply the democratisation of government through localisation of services. This was a philosophy centred on local civil society, structures from the golf club to the prayer breakfast, that became the bedrock of interaction within communities (see Avineri and de-Shalit 1992).

But the rosy pictures of community provision were somewhat unrealistic. Communities today are not the same as those that existed in the 1920s or the 1950s. Even in times now perceived as the halcyon days of community, there were marked differences in how well people banded together for the common good. Community provision in the past often reflected the underlying inequalities in society. Communities with resources had good provision while those without did not, reflecting to some extent the often middle-America/middle-England nature of civil society itself (Giddens 1999, 82).

Perhaps most crucially, the weaknesses of the community-focused idea were exposed during times of economic crisis, when the system was quickly overloaded. During Britain's Thatcherism-induced recessions of the 1980s, local community organisations, including churches, were quickly overloaded by the scale of social need amidst growing unemployment and childhood poverty. Drop-in centres, hot meals, and youth employment programmes helped some, but they could not tackle unemployment rates that approached 10 per cent and urban childhood poverty rates that approached 30 per cent. In the end, many local organisations had to turn to the state, and particularly its local governmental arms, for funding as they sought to address local needs. Several of the largest domestic charities in the country quickly became quasi arms of the state, still implementing local programmes, but in line with national policies.

The inability of community service providers to respond adequately to extraordinary social need is just as true in the developing world, as shown by the failure of traditional coping mechanisms, based on the extended family, to cope in Asia with the effects of the 1997 economic crisis (World Bank 1997, 59; Whaites and Commins 1998). State safety nets may not be as locally accountable as communitarian structures, but they do distribute the risk over the widest possible group of people.

No Magic Bullet

By the end of the 1990s civil society was no longer the perceived magic bullet, a reality summarised in one of the most important development books of the period, *Non-governmental Organisation – Performance and Accountability, Beyond the Magic Bullet* (Edwards and Hulme 1995). In the Western world there was a new appreciation that civil society is a complex and heterogeneous beast, capable of both good and ill. While the overloaded state may not have had all the answers, neither did the utopian resurgence of the Victorian charity mentality. In the developing world there was an increasing understanding that civil society forms a necessary but not sufficient part of both a healthy society and a healthy polity. The rise of civil society needed to be complemented by renewed attention to state structures and the underlying fabric of governance, such as the rule of law. While in some states civil society enabled people to gain their first experience of participation and community-based forms of organising, elsewhere civil society became a new vehicle for patrimonialism and clientelism. At worst, civil society enabled the manipulation of primordial hatreds and the rise of conflict.

The success stories or "poster children" of civil society became those movements that enabled poor communities to achieve a new kind of independence or to challenge powerful forces. The most widely known successes have been the Southern civil society movements that have risen to global prominence, such as the Grameen Bank, Narmada Dam campaign, and the Landless Peasants Movement of Brazil.[4]

By the end of the 1990s civil society had become an orthodoxy. Global institutions established civil society departments, boards, and councils, but this was as much for the benefit of those institutions as it was to enable real dialogue to take place (*The Economist* 2000, 23–29). Even so, while the anarchists of Seattle (at the World Trade Organization [WTO] meetings in November 1999) were linking arms to form a human chain around the building, other representatives of civil society (in suits and ties) were attending the meetings officially as accredited representatives.

Seattle marked a turning point for civil society, the point at which criticisms of civil society previously confined to academic journals reached more populist audiences. Civil society had for a decade been organising globally, often targeting the very governments and institutions that had encouraged its growth. Ironically, these new global movements that thrived by organising over the Internet and forging cross-border alliances also made globalisation one of their primary targets. The rise of global civil society exposed the inherent tensions of its heterogeneity. The Hegelian stresses of the more aggressive civil society groups, unrestrained by the safety valves of a global political framework, inevitably gave room to a violent minority.

THE CIVIL SOCIETY BACKLASH

Following the riots in Seattle and Prague (at the World Bank/IMF meetings of September 2000), civil society now faces a more sceptical and questioning world. The realisation of the limits of civil society has turned into a discussion of whether it might even be a cause of harm. This backlash, led by both established academics as well as fervently pro-liberalisation/globalisation journals like *The Economist* (Carrothers 1999–2000, 18–25; *The Economist* 2000, 23–29), has focused on questions of accountability and legitimacy (for an NGO response, see Bullard 2000). *The Economist* has argued that problems in both areas combined to make civil society less responsible and to question its moral right to speak on behalf of the people.

The legitimacy issue has been particularly acute for governments in developing countries, who have sometimes felt marginalised by the influence that civil society can wield. Should not elected governments (where they exist) be the primary voice for citizens of the developing countries? In truth, civil society is unusual in that it largely establishes its own governance structures, appoints its own boards, and claims legitimacy based on its aims rather than on any inherent attribute.

Ultimately, this is the luxury of a movement that remains more accountable for its fund-raising and its expenditure than for pronouncements that it will never need to risk implementing. The accountability gap has led even the strongest advocates for civil society to call for serious change. Alan Fowler, in a document prepared for the UN in 2000, touches on a number of areas that NGOs need to address to better connect with underlying society. He concludes:

> It is incorrect to assume that forces that create poverty, exclusion and injustice exist only in governments, public policies and market institutions. They lie within civil society as well. In other words, civil society encompasses contending power relations and group interests that can both advance and impede poverty reduction, equity, inclusion, justice and other social development objectives (Fowler 2000, 6–7).

Michael Edwards, a theorist key to the modern civil society movement and now director of the civil society and governance programme at the Ford Foundation, has suggested a series of reforms. His proposals include limiting the aid that can be directed through rich-country NGOs and introducing new codes of conduct for CSOs, effectively creating a certification for those deemed accountable (Edwards 2000).

Civil society exposed itself to criticism, allowing its own legitimacy to be challenged by realising only late in the day that its inclusion by governments and international bodies was not just an act of generosity. The World Bank, WTO, and IMF have been under increasing pressure to make themselves accountable to the people most directly affected by their activities, particularly the world's poor. In lieu of consulting directly with these constituencies, multilateral development institutions have seen NGOs as a useful substitute for listening to the communities and families at the grassroots.[5] NGOs thus serve as a labour-saving device, fuelled by their own tendency to identify with the people they claim to represent.

Currently, pressure is growing for governments and institutions to cut out the civil society "middlemen" and consult more directly with the social groups affected by change. The World Bank led the way in this change when at the end of the 1990s it commissioned the respected academic Robert Chambers to work with a team in surveying views of the poor in 60 countries.[6] The results were widely considered to be ground-breaking and certainly surprised many in the bank with the quality of the insights produced. This approach now needs to be institutionalised as an ongoing, continuous part of the decision-making framework within the bank.

Despite these innovations at the World Bank, doors of major institutions are likely to stay firmly open to at least some civil society groups. But the fact that major global institutions treat different NGOs differently has led to suggestions from influential NGO advocacy groups that these institutions are following a tried and true strategy of divide and rule. The goal is simple: to split civil society into "good" and "bad," "civil" and "uncivil." The "good" are those who accept the overall direction of globalisation . . . and behave nicely when they are invited to meet with the rich and powerful. The "bad" are those who don't (Bullard 2000).

Whatever the strategy of the UN, World Bank, IMF, and WTO toward civil society, experience suggests that the brush of civil society is simply too broad to produce anything coherent en masse. Amongst the squabbling and often contradictory voices of international environmental, developmental, human rights, and other groups, the voices of real grassroots movements from poor countries are often drowned out. Indeed, the small-issue focus of NGOs that made de Tocqueville see them as such a constructive part of democratic society is also the problem that makes it difficult for such NGOs to see the wider picture involved. NGOs tend to view the world by "scaling up" their own areas of expertise, usually leading to a lack of appreciation of the macro environment by which their own and everybody else's issues are shaped.[7]

CIVIL SOCIETY AND BUILDING HEAVENS

The idea that civil society needs in some way to be reformed reflects the Hegelian belief that civil society should be placed within a framework that regulates its most competitive and destructive forces. Civil society has become hugely diverse. If we take the development sector alone (leaving aside even related areas such as the environment), the range is from local community groups and service providers in the South, to large Southern NGOs, international and Northern groups, to emerging global players.

Groups seeking to transform the world village by village in the South can be affected by the proliferation of similar groups, and it can become harder to translate micro-scale, incremental change in the absence of an effective referee (usually the state) who can identify best practice and encourage its replication. The work of those who also aim to achieve change through influence and advocacy has become more complicated and more competitive. Today, countless voices seek to influence the practices of governments in the South, donors in the North, and intergovernmental agencies such as the World Bank and IMF.

We have also seen that the activist work of civil society, bringing practical change directly through projects and community work, can create social and developmental problems of its own, such as gap filling and state erosion. It is difficult not to conclude that, in the final analysis, civil society is not well placed to be the architect of a radically new vision of the world. This does not mean, however, that civil society is not building something better than we have today. Many small changes can transform our world, and certainly the negative should not cause us to lose sight of the de Tocquevillian positives. Civil society plays an important role as a means for people to articulate their concerns and lobby for social and political change. The violence of Seattle and Prague does not outweigh the huge good that civil society achieves in the developing and developed worlds, both politically and in direct provision of services to the poor.

Seattle and Prague simply remind us that civil society, like politics, is an imperfect and fallible construct of the modern world. When we look at the myriad protest groups that gathered in those cities to demonstrate, we are reminded that civil society provides an outlet for the deep human need to coalesce around causes that give identity and meaning. Anarchist groups, even violent anarchist groups, offer a form of community and affirmation that some will find appealing. None of us should be surprised by these dynamics. Civil society is, after all, not simply about activity, it is also about identity. Indeed, the search for identity within associative groups is not the exception; it has become the norm.

This aspect of civil society was first identified by J. N. Figgis, who played a seminal role in the development of both modern political theory and political theology. Figgis, writing in the years surrounding the First World War, noted that the atomisation of modern industrial society was not causing the alienation of humans, in a Marxist sense, but was leading rather to a search for new community. For Figgis, the golf club was the symbol of the new trend, and he envisaged a society emerging from a host of new associations (Nicholls 1994; Figgis 1910). The title of this chapter reflects the continuation of this trend, for as Manuel Castells has said, civil society is better at providing havens than heavens (Castells 1998, 64).

Castells may have a point, at least when it comes to civil society and the building of heavens. Heterogeneity and the lack of accountability of civil society, particularly when coupled to weak political contexts, create obstacles to it playing a fundamentally transforming role. This does not mean that positive change is not brought about, but rather that such transformation occurs "brick by brick." The anti-slavery movement, Jubilee 2000, and the Grameen Bank are good reminders that civil society has achieved much.

Nevertheless, these changes occur only incrementally. NGOs, as Giddens has reminded us, rely firmly on government (not the market) as the final agent of execution (Giddens 1999, 47–49). Focusing on the activist role of civil society is only part of the picture. It is equally important, if we want to understand the role of civil society in achieving social change, to look at identity.

BUILDING HAVENS?

To understand the full significance of civil society, we must recognise the truth encapsulated in the perspective of Figgis and Castells. Both argue that civil society is very much about our associational lives, which often revolve as much around our need for community and identity as around our altruistic aspirations. Put simply, everybody needs a haven sometime. In many Western countries this need has been amply demonstrated by the expansion of membership organisations. There is now a society, club, or association for everyone.

The middle strata of society flock to these groups. In my own country the largest non-religious mass membership movement is not a political party or a Trades

Union, or a radical environmental group; it has no declared aims for social transformation. It is the Royal Society for the Protection of Birds, an organisation that boasts nearly 2.5 million adult Britons as members. By associating with others of common interests, people form a sort of community and nurture a part of their identity.

Amartya Sen has recently pushed the issue of identity in the development process back onto the agenda. He has called for development economists, including those at institutions such as the World Bank, to recognise the critical importance of identity in shaping the decisions that people make in the South. The ability of civil society to create new identities for us through community, whether we are rich or poor, is in little doubt (Sen 2000). We associate with others almost instinctively when we discover new interests, talents, or concerns. The key to encouraging this change has been, in part, technological. The Internet chat rooms and e-mail lists allow us to go beyond Figgis's golf club into communities that may cover small population segments, but segments that nevertheless spread across the globe – although it would be wrong to see the changes as entirely technological (see Keck and Sikkink 1998).

The globalisation of civil society also enables groups to be in frequent contact – thus the great human chains that surrounded the G-7 in Prague or the Battle for Seattle. But as civil society mushrooms around a wider range of identities and concerns, civil society itself becomes ever more vast, diverse, and dissipated. The almost limitless growth of civil society ultimately mitigates against unified action. Equally, the growth of civil society contributes to a competition of voices that makes the early movements for social change (the anti-slavery society) appear to have been greatly blessed by a relatively free field. Even more than in the last two decades, the issue-centred groups of the future are likely to compete with innumerable others, all seeking change.

FROM HAVENS TO HEAVENS

Civil society therefore may play a role of social stability as it offers identity and community. While some CSOs, like the Royal Society for the Protection of Birds, have no great social vision, others seek to advance causes that would change society, and civil society invariably requires some form of government to achieve those changes. It was, for example, the state that actually abolished slavery, enforced temperance, and lowered third-world debt. To force or persuade the state to act, civil society relies either on the strength of its argument or on the power of public opinion. In effect, civil society is part of a bigger process, often the initiator of change but rarely the agent that actually implements and completes the process.

Can civil society move beyond providing identity, even beyond its activist role, towards something more fundamentally transformational? Can civil society save the world? Clearly, it depends on what kind of salvation we are seeking. If we see the world as having fundamental failings that require radical transformation, then the answer would seem to be no. Civil society is neither suited to the task nor unified on the issue of what such change would look like or mean. The best we can hope for is that it might make the world a better place gradually – something that it certainly does, community by community, project by project, in the developing world. To highlight its incremental nature is not to denigrate civil society. Indeed, the twin role of stability and social action makes civil society an invaluable part of any nation.

A second question is whether, even if civil society cannot save the world in the sense of fundamental transformation, can it at least save the world from itself? Can civil society, as a source of community, be an alternative to Coleridge's clerisy, providing social permanence that counterbalances eroding forces of market-induced change?

In this regard, civil society as provider of havens certainly has a role. Civil society can break down traditional and particularly primordial identities. Civil society can give voice to altruism, to personal creativity and interests. Within the framework of civil society, we can relax, or we can energise ourselves by committing to a cause. The parallels with Coleridge's clerisy are there, albeit without the Christian overtones he would have wished.

AND SAVING THE WORLD?

But is saving the world from itself enough, if we believe that radical change is needed? Here we must determine our ultimate goals. If Christians believe that the world needs saving in a radically transformational way, then civil society does not let the church off the hook. The Great Commission of Matthew's Gospel requires much greater responsibility in modelling and proclaiming the kingdom than just gaining individual souls. Saving the world certainly means addressing structural and systemic sin.

Does the world need saving? The unavoidable answer to the question of whether our current world is as Jesus Christ would want it to be must be no. Integral to this situation is the failure of our world to embrace a biblical sense of justice, understood here as a commitment within our polities to do unto others as we would have them do unto us. In today's world this might well mean a commitment to have the children of others grow up with as many opportunities, services, and resources as our own.

These injunctions point us to the issue of equality. Paul Tillich, in *Love, Power, and Justice,* suggests that love is made active in the social sphere through creative justice. Integral to Tillich's perception of justice is the notion of equality. Equality for Christians is not some cold, legal issue but rather an appreciation of the equality of God's love. Equality is therefore one of a number of justice issues that resonates deeply with the Christian message. We each have an equal vested interest in this joint venture called society, namely, our life and future. As Tillich states, no society can hope to achieve perfect equality economically and socially, but we can ask hard questions about whether our own polities and our wider world show any semblance of an equality of value (Tillich 1960, 57–71).

As an evangelical, I take the view that Genesis is true. God really did give the world equally to all humankind. He did not parcel it up, 80 per cent for the richest

20 per cent of the people and 20 per cent for the rest. The idea of jubilee, and the humane legislation of Deuteronomy 24:10 onwards, is difficult to reconcile with a world in which a half-dozen people hold greater wealth than the poorest 40 countries (UNDP 1998).

Such global inequality is only one symptom of a world that has lost touch with biblical principles of justice, but it is an illustrative one. In 1960 the gross domestic product in the richest 20 countries was 18 times that of the poorest 20; today it is 37 times greater. During the same period the proportion of our wealth spent on development has more than halved, and the quality of that expenditure has been doubtful (World Bank 1991, 50–51). Such inequalities sit uncomfortably in light of the harsh words of Amos or Zephaniah, and they look indefensible in the light of the injunction that there "must be no poor amongst you" (Deut. 15:4). In a world in which God's provision is sufficient for all, poverty is a damaging act of aggression by the rich against the poor. If divided equally, global wealth would put all people into the World Bank's middle-income category for countries. The evidence is that better wealth distribution actually accelerates overall economic growth by creating a better spread of demand (see Whaites et al. 1999).

N. T. Wright reminds us that Jesus's proclamation of the kingdom was real, practical, and intensely political (Wright 1996, 502–7, 592–611). The idea that the kingdom of Jesus must be concerned for justice in the here and now has, after all, been the basis for numerous traditions of political theology. In the last century F. D. Maurice, Henry Scott-Holland, and Charles Gore pointed to the continuing conflict between Christian principles and social injustice. In 1908 Bishop Gore called the church to penitence,

> a tremendous act of penitence for having failed so long and on so wide a scale to behave as the champion of the oppressed and the weak . . . for having so often been on the wrong side. And the penitence must lead to reparation while there is yet time, ere the well-merited judgements of God take all weapons of social influence out of our hands (Gore 1908, 6).

In effect, we have a problem, for the world does need saving – politically, socially, economically, and spiritually. How would a better world look? We could start by saying that it would model the kingdom through systemic justice rather than injustice, and that by modelling the kingdom it would point its citizens inescapably towards a realisation of Christ as Lord, saviour, and friend. In essence, a more Christian society would promote Christ and, in the process, be just in its treatment of the poor. If we can visualise such a world, we must also face up to the challenge of Gore's comments on the need for penitence on the part of the church: is the church up to the job?

CAN THE CHURCH SAVE THE WORLD?

Frank Field brings a similar discussion of social change back down to earth by reminding us that only God can save the world – before describing Christ's turning of that world upside down by taking the side of a tradition clearly suspicious of both wealth and power (Field 1987, 38–53). This reminds us that ultimately saving the world is a question of bringing it fully under God's influence. Rarely since the demise of the Christendom movement in the 1940s has the idea of polities being brought to submit to Christian principles been popular – it fits badly with the rampant secularism of the post-war years. The concept is simply that in Christendom "the world is no longer alien, but is seeking to conduct its secular affairs in the power of that life of which the church is the channel and trustee" (Temple 1917, 326).

William Temple believed that, to a degree, this could be brought closer by Christians coalescing around points of political unity. In effect, the church might be well placed to offer a unified voice representing a large (and politically powerful) segment of society. His view was centred on addressing issues of poverty. He called on the church to meet "men where they are," meaning that if we have no answers to the evils of which humans are conscious, then we are irrelevant. As a passionate proponent of the relevance of Christ to all aspects of human life (and an equally passionate advocate of personal evangelism) he stated:

> The church as witness to the Word of God must proclaim the divine law for man and the divine judgement. It may be that this is what the world now chiefly needs from it. That witness, like the message of the prophets, involves direct intervention in the political sphere (Temple 1943, 8).

As Archbishop of Canterbury, Temple modelled this idea, using his position to push the government of his day towards his vision of greater social justice. Temple marked a willingness of Christian leaders to use profile and privilege to speak out precisely for those who would otherwise be without a voice – not the church itself, nor Christians, nor middle England/middle-America, but rather the poor.

The Church's Problem

The problem, however, is that Temple's vision, despite his belief that it could be shared by all Christians, would not in reality be universally shared. The Bible-based call for social justice of Scott-Holland and Gore is, after all, primarily a European tradition that is ill at ease with the political objectives of some Christian lobby groups, particularly in the United States (Nelson 1991, chap. 7). If civil society is too fragmented to achieve such fundamental social change, can we honestly say, despite the call of Temple, that the church is any better placed?

The weaknesses of civil society described above revolve around its heterogeneity, lack of unified vision, and incremental approach to change. A similar review of the church would perhaps be at least as pessimistic, if not more so. The body of Christ suffers from as many divisions of opinion as any large population group (and often seems to generate more than its fair share). Politically, therefore, the lack of a unifying Christian agenda does weaken the churches' ability to play a truly transformational role. In some contexts we see churches preoccupied with a narrow set of personal moral issues. We also see churches that have firmly bought into a post-Enlightenment, neo-liberal economic worldview in which Adam Smith's voice has become the dominant prophetic voice. Elsewhere there are churches that accept secularisation and the marginalisation of the church in social and political life as a welcome sign of tolerance and liberalism. In its worst forms the church has become little more than an adjunct to other philosophies, particularly national-ism – a medium for political leaders to communicate with the masses (Whaites et al. 1999).

For Christians concerned with fundamental social change, the church in its in-stitutional and broader sense could be as unwieldy and problematic as civil soci-ety. Perhaps not surprisingly, this means that historical experience shows that, for Christians, incremental change has also traditionally been the more immediately viable route. Hence we have seen a long-standing marriage of civil society with a Christian agenda for change. It should be no surprise that Christians have played a prominent role in the anti-slavery movement, factory reform, the temperance move-ment, the Trades Union Movement in Europe, and, more recently, in establishing NGOs. In effect, civil society is a useful tool or vehicle through which Christians can promote their vision for social change.

Christians will therefore be amongst the competing voices of civil society, in-deed often contradicting one another. They may tend towards certain issue areas (roughly 25 per cent of international development NGOs are faith based) but will not necessarily work together in a co-ordinated approach. I have served in numer-ous NGO coalitions in which Christian NGOs have been at loggerheads with one another, while at the same time allied to secular counterparts. I have also been through the experience of trying to form an advocacy coalition of Christian agen-cies, a process that took 12 NGOs approximately 18 months to negotiate.

Where working together is concerned, Christian NGOs are as prone to schism as non-Christian ones. All NGOs need to go through a learning process based on the hard knocks of history before discovering what it takes to change the world. I have argued that all NGOs have an implicit or explicit ideology that drives their style and operational aims (Whaites 1999). We must be realistic enough to under-stand that Christian civil society may not necessarily pursue distinctively or uniquely Christian ideology or aims.

Conclusion – Is it Enough?

Civil society, far from saving the world in an active, transformational sense, can, in my view, only achieve slow, incremental change. This is very positive in itself, but not the stuff to save the world. Civil society has also served a role as a new source of community and identity. In this sense it has become a force for perma-nence, an alternative clerisy, balancing the breakneck social change wrought by dy-namic forces of the market and post-industrial culture. But if civil society is better at building havens than heavens, can the church do better? Because fault lines within civil society run as deeply as they do within the church, the heterogeneity of both mitigates against either fully leveraging its potential influence in the political and economic spheres.

Yet the challenge of fundamental change remains, a challenge from which Christians should not walk away. Some principles are intrinsic to achieving significant social transformation towards justice goals. The first of these principles for Christians is that God is bigger than the political and economic. Garvie reminds us that

> the spheres of economics and politics cannot be regarded as self-enclosed and self-sufficient, so autonomous as not to be subject to the moral law of God. . . . In both these spheres there has entered so much sin, so much defiance of and disobedience to the mind of Christ that the church in His name is justified in pronouncing a moral condemnation, and is called to offer in both the means of salvation. When we have done that we must confront the widely-spread opinion that for the world's ills there is no balm in Gilead, no Physician there, that Christianity has no adequate, effective remedy for social ills (Garvie 1934, 11).

The second of these basic principles is that neither civil society nor the church is the implementer of social, political, and economic change (although their work in social provision is valuable). Rather, they initiate in the hope that the state will complete. The state, therefore, should be a more significant focus for our discussion, for it is by refocusing the resources and power of government that change is achieved. The state should be seen as a vehicle, or tool, by which to achieve a more just society. Fundamental social change, as part and parcel of saving the world, therefore means harnessing national governments and global multilateral institutions.

The third basic principle is that the field of world salvation is very crowded, and therefore organisation is all important. Civil society cannot speak with a single voice because its mushrooming size has multiplied its heterogeneity. The church itself is no more unified, and therefore trying to leverage scale is unlikely to succeed. Instead, the key for Christians is to organise well around clear messages and be sure of the targets involved. For some, this will mean being very efficient in the civil society purpose of incremental change. Jubilee 2000 has had tremendous impact in a few short years, largely because its support was from politically powerful social groups that mobilised around very clear aims.

Christians and Christian NGOs should continue to chip away at the task of building a better world. Many small steps do amount to great journeys. Even so, if Christians want to see more radical change, and sooner, they must be willing to target government itself as the vehicle for the change that is needed. First, of course, as Anthony Giddens says from a secular perspective, "we need to know what society we would like to create and concrete means to achieve it" (Giddens 1999, 2). Charles Gore believed change would come through small groups of Christians, modelled on the early church, working towards focused goals (Gore 1908, 274–89). He went so far as to say of the early church that "in the everlasting opposition of rich and poor, beyond all possibility of question, it ranked and spoke for, the poor" (ibid., 278).

Gore's vision of Christians engaging in political life in a focused and determined way is a reminder of the role of political society asserted by Alfred Stepan and his Latin American colleagues. Christians must not look at civil society only as a tool for social change but must also look beyond it to those groups that move in and out of formal political power as the means to achieve social aims.

NOTES

[1] Alec Vidler's classic treatise on the impact of these changes on the church explores many of the pressures produced by these changes (*The Church in an Age of Revolution* [London: Penguin, 1971]).

[2] By the 1750s Britain had an executive drawn from its Parliament, a Bill of Rights, independent judiciary, and rule of law, making possible the emergence of situations in which policy change arose from popular demand, sometimes against powerful vested interests. The emergence at the end of the eighteenth century of a strong independent media and also what amounted to a two-party system aided the process of popular political organisation. Government decisions to use the Royal Navy against the slave trade in the early 1800s and the abolition of slavery in all British territories by the 1830s was testimony to the newfound power of the popular conscience.

[3] The Anti-Corn Law League was the world's first truly modern political pressure group. It brought together largely urban industrial interests to seek the removal of long-standing legislation that protected domestically grown wheat, thereby raising the cost of food for the rapidly expanding industrial workforce. The league was formed in 1838 and rapidly became a movement for free trade. Its proponents travelled the country speaking to large audiences on the benefits of free trade, even leading to the building of "free trade halls" in which meetings could be held. By the end of the 1840s the movement had gained its objectives but had also achieved fundamental change in the political and economic philosophy of the country. Perhaps the best-known legacy of the movement (apart from the neo-liberal schools of economics that owe much to it) is *The Economist* magazine, established as a voice for the free trade movement (see Kenneth O. Morgan, ed., *Oxford History of Britain* [Oxford: Oxford University Press, 1998], 497)

[4] The Narmada Dam campaign brings together local communities affected by a large-scale dam project in India, while the Grameen Bank in Bangladesh has become the "poster child" of the micro-finance movement. Brazil's Landless Peasants Movement continues to work in behalf of the rural poor in a country with one of the middle-income world's worst Gini coefficients (a measure of health inequalities).

[5] This includes both rich-country-based NGOs and also those many poor-country NGOs that are staffed by the articulate, educated, and urban middle class with whom the institutions are able to engage easily.

[6] Chamber's study has led to a three-volume series (*Can Anyone Hear Us?, Crying Out for Change,* and *From Many Lands*). See especially Deepa Narayan, Robert Chambers, Meerah K. Shah, and Patti Petesch, *Crying Out for Change* (Washington, D.C.: World Bank, 2000).

[7] Michael Edwards and David Hulme edited a volume of essays on this theme based on the first Manchester Conference, "Scaling-up NGO Impacts: Learning from Experience,"

SCF and the University of Manchester, January 1992. The book is entitled *Making a Difference: NGOs and Development in a Changing World* (London: Earthscan/SCF, 1992). I was struck by the impact of scaling up on policy recommendations when visiting the media room at the WTO Ministerial Meetings in Seattle in November 1999 (the infamous Battle for Seattle). The thousands of reports, leaflets, and briefings that had been left by NGOs in the media room were remarkably parochial, with seeing the complex area of trade only from their own specialist area perspective.

References

Avineri, Shlomo, and Avner de-Shalit, eds. 1992. *Communitarianism and Individualism.* Oxford: Oxford University Press.

Bayart, Jean Francois. 1993. *The State in Africa: The Politics of the Belly.* London: Longman.

Bayart, Jean Francois, Stephen Ellis, and Beatrice Hibous. 1999. *The Criminalisation of the State in Africa.* Bloomington, Ind.: Indiana University Press.

Beer, Samuel H. 1982. *Britain Against Itself: The Political Contradictions of Collectivism.* London: W. W. Norton.

Blair, Harry. 1997. "Donors, Democratisation, and Civil Society: Relating Theory to Practice." In *NGOs, States, and Donors – Too Close for Comfort*, edited by M. Edwards and D. Hulme, 23–42. New York: St. Martins; London: MacMillan.

Bullard, Nicola. 2000. "It's Time for 'Uncivil' Society to Act." In *Focus on Trade* 47 (March). Available online on the Focus on Trade website.

Cannon, Christy. 2000. "NGOs and the State: A Case-Study for Uganda." Reprinted in *Development, NGOs, and Civil Society*, a Development in Practice Reader, edited by D. Eade. Oxford: Oxfam Books. Books.

Carrothers, Thomas. 1999. *Aiding Democracy Abroad: The Learning Curve.* Washington, D.C.: Carnegie Endowment.

———. 1999–2000. "Civil Society." In *Foreign Policy* (winter): 18–25.

Castells, Manuel. 1998. *The Power of Identity.* Volume 2 of *The Information Age: Economy, Society, and Culture.* Oxford: Blackwell.

Chabal, Patrick, and Jean-Pascal Daloz. 1999. *Africa Works: Disorder as Political Instrument.* Oxford: James Currey.

Clapham, Christopher. 1996. *Africa and the International System.* Cambridge: Cambridge University Press.

Coleridge, Samuel Taylor. 1975. *On the Consitution of Church and State.* Vol. 10 of *The Collected Works of Samuel Taylor Coleridge.* Princeton, N.J.: Princeton University Press.

Deiniger, Klaus, and Lyn Squire. 1998. "New Ways of Looking at Old Issues: Inequality and Growth." *Journal of Development Economics* 57/2: 259–87.

Demant, V. A. 1936. *Christian Polity.* London: Faber and Faber.

———. 1939. *The Religious Prospect.* London: Frederick Muller Ltd.

Douma, Pyt. 1999. "Poverty, Conflict, and Development Interventions in Sub-Saharan Africa." Paper presented at Global Development Conference, Bonn, 5–8 December. Available online, multiple websites.

Economist, The. 2000 (23–29 September), 23–29.

Edwards, Michael. 1998. "Nailing the Jelly to the Wall: NGOs, Civil Society, and International Development." Paper produced for BOND (British Overseas NGOs for Development).

————. 2000. "Democratising Global Governance: Rights and Responsibilities of NGOs." London: The Foreign Policy Centre (June).

Edwards, Michael, and David Hulme, eds. 1995. *Non-governmental Organisation – Performance and Accountability, Beyond the Magic Bullet*. London: Earthscan/SCF.

Eliot, T. S. 1977. "Christianity and Culture" and "The Idea of Christian Society." In *Christianity and Culture*. San Diego, Calif.: Harvest Books.

Field, Frank. 1987. *The Politics of Paradise*. London: Collins.

Figgis, J.N. 1910. *The Gospel and Human Needs*. London: Longmans, Green, and Co.

Fowler, Alan. 2000. "Civil Society, NGDOs, and Social Development: Changing the Rules of the Game." United Nations Research Institute for Social Development (UNRISD). Occasional Paper no. 1 (January).

Garvie, A. E. 1934. *Can Christ Save Society?* London: Hodder & Stoughton.

Giddens, Anthony. 1999. *The Third Way*. London: Polity Press.

Gore, Charles. 1908. Paper for the Pan-Anglican Congress. CSU/Mowbray.

Griffin, Keith, and Amy Ickowitz. 1997 (November). "The Distribution of Wealth and the Pace of Development." Working Paper Series. UNDP (United Nations Development Programme). Available online at the UNDP website.

Islam, Iyanatul, and Anis Chowdhury. 1998. *Asia-Pacific Economies: A Survey*. London: Routledge.

Jefferies, Richard. 1993. "The State, Structural Adjustment, and Good Government in Africa." *The Journal of Commonwealth and Comparative Politics* 31: 1.

Jones, Sam. 1997. *Stolen Sovereignty: Globalisation and the Disempowerment of Africa*. Milton Keynes: World Vision UK.

Keane, John. 1988. *Democracy and Civil Society*. London: Verso.

————. 1998. *Civil Society: Old Images, New Visions*. Cambridge: Policy Press.

Keck, Margaret, and Kathryn Sikkink. 1998. *Activists Beyond Borders*. Ithaca, N.Y.: Cornell.

Kim, Kwan. 1997. "Income Distribution and Poverty: An Interregional Comparison." *World Development* 25/11 (November): 1909–24.

Leipziger, Danny M., and Vinod Thamas. 1993. *The Lessons of East Asia: An Overview of Country Experience*. Washington D.C.: World Bank.

Midgley, James. 1986. "Community Participation, the State, and Social Policy." In *Community Participation, Social Development, and the State*, edited by J. Midgley, H. Hall, and N. Hall. London: Methuen.

Migdal, Joel. 1988. *Strong Societies and Weak States: State Society Relations and State Capabilities in the Third World*. Princeton, N.J.: Princeton University Press.

Milanovic, Branko. 1999. "True World Income Distribution, 1988 and 1993: First Calculations Based on Household Surveys Alone." World Bank Policy Research Working Paper No. 2244. World Bank.

Nelson, Robert H. 1991. *Reaching for Heaven on Earth: The Theological Meaning of Economics*. Savage, Md: Littlefield Adams.

Nicholls, David. 1994. *The Pluralist State (The Political Ideas of J. N. Figgis and His Contemporaries)*. St. Antony's Series. Oxford.

OECD (Organisation for Economic Co-operation and Development)/DAC (Development Assistance Committee). 1995. *Participatory Development and Good Governance*. Paris: OECD/DAC.

O'Reilly, Siobhan. 1999. *The Contribution of Community Development To Peacebuilding*. Milton Keynes: World Vision UK.

Oxfam UK. 1995. *Former Yugoslavia: Towards a Durable Peace*. Oxford: Oxfam.

Peiris, G. H. 1999. "Poverty, Development, and Conflict in South Asia." Paper presented at Global Development Conference, Bonn, 5–8 December. Available online, multiple websites.

Robinson, Mark. 1993. *Governance, Democracy, and Conditionality: What Role for NGOs?* Oxford: INTRAC (The International NGO Training and Research Centre).

———. 1995. "Strengthening Civil Society in Africa: The Role of Foreign Political Aid." *IDS [Institute of Development Studies] Bulletin* 26/2.

Rodrik, Dani. 1999. "Democracies Pay Higher Wages." *Quarterly Journal of Economics* 114/3 (August): 707–38.

Sen, Amartya. 2000. *Freedom, Rationality and Social Choice*. Oxford: Oxford University Press.

Stepan, Alfred. 1988. *Rethinking Military Politics: Brazil and the Southern Cone*. Princeton, N.J.: Princeton University Press.

Temple, William. 1917. *Mens Creatix*. London: MacMillan.

———. 1943. *Social Witness and Evangelism*. London: The Epworth Press.

Tillich, Paul. 1960. *Love, Power, and Justice*. Oxford: Oxford University Press.

Tocqueville, Alexis de. 1835/40. *Democracy in America*. Volumes 1 and 2.

UK Department for International Development. 1997. "UK White Paper on International Development." London: UK Department for International Development.

UNDP (United Nations Development Programme). 1998. *Human Development Report*. New York: UNDP.

Vidler, Alec. 1971. *The Church in an Age of Revolution*. London: Penguin.

Whaites, Alan. 1995. "The State and Civil Society in Pakistan." In *Contemporary South Asia* 4/3: 229–54.

———. 1999. "Pursuing Partnership: World Vision and the Ideology of Development – A Case Study." *Development in Practice* 9/4 (August).

———. 2000a. "Conflict, Repression, and Politics: Dare NGOs Hope to Do Any Good?" In *Complex Humanitarian Emergencies: Lessons from Practitioners*, edited by M. Janz and J. Slead. Monrovia, California: World Vision Publications.

———. 2000b. "Let's Get Civil Society Straight: NGOs, the State, and Political Theory." In *Development, NGOs, and Civil Society*, a Development in Practice Reader, edited by D. Eade. Oxford: Oxfam Books.

Whaites, Alan, and Steve Commins. 1998. "Who Will Bail Out the Poor? The Impact of the East Asian Economic Crisis." Paper delivered to the Secretary of State for International Development, East Asian Crisis Seminar, 15 July, London. Available online at the World Bank websight.

Whaites, Alan, et al. 1999. *Urgent Issues for the New Millennium*. Monrovia, Calif.: World Vision Publications.

World Bank. 1991. *The World Development Report: Poverty*. Oxford: Oxford University Press.

———. 1995. "Equity and Growth in Developing Countries: Old and New Perspectives on the Policy Issues." World Bank Policy Research Working Paper No. 1563.

———. 1997. *Everyone's Miracle?* Washington, D.C.: World Bank.

World Bank/OUP. 1993. *The East Asian Miracle: Economic Growth and Public Policy*. New York: World Bank.

Wright, N. T. 1996. *Jesus and the Victory of God*. London: SPCK.

8

RELIGIOUS TRANSITIONS AND CIVIL SOCIETY IN LATIN AMERICA

Samuel Escobar

The post-Marxist era in Latin America coincided with a renewed general acceptance of democracy as the best form of government and of civil society as an important component of democracy. During the decade of the 1980s several military governments came to an end, and there was a general popular reaction against authoritarianism. Most notably in large and influential countries such as Brazil, Argentina, and Chile, civil movements emerged that were different from the popular mobilisations of the 1960s and 1970s. In those earlier decades the mobilisation of people through labour unions, political parties, or state-sponsored populism was conceived as the only way to involve the average citizen in public life. Long-term revolutionary projects and socialist dreams were the context of those movements. It was the belief that efforts such as "self-help" development projects, self-built housing, consumer or producer co-operatives, or community health care were "a piece meal approach (that) would not make a serious impression on poverty or social inequality" (Lehmann 1990, 151). These diverse forms of popular mobilisation failed both because authoritarianism undermined their basis and eliminated or persecuted their leaders, and also because of the collapse of real socialism in Europe. As Lehmann aptly describes:

> So, self-management, no longer presenting itself as a cosmetic façade or as a disguised form of government manipulation, appears in a more favorable light, untainted by official patronage. This forms part of a broader canvas in which the idea of the rebirth of civil society takes a prominent place, and it is an idea which has undermined many long-standing assumptions of radical thought (Lehmann 1990, 151).

This rediscovery of civil society as well as a new awareness about the decisive importance of religion for social and political life are two of the global trends that social scientists and observers of all kinds are now exploring in depth in Latin America. These trends are a challenge and an opportunity for Christian thinkers who are trying to understand the past and present history of Christian churches in this region in order to find better and more relevant ways of being witnesses to the gospel of Jesus Christ. In the 1960s and 1970s very few social scientists or political analysts considered Christian responses to human needs to be items worthy of their attention, for it was commonly thought that Christian action did not have any real relevance for the future of Latin American societies. The picture subsequently changed significantly for three reasons. First, the overwhelming nature of poverty and under-development made it evident that the state is incapable of addressing the need unless the whole of society also takes part in the struggle for survival and justice. Moreover, the bureaucratic inefficiency of state agencies contrasts with the efficiency and good stewardship of many religiously motivated NGOs, a reality that has caught the attention of international development agencies. Second, analysts of the relationship between religious life and political realities in Latin America agree that the reappearance of the notion of civil society owes much to the rise of new citizenship movements that began by questioning military authoritarianism (Comblin 1998; Mainwaring 1986). Many of these movements were inspired or initiated by progressive sectors within the Christian churches. Third, free from the ideological straitjacket of simplistic Marxism, social scientists are now approaching religious life and institutions from a different perspective, one that allows them to understand better the massive amount of data available about the relationship between church and society in Latin America.

The religious commitment of both the Catholic majority and the Protestant minorities has fostered the kind of active participation in the public arena that is at the core of what today is called civil society in Latin America. This new development must be understood within a long-term perspective that evolved through three distinct phases: First, spurred by the presence of Protestant minorities within the context of modernisation, a long process of religious transformation developed during the twentieth century; second, the social activism of Christians linked to revolution and liberation movements connected with the Vatican II *aggiornamento* of Roman Catholicism and its impact on Latin American Catholics; and third, the repercussions in Latin America of the sudden and profound changes in Eastern Europe, symbolised by the fall of the Berlin Wall in 1989, left a profound vacuum among leftist intellectuals and political parties that claimed to represent the poor and oppressed. Social and political leaders were unable to understand the social and religious dynamism boiling at the grassroots level during the decade of the 1980s. During this latter period four long-standing characteristics of Latin American politics seemed to be in the process of waning away; populism, academic Marxism, militarism, and protected economies with four digit inflation gave way to a modernisation process characterised by administrative reforms of the state, elected governments, ideological uncertainty, and openness to market economies. As a result, societies had to change, and churches had to change too.

My perspective is that of a member of a religious minority, an evangelical, in a society that has moved rather slowly towards acceptance of religious pluralism. This minority status does not imply that physical violence has been used as a means of coercion to force acceptance of the majority religious view, as happened in the days of the Spanish Inquisition or in the violent persecution of Protestants in Colombia in the 1950s. Nevertheless, evangelicals still face social discrimination.

For instance, in the official documents of the Roman Catholic hierarchy, numerical growth of Protestantism in Latin America, especially in its popular forms, has not been accepted as a legitimate movement towards more pluralistic societies. Anyone familiar with the daily life and action of NGOs in the fields of aid and development knows that whenever "the church" is mentioned or called to the scene, most government officials and the media actually mean the Roman Catholic Church, and this in spite of the fact that Protestants have been active and efficient in those fields for many decades. Under the Reagan administration in the United States, for example, the 1983–84 budget of the U.S. Agency for International Development (USAID) for development in Latin America was US$342 million, of which US$264 million went to Catholic Relief Services (77 per cent) and a meagre US$31 million went to eight evangelical agencies (Stoll 1990, 271). It is still an uphill battle for religious minorities to overcome restrictive and exclusive policies from the dominant religious force in Latin American societies.

On the other hand, it is now generally accepted that the presence of Protestant minorities was an important factor at key points in the movement of Latin American countries towards democratisation and modernisation. The ecclesial practice of Protestants in the daily life of their churches as well as the institutions they created were a form of civil society action at a time in which the state and its institutions were dominated by Catholicism. Protestants from a variety of denominational backgrounds adopted a prophetic but peaceful questioning of the status quo that may be described as an Anabaptist stance when they determined their role in society (Escobar 1975). They also developed their own alternative educational, medical, and relief and development institutions that became free associative and voluntary organisations of civil society. The social evolution of Latin America imposed new social and theological agendas for both Protestants and Catholics, and in both camps church leaders and theologians have tried to interpret critically the role of their churches in society and to determine new agendas for missionaries and pastors. Protestant minorities in particular have a critical and constructive role to play in their societies, but they must relate the wealth of their theological and institutional heritage to the changing situations these societies face. They must also be willing to change, for the challenge to develop viable nations in the context of the new global realities will require something new, the concerted effort of all Christians. Christian action and teaching can provide inspiration and motivation for activism in civil society, legitimation or delegitimation of political positions and regimes, and even active mediation in social conflicts (Garreton 1989). To understand how Latin American Christians might find their role in civil society, it is essential to gain clarity about the ways in which the various traditions of Christianity have interacted with Latin America's social history.

CONTRASTING REALITIES AND CONCEPTS

The first point to be established in a discussion about civil society in Latin America is that the concept is understood quite differently than it is in the United States. The intellectual sources of the concept, as well as the political experiences in Latin America, are clearly different from those in the Anglo-Saxon world, where the discussion about civil society has flourished in recent years. It is not out of place to remember at this point – as David Martin has reminded us – that "what happens now in Puerto Rico, or Brazil or the Philippines by way of mutations in culture and especially in religious consciousness, takes place within frames established in the long clash of 'Anglo' culture with Hispanic (or Lusitanian) civilization" (Martin 1989, 9). The centuries old confrontation between the Iberian and the Anglo-Saxon worldviews and ways of life still finds expression in the religious and political fields today. Howard Wiarda's chapter herein offers a helpful outline of contrasts between these two worldviews in relation to political concepts and practices. A clear example of these contrasting realities and discourses is that in the religious experience of North America there is no tradition of an established church. In Latin America, on the other hand, the relationship between religion and the social order is always perceived through the lens and the mental habits provided by the memory of almost five centuries of an established church. This contrast becomes evident in such areas as the role of volunteerism in churches, the giving habits of the faithful, and existing channels for social initiatives motivated by religious faith.

Comblin warns us that the concept of civil society is always presented within the framework of an overall system, and that many of the predominant systems and theories in Europe and North America may not be applicable or relevant to Latin American society. He then offers his own concept: "We take civil society to be simply the totality of relationships between citizens, whether institutionalized or not, in so far as they are independent of the state and the market" (in Comblin 1998, 134). This definition refers not only to a totality of relationships independent from the state but also claims independence from the market. Comblin is critical of the Iberian conquest to the point of stating that Latin America was born without a civil society, because the conquerors intentionally established a feudal order in which power was not understood to emanate from the people. There was thus no room for participation, a key attribute of civil society. When nation states developed after independence, this underlying structure remained. The state continued to be manipulated by an elite that used it for its own benefit. Though civil movements at different historical moments have made significant strides towards a participatory democracy, they frequently were co-opted by the elites, who were able to manipulate popular movements. For Comblin:

> Clientelism is still thriving: the elites think that the government is there to serve their private interests, and they choose public officials to carry out their orders. They make no distinction between public good and private good. They plunder the state as though it existed to solve the financial problems of their companies, to finance works on their properties, to nourish their political followers with favors and positions (Comblin 1998, 127).

These powerful elites were also able to adapt quickly to the new global situation. Comblin continues, "At the moment they have enthusiastically gone over to the privatization ideology; in it they have discovered a new way to appropriate public property for themselves" (ibid.).

There are important Latin American nuances affecting how the concept of civil society as a reality independent from the state is understood. This is evident, for instance, in a recent study by Nicola Miller about intellectuals and the question of national identity in Latin America. She traces the origin of the concept of civil society and the important role of Antonio Gramsci's ideas as a source for the development of a discussion that has been parallel but not equivalent to the one taking place in North America. Marx had attacked as fraudulent the concept of civil society "as an economic sphere separate from and in opposition to the state" (Miller 1999, 16). Lenin's contextualisation of Marxism in Russia emphasised the need for an overwhelmingly powerful state that after revolution could build a just and happy nation. Communist parties around the world adopted Leninist ideas, and their ideology found special receptivity in societies and cultures that had experienced centralised, authoritarian rule for many years, as had certainly been the case in Latin America. In her treatment of the development of the Western idea of civil society, Miller points out that "in Spanish America, the economic decentralization upon which the development of civil society is held to depend never fully took place; in the absence of a unified and self-conscious bourgeoisie, the state assumed the role of entrepreneur" (ibid., 18). Miller's treatment of Gramsci makes allowances for the more intellectually sophisticated brand of Marxism that he represented. However, though Gramsci's use of the term "civil society" was not always clear and consistent, at some points he "emphasized that civil society could function as part of the state, rather than, as in the liberal conception, in opposition to it" (in ibid., 17). Miller also places current debates about civil society as part of the rise of the New Right in Thatcher's England and Reagan's United States, which would explain why application of the concept of civil society is restricted to purely private interests, many times in opposition to the state and in tension with it. This would also explain why thinkers on the Left in Latin America, who dominated the intellectual discourse connected to political debate, remained suspicious of the Anglo-Saxon idea of civil society in the 1980s.

Some of the complexities of defining civil society in Latin America may be seen more clearly in how the term is described by a well-known theologian from Argentina. In his treatment of the relationship between "political power and the power of the gospel," José Míguez Bonino states: "If we make a distinction between political society (basically the State) and civil society (the totality of the associative life of a nation), it seems clear to me that from an Evangelical perspective the first should be at the service of the second and not the other way" (Míguez Bonino 1999, 34). For Míguez Bonino, civil society should enjoy peace, justice, solidarity and truthfulness through law, administration and equity at all levels. To that end, he goes on to say, the state has the duty "to encourage, insure, implement, recover, maintain and increase" those qualities. He thinks that the state should not relinquish those responsibilities, claiming to be "neutral" or "incompetent," but that it should fulfil a "regulatory" role and should also take initiatives in behalf of the poor when equity and fairness are in danger. He also argues that the church should be considered to be an autonomous but responsible part of civil society and that it should not be dependent on the state.

Míguez Bonino thus offers a helpful distinction between political society and civil society, and he makes the important point that the life of the church as part of civil society should be independent from the state. I am less enthusiastic than Míguez Bonino about the ability of the state to do for civil society all that he expects. Even so, Christian activism in civil society cannot substitute for the political responsibility Christians have towards the state itself. A great variety of collectivities function within the frame of civil society in an effort to achieve self-reliance and distance from an unfair and inefficient state. But as Lehmann says, "The state constrains the capacities of these collectivities in innumerable ways, great and small – ranging from outright repression to petty regulation" (Lehmann 1990, 152). In fact, civil society in Latin America must learn to move within a kind of dialectical relation with the state, neither fully independent of it nor dependent on it.

Sheldon Annis, a scholar who for several years has researched grassroots organisations in Latin America, formulated two simple but decisive questions in relation to this point, "Can small scale development be large scale policy? How large can small scale become?" These are questions that Christian NGOs that want to work within sustainability standards have to ask sooner or later: "Can a species of development flourish that maintains the virtues of smallness but at the same time reaches large numbers of people, transfers genuine political power to the poor, and provides high quality social services that are delivered by permanent, adequately financed institutions?" (Annis and Hakim 1988, 209). Annis notes that grassroots groups in Latin America perceive themselves to be in an adversarial relation with the state, and they often emphasise their independence and their non-governmental character. Yet he also observes that "in practice, nongovernmental organizations tend to be most numerous and most important where the state is strong; and generally the larger, more democratic, better organized and more prosperous the public sector, the greater are the incentives for the poor to barter for concessions or to co-produce with the state" (ibid., 213).

The kind of civil society that has been developing in recent years in Latin America is a good sign of democratisation, for it is a way of incorporating into the building of the nation sectors of people who were marginalised and forgotten in the past. Its emergence, by itself, will not solve all the social problems of Latin America. It cannot be conceived as an alternative to the need for stronger and efficient states, but it has demonstrated an ability to correct state policy, to provide checks and balances that have not been in place before, and to let people use their creativity to find alternative ways of responding to critical situations. The character of Latin American civil society today is intrinsically linked with developments in Latin American Christianity. The evolving Catholic tradition provides an important part of the story, but Protestant theology and practice have also made powerful contributions. The traditions have influenced each other, and both are also parts of global networks of institutions that link them, and their societies, with peoples and events around the world.

Religious Roots of Political Ideas

Political ideas in Latin America have deep roots in the religious consciousness of a church that was *Mater et magistra* (mother and teacher) during three centuries of Iberian colonial rule. When independence from Spain came in the early nineteenth century, it was natural for societies that had rejected the "mother" to transfer their allegiance to their new nations, ones that would be *Pater et magister* (father and teacher) and to expect everything from them, much as they had been taught to expect from Spain and the church. In one of the most perceptive works of cultural analysis of Latin America, Mexican thinker Carlos Monsivais shows how religious language and categories taken from the Catholic vocabulary became the way to refer to the nation *(la Patria)* and its institutions (Monsivais 2000). A transference of loyalties and admiration occurs at a quasi-religious level, from the sacred realities of the colonial times to the civil realities of nationhood as it was developing in the nineteenth century, often in tension with the church.

Such deep-seated attitudes of confidence and dependence on the state were rooted in the religious experience of societies in which the dominant church came to depend for its survival on the support and benefits it received from the state. Ivan Vallier's hypothesis about the opposition of the Roman Catholic Church to modernisation is based on an historical social analysis of the way in which the Catholic church was implanted in Latin America. At that time, there was a close relationship between conquest and evangelisation and church leaders tended to equate the growth of Christianity with the advance and establishment of the Spanish or Portuguese empires. As Vallier says, "Colonization equaled Christianization. For this reason the Church did not have to be preoccupied about the strength of its religious life at the grassroots. Unwittingly this lack of concern for strong religious motivations locked the Church into a position of extreme dependency on the secular order" (Vallier 1970, 48).

In contrast, the arrival and establishment of Protestantism in the nineteenth and twentieth centuries were marked by an emphasis on the call to personal conversion. Again, Míguez Bonino has provided a detailed socio-theological analysis of this individualistic emphasis at the base of the Protestant advance, which he argues was "in keeping with the theology and practice of the Anglo-American 'Evangelical Awakenings.' In comparison with Roman Catholic form and ritual Protestant preaching stressed the need for personal encounter with Jesus Christ, a vivid experience of forgiveness and a new moral life" (Míguez Bonino 1983, 60). For Míguez Bonino, the social impact of this religious process showed "clear signs of the transition from a traditional to a modern society, from the feudal to the bourgeois person," and he outlined a threefold set of social consequences. First, individualistic personal conversion is the origin of voluntaristic communities formed by people who have left behind social mediations. Second, while in traditional religion "religious categories are projected on a supernatural screen," in the Protestant experience "the supernatural is projected on the screen of subjectivity." Third, religious conversion is related to a transition in the moral realm. "The focus now is on internalization of duty, a sense of responsibility, and the virtues of early capitalism – industry, honesty, moderation, frugality" (ibid., 61). The social impact of this threefold direction of the Protestant conversion experience is summarised as follows: "Protestantism helps to create persons who correspond to and contribute to the change in social structures and mentality. It reinforces the liberal bourgeois utopia of the free moral agent" (ibid., 61).

The nineteenth century in Latin America was a time of nation building for the countries that had broken away from the Iberian colonial rule during the first two decades of the century. Liberal elites were active both in the independence movement and in the process of nation building. Jesuit historian Jeffrey Klaiber summarises the conflict that Liberalism had with the Catholic church during this process. "In the eighteenth and nineteenth centuries liberalism emerged as a new and powerful political force, and it constituted a new source of legitimacy. The church, which did not learn to change with the times, lost a measure of its own legitimacy in the eyes of liberals, positivists, and other reformers of advanced thinking" (Klaiber 1988, 5). The search for a participatory exercise of citizenship thus takes an anticlerical dimension more similar to what happened in the French Revolution than to developments in the Anglo-Saxon world. Modernising elites confronted the opposition of the Catholic church not only to democratic ideas but also to democratic practices. For its part, the church looked at democracy with great suspicion. Moreover, in their struggles against the new liberalising trends, conservative parties looked for legitimation in the Catholic church, and they usually found it.

Modernising elites admired the Anglo-Saxon way of life and democratic ideas, and for that reason they favoured the coming of Protestant missionaries, whose presence was seen as a source for democratic teaching and practices. One of the reasons the elite championed religious pluralism and freedom was to favour immigration from Anglo-Saxon and Protestant countries. In a study about Protestantism in Peru, for example, though a modern, democratic, and pluralistic society was an ideal embraced by the liberal elites, it could well have remained nothing more than an ideal. It only started to become a reality when there was a religiously motivated dissident community that was ready to stand in the face of legal discrimination and endure violent persecution (Escobar 1995–96). The same happened in relation to the incorporation of indigenous peoples into national life. While there were many literary and philosophical proponents of equality and human rights for aboriginals, their writings were considered to be nothing more than interesting literature. Only when Protestant missionaries immersed themselves in the lives of indigenous people did Protestant communities rise up and start to demand a right to exist. As a result, the human rights of indigenous peoples became a matter of national concern. In addition, more democratic legislation was passed and new social actors appeared on the scene (Escobar 1997).

PROTESTANTS AND DEMOCRACY

The presence of religious minorities that were carriers of democratic ideas, practices, and lifestyle inspired by the Anglo-Saxon model of society became a catalytic factor for the movements towards civil participation in the final part of the nineteenth century and the first decades of the twentieth, Protestants found themselves allies of political liberals in the struggle for a more participatory form of social life. During this time Protestant missionaries from mainline denominations engaged in practices that were similar to those of contemporary NGOs. They responded to the needs of marginal sectors of population, but at the same time they introduced democratic practices into the daily life of the communities they founded. These communities were able to survive religious persecution and to exert transformative influence in society because of their deep religious commitments.

The great Protestant gatherings of Panama 1916, Montevideo 1926, and La Habana 1929 were very explicit about the commitment to contribute to the creation of conditions for the development of a participatory, democratic society. The conviction about its modernising potential was rooted in the creed and self-understanding of missionary Protestantism, especially in the fostering of spiritual conditions that would be favourable to the spread of democracy (Escobar 1994a). For example, W. Stanley Rycroft, a British missionary who was an educator in Peru for eighteen years and later a mission executive in the United States, analysed Latin American social problems with the conviction that there was an intimate relationship between spiritual experience and social reality. He believed that Protestantism was destined to play a key role in the transition away from the old feudal order. Early in his career he wrote: "In its historical perspective the growth of democracy in Latin America is vitally related to the spread of Evangelical Christianity" (Rycroft 1942, 186). Later on, having outlined the main pillars of Protestant faith in contrast with the nominal and formal Catholicism of the region, he argued that "the four pillars of Protestantism, namely, the priesthood of all believers, justification by faith, the right of private interpretation and the authority of the Word of God, are also of fundamental importance in the development of a free democratic society" (Rycroft 1958, 152).

Socio-historical research has shown that Protestant missionary practice at the micro level contributed effectively to the creation of democratic attitudes and habits that are the basis for the existence of today's civil society. Democratic practices at the grassroots level were not encouraged by the established church, whose institutional life was based on an authoritarian concept of religious leadership. On the other hand, Protestant practice showed an alternative pattern of social participation linked to a concept of the church that had democratic elements. Rycroft's reference to the "priesthood of all believers" is significant. Jean Pierre Bastian (1989) and Rubén Ruiz Guerra (1992) have done extensive research about developments in Mexico. Though part of a very small minority, Protestant pastors, schoolteachers, lawyers, and journalists were active in the liberal clubs and the intellectual societies that were at the heart of the Mexican revolution. More recently, Juan Fonseca (2000) has done similar research for the case of Peru in the initial decades of the twentieth century, and he has come to similar conclusions about the social activism of the early Protestants.

A positive evaluation of the Protestant experience in these cases was usually connected with a tacit or explicit acceptance of the modernisation process through which Latin American societies planned to follow the development pattern of Western capitalist nations. According to this interpretation, the modernisation process was frequently set in contrast with the feudal order of the colonial days, which had persisted in spite of a century and a half of independence from Spain. Such interpretation tended to avoid questions about the validity or applicability for Latin America of those patterns of modernisation and democratisation, even though they were generally taken from the Anglo-Saxon and European models. In fact, they adopted the assumptions of the "liberal project" that had been the ideological frame of reference for political and economic developments until the Second World War. Such analysis stressed transformative processes at a micro level within the Protestant communities and assumed that the general direction of the historical development, the macro process of society as a whole, would almost naturally follow the pattern of Western development. The Cuban Revolution, the failure of the Alliance for Progress, and the dramatic social agitation of the 1960s would shatter this assumption and bring into question the idea of development, replacing it in the minds of many with the challenge of liberation.

Liberation movements and liberation theologies of the 1970s and 1980s reacted against the positive evaluation of the alliance of Protestantism and liberalism. Liberation theologians analysed social change from the critical perspective of the "socialist historical project" and the application of dependency theory. During the time in which Russia, China, and Cuba were depicted as positive models of alternative societies, the political programme of liberation was usually described in terms of the search for some kind of socialist project. Seen through this lens, the spread of Protestantism in Latin America appeared to be part of a new capitalist invasion to oppose socialism.

The most consistent and clear expression of this kind of analysis applied to Latin American Protestantism was provided by José Míguez Bonino in *Toward a Christian Political Ethics*. He evaluated the role of mainline and evangelical Protestantism within his critical appraisal of the liberal project and formulated his interpretation in some global statements about Protestantism in Latin America. According to his reading of history, the introduction of Protestantism became possible thanks to a "new colonial pact" that on the external front favoured relationships with the Protestant countries and on the internal front allowed the triumph of the modernising elites over the traditional ones. Protestantism thus is seen as a movement that, more than having a dynamism of its own, serves the purposes determined by the initiative and intention of the political liberal elites. "What is clear in relation to Latin America, is that Protestantism claimed and (within its limitations) assumed the role that the Latin American liberal elites had assigned it in the transition from a traditional society to the modern bourgeois world" (Míguez Bonino 1983, 62). Awareness of this fact produced a "crisis of conscience," says Míguez Bonino, who accepted the fact that Protestantism played a significant role in breaking the power of the traditional colonial mentality. But the precariousness of the Protestant position is brought to light when he reminds us of the Anglo-Saxon missionary base from which Protestantism came, and he poses the burning question, "Did we not in fact contribute to create the benevolent and idealized image of the colonial powers (mainly the U.S.A.) which has disguised the deadly character of their domination?" (Míguez Bonino 1975, 18). This critical reading of the role of Protestant churches in the history of Latin America was part of the new way of doing theology developed by liberation theologians. These new liberation theologians applied the same critical analysis to the history of the Catholic church.

CATHOLICS, SOCIALISM, AND DEMOCRACY AFTER VATICAN II

During the period under consideration, the Catholic church in Latin America went through a process of significant change. An adequate treatment of the relationship of Latin American Catholic history to the issue of civil society would require another chapter or even a book, so only a bare outline is offered here. The growth of evangelical Protestantism and especially the Pentecostal explosion were part of a larger phenomenon, the massive exodus of people from the dominant church. The Catholic church, whose structure of religious life and religious institution and pastoral practices had hardly changed for four centuries, was unable to cope with the challenges of the fast pace of social change brought by industrialisation, migration, and urbanisation. Political movements of peasants and workers, based on populist or Marxist ideas, were attracting potential leaders away from the church. In 1955 the first Latin American Council of Bishops (CELAM I) asked Catholics from other parts of the world to come and help them avoid the impending catastrophe that was upon them as a result of the insurgence of both Communists and Protestants. To everyone's surprise, the Catholic church changed. Jesuit historian Jeffrey Klaiber writes: "Against all predictions to the contrary, including those of Max Weber himself, the Catholic Church changed: it ceased to be a bulwark of the established order and turned into a force for social change" (Klaiber 1998, 5).

At the Second Vatican Council (1962–65) the hierarchy of the Roman Catholic Church acknowledged and made official the reforming and renewing pastoral and theological trends that had been developing in different parts of the world. The impact of Vatican II was registered in Latin America during the second assembly of the Council of Bishops (CELAM II), which met in the city of Medellín in Colombia in 1968. The name Medellín became a symbol of the transformations that were shaking the dominant church in the region. The challenge of Protestant growth, as well as a new type of missionary practice by Catholic missionaries from North America and Europe, brought an awareness that the Catholic church needed to revise its stance. Some influential liberation theologians in Medellín, such as Gustavo Gutiérrez and Juan Luis Segundo, were not first and foremost political activists but rather theologians concerned with the pastoral well-being of their church. But just as the Protestant theologians that we mentioned earlier reacted against the alliance of their churches with political liberalism, Catholic liberation theologians responded by proposing a new and critical reading of the social role that their church had historically played in Latin America. The bishops agreed to adopt a new stance described as "a preferential option for the poor." Different sectors of the church interpreted this option in different ways. The more radical sectors aligned with socialist political movements of the left, and some of them adopted Marxism as a way to interpret social reality. With the conviction that history was moving towards socialism, they threw their lot in with socialist and communist movements, as did key members of other churches who were influenced by their own versions of liberation theology. The more traditional sectors intensified efforts to provide assistance to the poor, channelling vast resources made available by Catholics from Europe and the United States into relief and development assistance.[1]

From the perspective of the development of civil society, the changes brought by Medellín were significant. Klaiber's historical study has the advantage of a long-term perspective that allows for a sober and objective look at a controversial and polarised period. A key issue for Klaiber is the role of the Catholic church in providing "legitimacy" to a particular social political regime. Using Weberian categories, Klaiber defines legitimacy as "the popular consent that undergirds power." He argues that in Latin America there has been a tension between authoritarian *caudillos* who offered charismatic and traditional legitimacy, on the one hand, and the liberals who wanted a democratic type of legitimacy based on equality before the law. According to Klaiber, the Catholic church enjoyed its own legitimacy based on religion, and it could thus provide legitimacy to the social order through what could be called a religious sanction. In his overview of how the Catholic church fulfilled this legitimising role and how that changed during the second part of the twentieth century, Klaiber offers a valuable summary of the process:

> In Medellín the bishops made a dramatic call to create a new social order based on justice and human rights. With this change the Church legitimised many of the ideals of the old liberals – democracy and human rights. . . . Most of all the church legitimized an entire popular movement that had been emerging since the end of the Second World War (Klaiber 1998, 5–6).

A central component of the "entire popular movement" to which Klaiber refers is the existence of the Christian Base Communities (CBCs). Some argue that CBCs are the most permanent and enduring result of the liberation theology movement. Theologians aware of the tight connection between theology and the practical Christian life realised the importance of the CBCs. Gustavo Gutiérrez thus said that these communities are "one of the most fruitful and significant events in the present day life of the Latin American church. . . . Their growth throughout our continent has helped to raise the hopes of the poor and oppressed" (in Torres and Eagleson 1982, 115). In 1979, eleven years after Medellín, the document of the third Council of Bishops, which met in Puebla, Mexico (CELAM III), referred to the CBCs as "the joy and hope of the Church." For the bishops, these communities "embody the Church's preferential love for the common people. In them their religiosity is expressed, valued and purified, and they are given a concrete opportunity to share in the task of the Church and to work commitedly for the transformation of the world" (Puebla Document 1980, 213). While there has been controversy within the Catholic community as to how that transformation takes place, with some Catholics stressing the religious dimension and others focusing on political activism, in several countries the CBCs have provided both the impulse and the means for Catholic participation in civil society movements.

There is a causal correlation between evangelical and Pentecostal growth in Latin America and the rise of the CBCs. This is especially evident in Brazil, where a popular and indigenous kind of Protestantism existed that did not depend on an educated clergy, sophisticated methodologies, or funds from abroad and where there were motivated pioneers of the CBCs such as José Marins (Escobar 1986). Pentecostalism was a movement coming from below, with its own religious and social dynamism and a great expansive power. Today, scholars trying to understand the role of religion in the life of the urban poor, or the relationship between democracy and religion in Latin America, are naturally drawn to comparative studies of the CBCs and the Pentecostals (Mariz 1994; Swatos 1995). The puzzling question for social scientists, church historians, and bishops in the 1980s was why, though the Catholic church was taking a preferential option for the poor, the poor themselves were taking an option for the Pentecostal churches.

PENTECOSTALS: PROMISE AND PRECARIOUSNESS OF A MOVEMENT

In the middle of the twentieth century analysts from mainline or historical Protestant denominations favoured the interpretation that saw Protestantism as a factor contributing to modernisation. This period of time corresponded to what we could call the first cycle of Protestant missionary activity, which reached its peak in the 1940s and 1950s and then began to decline. At that point there began a second cycle involving more conservative forms of Protestantism, missions influenced by the Cold War mentality, which brought about the significant numerical expansion of the Pentecostal movement. As we have seen earlier, the first wave of Protestant missionaries and national converts had a very explicit social agenda, which they implemented through their practice. Pentecostalism, on the other hand, was considered to be socially conservative and politically irrelevant because of its eschatological and spiritual emphasis, which appeared to observers to be "otherworldly." Besides that, Pentecostal expansion among the most marginalised urban poor, the noisy worship style, and insistence on miracles may explain why traditional Protestants often considered Pentecostals a sect.

Part of the unique social dynamics of Latin America after the 1960s was the relentless process of urbanisation that turned cities into massive labyrinths. Such urban growth brought to light the emergence of new segments of the population that in the past had been hidden in distant rural areas but who now had invaded the streets of capitals like Lima, Mexico City, Guatemala City, São Paulo, Caracas, and Bogotá. These emerging popular sectors demonstrated their ability to become social and economic actors without the tutorial paternalism of Marxist parties and their outdated theories. They constituted the appearance of "the other path," as economist Hernando De Soto called it, in a clear, contrasting allusion to the classic revolutionary way symbolised by the Maoism of Shining Path in Peru (De Soto 1989). De Soto has demonstrated that the vastness of informal economies prove that the poor have entrepreneurial abilities to survive and emerge in spite of oppressive bureaucratic control and inefficient socialising measures. Within this pattern of change, Pentecostalism as a new form of popular Protestantism thrived, and its rapid spread among urban communities became a surprising phenomenon.

A turning point in understanding the social and political significance of Pentecostals emerged from Emilio Willems's work on the Pentecostal church movement in Brazil and Chile (1967). He places the emergence and expansion of Pentecostalism within the context of rapid social changes generated by foreign immigration, urbanisation, and secularisation that were affecting the social structures and values of Brazilian and Chilean societies. As Pentecostalism developed, it became a factor contributing to social change, first because of its "Protestant ethics" value orientation, which challenges converts to function better in the new situation created by social change. But there was more to it than this, for Willems suggests that Pentecostalism was also a form of social protest. Its attraction among the lower classes could be interpreted as one of the ways open to masses to express a state of latent or overt rebellion or hostility against the Roman Catholic Church. In this view the Catholic church was seen by the people as a willing participant in the decaying structure that had always favoured the rich and powerful (Willems 1964, 103). Willems also applies the method of institutional analysis to his study of the life within Pentecostal congregations. This provides a better understanding of the links among liturgy, legitimation, and social change. He stresses the importance of the participative nature of Pentecostal liturgy and congregational life, that did not depend on literacy or education but on a disposition to be touched by the power of the Holy Spirit. Willems refers especially to the significance of the *tomada de Espíritu* or "seizure" by the Spirit that "puts a seal of divine approval on the individual who can now be elected or appointed to any office" (ibid., 106–7).

The seizure became a form of legitimation within Pentecostal congregations validated by energetic and successful proselytism. The seizure had an integrative effect allowing thousands of persons from the lower social classes to become part of an organised group in which they could enter in community, participate freely, and receive affirmation, comfort, and a sense of belonging. The seizure experience also had an egalitarian effect, as participation in the community did not require the symbols of status like money, education, or even verbal articulateness. What started at the level of liturgical participation was thereby extended to the level of inclusion in decision-making processes in the community. Willems concludes: "The principle of unrestricted social mobility embodied by the Pentecostal sects is obviously at variance with the limited opportunities for upward mobility within the general society" (Willems 1964, 107). Research carried out in the decades following Willems's key insights has confirmed his analysis. For the marginally poor within the urban explosion, entering Pentecostal churches became a way of being accepted in a community, gaining a new sense of dignity and self-worth, and rearranging their priorities in life. Those effects that were not explicit aspects of a Pentecostal social creed, but rather were part of a Pentecostal socio-religious experience, which became an excellent training ground for participation in the secular society where a democratisation process was taking place.

The numerical growth of Pentecostals fostered upward mobility and created conditions that brought the political question to the foreground of sociological observation and theological reflection. Willems's analysis demonstrated the sociological potential of conversion to Pentecostalism by emphasising how the very character of converts changed as an indication of "the change of life." This important component of the Pentecostal message was considered an evidence of the redeeming power of Christ. As in the case of evangelical Protestants, Pentecostals presented the convert with specific prohibitions against the use of alcohol and tobacco. But what was especially significant in the Pentecostal practice was that the prohibitions were accompanied by the strong emphasis on an emotional experience of conversion, a seizure from God's power. In some cases the seizure was the key point of breaking away from old vices like alcoholism, which were prevalent among the masses of the urban world. In the Pentecostal experience the ascetic lifestyle included in conversion was also accompanied by a celebrative form of worship and communal life that was a great help for the converted in maintaining their new lifestyle. This change of lifestyle also had economic and social consequences in the improvement of housing conditions and eating habits. Savings were generated and were sometimes matched with a newly discovered ability for entrepreneurship that brought upward mobility. "The economic significance of Protestant asceticism lies in the fact that it frees part of one's income for the acquisition of things that symbolize a higher level of living" (Willems 1964, 251).

In many ways these popular Protestant churches have become alternative societies that have created a closed world where people are accepted and become actors, not on the basis of what gives them status in the world around them, but on the basis of values that come from their vision of the kingdom of God. Observers and scholars had to come to terms with the fact that, in spite of reputable theory and good intentions, many actions of Christians in favour of the poor were tainted by a paternalistic approach. Social and political conscientisation took the form of a struggle for the poor, trying to create a more just society *for* them rather than *with* them. Both the Catholic church and historical or mainline Protestant churches were connected to world communities and denominational families, but they used their access to funds, the foreign press, and even diplomatic ties to help the victims of poverty or state terrorism. Though incarnation among the poor has often been the source of these movements, they nevertheless failed in mobilising the poor themselves.

By contrast, the popular Protestant churches are popular movements in themselves. Their pastors and leaders do not have to identify with the poor; they *are* the poor. They do not have a social agenda but an intense spiritual agenda, and it is through that agenda that they have been able to have a social impact. As sociologist David Martin observes in his now classic study about the impact of the Pentecostal experience: "Above all it renews the innermost cell of the family and protects the woman from the ravages of male desertion and violence. A new faith is able to implant new disciplines, re-order priorities, counter corruption and destructive machismo, and reverse the indifferent and injurious hierarchies of the outside world" (Martin 1990, 284).

After long years of academic and journalistic hostility and misrepresentation against Latin American evangelicals and Pentecostals, a new generation of social scientists working at the micro level brought to light the transforming nature of the spiritual experience offered by these churches (Escobar 1994b). David Martin summarised and interpreted a vast amount of data from the accumulated research of the 1970s and 1980s. He found the massive migration from countryside to megacity to be the background for the religious transformation. "The new society now emerging in Latin America has to do with movement, and evangelicals constitute a *movement*. Evangelical Christianity is a dramatic migration of the spirit matching and accompanying a dramatic migration of bodies" (Martin 1990, 284). There is consensus that the field is ready for a revision of assumptions (Cleary and Stewart-Gambino 1997) and that the methodologies also have to be revised. Historians and social scientists such as Scott Mainwaring from the University of Notre Dame and Cecilia Mariz from the Universidad Fluminense in Niteroi, Brazil, concur that the Marxist analysis prevalent in the 1960s and 1970s was seriously deficient. They also concur that a return to a Weberian approach would provide methodological ideas more adequate to their object of study (see Mainwaring 1986). Mariz is very specific:

> Marxist-oriented studies about religions are concerned with an ideological critique of their beliefs and worldviews. Ideological critiques and the historical materialist concepts of "alienation" and "false consciousness," however, do not take into account the standpoint of the poor and thus they limit our ability to understand the reasons for the popularity of religion among the poor. . . . The Weberian approach, which tries to understand how religion can ascribe meaning to economic activities, is more helpful for our purpose than the Marxist approach (Mariz 1994, 6–7).

Peter Berger agrees that the current resurgence of religion on a global scale and its connection to world politics requires an "un-reconstructed Weberian" approach (Berger 1999, 16–17).

As we explore the social mobility that the Pentecostal experience fosters, as well as its impact on participation in civil society, questions arise about its long-term effect. Martin's analysis and interpretation is helpful, because it provides clues from the history of Protestantism, taking as background a sociological interpretation of the evolution of Protestantism in Europe and especially in the English-speaking world, including the United States. He is aware that there is no historical continuity between all forms of popular Protestantism in Latin America and Protestantism in the English-speaking world, but he thinks that the evolution of Methodism and of the Wesleyan movement offers enough parallels to provide helpful sociological patterns of interpretation for understanding the future of Pentecostalism in Latin American. The Pentecostal experience is explained by Martin as a way in which "millions of people are absorbed within a protective social capsule where they acquire new concepts of self and new models of initiative and voluntary organization" (Martin 1990, 85). His analysis coincides at many points with that of

Willems. Martin thinks that, like Methodism at the beginning of the Industrial Revolution in Britain, Pentecostalism thrives today in Latin America as a "temporary efflorescence of voluntary religiosity which accompanies a stage in industrialization and/or urbanization" (ibid., 294). Methodism had a long-term social and political impact upon life in some of the English-speaking countries, but the context in which it appeared was very different from Latin America, and Martin is cautious to point out that the European experience may not necessarily provide a universal paradigm.

When Protestants of the older denominations have critically evaluated the Pentecostal movement, it has usually been from a theological perspective emphasising belief. But the massive numerical growth of the movement calls for the attention of social scientists and political analysts as well. Evangelical observers and interpreters from Latin America have begun to pose critical questions about the long-term social impact of the Pentecostal experience, especially in the countries where the growth of this kind of popular Protestantism has been more visible. Valuable studies covering several decades in Chile and Brazil employ a sophisticated socio-theological approach in an effort to probe the social life of these churches and their structures.[2]

Brazilian Paul Freston, a scholar who has conducted the most exhaustive and systematic study of Brazilian Pentecostalism and its expressions in relation to politics, combines theological training with rigorous work in the social sciences. His research is prompted by an ethical and pastoral concern. Summarising research from a variety of sources, he concludes that "the new evangelical political participants in Brazil do not have a project; they only feel, and perhaps justifiably, that the future belongs to them" (Freston 1992, 30). This is in open contrast with the beginning of the twentieth century, when Protestantism presented itself as the carrier of modernisation. "The current majority political project of Brazilian Protestants, that of the Pentecostal leadership, far from being the future opening up before the nation is sombre, tinged with apocalyptic chaos, and barely goes beyond a church-growth strategy" (ibid.).

In spite of the forces moving Pentecostals to greater civil participation and towards a more democratic and inclusive society, there are also forces that pull Pentecostals towards the more traditional Latin American social-political models. The lack of a political project means that Pentecostal politicians may be tempted to follow the path of expediency and the patterns of clientelism typical of Latin American politics. In the same way, the lack of an articulate ecclesiology leads Pentecostal pastors to adopt patterns of political *caudillos,* to organise their churches following patriarchal, corporatist patterns that correspond more to the conservative Catholic tradition centred on an almost infallible priest than to a new democratic tradition. Freston has uncovered these trends through an analysis of the discourse of Pentecostal politicians, of their participation in Congress, and of their voting patterns. They seem to be lending to the forces of political conservatism "the phenomenal contribution of [its] cultural and rhetorical resources, and enviable human and organizational base resources" (Freston 1992, 28–29). Moreover, they have fallen into politically corrupt practices that non-evangelicals have been eager to criticise. During sessions of the Brazilian Constitutional Assembly an article in a well-known newspaper pointed to facts widely known by the public. According to Freston the conclusion of the article stated that "a considerable number of evangelicals makes the task of preparing a new Constitution a large and profitable business bartering votes for benefits and privileges for their churches and often for themselves" (ibid., 32). Freston's theological and ethical reflection takes Jesus' words into this context:

> The Pharisees who faithfully gave their tithes, were notwithstanding, "lovers of money" (Luke 16:14). Once they had given their tithe, they had no criteria for the use of the rest of the money. When the legalist finds himself in a situation where there are no rules, he becomes literally ."unruly." That is why he easily falls prey to public favours and vote-selling in congress. Legalism which only teaches rules, produces people without principles. When a legalist goes into politics, it is very likely that he will become "a lover of money" (Freston 1994, 137).

On the other hand, the emergence of civil society has often brought together Catholic activists from the CBCs and Pentecostal or evangelical leaders involved in networks of mutual help or defense of common local interests. The interaction tends to be mutually enriching and makes it possible to achieve limited common goals in areas such as human rights, disaster relief, implementation of food banks, and protest against violence or government policy (Yamamori et al. 1997). In both Catholic and evangelical communities there is a common volunteer dynamic necessary for mobilisation. What has to be explored for the future is the possibility of a more concerted effort of all Christians to dialogue about their practice and to agree on long-term goals. To that end, a first step is intra-Protestant dialogue among activists from different denominations in an exploration of a common biblical and theological heritage. The Latin American Theological Fraternity has been a forum for the exchange of experiences and theological reflection among Pentecostals, evangelicals, and Protestants from the older denominations. The underlying premise of this forum is the conviction that there is much common ground still awaiting careful exploration as churches respond to new historical challenges. Using a metaphor from Míguez Bonino, these different "faces of Latin American Protestantism" are like masks of one subject which allow diversity to exist within a unique identity that is specifically Protestant. But theological reflection is only part of the task ahead. Compendiums of congresses and consultations organised by the fraternity are evidence not only of theological reflection but also of a variety of projects of service. These are activities that move in the direction of a type of social participation that is at the base of civil society (Padilla 1991; Fraternidad Teológica Latinoamericana 1992). In a few cases the intra-Protestant dialogue has joined in common action with Catholic activists, such as in the defense of human rights in Peru (López 1998). NGOs of Protestant origin have provided many Pentecostals with the first opportunity for active participation as volunteers in social and economic projects that also bring "conscientisation" for further political practice.

My own comparative study has brought me to the conclusion that the persistence of religious commitment at the grassroots level, in both Protestant and Catholic traditions, is a reality that anyone interested in civil society has to take into account in Latin America (Escobar 1997). Religious commitment along Protestant lines, marked by a strong emphasis on the individual, has been a means of understanding modernisation as well as a source of empowerment of persons through a change in values. Both allow believers to function better within modernising or globalising societies. Emphasis on conversion has been key for the personal transformation of people among the poor and marginal classes who lived under fatalism about their own condition, with no hope of change or escape. Their new practice of faith has contributed to the formation of character and habits that have allowed converts to recover a sense of dignity and worth and to develop a sense of mission in the world. This new mission includes both proclaiming the truth of the gospel and changing their social environment, beginning at the personal and family level. In the case of the popular Protestantism that has grown more recently in Latin America, however, this form of religious dissidence has not produced an analysis of social structures, a logical discourse of political criticism, or an agenda for political action in accordance with a biblical and theological perspective related to the Protestant experience. Protestants have been relatively open to accommodate to and try to function within new systems. The rise of civil society has allowed them to see new possibilities for their limited actions, and they have put their important quota of volunteerism to many civil society purposes.

In the Catholic case there is a tradition of popular religious commitment as a form either of resistance to modernisation or a messianic questioning of the social order, both of which have been evident since colonial times. After the reforms of Vatican II and the rise of liberation theology, some Catholic sectors have participated decisively in civil society actions promoting social change, defending human rights, and offering an articulate criticism and protest against social and political conditions, including the effects of modernisation and globalisation. These sectors are still a minority within the Catholic church, and in recent years there has been a backlash from the more conservative sectors. Catholics also have a strong sense of the importance of community as well as the individual, and because of their tradition and their dominant role in society, it is more natural for them to think in political terms. In important areas such as responsible parenthood, gender issues, use of state resources, and acceptance of pluralism, even progressive Catholics may find themselves at odds with the position of Protestants or activists from secular sectors.

If there is going to be an effective Christian presence and action in the development of civil society in Latin America, the contributions of both Catholics and Protestants are necessary. Thus far civil society has opened new avenues for all kinds of Christians to express their faith and to volunteer their spiritual human resources in the struggle for justice, freedom, and peace in the century that has just begun.

NOTES

[1] For a liberation theology perspective, see Gustavo Gutiérrez,"Expanding the View," an introduction to the fifteenth-anniversary revised edition of *A Theology of Liberation* (Maryknoll, N.Y.: Orbis Books, 1988). For an American academic perspective, see Paul Sigmund, *Liberation Theology at the Crossroads* (New York: Oxford University Press, 1990). For an evangelical perspective, see Samuel Escobar, *La fe evangélica y las teologías de la liberación* (El Paso: Casa Bautista de Publicaciones, 1987).

[2] For Chile, see Humberto Lagos, *Crisis de la esperanza* (Santiago de Chile: Presor-Lit, 1988). For Brazil, see Paul Freston, *Evangelicos na politica brasileira. Historia ambigua e desafio etico* (Curitiba: Encontrao, 1994).

REFERENCES

Annis, Sheldon, and Peter Hakim, eds. 1988. *Direct to the Poor: Grassroots Development in Latin America*. Boulder, Colo.: Lynne Rienner Publishers.

Bastian, Jean Pierre. 1989. *Los disidentes: sociedades protestantes y revolución en Mexico*. Mexico: El Colegio de Mexico-Fondo de Cultura Económica.

Berger, Peter L., ed. 1999. *The Desecularization of the World*. Grand Rapids, Mich.: Eerdmans.

Cleary, Edward L., and Hannah Stewart-Gambino, eds. 1997. *Power, Politics, and Pentecostals in Latin America*. Boulder, Colo.: Westview Press.

Comblin, José. 1998. *Called for Freedom: The Changing Context of Liberation Theology*. Maryknoll, N.Y.: Orbis Books.

De Soto, Hernando. 1989. *The Other Path*. New York: Harper.

Escobar, Samuel. 1975. "The Kingdom of God, Eschatology, and Social and Political Ethics in Latin America." *Theological Fraternity Bulletin* 1: 1–42.

———. 1986. "Christian Base Communities: A Historical Perspective." *Transformation* 3/3 (July-September): 1–4.

———. 1994a. "Conflict of Interpretations of Popular Protestantism." In *New Face of the Church in Latin America*, edited by G. Cook, 112–34. Maryknoll, N.Y.: Orbis Books.

———. 1994b. "The Promise and Precariousness of Latin American Protestantism." In *Coming of Age: Protestantism in Contemporary Latin America*, edited by D. R. Miller, 3–35. Calvin Center Series. Lanham, Md.: University Press of America.

———. 1995–96. *Metodistas y Adventistas: Dos Modelos de Proyecto Protestante en el Perú, 1877–1915*. Lima: Cátedra de Misiología.

———. 1997. "Religion and Social Change at the Grass Roots in Latin America." In *Annals of the American Academy of Political and Social Science* (November): 81–103.

Fonseca, Juan. 2000. *Entre el Conflicto y la Consolidación: Protestantismo y Modernización en el Perú (1915–1930)*. Thesis for a licenciate degree. Pontificia Universidad Católica del Perú, Lima.

Fraternidad Teológica Latinoamericana. 1992. *Todo el Evangelio, Para Todos los Pueblos, desde América Latina*. Compendio CLADE III. Quito: Fraternidad Teológica Latinoamericana.

Freston, Paul. 1992. "In Search for an Evangelical Political Project for Brazil." *Transformation* 9/3 (July/September).

———. 1994. *Evangélicos na Poítica Brasileira: História Ambígua e Desafio Ético*. Curitiba: Encontrao Editora.

Garreton, Manuel Antonio. 1989. "Political Realities and the Witness of Religion." In *Theology, Politics and Peace*, edited by T. Runyan. Maryknoll, N.Y.: Orbis Books.

Klaiber, Jeffrey, S.J. 1998. *The Church, Dictatorships, and Democracy in Latin America.* Maryknoll, N.Y.: Orbis Books.

Lehmann, David. 1990. *Democracy and Development in Latin America.* Philadelphia: Temple University Press.

López, Darío. 1998. *Los evangélicos y los derechos humanos: La experiencia social del Concilio Nacional Evangélico del Perú 1980–1992.* Lima: CEMAA-Puma.

Mainwaring, Scott. 1986. *The Catholic Church and Politics in Brazil 1916–1985.* Stanford, Calif.: Stanford University Press.

Mariz, Cecilia Loreto. 1994. *Coping With Poverty: Pentecostals and Christian Base Communities in Brazil.* Philadelphia: Temple University Press.

Martin, David. 1989. *Tongues of Fire: The Explosion of Protestantism in Latin America.* Oxford: Basil Blackwell.

———. 1990. *Tongues of Fire: The Explosion of Protestantism in Latin America.* Oxford: Basil Blackwell.

Míguez Bonino, José. 1975. *Doing Theology in a Revolutionary Situation.* Philadelphia: Fortress Press.

———. 1983. *Toward a Christian Political Ethics.* London: SCM Press.

———. 1999. *Poder del Evangelio y poder politico.* Buenos Aires: Kairos Ediciones.

Miller, Nicola. 1999. *In the Shadow of the State.* London: Verso.

Monsivais, Carlos. 2000. *Aires de Familia: Cultura y Sociedad en America Latina.* Barcelona: Anagrama.

Padilla, C. Rene, ed. 1991. *De la marginación al compromiso.* Buenos Aires: Fraternidad Teológica Teologica Latinoamericana.

"Puebla Document." 1980. In *Puebla and Beyond*, edited by J. Eagleson and P. Scharfer. Maryknoll, N.Y.: Orbis Books.

Ruiz Guerra, Rubén. 1992. *Los Hombres Nuevos: Metodismo y Modernización en Mexico (1873–1930).* Mexico: Casa Unida de Publicaciones.

Rycroft, W. Stanley. 1942. *On This Foundation: The Evangelical Witness in Latin America.* New York: Friendship Press.

———. 1958. *Religion and Faith in Latin America.* Philadelphia: Westminster Press.

Stoll, David. 1990. *Is Latin America Turning Protestant?* Berkeley and Los Angeles: University of California Press.

Swatos, William H. Jr. 1995. *Religion and Democracy in Latin America.* New Brunswick, N.J.: Transaction Books.

Torres, Sergio, and John Eagleson, eds. 1982. *The Challenge of Base Christian Communities.* Maryknoll, N.Y.: Orbis Books.

Vallier, Ivan. 1970. *Catholicism, Social Control, and Modernization in Latin America.* Englewood Cliffs, N.J.: Prentice Hall.

Willems, Emilio. 1964. "Protestantism and Social Change in Brazil and Chile." In *Religion, Revolution and Reform*, edited by W. V. D'Antonio and F. B. Pike. New York: Prager.

———. 1967. *Followers of the New Faith: Culture Change and the Rise of Protestantism in Brazil.* Nashville, Tenn.: Vanderbilt University.

Yamamori, Tetsunao, B. Meyers, K. Bediako, and L. Reed, eds. 1997. *Serving with the Poor in Latin America.* Monrovia, Calif.: MARC.

9

CIVIL SOCIETY AND HUMAN DEVELOPMENT

James W. Skillen

As even a cursive review of the literature clearly shows, there is vagueness, ambiguity, and multiple meanings to the term *civil society*. Thus it is important to bear in mind the need to keep the term fluid, open to development. In so doing, we may also avoid a danger pointed out clearly by Gertrude Himmelfarb, who writes, "I am also wary of civil society used as a rhetorical panacea, as if the mere invocation of the term is a solution to all problems – an easy, painless solution, a happy compromise between two extremes" (Himmelfarb 1998, 117).

Keeping in mind this caution about the amorphous meaning of *civil society*, we turn to an exploration of both the "domain" and the "organisations" of civil society in a way that can offer some normative guidance for Christians working to promote economic, social, and political development in the Third World. We start by summarising the thesis to be developed.

The historical unfolding or differentiation of human institutions and associations that we have experienced in the West has led inevitably to the need for an ever sharper identification of the distinguishable identities and responsibilities of those institutions and associations. This differentiation process has also created the need for answers to the question of how the diverse types of organisations ought to be properly interrelated. The historical process of social differentiation and integration is evident now throughout the world, albeit in different ways, yet almost always influenced by Western-led globalisation. There are, for example, the ongoing domestic and international public-legal struggles to distinguish the responsibilities of governments and of business corporations in relation to one another and in relation to all the other responsibilities and relationships people have.

The "space," "domain," or "intersection" of all the different institutions and relationships is one and the same for all of them, though it is variously referred to as the public square, the commons, the market, or the open space of free societies. This space is made possible by law-making and law-enforcing governments, both domestic and international, whose responsibilities, normatively stated, are precisely to do justice to all – to everything and everyone at the same time and in the same public space. Thus, the market (both domestic and international) is part of the public domain as defined by rules that govern economic life: the rules of trade and commerce, of weights and measures, of incorporation and taxation, of loans and investments. But in that same public commons there are also many non-governmental and noneconomic organisations and relationships that must also be distinguished, identified, and protected in public law in order to be free to fulfil their own responsibilities. Each non-governmental and noneconomic organisation has its own identity and purpose – family, friendship, university, hospital, church, sports club, political interest group, community organisation, and thousands more.

Part of the ambiguity in the use of the phrase *civil society* arises because of a desire to group everything that is *neither* economic *nor* governmental into one category for easy reference. That desire may be pragmatically useful for purposes of *negative* identification, but it does not provide much help for identifying actual organisations and relationships of human society that are so diverse in character and purpose. Using the phrase *civil society* as Benjamin Barber does, to refer to a "third sector" whose function is to mediate "between our specific individuality as economic producers and consumers and our abstract collectivity as members of a sovereign people" (in Dionne 1998, 2–3), is, from my vantage point, both misleading and ultimately dehumanising. Human identity is not adequately captured by the idea of a consuming/producing individual who only "abstractly" belongs to a sovereign collectivity and is thus "mediated" to that abstraction by a "third sector." No. Human beings *are* the image of God, created with an amazing range of responsibilities that can be realised only multi-generationally in the course of the historical differentiation and integration of all those capabilities and responsibilities in service to God. Healthy societies and a healthy globe, in other words, can be realised only by way of the proper differentiation, integration, and fulfilment of a diverse range of institutions and relationships, which require room, a common public space, in which justice is done to all. The just treatment of all and the maintenance of the public square for all are the responsibilities of public-legal governance.

What we need, then, from a biblical point of view, is a normative framework for understanding and developing the following:

1. the proper historical differentiation and integration of human responsibilities in God's creation;
2. the proper exercise of the particular and necessary responsibility of governing the open, densely occupied, and highly interactive public square;
3. human identity as the image of God, resisting both the reduction of individuals to their role as consumers, producers, and citizens, and the reduction of non-governmental and noneconomic organisations to a mere "mediating" function; and
4. the proper interlinking of all institutions and relationships in a just society.

DIVERSE CONTEXTS

In *Rights Talk* Harvard law professor Mary Ann Glendon argues that our American focus on the rights of individuals as the highest principle of law and politics makes it difficult, if not impossible, to obtain an adequate recognition and protection of civil society. "Our legal and political vocabularies," she writes, "deal handily with rights-bearing individuals, market actors, and the state, but they do not afford us a ready way of bringing into focus smaller groups and systems where the values and practices that sustain our republic are shaped, practised, transformed, and transmitted from one generation to the next" (Glendon 1991, 120). What Glendon means by smaller groups and systems is "families, neighborhoods, workplace associations, and religious and other communities of obligation" (ibid.). Other American theorists and social commentators have referred to these kinds of institutions and relationships as "mediating structures" (Berger and Neuhaus 1977), the "social sector" (Drucker 1994, 53–80), the "third sector" (Dionne 1998, 3), "seedbeds of virtue" (Council on Civil Society 1998, 7), a "buffer" (Wolfe 1998, 17), and simply "civil society" (Wolfe 1989).[1]

In European discourse, especially after the liberation of Eastern Europe from Soviet communist control, the phrase *civil society* has more often been used to refer to a narrower range of organisations and institutions – the ones that give people an organised public voice and identity over against totalitarian governments. The Catholic church and Solidarity in Poland, for example, and underground newspapers, civic organisations, and intellectual networks in Hungary, Czechoslovakia, and Russia served as the seedbeds of revolution. Beyond Europe and America, both the public and the private meanings of *civil society* have been featured in discussions of third-world development, as is much in evidence in other essays in this volume.

A report from the International Jacques Maritain Institute in Rome titled "Globalisation: A Challenge for Peace, Solidarity or Exclusion?" highlights the "democratic deficit" inherent in the current process of globalisation. The report calls for a new international social contract in which "the world is seen as a global civil society." Fundamental to this reform, the report argues, are NGOs "which are not subject to political or economic interests and, more generally . . . are the bringers of human, religious, ethical and cultural values. . . . These are the institutions that normally help people to become aware of themselves, of their own values and their own most profound needs." At a global level, the report goes on to say, "the organisations of civil society must be recognised and not authorised by governments." Furthermore, those organisations "must not stop at simply reporting wrongs and advocating solutions but must become true monitors of the activities of transnational companies and the international institutions" (International Jacques Maritain Institute 1999, 56, 58–59).

To conceive of civil society in these diverse ways poses difficulties. In the view of some, the associations of civil society exist primarily to mediate between individuals and governments, or between individuals and the market. For others, their primary function is to serve as "seedbeds of virtue" or as seedbeds of citizenship. Still others emphasise the moral haven provided by these more intimate human communities in the context of an impersonal, perhaps even "un-virtuous" world of politics and market competition. Yet, if all these meanings can be lodged in *civil society,* is there no significance at all to the differences between a family and a political party, a church and a human rights watchdog organisation, a service organisation that feeds the hungry and a neighbourhood?

Robert Putnam appears, at first glance, to address this question. There is an important difference, says Putnam, between two types of social capital. One is "bonding" (exclusive) and the other is "bridging" (inclusive) (Putnam 2000, 22). Apart from the development of social capital, he says, political society will become ever more divided and people will further retreat from tolerance and civic engagement. Americans now watch too much television instead of talking with their neighbours over the fence; they bowl alone instead of in leagues. Putnam's argument, however, is not that Americans should intensify the development of smaller, more intimate, non-governmental "bonding" relationships for their own sake. Instead, he wants Americans to increase their "connectedness" as citizens so that each person can feel included in the American community regardless of the private social and moral differences they may have. When, for example, Putnam calls for a new "great awakening," he is referring not to a spiritually deep evangelical revival, like those of America's past, but to a civic awakening that is "pluralistic" and "socially responsible." This means, among other things, that the goodness of any particular spiritual community should be judged by the extent to which it encourages its members to be "more tolerant of the faiths and practices of other Americans" (ibid., 409).

In Putnam's view, bonding in a family or religious community is not necessarily good for the larger civic order because that only "bolsters our narrower selves" (Putnam 2000, 23). What America needs is more of the kind of bridging social capital that "can generate broader identities and reciprocity" (ibid.). Bridging, as Putnam describes it, reflects and nurtures the highest value of liberal society, namely toleration, which amounts to each person respecting the other's autonomy in the broader society (ibid., 350–63). Strong family and religious bonds may have a utilitarian value to the extent that they teach people to become tolerant of one another. However, if those institutions teach children to be intolerant of certain behaviours of other members of society, or train them, for example, to believe "narrowly" that the meaning of life is to be found in giving oneself wholeheartedly to Jesus Christ, then they may prove to be counterproductive to the building up of the bridging type of social capital that Putnam believes is so essential for our modern society (ibid., 362–63; see also Hoksbergen 1999, 13). Putnam admits that much evidence points to the mutually reinforcing character of bonding and bridging social capital: "Those who reach out to friends and family are often the most active in community outreach as well" (ibid., 362). But this is not always the case. "Some kinds of bonding social capital may discourage the formation of bridging social capital and vice versa. That's what happened in the case of busing" (ibid.).[2]

From the standpoint of the normative framework we are seeking, Putnam's argument reduces bonding social capital to a means – a means to the end of bridging social capital, which is the role he praises for civil society. But if American society is in danger of disintegrating under the impact of individualism and self-seeking, then encouraging individuals to be more publicly tolerant of other self-seeking individuals does not look like much of an answer to the problem. A political order that exists primarily to promote the social norm of individual autonomy and the market norm of consumer satisfaction may be able to maintain itself as long as everyone can rely on healthy bonding social capital built up in the past. But how does bridging social capital help to restore the bonding relationships on which it depends? (see Seligman 1992).

Some NGOs do indeed appear primarily to serve a bridging, connecting, or mediating purpose, organising and mobilising individuals for civic or public-influence purposes. No doubt certain of these NGOs need to be strengthened in the United States and around the world today. However, the family and the church appear to have an original, internal, exclusive identity and purpose that is not reducible to a mediational or bridging purpose. Moreover, from a Christian vantage point these institutions are essential to the healthy identity of human beings and are not simply a means to other ends. Putnam has not given us much help to specify the identity of civil society or to explain how the diverse institutions and relationships of society ought to hold together.

MORE THAN MEANS TO AN END

If, instead of emphasising the negative reference and the means-to-an-end role of civil society, we were to consider each so-called social-sector institution and relationship in its own right, what would we look for and what would we find?

The wide variety of social bonds displays quite different types in terms of their commitments, obligations, sizes, purposes, and degrees of intensity, cooperation, and endurance. If there is any common denominator among them, it would appear to be simply that all are human and social. Yet that denominator does not distinguish them from political and economic institutions. Businesses and political communities are made up of humans, even if the obligations that obtain in those spheres are different in kind from the obligations that hold for families, friendships, and churches. It seems quite illegitimate, then, to describe NGOs in particular (as the report from the Jacques Maritain Institute does) as "bringers" of human, ethical, and cultural values, implying that political and economic institutions do not also do the same. At this point, therefore, we need to step back to ask why the civil society question has been posed the way it has in the West and whether an appeal to the virtues of civil society is adequate to help guide social, economic, and political development in non-Western, especially third-world countries.

Consider first the argument of Amartya Sen. Sen contends that the direction of the West's "development" should itself be questioned. We should not simply assume that the West has arrived and has provided for all people of all time the normative meaning of social, economic, and political development. Among other things, Sen rejects the idea that some activities or institutions serve simply and chiefly as the means to the higher end of economic or political development. Instead, he contends that development ought to be conceived as the expansion of human freedom or "agency" and not primarily as a means of bringing help to "patients." This leads to his argument in favour of developing human *capabilities*, the "substantive freedom" that makes it possible for people to "lead the lives they have reason to value and to enhance the real choices they have." This is different from developing human *capital*, understood primarily as "augmenting production possibilities" (Sen 1999, 293). The goal of development is freedom, as Sen sees it, and not simply obtaining more goods and services.

> While economic prosperity helps people to have wider options and to lead more fulfilling lives, so do more education, better health care, finer medical attention, and other factors that causally influence the effective freedoms that people actually enjoy. These "social developments" must directly count as "developmental," since they help us to lead longer, freer and more fruitful lives, in addition to the role they have in promoting productivity or economic growth or individual incomes (Sen 1999, 295).

From Sen's point of view we might say that pursuing economic and democratic development in the Third World so that individuals can have a higher level of income and enjoy the protection of individual rights is insufficient as a development goal. The pursuit of those ends at all cost may actually lead to the degrading of human life and community in other respects. Strengthening families, schools, voluntary associations, medical care, and civic action should be seen as ends in themselves, because they expand and express human capabilities. If this is true, however, it takes us back to the original question about what constitutes civil society and whether that phrase even identifies a meaningful aggregate. It also heightens the importance of our concern with human identity. Sen is clearly trying to find a way to overcome an economic reductionist view of human beings that treats them as little more than producers and consumers. But who are human beings, and what should their development aim for?

Let's return for a moment to the United States. Organisational development guru Peter Drucker discovered the importance of what he calls the "social sector" in the process of evaluating the development of Western organisational management and economic change. "Before the First World War," writes Drucker, "farmers composed the largest single group in every country" (Drucker 1994, 54). Today, "*productive* farmers make up less than half of the total farm population" and "no more than two percent of the work force in the West" (ibid.). The second-largest group in Western populations around 1900 were live-in servants. Today there are scarcely any live-in domestic servants in the developed countries. The transformation that has taken place is, of course, the fruit of the Industrial Revolution. Yet that revolution was brief. "No class in history has ever risen faster than the blue-collar worker. And no class in history has ever fallen faster" (ibid., 56). In the first decade of the twenty-first century, Drucker predicts, industrial workers in countries with well-developed free-market societies will shrink to constitute only one-eighth of the work force. Today a new "knowledge society" is emerging along with an expanding service economy. Add to this the increasing mobility of people everywhere and one can easily understand why there are fewer and fewer of the older human relationships that were constituted by local community, extended family, and neighbourhood. In other words, the institutions of an older society in the West are disappearing.

Who then attends to, or will attend to, the needs once met by local communities, families, and neighbourhoods? Drucker asks. Two answers to this question about community well-being and the service of people's needs were proposed in the twentieth century. The first solution was that government, through the welfare state, would meet the needs once met by local communities or civil society. Although Drucker does not say so, this was also the answer assumed by many Western foreign-aid plans in the 1960s and 1970s to be correct for third-world nations.

The second solution, according to Drucker, was that the "workplace community" or corporate organisation would meet the human needs once supplied by earlier forms of more personal community. For a time, this was also assumed by the West to be the answer to the question about third-world development: Large-scale economic development would supply jobs and countless human benefits would trickle down to all.

Drucker concludes, however, that both solutions proved to be wrong or at least insufficient. "The right answer to the question Who takes care of the social needs and challenges of the knowledge society? is neither the government nor the employing organisation. The answer is a separate and new *social sector*" (Drucker 1994, 75). In the United States, according to Drucker, this third, nonprofit sector comprises religious organisations but not churches. These organisations aim to change human beings, to create health and well-being. They also "serve a second and equally important purpose. They create citizenship" (ibid., 76).

To some degree Drucker has here posed the question of this volume: Should the hope for development in poorer countries now be grounded in the push for the creation and strengthening of a social sector, or more social space, or a greater number and variety of NGOs in those countries? And if so, what kind of organisations ought to be promoted and towards what ends?

Whether or not Drucker is right about the identity and role of the social sector in the West, and particularly whether such a sector is *new*, one can see how he came to discover it. Drucker takes a fairly utilitarian approach to development, and the social sector is the source of certain important human services (for "patients," Sen would say). The "new" social sector has emerged, in Drucker's view, as a *means* to an old end; that is, to meet needs left unmet or left behind by ongoing technological, economic, and political developments, which are the chief motors of social change and ought not to be stopped. Yet here we need to turn Sen's argument around in order to question Drucker: Is it not the case that economic, political, and social-sector organisations *all* meet human needs – the need for jobs, the need to develop one's talents, the need for police protection, transportation, and intellectual development? We may certainly question whether the direction of Western development has been healthy and whether economic growth should be expected to take the lead, but surely the economic and political sectors as well as the social sector are arenas of interdependent human development.

Keeping in mind the contrasting arguments of Sen and Drucker, let's now draw Jean Bethke Elshtain into the discussion. Her assessment of the family in relation to modern political development in the West is crucial at this juncture. Democracy,

Elshtain explains, arose out of opposition to kings and chiefs and other traditional, unchosen, patriarchal authorities (Elshtain 1990, 49–56), and ideals of equality and hopes of self-government gradually took hold. But what also took hold was a questioning of any and all traditional bonds, those bonds of social life not contracted or freely chosen by individuals which are the history of modern, secularising liberalism. Yet how do individuals achieve sufficient maturity to become rational and self-governing? Elshtain asks. They do so only by growing up in families from helpless infancy, and the family is one of the most traditional and undemocratic institutions of society. That is why, from Plato onward, those with ideas about radically redesigning society and government have had to fight the family. This is an error, however, even for those who most want to build a society composed of autonomous individuals. If children do not experience strong, loving, parental authority in families, they will not become independent adults. "Families are not democratic polities," yet any "further erosion of that ethical life embodied in the family bodes ill for democracy" (ibid., 56). The crisis produced by Western individualism, says Elshtain, is that the very foundation for the development of mature persons is being undermined in the quest for greater freedom and independence of those individuals. "Located inside a wider ethos that no longer affords clear-cut moral and social support for familial relations and responsibilities, young people, unsurprisingly, choose in growing numbers to postpone or evade these responsibilities" (ibid., 57). Like Michael Sandel, who criticises the faulty liberal ideal of the "unencumbered self" (Sandel 1982; for a wider debate see Sandel 1984), and like Glendon, who tracks the same history of liberalism to the apparent triumph of individualist "rights talk" (Glendon 1991), Elshtain rejects as illusory the ideal that democracy and free markets can survive without undemocratic institutions such as the family.

Does this mean that Elshtain is simply nostalgic for an earlier period in history, prior to the Industrial Revolution, when most people lived in small towns and on family farms? No, to the contrary, she supports the ongoing development and differentiation of society and of human responsibilities. The family should not be absolutised any more than the democratic polity should be absolutised. In actually nurturing children to adulthood, Elshtain explains, families teach "that no authority on this earth is omnipotent, unchanging, and absolute" (Elshtain 1990, 57). A proper democratic attitude toward society "involves a rejection of any ideal of political and familial life that absorbs all social relations under a single authority principle" (ibid., 56). Nothing should be absolutised and nothing made to serve only as a means to other ends, Elshtain implies.

To those who criticise her for being nostalgic for an earlier time, Elshtain responds by challenging her critics' "triumphant progressivism" (Elshtain 1998, 27; see also Fox-Genovese et al. 2000). Triumphant progressives are those who refuse "to come to grips with the fact that federal-government-centered solutions don't solve all problems or even, more disturbingly, that not all of our problems are fixable. . . . Many of our troubles are troubles that will plague any mass postindustrial democracy. Civil society isn't so much about problem solving as about citizen and neighbor creating" (Elshtain 1998, 27). Civil society, writes Elshtain, "reminds us that this is a world of ties that bind. You cannot have all the good things of democratic life and culture without accountability and duty" (ibid., 28). Without families, schools, churches, unions, and all the rest, including state and local governments, "there is no democratic culture and, indeed, nothing for the federal government to either correct or curb or serve" (ibid., 29).

From Elshtain's point of view we can draw the conclusion that the historical differentiation and development of diverse social, economic, and political institutions is essential for the full realisation of human life. At the same time, exclusive bonds cannot be replaced by "bridging" connections among free citizens. Strong, undemocratic families are essential to an open society. All of this has important implications for development strategies in more traditional societies that may still be dominated by family and clan ties. In those countries where exclusive family and clan bonds are still the strongest, governments often cannot or will not rule in the public interest in a disinterested fashion. They do not encourage the differentiation of independent social institutions and voluntary organisations. Instead, many such governments are led by authoritarian autocrats who rule in their own interests and in the interests of those closely related to them. The political order has not become sufficiently differentiated from the rest of society and strong enough to fulfil a responsibility of upholding equal justice for all. It does not function to "correct or curb or serve" all citizens in the full diversity of their social and economic life. Alan Whaites in Chapter 7 makes the same point, that the celebration of the decline of the state in parts of Africa, for example, has been a mistake. The government of a weak state that is unable to keep competing groups apart and dedicated to a larger common good creates a highly dangerous situation because civil society groups in many third-world countries are based on "primordial identities." Proliferation of conflict throughout the 1990s, writes Whaites, fed on these identities that became "the focus for entirely selfish group competition." Of course, to make a critical judgement like this implies not only a normative standard for government; it also implies a normative rationale for the ongoing differentiation of societies so that a greater diversity of human capabilities can be realised. Family or clan independence must not be the highest development goal of human society.

What is gradually emerging from our conversation with these diverse voices is an initial outline of a normative framework for evaluating healthy human development. People the world over need to achieve sustainable balance among multiple, differentiating responsibilities, some of which can be fulfilled only through independent institutions and organisations, each of which needs to be developed in its own sphere. In other words, to affirm healthy societal differentiation is to reject the idealisation of older, less-differentiated social, political, and economic communities. In order for ongoing historical development to occur, it is essential that disinterested, public-legal authorities (governments) emerge to govern political communities in which independent, non-government institutions and organisations can be recognised and protected.

To argue in this way obviously entails making normative judgements about what constitutes a just political community, a sound economy, and a healthy society. Societal differentiation, in other words, does not by itself guarantee the normative development of each differentiated institution. The more kinds of responsibility people have, the more ways they can do wrong as well as right. One of the aims of the normative framework we are seeking, therefore, is to avoid or to overcome the absolutisation of the family, the state, the market, and the individual in order to promote societal differentiation and integration in a well-balanced and just fashion. If a healthy society needs both undemocratic families and a democratic government, both disciplined schools and profit-making enterprises, both strongly encumbered selves and free-choice consumers, then how do we derive the norms for all of these different relationships and institutions? If each institution has its own character and none should be all-embracing or omni-competent, then what ought to be the right balance and relation among them? How ought they to be both differentiated in their own right and integrated together in harmonious societies and a just global order? Underlying all of these questions, certainly, is the question about the meaning and purpose of human life in its entirety. These are the big questions, the questions of greatest importance, not only for development in the South but also for reform in the North.

SEEKING BIBLICAL WISDOM FOR HUMAN DEVELOPMENT

It should be evident by this point that the questions we are asking and the criticisms we are levelling arise from a Christian point of view. But let's take the initial exploration further and ask more pointedly what is entailed in a Christian view of human development. In taking this step, I intend something different than does David Bronkema, who uses the word *Christian* in the phrase *Christian NGOs* to mean "those organisations that draw their inspiration from the Christian faith and church, and reflect that inspiration at the very least in their rhetoric" (Chapter 11, n. 3). I do *not* want to confine civil society to the narrow circle of development NGOs; neither do I believe that the adjective *Christian* should be used primarily to refer to the subjective, sociological reality of those people and churches inspired by Christian faith.

I use *Christian* or *biblical* in what follows to refer primarily to God's normative purposes, standards, and revelation that constitute and define the whole creation for all people. Many or most people in the world may not understand their lives and the world in this Christian light, but those who do and who, by faith, are members of Christ's body do not merely bring an "inspiration" to a reality that otherwise has its own "secular" meaning. Christians confess, or ought to confess, a meaning of the world, including all of its institutions and relationships, that comes from and is held accountable to God through Jesus Christ.

Biblically speaking, then, the meaning and value of family life, of the education of children and adults, of the service of neighbours in need, of the work of medical and other professions, and of organisational efforts to promote justice in society, the meaning and value of these is *not*, first of all, that they are means to the end of economic growth, or democratic government, or the evangelisation of the lost. The pressure to orient all of life towards the economic and political maximisation of human freedom, for example, distorts the real meaning of human life in *all* spheres, including the economic and the political. Economic growth for the sake of more consumption, and politics reduced to rights talk also represent distorted forms of economic and political life. So the aim of social recovery and healthy develop-ment, from a Christian point of view, must not be simply to strengthen so-called seedbeds of virtue and watchdogs of government so that the market and democ-racy can survive. Nor should the so-called Christian aim be to use various NGOs as tools to evangelise and serve people so they will better be able to influence government. The Christian aim must be the reformation of all of life through ori-entation of every sphere to its true purpose. And the ultimate aim of all of this, the true purpose of all dimensions of human life, is to show forth and celebrate the glory of God, to enjoy fellowship with God and all our neighbours in Jesus Christ, by the power of the Holy Spirit, by praising God with all that we are and have.

The diverse institutions and relationships often identified as civil society should not be approached first of all, therefore, from the viewpoint of how they affect or undergird economic development, but rather out of concern for their own norma-tive development as part of the full breadth and depth of human meaning. If the full meaning of human life cannot be properly realised apart from service to neighbours, apart from the development of musical talent, teamwork in scientific laboratories, and the worship of God, and apart from the deep intimacy of human friendships, marriages, and multi-generational family life, then all of the activities and organisations that are necessary to realise these ends must be seen as meaningful in their own right. This is what development should mean in any country or culture in the world.

Economic development and democracy should therefore be viewed, at least from one angle, as means to ends beyond themselves. A society in which an open market allows for more human entrepreneurship and creative activity is a society in which more human talents can be developed and interrelated. A society in which the political authorities are held accountable by citizens to protect their rights to speak, to worship, and to pursue many different human activities is a society in which a greater number of dimensions of human life can develop simultaneously. In this sense democratic politics and open markets both *aid* and *express* human development.

At the same time, we should see commerce, industry, politics, and government as meaningful, God-given dimensions of human life-in-community and not merely as means to other ends or as evils to be curbed by civil society. Those with gifts in the art of sales, industrial organisation, advertising, political organising, conflict resolution, and public administration are called to develop important human tal-ents and fulfil valuable human aspirations in those avenues of service. The chief question behind all human development, therefore, is this: What is the purpose of human life, and how ought the many different dimensions of human experience to be developed simultaneously and interdependently throughout the globe in order for humans adequately to express the image God, to know themselves truly, and to praise God? Or to put it another way, what is the meaning of life in this world which God loves so much that he sent his only Son to save it? Who are these human beings whom God loves so much and who were created to reveal God as God's image?

Amartya Sen speaks of human beings needing not simply more "utilities" or "primary goods" but more "substantive freedoms" – "capabilities . . . to choose a life one has reason to value" (Sen 1999, 74). There is a diversity of human "functionings" that needs to be kept in view with regard to substantive freedom, he argues. Consequently, a "person's 'capability' refers to the alternative combinations of functionings that are feasible for her to achieve. Capability is thus a kind of freedom: the substantive freedom to achieve alternative functioning combinations (or, less formally put, the freedom to achieve various lifestyles)" (ibid., 75).

Sen is on to something here. Nevertheless, from a biblical point of view, he is on to it in an inadequate way. While trying to be empirical in one respect, his attempt to generalise with value-neutral terms leads to an abstraction from the real *valuational* struggle in which humans are always engaged. The fact is that some people want to pursue wealth above all else, while others choose a life of poverty. Some discover musical talent within themselves, and others do not. Some decide to balance many "functionings" of work, family life, voluntary service, hobbies, and recreation, while others give themselves to only one cause. Some value community most highly; some seek to live with few if any obligations to others. Why are humans like this? How should we judge what is good and bad about any of these patterns of life? How do people with different talents benefit one another? Sen's abstractions of "capabilities" and "functionings" do not adequately address these questions and do not help to illuminate standards by which to judge normative and anti-normative functionings.

The concern about moral standards and not just about freedom and functionings is one of Gertrude Himmelfarb's chief concerns with respect to the loose use of the term *civil society*. What is required today, she argues, "is not only a restoration of civil society but the far more difficult task of reformation – moral reformation. Even to articulate the problem is difficult, because the language of morality has become suspect. One of the reasons the idea of civil society is so attractive is that it is couched in the language of sociology" (Himmelfarb 1998, 119). From a biblical point of view, then, what are the foundations for a moral viewpoint, for the language of moral judgements about normative and anti-normative development patterns?

It is possible to keep meat on the bones abstracted by sociological and economic analyses and to speak about human obligations quite concretely if we speak in terms of talents, callings, and responsibilities rather than in terms of functionings and capabilities. God has constituted human beings with many different talents and callings with which to respond to the One in whose image they have been created. All human responsibilities are ultimately a response to God. The image of God – male and female, in their generations – is a complex creature *called* to fill the earth and to develop the whole creation in order to know and praise God and thereby to come to true self-knowledge as the image of God in community. The ability to make music, pursue agriculture, build bridges, fly to the moon, raise children, write public laws, nurture love in an intimate friendship, invent millions of types of machines, and play in the backyard or on a stage – all of this and much, much more *reveals something about both God and the image of God*. To develop any of these human talents or interests properly is to pursue a calling from God. And the pursuit of such callings both depends on and requires service together with fellow humans and other creatures. In fact, when properly analysed, every talent and calling is to one degree or another a shared, communal activity exercised in response to normative standards that bind creatures to their Creator in a covenant relationship.

Talents and callings are not merely the functionings or capabilities of free selves, as if freedom has an original, creative meaning prior to, or apart from, those talents and responsibilities given by God. Neither civil society nor any other part of human life is merely a realm we create for ourselves. The variety of human callings is constitutive of the image of God who exists only in complete dependence on God. Altogether the diverse kinds of abilities and exercises of human responsibility arise from a depth that is nothing less than the revelatory connection, the covenant communion, between God and the image of God. Humans have their identity as the image of God, and everything they are and do reveals something about the deepest meaning of life. Sen's phrase "substantive freedom" is thus an abstraction that allows for very limited normative content. The content that he gives it throughout his book comes from the fact that he is exploring dimensions of creaturely life on earth that must be accounted for in terms of an origin and a destiny that can only be grasped by humans in communion with God, the One whom they image. And the modes of that communion in this age are not just prayer and worship but include a full life of earthly stewardship, service, and development. Thus, *human development may be defined as the unfolding, diversifying, and complexifying exercise of all the responsibilities that belong to the generations of the image of God, and this occurs in a healthy fashion only when humans steward the earth creatively with all of their talents in obedience to and in fellowship with the One who has called them into service toward the destiny of face-to-face fellowship with God.*

From this point of view it becomes possible to see why economic development is itself an important and essential human calling, but one that, if absolutised or distorted, can cripple other aspects of human development as well as the very meaning of stewardly enterprise. From this point of view one can see how crucial a just political system is, in order to achieve the right public-legal integration of a differentiating society. A just political order will have to do more than merely protect individual freedom and protect an open market. The public square is more than a market. Likewise, authoritarian governments, which serve the interests of one family or clan, of one corporation or another, must also be judged inadequate and even dangerous for human well-being in differentiating societies. Governments that deny people the right to exercise God-given responsibilities to educate their children, to worship as their conscience leads them, or to organise freely are governments that inhibit genuine human development as a responsible service to God.

If either government or the market in a given society or at the global level suppresses human responsibility in other spheres of life, one can understand why the conviction might arise that civil society can save the world. For it is certainly true that if the richness of human creativity and responsibility is nurtured among people in a healthy, balanced way, there will, over time, be positive economic and political consequences. Nevertheless, these positive consequences do not follow naturally or inevitably. Economic and political responsibilities must themselves be exercised in normative ways to help realise properly balanced patterns of development.[3]

CONCLUSION

The implications of the foregoing discussion are vast. The following offers a brief outline of some of those implications.

1. The historical emergence of disinterested governments called to govern political communities with "justice for all" is a development that must go hand in hand with the differentiation of other institutions and associations, including some form of economic marketplace. Civil society cannot save a people from oppressive, unjust governments, but neither can such governments be changed without the emergence of a sense of civic purpose and the ability of citizens to mobilise in order to reform or replace such governments. For the latter to occur, people must be literate, publicly engaged, and willing to act in the public interest, and this is where mediating civil society institutions play a critical role. Opening free markets and opening a society to foreign investment will not inevitably lead to just governments and a flourishing civil society that includes a free press, independent political parties, and so forth (see Skillen 1994). As with all historical development, however, well-balanced societal differentiation and integration never occur without the opening of markets for free exchange. So the question will always be one of how to bring balanced social, economic, and political development where it does not exist. In that sense the aim to encourage the development of a variety of civil society institutions in poor countries, which currently may be over-controlled by arbitrary, authoritarian governments and/or by domestic or international economic forces, should be pursued with utmost diligence. Political and economic changes in themselves are not sufficient, nor will the reform of those public institutions be possible without the multi-dimensional social development of the people. Michael Walzer makes this point well:

> The network of associations incorporates, but it cannot dispense with, the agencies of state power; neither can socialist cooperation or capitalist competition dispense with the state. . . . Citizenship is one of the many roles that members [of society] play, but the state itself is unlike all the other associations. It both frames civil society and occupies space within it. It fixes the boundary conditions and the basic rules of all associational activity. . . .
>
> Only a democratic state can create a democratic civil society; only a democratic society can sustain a democratic state. The civility that makes

democratic politics possible can only be learned in the associational networks; the roughly equal and widely dispersed capabilities that sustain the networks have to be fostered by the democratic state (Walzer 1998, 138, 140; see also Himmelfarb 1998, 121; Chaplin 1997, 1998, and 2000).

2. The work of NGOs should not be thought of as necessarily in conflict or in tension with economic organisations and a free market, such that NGOs have to save people from markets and corporations. A mistaken absolutisation of capitalism or of the goal of economic growth will certainly distort human communities and associations that are not economically or politically qualified. But those distortions are a sign of a faulty, anti-normative development of the economy and of the laws that govern business and the economy. The fact is that an open society with an open market is one of the important ingredients for human flourishing. Without such freedom of exchange, many of the talents and callings that belong to people will not be able to be developed and interwoven with one another. The moral import here is that the *simultaneous* development of healthy, limited markets *and* of healthy families, schools, voluntary associations, and social-action organisations is necessary, with each being developed in accord with its own normative purpose (see Goudzwaard and de Lange 1995; Goudzwaard et al. 2001).

3. With respect to both a healthy political community and a healthy market we might use the analogy of a choir or orchestra, as long as we don't stretch the analogy too far. It takes many different voices, many different kinds of instruments, to make certain kinds of music. Each voice or instrument needs to be developed in accord with its own character and purpose. Not everyone can aspire to be the soloist or the conductor. This is not to suggest that a government, stockmarket, or central bank is the conductor of a single social purpose (a single piece of music), because the public-legal interweaving of society or the simultaneous movement of many market exchanges is more complicated and diversified than a musical concert. Only God, not the state or the market, is the conductor of human life in the world. The point of the analogy, however, is to say that a government which suppresses families, the media, and/or political advocacy will distort human life for everyone, much as a conductor would destroy a symphony if he or she refused to allow the violins to come on stage and made the horns play the parts of the woodwinds. A market that allowed only multinational corporations to participate and denied a place to nonprofit organisations would be like a choir with a very limited repertoire that kept many potential vocalists from ever being able to develop their talents.

4. An important note about "self-interest" and "selfishness" must also be entered here. Sometimes the market and economic enterprising as well as interest-group politics, and even government itself, are viewed as selfish and self-serving, while civil society efforts are valued as constructively oriented toward the good of others and not self-serving. A corporation's aim to make a profit is seen as self-serving, while the aim of a nonprofit job-training programme is seen as other-serving. Civil society is the "good guy" who will, in this context, save the world from the clutches of the "bad guy," the evil corporations and governments of this

world. These distinctions harbour both truths and falsehoods, but they do not help clarify the norms that hold for different institutions and relationships. Consider the following examples:

a. Parents in a family legitimately bear responsibility for their children. It is not selfish, then, for them to look after the interests of their children and of their family. When questions of public policy arise that touch on the family, nothing could be more legitimate than for parents to want those public policies to be good for their children. Love of one's own children, like proper self-love, is perfectly legitimate. It is one of the bases for learning how to love others as ourselves. Where selfishness supplants proper self-love and love of one's own, however, is when parents seek only the benefit of their children and do not rise beyond that motivation to see that they and their children are also neighbours, citizens, and friends of others, including other children. Public policies or neighbourhood-watch groups must serve all families and all children, and there is always a point at which true parental love must show itself by the way parents teach their children to love others, sometimes sacrificially and regardless of themselves.

b. For a business to try to increase its sales or to seek adequate legal protection and the best tax policies for its own benefit is not selfish or greedy. Only by producing and selling its product in an encouraging environment can it employ people, serve customers, and do all kinds of other good things. That is what a business does to fulfil its own purpose and to be of service to others. Yet if the only thing business people do is to seek the interest of their own businesses and lobby for benefits to help their businesses regardless of all else, then they turn proper self-care into unjust and unstewardly selfishness. They fail to see that in their civic capacity, for example, they should be seeking justice for all businesses, all labourers, all citizens, all nonprofit organisations, and the environment. Even within their businesses there is more to success than self-service. As Sen comments, it is incorrect "to conclude that the success of capitalism as an economic system depends only on self-interested behavior rather than on a complex and sophisticated value system that has many other ingredients, including reliability, trust, and business honesty (in the face of contrary temptations)" (Sen 1999, 279).

The myth of the "invisible hand" has become, for many people, a political philosophy that confuses the legitimacy of businesses pursuing their own ends with the idea that the public good is best achieved only as an indirect outcome of everyone seeking his or her own interests. The element of truth in this myth is that if every family nurtures love within itself, if every school succeeds at its teaching, if every business is stewardly and productive in its own quest for success in a free market, and if every voluntary association tends to its own purpose diligently, then all of this will add up to something good for everyone. But the element of error in the myth is the assumption that the common good of the entire public order can be achieved indirectly without anyone paying attention to it or nurturing it in its own right. This is mistaken. A political community has its own calling, its own offices, its own purposes, its own normative standards of justice for the public square. The health of the political order is not guaranteed as an indirect consequence of the action of other organisations and institutions, even when they behave normatively in their own spheres. There is more to the common good than an accumulation of multiple private goods. And, in fact, no differentiated private good can be achieved outside the context of a public-legal governance structure that upholds and protects it.

c. Internationally, too, there is nothing wrong with states seeking to protect their own national interests. After all, governments have primary responsibility for their own citizens; they do not govern the citizens of other countries. But here again, if everything a government does is oriented only towards its own interests, narrowly conceived, regardless of what is good for other states or for the international order, it will fail to take seriously the responsibility it bears, *together with other states*, to do justice internationally and transnationally. Governments, in other words, are no more free, in God's creation, to be entirely self-occupied within their own borders than are people within their own homes or businesses. God's purposes for human beings and the responsibilities they have from God do not allow for the absolutisation of state sovereignty, as Lowell Ewert argues in his discussion of human rights in Chapter 5. Proper self-regard and self-care of states amounts to something different than nationalistic self-preoccupation and self-centredness. And in a shrinking globe it becomes more and more apparent with each passing day that the national interests of any state depend very much on a healthy and just world order.

As Ewert points out, even though the UN's Universal Declaration of Human Rights was adopted as a non-binding resolution, the declaration soon began to take on a binding, normative character because of the yearning for respect for human rights that the document unleashed. On the other hand, Ewert's argument that civil society ought to be grounded in basic international respect for human rights gives too little attention to the fact that rights can be upheld and enforced only by rights implementers and law enforcers. It is not enough to pit the universality of human rights appeals against unjust governments; it is not enough to appeal to civil society as the means of achieving international justice. One must also make the case for the just governance of states and the just enforcement of international law and human rights. And this can be done only by states or international authorities enforcing international law.

d. While it is true that the institutions and organisations of civil society tend to be viewed as worthy empowerment vehicles, they themselves can act in selfish, unjust ways that are bad both for people and for the larger society. A desire to protect the environment, for example, does not guarantee the wisdom and justice of every lobby effort by environmentalists, particularly if they do not recognise that governments must deal with more than environmental protection. Families that fail at being families do not thereby serve as seedbeds of virtue. "The family, the most basic and intimate unit of civil society," says Himmelfarb, "is hardly a paragon of virtue" (Himmelfarb 1998, 118). Those who serve the poor with job training or financial support can do so in ways that instill in recipients a sense of victimhood or of class hatred. Whaites makes the point that NGOs in the Third World tend to see the world made better "by 'scaling up' their own areas of expertise, usually leading to a lack of appreciation of the macro environment by which their own and everybody else's issues are shaped. . . . The heterogeneity and the lack of accountability of civil society, particularly when coupled to weak political contexts, create obstacles to it playing a fundamentally transforming role" (Chapter 7 herein). Just as political and economic institutions need to develop in accord with normative standards, all other organisations must do the same.

The aims of social analysis and responsible action, therefore, must be to clarify the norms or standards that should guide those who bear responsibility in families, schools, businesses, nonprofit organisations, and governments. Only by means of the normative development of each such institution and organisation *simultaneously* and *together* can a healthy and just society be sustained and further developed. Civil society cannot save the world, but people who respond to God obediently to build just states, to nurture loving families, to perfect good schools, to meet the real needs of the poor or handicapped, and to build sound, stewardly businesses can together, by God's grace, give evidence of the whole creation being redeemed.

5. Finally, the differentiation of society, which includes the development of countless talents and callings in thousands of fields of music, art, industry, commerce, science, technology, education, leisure, government, and politics, means increasing opportunities for every person to use his or her gifts to the praise of God. And this should be as true for women as it is for men. One of the important fruits of societal differentiation and public-legal integration is that people can exercise many different responsibilities all at the same time. Less differentiated societies often have relatively few fixed roles for individuals. It has been possible in different societies at different points in history to think in terms of permanent classes and gender roles. Yet even with a high view of marriage as a lifelong, intimate bond and of family as the most fundamental of social relationships, one can see that the marital and family roles do not exhaustively define women any more than they exhaustively define men. With changes in employment patterns, social attitudes, and public laws it is possible within relatively well-balanced, differentiated societies for women as well as men to enter into marriage and build strong families while also developing a diverse range of talents and fulfilling diverse responsibilities outside the home. In so far as we see men and women together as the image of God, called to serve God with all that they are and have, we must seek diligently to make it possible for every person, in community, to develop and bring to light his or her gifts and abilities (Fox-Genovese et al. 2000).

A Christian view of civil society and of human development most broadly begins, therefore, with creation, with God's purposes for the image of God, male and female, and it ends by looking with expectation to the final unveiling of the City of God, in which every dimension of human life will be fulfilled in perfect balance and harmony to the glory of God and praise of Jesus Christ, our elder brother, friend, vineyard keeper, shepherd, teacher, guide, high priest, corner stone, messiah, lord, and king.

Notes

[1] For a good introduction to the different meanings of the phrase *civil society* relative to the concern for a Christian contribution, see Roland Hoksbergen, "Give Them a Fish, Teach Them to Fish, or Organize a Fishing Club? NGOs, Civil Society and Economic Development," *Faith and Economics* (fall 1999): 11–18.

[2] Putnam seems not to see why the very idea of a civic community of tolerant individuals may be the cause of damage to certain kinds of non-governmental associations that build strong bonding social capital. For an assessment of this problem as regards racism and busing, see James W. Skillen, "Evangelical Cooperation in the Cause of Racial Justice," in *Religion, Race, and Justice in a Changing America*, ed. G. Orfield and H. J. Lebowitz, 115–36 (New York: Century Foundation Press, 1999).

Alan Wolfe, like Putnam, also seems less concerned by the evident decline of bonding social capital, believing that "the capacity of Americans to reinvent their worlds" will fill the gaps. "Less likely to find civil society in neighborhoods, families, and churches," says Wolfe, "Americans are more likely to find it at the workplace, in cyberspace, and in forms of political parties." The question that Wolfe agrees cannot be answered now, however, is whether "these newly emerging forms of civil society" can serve as a sufficient "buffer between the market and the state, protecting Americans from the consequences of selfishness on the one hand and coercive altruism on the other" (Alan Wolfe, "Is Civil Society Obsolete?" in *Community Works*, ed. E. J. Dionne Jr. [Washington, D.C.: The Brookings Institution, 1998], 22).

[3] Thus, Himmelfarb's point that "when we speak of the breakdown of the family, it is a moral breakdown we are talking about. And when we speak of the restoration of civil society, it is a moral restoration we should seek. That restoration may actually take us outside the realm of civil society, for the mediating structures of civil society are themselves dependent on the well-being of the individuals who participate in them and of the state that protects and legitimises them" (Gertrude Himmelfarb, "Second Thoughts on Civil Society," in *Community Works*, ed. E. J. Dionne Jr. [Washington, D.C.: The Brookings Institution, 1998], 117).

References

Berger, Peter L., and Richard John Neuhaus. 1977. *To Empower People: The Role of Mediating Structures in Public Policy*. Washington, D.C.: The American Enterprise Institute.

Chaplin, Jonathan. 1997. "Subsidiarity and Sphere Sovereignty: Catholic and Reformed Conceptions of the Role of the State." In *Things Old and New: Catholic Social Teaching*, edited by Frank McHugh and Samuel Natale, 175–202. Lanham, Md.: University Press of America.

———. 1998. "Religion and Democracy." In *Contemporary Political Studies 1998*, vol. 2, edited by A. Dobson and J. Stanyer, 988–1003. Nottingham: Political Studies Association of the United Kingdom.

———. 2000. "Beyond Liberal Restrain: Defending Religiously Based Arguments in Law and Public Policy." *University of British Columbia Law Review* 33/2.

Council on Civil Society. 1998. *A Call to Civil Society*. New York: Institute for American Values.

Dionne, E. J. Jr., ed. 1998. *Community Works*. Washington, D.C.: The Brookings Institution.

Drucker, Peter F. 1994. "The Age of Social Transformation." *The Atlantic Monthly* (November): 53–80.

Elshtain, Jean Bethke. 1990. "The Family and Civic Life." In Jean Bethke Elshtain, *Power Trips and Other Journeys: Essays in Feminism as a Civic Discourse*, 49–56. Madison, Wis.: University of Wisconsin Press.

———. 1998. "Not a Cure-All." In *Community Works*, edited by E. J. Dionne Jr. Washington, D.C.: The Brookings Institution.

Fox-Genovese, Elizabeth, et al. 2000. *Women and the Future of the Family*. Grand Rapids, Mich.: Baker Books.

Glendon, Mary Ann. 1991. *Rights Talk: The Impoverishment of Political Discourse*. New York: The Free Press.

Goudzwaard, Bob. and Harry de Lange. 1995. *Beyond Poverty and Affluence: Toward an Economy of Care*. Grand Rapids, Mich.: Eerdmans.

Goudzwaard, Bob, et al. 2001. *Globalization and the Kingdom of God*. Grand Rapids, Mich.: Baker Books.

Himmelfarb, Gertrude. 1998. *Second Thoughts on Civil Society*. In *Community Works*, edited by E. J. Dionne Jr., 117. Washington, D.C.: The Brookings Institution.

Hoksbergen, Roland. 1999. "Give Them a Fish, Teach Them to Fish, or Organize a Fishing Club? NGOs, Civil Society and Economic Development." *Faith and Economics* (fall): 11–18.

International Jacques Maritain Institute. 1999. *Notes and Documents* 24/54–55 (January-August): 42–65.

Putnam, Robert. 2000. *Bowling Alone*. New York: Simon and Schuster.

Sandel, Michael. 1982. *Liberalism and the Limits of Justice*. Cambridge: Cambridge University Press.

Sandel, Michael, ed. 1984. *Liberalism and Its Critics*. New York: New York University Press.

Seligman, Adam. 1992. *The Idea of Civil Society*. Princeton, N.J.: Princeton University Press.

Sen, Amartya. 1999. *Development as Freedom*. New York: Anchor Books.

Skillen, James W. 1994. *Recharging the American Experiment*. Grand Rapids, Mich.: Baker Books.

Walzer, Michael. 1998. "The Idea of Civil Society." In *Community Works,* edited by E. J. Dionne Jr. Washington, D.C.: The Brookings Institution.

Wolfe, Alan. 1989. *Whose Keepers? Social Science and Moral Obligation*. Berkeley and Los Angeles: University of California Press.

———. 1998. "Is Civil Society Obsolete?" In *Community Works*, ed. E. J. Dionne Jr. Washington, D.C.: The Brookings Institution.

Part 3

IMPACT, INFLUENCE, AND POTENTIAL

The Role of Christian NGOs in Strengthening Civil Society

———————◆———————

10

A Christian NGO Faces Globalisation

CRS as Development Agent

Denis Goulet

The Changing World of NGOs

Following the end of World War II the pursuit of development became an explicit policy goal of national governments and international institutions. NGOs created earlier to provide emergency assistance in the wake of other wars, population displacement, and natural catastrophes gradually expanded the scope of their activities to include helping people "develop" the capacity to provide for themselves.

We see today, however, that their original role did not disappear. On the contrary, with the increased numbers of internal conflicts, civil wars, and enforced migrations, humanitarian assistance has grown astronomically. To a considerable degree, development itself has come to be viewed as the step to take after emergency relief. As the regnant development model shifted away from assigning central roles to state action and international resource transfers and towards primary reliance on markets, export-driven economic strategies, and integration into global trade competition, the relative importance of NGOs as development agents has grown.

This shift has given rise to a troubling paradox. In earlier days NGOs operated mainly at the local project level and drew praise for being closer to the people and more sensitive to the real needs of the poor than were governmental or international planning, technical, or financial agencies. More important, NGOs were seen as committed to development for ethical reasons and not to secure ideological, political, strategic, or bureaucratic advantages – motives usually imputed to official aid providers and interstate bodies. But as these older NGOs, together with thousands of new ones springing up mainly in the South, took on welfare functions increasingly abandoned by states and public agencies, NGOs became increasingly

Grateful acknowledgment is made to Jaco Cilliers and Mary Mulvihill for facilitating interviews at CRS and for their assistance in obtaining documentation. Thanks also extend to all CRS personnel, present and past, interviewed.

dependent on funding from governments and international agencies. Raymond Offenheiser contends:

> The increased funding to NGOs in the 1980s and 1990s resulted in a great interest among NGOs to tap into these funds to further their respective mandates as well as a substantial increase in the number, density, and capacity of NGOs. NGOs can lay claim to some significant successes in fostering democratic change, in complementing the state in providing quality social services, in assuming responsibility for organising credit programmes for the rural poor, in leveraging policy reforms in a wide range of key policy areas, in supporting free and fair electoral processes, and in assisting in processes of building decentralised governmental structures. Southern NGOs are now more capable of formulating and voicing their own visions for their societies. These developments raise serious questions of what the mission and role of Northern development NGOs, both secular and faith based, should be in the future (Chapter 1 herein).

Even friendly critics wonder if NGOs are becoming mere subcontractors to governments and international agencies in the provision of social services. And where now is the NGOs' initial distinguishing trait – the commitment to empower non-elites and the poor in a participatory mode respectful of cultural differences and sensitive to local factor endowments and environmental demands? Can NGOs still plead ethical superiority over politically motivated or geo-strategically driven assistance programmes conducted by bilateral and multilateral aid agencies? Can they credibly present themselves as agents of genuine human development and not merely as purveyors of relief supplies or of technical, financial, or managerial expertise? Are NGOs promoting sound alternative development to serve as a counter or a corrective to dominant patterns of development widely criticised as ethnocentric, elitist, and economically reductionistic? A recent fictional work gives voice to the growing scepticism about the beneficence of NGOs as aid agents:

> It [the NGO] fosters *efficacy*, or *effectiveness* in the aid field. In aid work, *effectiveness* is pretty much the gold standard. Compassion's a given. . . . [It] addresses the thorny question of how much of each dollar from each donor nation actually reaches its target, and how much wasteful overlap and unhelpful competition exists between agencies on the ground. It grapples, as we all do, alas, with the aid world's three Rs: reduplication, rivalry, rationalisation. It balances overheads against productivity and . . . it sat well with calls for greater transparency and an ethical foreign policy and other questionable nostrums of the day, so we pushed it for all it was worth. There are those who say the U.N. should do the job. Others say the U.N. already does it. Others again say the U.N. is part of the disease (Le Carré 2001, 84).

Critical questioning of development reached the public at large through striking images such as the champagne glass that illustrated inequalities in income distribution (UNDP 1992). Development was shown as benefitting the few to the exclusion of the many, and as accelerating disparities in income, living standards, and quality of life. Development was likewise blamed for destroying more liveli-hoods than it created, for diluting fragile cultures in the name of technological or market imperatives, and for damaging environments (Haque 1999; Sachs 1992).

Not surprisingly, voices arose urging NGOs to "'return to their roots' if they are to promote poverty reduction on a mass scale" (Hulme and Edwards 1997, 20). In a world increasingly globalised, however, populated by thousands more NGOs than in earlier times, a world in which rich nations show little inclination to transfer re-sources to poorer ones, it is no easy thing for NGOs to return to their root values and modes of action. Nor can returning to their roots mean restoring past patterns of local project work in micro arenas. On the contrary, the change needed requires NGOs to institutionalise and operationalise their values in a complex globalised world in which micro activities are affected by and in turn affect larger forces at work in macro and intermediate meso arenas of action. In the numerous settings of conflict in which NGOs perform their relief and development tasks, they have also been thrust (wittingly or not) into playing political roles. Stephen Commins warns:

> Owing to the rapid changes in the international political economy, and to the deeply embedded political and social factors in each complex emergency, NGOs are in danger of becoming increasingly marginal in terms of the im-portance of their work, to put it in stark terms, they are becoming the deliv-ery agency for a global soup kitchen, handing out meagre comfort amidst harsh economic changes and complex political emergencies, in a world that is characterized by global economic integration and the social exclusion of low-income communities, as well as continuing and widespread levels of civil strife. In effect, NGOs are handing out bits of comfort, doling out cups of soup, to the victims of massive economic changes and to the survivors of brutal civil wars. While NGOs have claimed the right to a moral as well as programmatic voice in international affairs, their organizational legitimacy and operational impact are in fact being weakened.
>
> For the past two decades, NGOs have occupied a privileged position in the industrialized countries, both in the public eye and with bilateral donors. NGOs have presented themselves as having a significant impact in shaping donor policies and humanitarian responses. Particularly during the latter part of the 1980s and the early 1990s, NGOs were seen as the most effective and efficient entities for delivering international relief and development programmes. That perception is now changing, which raises questions about the future of the NGO sector (Commins 2000, 70–71).

NGOs have grown geometrically in number in recent decades. One estimate now places the number of international NGOs at 35,000, along with one million local NGOs (Tirman 1998–99, 3). *The Economist* cites a 1995 United Nations report that suggests: "By one estimate, there are now two million [NGOs] in America alone, most formed in the last 30 years. In Russia, where almost none existed before the fall of communism, there are at least 65,000. Dozens are created daily; in Kenya alone, some 240 NGOs are now created every year" (*The Economist* 2000, 25). NGOs are pressured by events to re-examine multiple possible roles they may play in global civil society – service provision, capacity building and empowerment, policy advocacy and formation, serving as beacons or pilot demonstrators of alternative pathways to human development.

Because their existence rests explicitly on ethical and religious values, Christian NGOs are acutely affected by the new conjuncture, the new criticism, and the newly felt need to situate themselves as constructive development agents in a globalising world (Lewis 2000; Simmons 1998; Fisher 1998; Edwards and Hulme 1996; Weiss and Gordenker 1996). Like NGOs at large, Christian NGOs are themselves highly diverse in size, age, arenas of action, philosophy, and practice of development.

Here we explore the culture of development at one Christian NGO, Catholic Relief Services (CRS), and analyse how it is shaping its institutional responses to challenges posed by today's constellation of conditions: globalisation, the new potential importance of civil society organisations in matters of governance, and the search for ways of promoting sustainable, people-centred, development. What new self-understandings and decision-making criteria inform and guide CRS in its rationale for doing what it does and in how it translates this rationale into practice? How does CRS choose where and how to work, with whom, and at the service of what policies? Finally, what is CRS' view of civil society and globalisation? The aim is to identify and explicate the ethical framework of development that CRS follows in theory and practice (Goulet 1995). This ethic, the centrepiece of CRS' culture of development, offers clues as to whether NGOs at large can successfully perform as agents of sustainable human development.

Thierry Verhelst, former director of the Belgian NGO Broederlijk Delen and editor of the bilingual journal *Cultures and Development*, has defined development as "an all-inclusive process that is, in the final analysis, cultural. *For it is the idea of culture that gives both meaning and direction to economic activity, political decisions, community life, social conflict, technology, and so on. It is in fact culture that gives development its raison d'être and its goal"* (Verhelst 1987, 159–60). All development models, Verhelst adds, "whether left-wing or right-wing, have been based on Western preconceptions. The indigenous cultures of the peoples of the Third World have been largely neglected. . . . They must be studied much more closely" (ibid., 22). The culture of Western NGOs likewise needs to be studied to assess what prospects exist for them, as actors in civil society, to promote human development in a globalised world. "Culture," as used here, is the array of preferred definitions, self-understandings, values, shared assumptions, criteria for decisions and evaluations, institutional arrangements, and modes of action pursued by NGOs in development arenas. Older NGOs possess a "culture" in this sense, an examination of which brings to light their philosophy of development and their role in civil society.

Moreover, a new globalisation culture is itself emerging – a culture of transparency, accountability, and legitimacy accorded to citizens' groupings to act in political arenas through channels not themselves part of formal political institutions (government agencies, legislatures, courts), but through media disclosure, advocacy, monitoring, demonstrations, advertising, acting as observers at international negotiation conferences, and citizen diplomacy.

In 1980 the large Sri Lanka NGO/social movement Sarvodaya found itself at a crucial crossroad. After more than two decades of rapid expansion and successful revitalisation of hundreds of villages into agents of "people's development" in harmony with local values, Sarvodaya aspired to change the direction and quality of macro-development policies then being pursued by its national government. It seemed that Sarvodaya faced a challenge to its "survival with integrity" (Goulet 1981). Could it retain its distinctive value orientation and participatory thrust as it entered larger, more complex, macro arenas of development at the national level? In view of the mandate that CRS has now given itself – to promote, in a globalised world, a pattern of sustainable, peaceful development rooted in justice – a partial analogy exists with the *problématique* Sarvodaya faced in 1980. As it faces new challenges posed by globalisation, can CRS survive with integrity? Offenheiser (Chapter 1) endorses Michael Edwards's view that "harnessing the forces of globalisation to a vision of social justice is THE political project of the 21st century" (Edwards 2000, 14). Will CRS and other value-based NGOs prove able to promote integral human development which is socially just, environmentally sustainable, culturally protective, human rights and freedom enhancing in the larger globalised world?

In the following we make extensive use of the precise language (mainly internal) employed in documents crafted by CRS officials and internal evaluation teams in the wake of critical reflections on their agency's identity, mission, and relations with other developmental agents. Taken cumulatively, these lengthy quotations constitute a phenomenological portrait of the values, principles, critical definitions, criteria of decision-making, and evaluation standards which comprise CRS' ethic and culture of development.

CRS as Development Agency

Mission

CRS, a large Catholic NGO with approximately 4,000 personnel, of whom nearly 10 per cent are located at headquarters in Baltimore, Maryland,

was established in 1943 by the Roman Catholic Bishops of the United States. Its mission is to provide assistance to those in need outside the United States. All assistance is provided on the basis of need, without regard to creed, race or nationality. In 1943, during World War II, the agency began its work just as the resettlement of war refugees in Europe was taking place. In the 1950s, as Europe regained its balance, the agency began to look at other parts of the world that could benefit from the assistance of Catholics in the United States.

In the 1960s and 1970s Catholic Relief Services began to expand its operations and opened offices in Africa, Asia and Latin America. Building on its tradition of providing relief in emergency situations, Catholic Relief Services also began to seek ways to help people in the developing world break the cycle of poverty through community-based, sustainable development initiatives. These programs, which include agricultural assistance, small business loans for the poor, health education and clean water projects, ensure that the local population is the central participant in its own development and that a project can be sustained through the effort and resources of the local community.

Over the past half century, Catholic Relief Services' mission of helping people in times of need through emergency aid, following natural disasters like Hurricane Mitch in Central America as well as through development programs – has sought to inspire the U.S. Catholic community to live out our spiritual tradition of compassionate service to the world. Today, as we look to the next millennium and a renewal of our commitment to the most vulnerable members of the human family, we continue to reassess our mission. We do so always, with a view to fulfilling our gospel mandate in a way that most clearly reflects the principles of Catholic social teaching, which is the foundation on which our work is built (CRS 2000a).

Catholic Relief Services reaches out to more than 80 countries and territories around the world to alleviate poverty and suffering. The core of our work at Catholic Relief Services is to honor the dignity of the human person, and to work for a world in which all flourish in accordance with that dignity (CRS 2000b).

Philosophy

The remote source of CRS' development philosophy is the traditional Catholic view on the essential goodness of human nature, albeit a nature flawed by inclinations toward evil. This view of human nature places a positive valuation of human efforts on history to gain knowledge, create beauty, achieve personal fulfilment, and construct a societal common good. Human activities in time and space are valued for themselves and not merely as occasions or springboards for humans to fulfil what Catholics regard as their ultimate purpose – gaining lasting, joyful union with God. Human work and accomplishments – individual and collective – are valued as ends and not as mere means. The Catholic philosopher Jacques Maritain calls them "infra-valent ends" (Maritain 1973, 133–34). Accordingly, the mission of relieving human misery and enabling men and women to live a better life is viewed by CRS not as a platform for proselytising, but as a valid work for its own sake. Nevertheless, as Eileen Egan, a long-time worker at CRS and historian of its early years explains, it is its religious faith that propelled CRS into its humanitarian and developmental mission.

Through communicating to Americans the agony of Christ in its twentieth-century expression, the agency helped generate an explosion of mercy on behalf of the homeless, the uprooted, the war-ravaged and those whose basic human rights had been violated and were still in peril. . . .

The explosion of mercy did not abate as larger challenges presented themselves. It grew to encompass former enemy as well as friend, to meet more and more of the needs and agonies of the world's peoples, confronting their hunger, their disasters, whether natural or man-made, and their entrapment in oppression and underdevelopment. Mercy, after all, is only love under the aspect of need, reaching out to console, shelter, feed and rescue the person loved. And love is the central teaching and command that Jesus left with his followers (Egan 1988, xiii).

In later formulations of its self-understanding, CRS declares:

- Catholic Relief Services work is founded on the belief that each person possesses a basic dignity that comes directly from God. Because of this belief, we advance the intrinsic value and equality of all human beings, and strive for systems and procedures which demonstrate fair and equitable treatment of all people.
- We understand ourselves to be a part of a wider global family and believe that our responsibilities to one another cross national, cultural, and religious boundaries. Our work worldwide is a concrete expression of the interdependence of all people in community with each other as we seek to fulfil our responsibilities to our brothers and sisters worldwide.
- We believe that the development of economic, social, political, material, spiritual, and cultural conditions are necessary for all people to flourish and reach their full human potential and we accept our responsibility to promote the common good of the larger society.
- The poor and marginalized have the most urgent claim on our mission and their vulnerability and oppression harms us all. We seek to stand alongside suffering communities in solidarity, sharing our talents, resources, and time with them, and analyzing and addressing structural causes and systems that continue to impoverish them (CRS 2000c).

The proximate source of values, principles, and models of action informing CRS' institutional culture is Catholic social teaching (CST) (Williams and Houck 1993; O'Brien and Shannon 1992; Hobgood 1991; Henriot, DeBerri, and Schultheis 1985; Houck and Williams 1984; Cronin 1950), whose central tenets, as these apply to development and relief, are universal solidarity (each of us *is* his or her "brother's keeper"[USCC 1998]); the subsidiarity principle (solutions to problems are to be sought first at the lowest level or that most directly linked to human experience and community); and the poor have special claims in justice, and not merely in charity, on individuals and corporate bodies in lesser need, as well as on society at large. These values are synthesised by CRS through its adoption of a "justice lens" as normative of all its activities. Internal CRS documents inform us that:

> Catholic Relief Services takes its definition of justice from the above Hebrew and New Testament Scripture, as well as Catholic Social Teaching. Justice is about the establishment and promotion of right relationships between all members of the human family, as well as the transformation of society's unjust structures and institutions. Justice includes the fair balancing of one's rights and responsibilities in the relationships in which one participates. . . .
>
> • Justice as the focus for CRS' work requires an in-depth understanding of the wide variety of relationships that can exist at various levels. The question of determining if and to what degree these relationships are right relationships is a difficult one and requires a great deal of sensitivity. One place to begin would be to evaluate them in light of Catholic Social Teaching, which helps to define the content of justice and how it is promoted. These teachings include: dignity and equality of the human person, rights and responsibilities, social nature, the common good, solidarity, the option for the poor, subsidiary, and stewardship. . . .
>
> • In addition to the teachings mentioned above, the Church's teaching on solidarity is integral for CRS' understanding of justice. Because justice goes beyond the claim on rights and includes the fulfillment of responsibilities, *solidarity* – the sense of duty to others within the human community – is an important pre-condition to CRS's work of justice. This profound commitment to others requires that we reflect on relationships within society, including the structures and systems of which we are a part or from which we benefit. Living in solidarity with others requires that we pursue justice and stand on the side of those who do not share fairly in the rewards of these systems and structures or who are oppressed by them. Genuine solidarity requires us to work to remove barriers to participation and inclusion and to create instead an environment in which right relationships flourish.
>
> • . . . Living in solidarity with others obliges us to work to remove barriers to participation and inclusion, and establish in their place an environment where right relationships flourish. By virtue of our membership in the human family, we have a responsibility to work alongside our brothers and sisters so that all may share equally in life's goodness and participate in the institutions that shape our world.
>
> • The concept of peace is directly related to the promotion of justice and is also extremely important in the context of CRS' work. True peace is not simply the absence of war or violence. Rather, it is the fruit of just and right relationships. It can be achieved only through the establishment of right relationships among members of the human family and through the transformation of society and unjust structures. . . .
>
> • CRS has adopted a "Justice Lens" through which it views and examines

all of its work and relationships. The idea behind the Agency adopting a Justice Lens is to have a tool to help view the situations and events around it differently – with a new eye and a new focus on justice to help CRS analyze the world around it. The Justice Lens helps CRS set priorities, sharpen responses to injustice, and apply consistent values internally and externally in all of its decisions (CRS 1999a, 4–5).

All CRS personnel attend workshops and training sessions to help them understand and apply the justice lens.

- Numerous staff and directors have started to apply the Justice Lens to the work in their own departments and programs, and are starting to experiment with what it means to promote justice through their work.
- The commitment to justice has also led the Agency to a re-examination of CRS' relationships to domestic constituencies in the United States. This is encouraging a new look at how to promote solidarity with others in the wider human community, and the role of our own country and citizenry in the allocation of income, resources, and power among peoples and nations.
- CRS also recognizes that genuine pursuit of justice in its work in the world requires the same pursuit of justice for us as individuals and as an organization internally. As a result, it will be essential to apply the Justice Lens to our own internal systems and structures as we work toward the promotion of a just work place.
- In the past, CRS has mainly focused its attention on issues of distributive justice. We are now beginning to focus more on issues of social justice and addressing the systemic causes of injustice. We are gaining capacity in areas such as advocacy and public policy, and continuing to examine ways in which the Agency can be an agent of change in such a large and daunting task.

As stated above, the teachings found within Catholic Social Teaching mandate the Agency to work toward the establishment of justice and peace, and also provide basic values and principles that assist in this work. The Agency also recognizes that many staff, partners, and programme participants represent numerous faith traditions and beliefs, and in order to develop a common language in this pursuit of justice, the Agency must ensure that CRS values and principles incorporate this diversity to the greatest extent possible without compromising the principles outlined in Catholic Social Teaching (CRS 1999a, 7–8).

Although it still engages heavily in humanitarian assistance, in earlier times called relief work, CRS assigns increasing emphasis and resources to development work aimed at empowering populations to provide for themselves in sustainable fashion. The boundary lines between assistance and development are fast disappearing, however, for humanitarian work is increasingly carried out according to principles of development. As David Bryer, former director of Oxfam/UK writes, "We have increasingly found the conventional concepts of 'development' and 'relief' no longer relevant; to maintain the traditional distinction between the two would be a hindrance" (Bryer 1995, xiii-iv).

Decision-making Criteria

What criteria does CRS follow in choosing where to work; in taking on specific projects, programmes, and policies; in selecting institutional partners in precise countries or regions? What role does it assign to country directors and teams, and how do these relate to headquarters personnel in decision-making processes? CRS answers:

> Injustices exist in all societies. Some result in violence or destructive conflict while others exist at structural or social levels and form the basis of inequity. A focus on justice is therefore applicable in all countries and in both relief and development programs (CRS 1998a, i).

> Catholic Relief Services is committed to the promotion of social justice, a commitment that requires the efficient use of resources to effect the greatest change in the lives of the poor and marginalized. Being efficient and effective in making change means developing global capacity to respond to selected needs. When the poor and marginalized have other needs, it means responding locally, and/or facilitating connections to others. Developing global capacity means building staffing and project selection and evaluation systems that enable excellent programming in the selected "core competencies." . . .
> CRS' partner of preference is the local Catholic Church, usually through its social action agencies, because of our common commitment to justice as an active and life giving virtue which defends the dignity of all persons. We also collaborate with other faith-based and secular organizations (including private, government, community, and intermediate entities) in recognition of the role they play in promoting justice and reconciliation, and of the fundamental values which are frequently shared by other faith and humanitarian traditions.
> All of CRS' partnerships assign responsibility for decision making and implementation to a level as close as possible to the people whom decisions will affect; this is the principle of subsidiarity (CRS 1998a, 8).

> CRS' investments must increase the institutional capacity of CRS and its partners to identify and redress gender imbalances. Gender responsive programmes require corresponding and consistent internal CRS policies (CRS 1998a, 11).

Illustrative Practices

The CRS philosophy and its criteria of decision-making are shown in its concrete practices. CRS strives to conduct relief "developmentally" by providing residents of refugee camps with seeds and tools for future food production, by conditioning further aid on contributions in labour from refugees, and by associating assisted populations in planning future efforts so as to reduce their dependence on relief. Getting victim populations "back on their feet" takes diverse forms. In drought-affected regions of India CRS helps victim populations survive during emergencies and builds up their capacity to cope with future droughts.

> CRS is working with local partners to reorient and strengthen water harvesting and drought mitigation projects. As a supplement to the Indian government supply of water, which is available every few days and sometimes for only fifteen to twenty minutes a day, the agency is working to reallocate resources within existing watershed projects and build water conservation systems for this monsoon season. . . .
> Plans also include training young village people in the construction of solar stills for families in areas where potable water is no longer available. Additionally, assistance will be offered to plant fodder grasses and drought-tolerant vegetation for fodder as well as construct sheds and pole barns to protect livestock and reduce free grazing (CRS 2000d, 1).

Post-relief developmentalism in Ethiopia takes the form of micro-finance projects benefitting women.

> Development programs operated by Catholic Relief Services throughout Ethiopia include a women's savings and credit program, based on the Grameen Bank model, whose goal is to improve the income of vulnerable women by making small loans for petty trading such as the sale of cereals, food and beverage, and handicrafts. The resulting income enables participants to access more food and health care, pay school fees and build assets. And it provides an alternate source of income so families are able to survive when crops fail (CRS 2000e, 1).

After Hurricane Mitch, efforts in Nicaragua centred on creating and supporting Peace Commissions.

> Peace Commissions are essentially community organizations trained in civic responsibility, citizens' and children's rights, tolerance, and in understanding the flow of government in a democratic society. Democracy is a new concept in Nicaragua, born from a history of violence that plagued the country throughout the 1980s. The Peace Commissions first emerged in 1995 as a means to build peace in the country, little by little, within the local municipalities. Working with local Catholic dioceses, Catholic Relief Services of-

fered training in working toward peace and reconciliation in families, neighborhoods and communities. The resulting Peace Commissions provided the citizens with a new sense of empowerment and the capacity to work together for a better life (Brown 2000, 3).

By creating and nurturing Peace Commissions, CRS gives concrete expression to its principled commitment to conflict transformation and peacebuilding:

Conflict transformation/peace building (CT/PB) promotes the changing of relationships and structures for the benefit of those who suffer most from injustice. It can be viewed as an overarching framework, with the potential to incorporate other focus areas in a dynamic process of transformation applied to situations of both latent and manifest conflict. Conflict transformation processes utilise strategies of non-violence and promote just structures.
Conflict transformation/peace building programs include:
- Skills and capacity building in non-violent forms of dealing with conflict
- Education in values and attitudes of peace building and mutual respect in diversity
- Mediation services
- Fostering/strengthening of fora for dialogue and consensus building.
Programming in CT/PB is implemented through pastoral agents, grass roots organizations, NGOs and state institutions (CRS 1999b, 4–5).

In its properly socio-economic developmental activities CRS assigns priority to agriculture, health, and microfinance.

Agriculture
Values and norms underpinning the agency's approach to agriculture are shown in a mission statement declaring that:

CRS agriculture projects are part of larger, integrated programs that:
- conserve and protect natural resources;
- foster full partnership with the poor;
- strengthen the capacity of farm families/communities to take control of their own development;
- strengthen the capacity of local partners to serve marginalized communities;
- help rehabilitate farming systems disrupted by manmade/natural disasters; and
- foster linkages with other organizations to supplement and complement CRS resources (Burpee 2000, 1).

One of the rare projects implemented by CRS without partners – "because there are no local development organisations that can serve as counterpart" (Burpee

1999, 2) – is a three-year pilot project to benefit 300 native families by empowering women producers living near Ecuador's Chimbortazo Volcano. The centrepiece of the project is the support of women's community banks and small-scale irrigation systems by forming technical assistance groups (TAGs).

TAGs are agricultural training and information-sharing groups open to all adults in a community. Each TAG focuses on a different topic, for example:
- composting and vermiculture (cultivating worms in compost);
- cage micro-livestock and forage production;
- greenhouse construction and horticulture (vegetable) production;
- marketing;
- animal husbandry (Burpee 1999, 4–5).

TAGs:
- Provide ongoing, rather than on-off, technical assistance, while promoting development of local expertise to ensure success of technical innovations
- Improve knowledge and productivity of adults in project communities (ibid., 5–6).

Health

CRS emphasises community health, which is seen as promoting social justice, human rights, and meeting basic health needs. "Priority is given to community-based, focused health interventions that have been demonstrated to have high impact, and to the establishment of sustainable community structures that are capable of coordinating community activities with all health and development partners" (CRS 1998b, 13). Projects are designed jointly with local partners and great importance is attached to installing management information systems which combine "the collection of quantitative and qualitative data for problem identification" (ibid.).

HIV/AIDS receives special attention, as illustrated in the case of CRS/Egypt, which supports

a program that provides counseling for people with HIV/AIDS and information on AIDS prevention, including how HIV is transmitted by both men and women and under what conditions. It seeks to support individuals with HIV/AIDS as they face the emotional stresses of the disease (*e.g.*, financial difficulties for their families, social ostracisation, *etc.*) and to encourage an open discussion of AIDS within their families (CRS 1998a, 10).

Microfinancing

A CRS senior advisor on microfinance reports that "CRS is one of the largest PVO microfinance lenders in the world, reaching nearly 220,000 clients in 33 countries" (Wilson 2000, 15). Six principles inform CRS micro-financing activities: service to the poorest; linking loans to the level of savings made by clients (so that they may build assets as they borrow); the use of solidarity guarantees, which tie new loans to repayment of earlier ones and engage a group promise of responsibility for each individual's loan; active involvement of clients in the administration of overall loan service operations; an explicit strategy of reaching a scale of loan operations and clients suited to heighten self-sufficiency "through efficient operations and by charging interest at market rates"; and institution-building to achieve long-term survival and vitality of loan programmes ("Permanence may include creating a formal financial institution, helping partners transform programs in to specialised micro-finance institutions, or consolidating pilot activities into larger local entities" [CRS 2000f]).

The CRS strategy is to use microfinance as a steppingstone to open up access for poor clients to more mainstream sources of credit.

Civil Society and Globalisation

In writings on civil society and globalisation no commonly accepted definition of either phenomenon has yet imposed itself. A recent work exploring new links between civil society and market institutions registers several quite different views of civil society.

Leaders in postcommunist nations began the resurrection of civil society; they called for a moral restoration of the whole economy by organizing a different system of sharing power. For them, civil society meant minimum government control and the development of civil associations wherein they governed themselves, autonomous from the state. Advocates defined civil society as a social matrix of voluntary groups and self-governing associations.

In capitalist societies, other analysts identified civil society with the Third Sector, distinguishing it from government and business. The Third Sector included nongovernmental organizations, people's movements, citizens' groups, consumer associations, religious institutions, women's organizations, indigenous people's associations, civic groups, leagues, alliances, and confederations. . . .

Not everyone defined civil society as the "Third Sector." Conservative analysts saw it as composed of a democratic government with a voluntary sector that included business as well as nonprofits. Philosophers saw civil society as a "public sphere" (not government) emerging within the "private sphere" of society. Cultural theorists saw it as the resolution of tensions between opposing principles in modernity (e.g. individual vs. community, public vs. private) leading toward a postmodern society.

For many advocates, civil society is visualized today as a decentralised, voluntary, self-regulating system of civil associations based on a democratic and moral order. Salamon and Anheir described it as the great social innovation of the twentieth century, but they were puzzled by how it connected with the business sector. Civil-society analysts in this line of thought wondered how business could be a moral order. How could civil-society associations fit the reality of a competitive corporate economy? (Bruyn 2000, 7–8).

CRS understands civil society to be

those individuals and organizations in a society which are independent of the government and which are able to exercise rights of free speech and association. Where there is an active civil society citizens can openly organize and advocate for their beliefs and causes. In some countries where CRS works, governments are not yet supportive of an active civil society (*The Burden of Anonymity*, n.d.).

Executive Director Kenneth Hackett considers that "by implementing programs that emphasize holistic development and the growth of civil society, NGOs can play a critical role in preventing future conflicts" (Hackett 1996, 269). For CRS, contributing to the growth of civil society consists of:

1. increasing the awareness of individuals of their rights and responsibilities,
2. strengthening the capacity of local organizations to advocate for improved government services to meet basic needs or for structural changes needed to address the underlying causes of poverty, and
3. activating citizen involvement (CRS 1998a, 8).

CRS has defined

a new framework for local capacity building based on three key pillars: partnership, organizational development, and strengthening civil society. . . .
   In the past, CRS has undertaken "institution building" with civil society partners, but this was usually limited to providing the physical goods or infrastructure (such as a vehicle or a computer) needed to undertake a particular CRS project, or training in a particular field required mainly to meet CRS project goals or reporting requirements (such as accounting). The "local capacity building" concept shifts efforts such as these to a higher level in that it stresses the need for local organizations to develop skills in areas such as strategic thinking and planning, advocacy, organizational management, and project development and management. Building capacity at the local level is a critical step toward making development efforts sustainable (CRS 1999c, 2–3).

For the Latin America and the Caribbean Regional Office (LACRO) of CRS, building up civil society centres on advocacy.

Through the advocacy focus area, CRS/LACRO seeks to motivate processes which influence situations of power at local, national and international levels to achieve changes in systems, practices, and policies which favor just, dignified and peaceful relations in society.

This is accomplished through the generation and facilitation of participatory processes including analysis, proposal formulation and the development of negotiation and consensus building strategies with community leaders, grass roots organizations, authorities, and institutional representatives at all levels. The advocacy process is oriented toward serving those populations whose rights are most seriously affected (CRS 1999b, 5).

In reporting on geographically wider activities in domains of civil society, CRS points to activities in Cameroon to educate citizens on their rights; projects in Latin America that provide legal advice and protection in support of human rights; programmes in the Philippines that assist dwellers wronged by eviction gain redress by lobbying the government for protection. The Parent-School Partnership (PSP) project in Macedonia (Mulvihill 2000) involves the local community and the national ministry of education to strengthen civil society through increased parental involvement in their children's education (through the medium of inter-ethnic dialogue and joint action to repair schools, jointly plan curriculum improvements, and engage government in efforts at improvement) (CRS 1998a, 8–9).

CRS regards advocacy in behalf of victims of poverty, violence, and human rights violations conducted for the purpose of inducing governments and international organisations to change their policy or their practices as "normal" activity consistent with its mandate. It has engaged in advocacy in behalf of landless groups in Northeast Brazil and of internally displaced populations in African emergency relief sites to win access to emergency food and relief supplies. CRS has worked in various countries to win access to water, to secure the rights of poor farmers, to obtain more generous policies on migration, to protect workers' rights, and to promote fair trade.

Jointly with CIDSE (International Cooperation for Development and Solidarity), CRS has also conducted broad-gauged advocacy campaigns aimed at International Financial Institutions (IFIs) and creditor governments in behalf of third-world debt relief. CIDSE, "a network which brings together sixteen Catholic development organizations located in Europe, North America, and New Zealand, along with CI (Caritas Internationalis), a network of 146 national relief, development, and social service organizations in 194 states and territories throughout the world," has prepared a guide to advocacy and citizen mobilisation entitled *Putting Life Before Debt* (CIDSE and CI 1998).

Other partnerships are also sought.

Partnering with government agencies at various levels (such as ministries or mayoral or district offices) and through various means (such as projects or training programmes) can strengthen civil society-government understanding and cooperation. By encouraging such intersectoral collaboration, CRS positively influences governing bodies to improve service delivery and contributes to raising awareness of and stimulating new approaches to addressing injustices . . .

The Option for the Poor, as emphasised in Pope Paul VI's *A Call to Action*, has as its central tenet the need to ensure the right of all to participate in society and to take political action where appropriate. The right and responsibility to participate in society are the foundation of a healthy civil society and must be central to CRS' approach to local capacity building (CRS 1999c, 8, 10).

CHALLENGES AND NEW DIRECTIONS

In recent years CRS has conducted a wide-ranging process aimed at redefining its mission, reconceptualising the rationale for that mission, and critically evaluating its institutional and operational responses to challenges posed by the present world conjuncture. As a relief and development NGO, CRS is particularly attentive to three elements that characterise this conjuncture: changes in the international geo-political system after the end of the Cold War, the growing number of intra-state violent conflicts, and globalisation. The rethinking of development is not a phenomenon unique to CRS; it has occurred as well in many IFIs, bilateral aid agencies, regional organisations, business firms, NGOs, and other collective actors in civil society. The re-examination conducted by development "practitioners" finds its reflection in, and draws conceptual resources from, theoretical and normative writings that explore how to think of development and aid in the new setting (Putterman 2001; Harris 2000; Lancaster 2000; Munck and O'Hearn 1999; Rist 1997; Wolfe 1996; Escobar 1995; Rodwin and Schön 1994; Norgaard 1994; Galli et al. 1992; Manor 1991; Oman and Wignaraja 1991; Vachon 1988; Apter 1987). For CRS, the principal source of normative guidance has been CST, especially its emphasis on a few core values: the intrinsic dignity and worth of each human person; the universality of the common bond which ought to exist among all human persons and societies; the principle of subsidiarity; the priority of the demands of justice over "laws" of economics or politics.

By embracing CST values – in theory, field practice, and its internal workings – CRS is in effect returning to its NGO roots. As R. J. Kupke writes, CRS was created "to help bring American riches and technology to bear on the problems of humankind" (Kupke 1995, 3). In a doctoral dissertation on the life and work of James Norris, a layman who served as special assistant to the first three executive directors of CRS (all of whom were ecclesiastics) and directed the agency's relief operations for nearly two decades, Kupke recalls:

Norris felt it was essential that the staff be firmly grounded in concepts of Catholic social justice, and he often participated himself in the orientation programs of new staff members to ensure that this orientation was sound. Just as he had been conscious of protecting the image of the Catholic Church among the refugees and the other voluntary agencies, Norris was also conscious of the image the individual employee projected (Kupke 1995, 197).

By 1960, war-related relief had largely given way to assistance to victims of natural disasters, and CRS had expanded its efforts beyond Europe and Mexico to Africa and Asia. More significantly, it had begun to move beyond relief into development. Kupke cites with approval Daniel Martin's view that

> 1960 was clearly the turning point. The Foreign Aid Bill amendment led to increased cooperation between the government and voluntary agencies. Programs everywhere began to emphasize rural education, development, housing, credit unions and cooperatives. In Latin America the Alliance for Progress had a similar effect.
>
> For the following years, development became the catch-word of all the voluntary organizations. The CRS "resettlement" offices were closed in Europe and more and more attention was focused on the 3rd World (Kupke 1995, 266).

During the Cold War, CRS judged itself, as did US society at large, to lie on the ethically "good side" of the democracy/freedom/competing development models divide. There seemed to be no compelling reason for CRS to question its collaboration with the US government, which had proved fruitful and effective during the relief years, or to challenge the development model and aid patterns favoured by governments of the "free world" and by international organisations. That development model aimed at helping poor countries achieve rapid and self-sustained economic growth through industrialisation and the diversification of economic production. Poor countries were to be helped by resource transfers to carry out priority projects and programmes. The "proper developmental niche" of CRS and other NGOs was local project work at the micro level. At that time macro policies pursued by national governments in the free world bloc and by international organisations left ample room and freedom for NGOs to work at the micro level in consonance with their own value preferences. Micro-level activities of NGOs seemed complementary to, not competitive with, the macro policies then in force. Accordingly, there seemed to exist little reason for NGOs to engage in critical advocacy in behalf of different macro policies.

In 1983, after being headed by ecclesiastics for forty years, CRS named Lawrence A. Pezzullo, a long-term State Department career officer and former U.S. ambassador to Uruguay and Nicaragua, as its first lay director. Pezzullo's decade in CRS was marked by a drive to professionalise the staff and to achieve greater managerial efficiency throughout the organisation. During this period there was little talk of CST or the justice lens. It seemed quite enough for CRS to respond to the growing number of development demands placed upon it in multiple field sites and to endow the agency with professionally trained staff and with structures and operating modes comparable to those found in high-quality national and international development agencies. As one perceptive student of religious social movements observes:

> For much of CRS's history, the "apostolate of helping those in need" translated into traditional charitable works, such as responding to victims of natural

and man-made disasters and providing assistance to the poor and to victims of conflict to alleviate their immediate needs. Until recently, however, its worldwide staff tended to think of themselves as members of a voluntary and professionalized social service agency working under religious auspices rather than as religious or humanitarian actors educated in the social teaching of the Catholic Church and trained to mediate conflict and build peaceful relations in local communities.

In this regard the experience of CRS workers in Rwanda, a nation that is 62 percent Roman Catholic, may have been a turning point. The agency had placed fieldworkers there since the 1960s, yet few had developed a sophisticated understanding of the social dynamics that led to the genocide of 1994. "We were taken by surprise by the violence and its terrible intensity," one CRS official admitted. "And we asked ourselves how this could have happened, and what we needed to do to integrate ourselves into the whole life of the communities we served." The Rwanda massacres occurred just as CRS was reviewing and beginning to reconceptualize its mission (Appleby 2000, 52).

With the collapse of "real" communism and of competing Cold War development models in 1989, the world in which CRS worked changed dramatically. Unitary thinking centred on liberalisation of markets, privatisation, and the withdrawal of government intervention, except to provide stimuli to markets, gained a near monopoly in development policy circles. The nature of violent conflicts likewise changed: most conflicts erupting were now internal, and the major beneficiaries of relief efforts were internally displaced populations, not trans-border refugees. More important, globalisation – economic, technological, financial, and cultural – was spreading rapidly and revealing its twofold nature as simultaneous creator of wealth and poverty, of new jobs and massive destruction of livelihoods, of new networks of solidarity both in the pursuit of profit and in mobilisation of resistance to its visibly harmful effects. Along with other NGOs, CRS found itself summoned to reconsider its place and its role in this different kind of world. In conflict areas, relief work became highly politicised, either because of the collapse of legitimate state authority or open competition among warring factions for setting rules of access and delivery of humanitarian relief supplies. There was much talk of promoting democracy, of new roles for NGOs as actors in civil society, of an alternative development that was socially equitable and environmentally sustainable, of bringing fairness and justice to play in competitive economic arenas.

It was no coincidence, therefore, that in 1993 CRS named as its director Kenneth Hackett, a lay professional and long-time director of the agency's operations in Africa, the continent most severely victimised by conflict and by the privatisation/ globalisation model of development. One CRS official, who spoke on condition of anonymity, commented to this author that Hackett "re-Catholicised" CRS. In the new globalised context, CRS needed to gain clarity of vision and normative direction and that need led it to return to its Catholic roots, values founded on CST. This it did in a more conscious, deliberate, and explicit fashion than it had done in the previous "professionalising" decade. By then CST was itself an enlarging and evolving *corpus* of principles, norms, and recommendations bearing on economic life, work, technology, environment, peace, and social justice. And inasmuch as the United States was the main promoter of the privatisation/ globalisation development model, as well as the global actor richest in power, resources, and influence, CRS as a US-based NGO felt itself powerfully challenged to question, if not to criticise, its collaborative partnership with the US government and its promotion of that development model. After the collapse of communist regimes in 1989, the patriotic (and apparently ethically defensible) rationale for partnership with the US government which had long served CRS well had partially evaporated. As for its "niche" in development arenas or in the "aid industry," CRS as a large NGO working in many countries and in many different sectors had to reconsider, as did other NGOs, what role, if any, it should play in macro arenas.

This seemed all the more important as influential policy-makers were launching proposals to co-opt independent NGOs into becoming de facto subcontractors of the US government in dispensing foreign aid. Early in the year 2001

> Senator Jesse Helms, the most powerful critic of foreign aid in Congress, said that he would champion an increase in international assistance – but only if all future United States aid was funneled to the needy through private charities and religious groups instead of a government agency . . .
>
> But his most provocative proposal was to abolish the Agency for International Development and shift responsibility for overseeing $7 billion a year in economic and humanitarian aid to a quasi-governmental foundation, which would deliver grants to private and community relief groups.
>
> The plan envisions replacing the aid agency and its 7,300 employees with a smaller, streamlined International Development Foundation with lower expenses. The secretary of state as well as relief groups would oversee the foundation's activities, Mr. Helms' aides said, to provide oversight and co-ordination with American foreign policy goals . . .
>
> Under his plan, Mr. Helms said, the groups that could receive grants include World Vision, Save the Children, Hadassah, Catholic Relief Services and Samaritan's Purse (Schmitt 2001, A4).

The Helms and similar proposals lend special importance and urgency to CRS' explorations into its proper developmental role. Should it abandon its independence to become an implementing agent of US governmental interests or of international aid agencies? (Reusse 2001) Or should its chosen role consist of advocacy, critique, participation in policy-setting, or coalitional governance in behalf of authentic human development (Goulet 1991, 1996)? One official at CRS headquarters thought it was likely that in future years CRS "would become increasingly Oxfam-ised," referring here to the activist role played by Oxfam in pressuring macro-development agencies (IFIs, the UN, the European Union, and national governments) to give it a voice in shaping policy and in redressing harmful consequences following upon their development strategies. Nor has Oxfam shrunk from publicly denouncing large international pharmaceutical firms for their exploitative operations in poor countries to block indigenous production of generic drugs for the treatment of AIDS and other diseases.

Campaigners like Oxfam have demanded that poor countries be allowed to change their patent laws so that they can import, without fear of trade retaliation, cheap generic versions of anti-AIDS drugs, powerful antibiotics and other lifesaving medicines made in Brazil, Canada, India or Thailand (McNeil 2001, A5).

More ambitiously still, just as the World Bank and the UN have, through their publications, taken on the role of serving as theorists of development and educators of the public at large, so too has Oxfam embarked on theoretical and conceptual work to win legitimacy for its expanded vision of development (Eade and Williams 1995).

In 1996 CRS officially adopted the justice lens as its organising vision to provide normative guidance for its internal and external activities. Even after organising numerous training sessions, leading workshops, and disseminating educational and explanatory materials, CRS acknowledges that not all staff and field workers fully understand what the justice lens entails in practice. Nor do they possess deep and thorough knowledge of the CST which serves as the doctrinal and value basis of the justice lens. Moreover, not everyone in CRS agrees that justice should be the central focus. Some plead for peacemaking as the central focus (Reilly and Cilliers 2000). Others, while acknowledging the dangers that their preferred stance poses to continued resource flows and to peaceful relations with governments and partners, nonetheless advocate a posture of "prophetic advocacy and critique" (Selvaggio 2000). Still others ask what their agency's relations with government should be (Gary 2000), or favour a more capacious criterion of selection of partners in field operations. On this point they argue that the CRS predilection for Catholic organisational partners excessively circumscribes its potential influence as a change agent which promotes, in deed as well as in word, authentic human development and not mere economic development. It is useful to recall here the distinction between ends and means made by the UNDP:

Human development is the end – economic growth is a means. So, the purpose of growth should be to enrich people's lives. But far too often it does not. . . .

Growth has been failing over much of the past 15 years in about 100 countries, with almost a third of the world's people. And the links between growth and human development are failing for people in the many countries with lopsided development – with either good growth but little human development or good human development but little or no growth (UNDP 1996, 1).

Nevertheless, Harbison and Myers, specialists in human resource planning, noted in the 1960s that "there need be no conflict between the economists and the humanists. . . . The development of man [sic.] for himself may still be considered the ultimate end, but economic progress can also be one of the principal means of attaining it" (Harbison and Myers 1964, 13). To avoid inverting means and ends it seems essential that NGOs, as civil society actors contributing to normative governance of the forces and institutions of globalisation, heed the distinction made in the 1950s by Karl Mannheim, who explains that

> competition and cooperation may be viewed in two different ways: as simple social mechanisms or as organizing principles of a social structure.
>
> Competition or cooperation as mechanisms may exist and serve diverse ends in any society, preliterate, capitalist, and non-capitalist. But in speaking of the capitalist phase of rugged individualism and competition, we think of an all-pervasive structures principle of social organization. . . .
>
> This distinction may help to clarify the question whether capitalist competition – allegedly basic to our social structure – needs to be maintained as a presumable activating force. Now, one may well eliminate competition as the *organizing principle* of the social structure and replace it by planning without eliminating competition as a *social mechanism* to serve desirable ends (Mannheim 1951, 192).

The reason why market competition must not be taken as the organising principle of economic life, as Barbara Ward points out, is that

> a market system, wholly uncorrected by institutions of justice, sharing, and solidarity, makes the strong stronger and the weak weaker. Markets as useful tools in a functioning social order have a positive and decentralizing role to play. Markets as masters of society enrich the rich and pauperize the poor (Ward 1976, xii).

It is in two arenas – (1) what kind of development NGOs advocate and carry out, and (2) what modes of global governance they help institute, in collaboration with other civil society actors, governments, international organisations, business firms, and associations – that the value commitments of NGOs will be most severely put to the test. For the sociologist of business organisations Severyn T. Bruyn, the primary arena of testing is the encounter between NGOs and other Third Sector actors with business firms. Bruyn writes:

> The development of civil society is connected to capitalism and represents a major change in the formation of markets. The crucible of change, the severe test of development, takes place between the connected fields of business and the Third Sector. The Third Sector – composed of nonprofit organizations and grassroots movements – stands in tension with the business actors. This tension is the location for major changes taking place in the institution of the market place (Bruyn 2000, 3–4).

CRS is actively re-examining its posture toward business. It recently became a member of ICCR (Interfaith Center on Corporate Responsibility). Created in 1971, the ICCR is

> an association of 275 Protestant, Roman Catholic and Jewish institutional investors, including national denominations, religious communities, pension funds, endowments, hospital corporations, economic development funds and publishing companies. . . .
>
> As responsible stewards, they merge social values with investment decisions, believing they must achieve more than an acceptable financial return. ICCR members utilize religious investments and other resources to change unjust or harmful corporate policies, working for peace, economic justice and stewardship of the Earth. . . .
>
> Rather than simply selling stock when company policies or practices are harmful to people or the environment, ICCR members press corporations to change. They use their investments to open doors at corporations and attempt to raise concerns at the highest level of corporate decision making.
>
> They use the power of persuasion backed by economic pressure from consumers and investors to hold corporations accountable. They sponsor shareholder resolutions; meet with management; screen their investments; divest stock; conduct public hearings and investigations; publish special reports; and sponsor actions such as prayer vigils, letter writing campaigns and consumer boycotts. ICCR members also make investments to promote economic development in low income and minority communities (ICCR 2001).

As the "foreign aid" arm of the US Catholic church, CRS adheres to the socially responsible investment guidelines adopted in 1991 by the National Conference of Catholic Bishops/US Catholic Conference (NCCB/USCC). Of special relevance to CRS in this detailed set of normative prescriptions is the injunction

> to develop alternative investment policies, especially those which support enterprises that promote economic development in depressed communities and which help the Church respond to local and regional needs . . . ; [that is,] investments which may result in a lower rate of growth, but which nevertheless are chosen because they give expression to the Church's preferential option for the poor or produce some truly significant social good (NCCB/ USCC 1991, nos. 1, 2).

On another corporate front, investment by multinationals in developing regions, CRS plans to monitor the Chad-Cameroon Pipeline Project (CCPP). The project, sponsored by a consortium made up of Exxon (40 per cent), Shell (40 per cent), and Elf (20 per cent) will extract oil from Chad and transport it to the Atlantic in a pipeline crossing Chad and Cameroon. CRS is formulating overall guidelines for the full range of its dealings and relationships with business firms in developing areas. Possibilities of co-operation in diverse forms – joint ventures, joint funding, technical assistance – are being studied. The significant point, for CRS as an agent of development, is that it is engaging business corporations in properly developmental arenas, in clear recognition of the dominant role played by corporations in economic, financial, and technological globalisation.

Thanks to its great institutional strengths and its large and solid constituency, the survival of CRS is not seriously jeopardised. Success in implementing its ideals, however, defined as the effective institutionalisation and operationalisation of the justice lens in the whole gamut of CRS operations, including new roles of advocacy in macro arenas, prophetic critique and governance in realms of globalisation, and innovative approaches to peacekeeping and participatory development, may prove difficult to achieve in full. CRS clearly takes integral implementation of the justice lens seriously, and it is striving with great energy and imagination to find ways of implementing it concretely. Its director, Kenneth Hackett, has commented in lucid terms on the larger tasks facing NGOs:

> As NGOs take on the challenge of supporting development in a manner that builds lasting peace, they must look for transformative processes that repair and strengthen relationships and resolve societal tensions, as well as those that increase equity and establish just structures. They must become more proficient in supporting these processes. International and indigenous NGOs operating in partnership in this way should be widely supported by governments and the international donor community. In order to prevent future conflicts in an environment of decreasing resources, it is vital that investments be made in PVOs [private voluntary organizations] that have years of experience, access to local structures, and an improved development or peace-building practice. At the same time, PVOs must coordinate their efforts well with the full range of players in this process, UN agencies, governments, and each other.
>
> As the international community does this, it must look at a new diplomatic paradigm for peace just as it looks for new paradigms for humanitarian and economic assistance before and after situations of conflict. It is imperative to look outside the foreign service or international banks for solutions to such emotionally charged problems. For it is not in the language of statecraft or economic models or in transplanted Jeffersonian democracy that lasting solutions will be found. It may be in solutions that flow from dialogue with Mullahs, with Bishops, or with community leaders and individuals who live deeply in the emotions that often fuel the problems. The challenge is to build on existing traditions of social organization, not purely those that are externally conceived. If one searches, the right individuals and processes will be identified, and if those concerned are smart, they can help these individuals and processes work toward peace (Hackett 1996, 283).

At its organisational summit held in Tampa, Florida, 8–13 October 2000, CRS emphatically ratified value commitments made when adopting the justice lens in

1996 and explicitly gathered other important value emphases (peacekeeping, wider partnerships, stronger advocacy in behalf of alternative development) under the umbrella of the reconfirmed justice lens. It traced its reason for doing so to its diagnosis of new global conditions:

> Partly because of the international dimensions of globalization and partly because of shifting roles between states and civil society, many national governments have not been able to fulfill their legitimate roles in promoting the well-being of all of their citizens – some cannot, while some choose not to. At the same time, there is a lack of effective mechanisms for civil society to articulate and advocate for their needs and interests to the State at all levels.
>
> These complex global realities compel CRS to re-envision its role and responsibilities in the 21st century. Modified strategies and programming, expanded partnerships, effective technologies, an internal working environment that can more effectively respond to the situation, as well as greater resources are but a few of the elements that will be needed. In this regard, CRS seeks to act as a servant leadership team that will more efficiently and effectively address the root causes of these unjust realities and prevent similar situations from occurring.
>
> With a solid financial base, more than 4,000 CRS staff members, partnerships throughout the world and countless people who share our values and principles, Catholic Relief Services must courageously face these challenges with a new visionary commitment for justice, peace, equality, and dignity (CRS 2000g, 2).

To the "justice lens" is added a more explicit commitment to building peace.
Visionary Statement: CRS will build a culture of peace throughout the world based on a foundation of justice and reconciliation.
Description: Peace does not consist merely in the absence of war but rather, sharing the goodness of life together. Peace must be built, not declared. Peace is built on the global common good, social and economic development and solidarity. The pursuit of a culture of peace also includes values-based education, conflict prevention, resolution, transformation, and reconciliation. These are essential because they affect the way we think and act in terms of our obligations as members of a global community. Within CRS, peacebuilding must be a driving determination, from the language we use to our spirituality, from our operating ethos to our support for programs (ibid., 3).

CRS also seeks to expand the circle of its working partners, in the field, engaging itself to:
Change and improve the way we work overseas:
  • support old and new types of partners to contribute to policy formation in their countries

- develop programs that have a higher level of interaction between government and civil society
- empower communities to participate more actively in government
- support awareness campaigns
- develop a framework and capacity for actively engaging US state, local government and transnational corporations on international justice agenda (ibid., 7).

CRS likewise aims at activating its US constituencies into the new arenas it has entered overseas:

A world transformed by solidarity into one that is characterized by justice and peace requires relationships between individuals, institutions and communities based on common ground that is more radically inclusive. For CRS, these relationships begin within U.S. Catholic networks because of shared values. Within these networks, CRS will seek a servant leadership role to mobilize an increasingly vibrant Catholic movement. At the same time, these relationships must necessarily cross lines of faith to embrace interfaith and ecumenical relationships as well as others of good will across economic, racial, ethnic and class divisions. From these relationships, CRS will create opportunities to promote action, advocacy, education, exchange dialogue and volunteerism on behalf of and with the poor. These opportunities will examine issues related to poverty and injustice, promote networks and develop actions to address them from both a global and local perspective. In order to build an expanding network of partners CRS will need to reflect upon and embrace its own limitations and biases in a spirit of humility (CRS 2000g, 7).

As it looks beyond its Tampa planning and evaluation meeting, CRS looks ... to continue this process through the development of a strategic plan, operating plans and individual plans. The approach moves from broad to narrow, beginning with a worldwide view and getting more specific to the organization and more detailed at each tier. It is at these next stages where the definition of the specific steps will be determined through which CRS will move the vision forward into reality (ibid., 9).

Operationalising the justice lens, deepened and widened to answer challenges posed to CRS by globalisation, is quite clearly a work in progress. The same can be said of efforts made by other civil society actors as they respond to these same challenges.

References

Appleby, R. Scott. 2000. *The Ambivalence of the Sacred*. Lanham, Md.: Rowman and Littlefield Publishers.

Apter, David. 1987. *Rethinking Development: Modernization, Dependency, and Post Modern Politics*. Newbury Park, Calif.: Sage Publications.

Brown, Kathy. 2000. "Commissions Give Birth to Hope in Nicaragua." *Catholic Relief Services Quarterly* 6/2 (summer).

Bruyn, Severyn T. 2000. *A Civil Economy, Transforming the Market in the Twenty-first Century*. Ann Arbor, Mich.: The University of Michigan Press.

Bryer, David. 1995. "Foreword." *The Oxfam Handbook of Development and Relief*. Vol. 1. Oxford, UK: Oxfam.

Burden of Anonymity, The. n.d. Baltimore, Md.: CRS.

Burpee, Gaye. 1999. *Doing It Right: The Messarrumi Project in Ecuador*. Baltimore, Md.: CRS (July).

———. 2000. *CRS Agricultural Principles*. Baltimore, Md.: CRS (January).

CRS (Catholic Relief Services). 1998a. "Applying the Justice Lens to Programming." Occasional paper. Baltimore, Md.: CRS (July).

———. 1998b. "Programming Quality Statements for Overseas Development Programming." Baltimore, Md.: CRS (March).

———. 1999a. *CRS' Justice Lens*. Baltimore, Md.: CRS (October).

———. 1999b. "LACRO Civil Society and Human Rights Quality Statement." *LACRO CH/HR Regional Summit Conference Proceedings,* Lima, Peru, 7–11 December 1998.

———. 1999c. "Partnership and Local Capacity Building: Foundations for a CRS Strategy." Occasional paper. Baltimore, Md.: CRS (January). Available on the CRS website.

———. 2000a. "Who We Are: CRS History." An updated version of this document is available on the CRS website.

———. 2000b. "Where We Work." Available on the CRS website.

———. 2000c. "What We Believe: CRS Guiding Principles." Available on the CRS website.

———. 2000d. "Drought Afflicts India." *Catholic Relief Services Quarterly* 6/2 (summer).

———. 2000e. "Striking a Balance in Drought-Stricken Ethiopia." *Catholic Relief Services Quarterly* 6/2 (summer).

———. 2000f. "CRS Microfinance Principles." In *Microfinance Status Report 2000* 6:1. Baltimore, Md.: CRS.

———. 2000g. "World Summit Summary and Recommendations." CRS World Summit Conference, Tampa, Fla., 8–13 October.

CIDSE (International Cooperation for Development and Solidarity) and CI (Caritas Internationalis). 1998. *Putting Life Before Debt*. Brussels and Rome: CIDSE and CI.

Commins, Stephen. 2000. "NGOs: Ladles in the Global Soup Kitchen?" In *Development, NGOs, and Civil Society,* edited by Jenny Pearce. Oxford, UK: Oxfam GB).

Cronin, John Francis, S.S. 1950. *Catholic Social Principles*. Milwaukee, Wis.: The Bruce Publishing Company.

Eade, Deborah, and Suzanne Williams, eds. 1995. *The Oxfam Handbook of Development and Relief*. 3 vols. UK and Ireland: An Oxfam Publication.

Economist, The. 2000. "Sins of the Secular Missionaries." 29 January.

Edwards, Michael. 2000. Speech given at Oxfam America's 30th Anniversary Celebration, 6 October.

Edwards, Michael, and David Hulme, eds. 1996. *Beyond the Magic Bullet, NGO Performance, and Accountability in the Post–Cold War World*. West Hartford, Conn.: Kumarian Press.

Egan, Eileen. 1988. *Catholic Relief Services, The Beginning Years*. New York: Catholic Relief Services.

Escobar, Arturo. 1995. *Encountering Development: The Making and Unmaking of the Third World*. Princeton, N.J.: Princeton University Press.

Fisher, Julie. 1998. *Nongovernments: NGOs and the Political Development of the Third World*. West Hartford, Conn.: Kumarian Press.

Galli, Rosemary E., Lars Rudebeck, K. P. Moseley, Frederick Stirton Weaver, and Leonard Bloom, eds. 1992. *Rethinking the Third World*. New York: Crane Russak.

Gary, Ian. 2000. "Bringing the State Back In: Implications for CRS and Its Partners." Issue papers. CRS World Summit Conference. Tampa, Fla., 8–13 October.

Goulet, Denis. 1981. *Survival with Integrity: Sarvodaya at the Crossroads*. Sri Lanka and Washington, D.C.: Marga Institute and ODC.

———. 1991. "On Authentic Social Development: Concepts, Content, and Criteria." In *The Making of an Economic Vision,* edited by O. F. Williams, C.S.C. and J. W. Houck. Lanham, Md.: University Press of America.

———. 1995. *Development Ethics: A Guide to Theory and Practice*. New York: The Apex Press.

———. 1996. "Authentic Development: Is It Sustainable?" In *Building Sustainable Societies*, edited by D. D. Pirages. Armonk, N.Y.: M. E. Sharpe.

Hackett, Kenneth. 1996. "The Role of International NGOs in Preventing Conflict." In *Preventing Diplomacy, Stopping Wars Before They Start,* ed. K. M. Cahill. New York: Basic Books.

Haque, M. Shamsul. 1999. *Restructuring Development Theories and Policies: A Critical Study*. Albany, N.Y.: State University of New York Press.

Harbison, Frederick Harris, and Charles A. Myers. 1964. *Education, Manpower, and Economic Growth*. New York: McGraw-Hill.

Harris, Jonathan M. 2000. *Rethinking Sustainability: Power, Knowledge and Institutions*. Ann Arbor, Mich.: University of Michigan Press.

Henriot, Peter J., Edward P. DeBerri, and Michael J. Schultheis. 1985. *Catholic Social Teaching: Our Best Kept Secret*. Washington, D.C.: Center of Concern.

Hobgood, Mary E. 1991. *Catholic Social Teaching and Economic Theory*. Philadelphia: Temple University Press.

Houck, John W., and Oliver F. Williams, C.S.C., eds. 1984. *Catholic Social Teaching and the U.S. Economy*. Washington, D.C.: University Press of America.

Hulme, David, and Michael Edwards. 1997. "NGOs, States, and Donors: An Overview." In *NGOs, States and Donors: Too Close for Comfort?* edited by David Hulme and Michael Edwards. New York: St. Martin's Press.

ICCR (Interfaith Center on Corporate Responsibility). 2001. "About ICCR." Available on the ICCR website.

Kupke, Raymond J. 1995. "James J. Norris: An American Catholic Life." Ann Arbor, Mich.: University of Michigan Dissertation Service.

Lancaster, Carol. 2000. "A Fresh Start for Foreign Aid." *Foreign Affairs* 79/5 (September/October).

Le Carré, John. 2001. *The Constant Gardener.* New York: Scribner.

Lewis, David, ed. 2000. *New Roles and Relevance: Development NGOs and the Challenge of Change*. Bloomfield, Conn.: Kumarian Press.

Mannheim, Karl. 1951. *Freedom, Power and Democratic Planning*. London: Routledge & Kegan Paul.

Manor, James, ed. 1991. *Rethinking Third World Politics*. London and New York: Longman.

Maritain, Jacques. 1973. *Integral Humanism*. Notre Dame, Ind.: University of Notre Dame Press.

McNeil, Donald G. Jr. 2001. Oxfam Joins Campaign to Cut Drug Prices for Poor Nations. *New York Times International* (February 13).

Mulvihill, Mary. 2000. "Background Information Document." Prepared for CRS Diocesan Directors. Baltimore, Md. (Spring).

Munck, Ronaldo, and Denis O'Hearn, eds. 1999. *Critical Development Theory*. London: Zed Books.

NCCB/USCC (National Catholic Bishops Conference/US Catholic Conference). 1991. "Socially Responsible Investment Guidelines." *Origins* 21 (November 28): 25.

Norgaard, Richard B. 1994. *Development Betrayed: The End of Progress and a Coevolutionary Revisioning of the Future*. London and New York: Routledge.

O'Brien David J., and Thomas A. Shannon. 1992. *Catholic Social Thought: The Documentary Heritage*. Maryknoll, N.Y.: Orbis Books.

Oman, Charles P., and Ganeshan Wignaraja. 1991. *The Postwar Evolution of Development Thinking*. New York: St. Martin's Press.

Putterman, Louis G. 2001. *Dollars and Change: Economics in Context*. New Haven, Conn.: Yale University Press.

Reilly, Annemarie, and J. Cilliers. 2000. "Champion for Peace: The Role of CRS in Times of Violent Conflict." Issue papers. CRS World Summit Conference, Tampa, Fla., 8–13 October.

Reusse, Eberhard. 2001. "What Was Wrong with Structural Adjustment?" *Development and Cooperation* 1 (January/February).

Rist, Gilbert. 1997. *The History of Development*. London: Zed Books.

Rodwin, Lloyd, and Donald A. Schön, eds. 1994. *Rethinking the Development Experience*. Washington, D.C.: The Brookings Institution.

Sachs, Wolfgang. 1992. *Development Dictionary: A Guide to Knowledge as Power*. London: Zed Books.

Schmitt, Eric. 2001. "Helms Urges Foreign Aid Be Handled by Charities." *New York Times* (January 12).

Selvaggio, Kathleen. 2000. "Advocacy at CRS: Giving Voice to Justice." Issue papers. CRS World Summit Conference, Tampa, Fla., 8–13 October.

Simmons, P. J. 1998. "Learning to Live with NGOs." *Foreign Policy* (fall).

Tirman, John. 1998–99. "Forces of Civility: The NGO Revolution and the Search for Peace." *Boston Review* (December/January).

UNDP (United Nations Development Programme). 1992. *Human Development Report 1992*. New York: Oxford University Press.

———. 1996. "Overview." *Human Development Report 1996*. New York: Oxford University Press.

USCC (United States Catholic Conference). 1998. A Statement of the National Conference of Catholic Bishops with Parish Resources. *Called to Global Solidarity, International Challenges for U.S. Parishes*. Washington, D.C.: USCC.

Vachon, Robert. 1988. *Alternatives au Dévelopment*. Montréal. Québec: Institut Interculturel de Montréal.

Verhelst, Thierry. 1987. *No Life Without Roots*. London: Zed Books.

Ward, Barbara. 1976. "Foreword." In Mahbub ul Haq, *The Poverty Curtain*. New York: Columbia University Press.

Weiss, Thomas G., and Leon Gordenker, eds. 1996. *NGOs, the UN, and Global Governance*. Boulder, Colo.: Lynne Reinner Publishers.

Williams, C.S.C., Oliver F. and John W. Houck. 1993. *Catholic Social Thought and the New World Order*. Notre Dame, Ind.: University of Notre Dame Press.

Wilson, Kim. 2000. "Principled Practices in Microfinance." Baltimore, Md.: CRS (October), quoting CRS Microfinance Unit. *Microfinance Status Report 2000* 6:2. Baltimore, Md.: CRS (August).

Wolfe, Marshall. 1996. *Elusive Development*. London: Zed Books.

11

FIRM FOUNDATIONS

Christian Development NGOs, Civil Society, and Social Change

David Bronkema

Two key questions pertaining to the ongoing discussion about civil society: First, what is the relationship between civil society and development? Second, is there anything unique that Christian NGOs can and should be doing to promote development through a focus on civil society building?

To address these questions, we need to examine the role that Christianity has played in development thinking and how the concept and use of civil society has emerged in development circles. It is helpful to consider the history of development through the lens of US Protestant mission efforts to Latin America and then analyse two case studies of faith-based development NGOs in Honduras that have been particularly active in civil society building. In the process, I make the following arguments:

1. The current focus on civil society as a development strategy, far from being a passing fad, is a step in the evolution of development strategies and techniques that are based on increasing awareness of the political nature of development and are applied to changing global and national conditions.
2. The effectiveness of development strategies that focus on civil society is highly dependent on elements of previous development strategies and techniques that emphasise basic needs and capacity building.
3. Development strategies as a whole, including those focusing on civil society, are deeply flawed in terms of their effectiveness due to their blindness to the implications of human sinfulness, their faith-like reliance on social science and techniques designed to produce intended outcomes, and their concomitant disregard for the spiritual side of the human person.
4. Christian development NGOs should base their development approaches on firm biblical foundations, adopt community building as an end in and of

I would like to give special thanks to Roland Hoksbergen, Lowell Ewert, and Carlos Mejia for their valuable comments on previous drafts.

itself, promote a focus on principles and values rooted in obedience to Christ, and practise "development evangelism."

A History of Development

To understand the history of development,[1] especially the actions of NGOs, one must acknowledge the fundamental role played by Protestant Christianity. Indeed, Protestant beliefs about Christian responsibility to serve others were the key motivator driving the creation and evolution of a "nonprofit," or "third sector" dedicated to social service and social change. (James 1987; Jeavons 1994; Hall 1992; see also Hatch 1990). The Protestant missionary movement of the nineteenth and twentieth centuries internationalised the provision of social service as part of its evangelistic endeavour, creating strategies and techniques that became the hallmarks of community development (Curti 1963). At the same time, it played a major role in the establishment of the "thick web of organisations" now associated with international development (Firth 1981).

Today, churches, para-church organisations, and faith-driven individuals continue to be omnipresent in development and social change projects. These actors have produced volumes of material composing a rich and valuable source of analysis and self-reflection not only on Christianity's role in development but also on general development issues.[2]

The brief history of development that follows looks specifically at the evolution of mainline US Protestant mission efforts to Latin America to glean insights into how the current focus on civil society among NGOs fits into broader approaches to development.[3] These mission efforts began by approaching social change in a holistic way in which evangelism and social service were intimately linked, but they gradually moved to an approach that dropped the spiritual component and came to see social change as a technical problem to be solved by professional development organisations through the application of social science and related techniques.

Protestant Missions to Latin America:
A Holistic Approach to Social Change

When Protestant missions began in Latin America in the nineteenth century, missionaries were no strangers to the idea of social progress. Already in other parts of the world, "agricultural," "medical," and "industrial" missionaries were an integral part of mission teams that had opened up schools, universities, and hospitals in places where none had existed before (see Hutchison 1987; for an anthropological view, see Comaroff 1991).

Latin America was a relatively late target of the Protestant missionary movement. For many years the Catholic church had exercised a jealous protection of Latin America by using the Inquisition to root out attempts to establish a Protestant presence. The persecution of Protestants was a feature of life as late as the 1960s in countries like Colombia (see *Latin America New Letter* 1956). Moreover, European Protestant churches, with the exception of British-based churches, had

reached an understanding with the Catholic church concerning spheres of influence in Europe and had accepted the Catholic church's claim that Latin America
was already evangelised (Deiros 1992, 663).

Protestant mission work in Latin America received a tremendous boost in 1916
with the convening of the Congress on Christian Work in Latin America in Panama
City. Organised by the Committee on Cooperation in Latin America (CCLA), an
organisation founded in 1913 by representatives of the majority of the US mission
boards working in Latin America, the Panama conference laid the groundwork for
the co-ordination and co-operation between mission agencies and an increase in
resources dedicated to Latin America missions.

Mission work coordinated by the CCLA was based on the "scientific" approach
to missions that had characterised the World Missionary Conference in Edinburgh
in 1910. This approach drew on the social science research methods that had been
used by the church to devise responses to the Industrial Revolution in Britain and
the United States, responses that became known as Social Christianity or the Social Gospel (Hopkins 1940; May 1949). It combined them with the scientific philanthropy movement, which stressed the application of business and management
principles to philanthropic endeavours (see Hall 1992, 116–30). The goal of this
social analysis was to ensure the effectiveness of mission efforts. As stated by one
of the participants in the Panama conference:

> We are really trying to apply this [scientific] method in this Congress . . . an
> attempt to carefully survey the field, to get at the facts, to classify the facts,
> to see what laws underlie the facts, to discern the conditions involved in the
> laws, and then, upon fulfillment of these conditions, to be able to count upon
> results (*Christian Work in Latin America* 1917, 1:293).

The inherent tension between relying on science to produce results and giving
results up to God was not evident in these circles, at least not as reflected in the
conference reports. There was instead an underlying assumption that the scientific
approach was a God-given tool to promote God's work, so there seemed to be no
need to question its use. Rather, the tension in Protestant circles lay in the struggle
between those who wanted to "save souls" and those who wanted to "change
society,"[4] but the CCLA managed to combine these potentially conflicting views
into a holistic approach to social change that drew deeply on the Social Gospel
insights:

> With this new light which has broken forth from the newly understood Bible
> to meet the new social needs of the new civilization, missionaries and minis-
> ters of the gospel everywhere are discovering that it is their business not
> only to win individual souls to Christ, but create a Christian civilization, and
> it has been conspicuously demonstrated at home and abroad that social work
> is as helpful to one as it is essential to the other (*Christian Work in Latin
> America* 1917, 1:292).

Or, as another delegate to the Panama conference put it, "Let there be no striving between the individual gospel and the social gospel, for we be both brethren. . . . The two gospels must never be separated" (*Christian Work in Latin America* 1917, 1:356).

In the eyes of the delegates, Protestantism was the solution to present and future problems of Latin America, for it held the key to progress and prosperity. The reasoning was simple: Religion was the key variable to effective social change:

> As religion is the soul of history, the character of the coming development of Latin civilization depends in supreme degree upon the quality of its moral and spiritual life. Only upon a sound religious basis can the Latin character and the Latin culture rise to their full possibilities (*Christian Work in Latin America* 1917, 1:248).

The Catholic church, according to these analyses, had done a poor job of evangelising the two groups that held the keys to social transformation, Latin American intellectual classes and students. According to this view, by refusing to deal with modern thinking and instead aligning itself with repressive sectors of society, the Catholic church had left "thinking men . . . without any program to point the way for them to be at once Christians and yet true to the laws of the mind and to the accepted facts of modern knowledge with which their best institutions of higher learning are abreast" (*Christian Work in Latin America* 1917, 1:77). The result was that intellectuals and students had "dismissed the subject of personal religion as unworthy of the consideration of the educated," leading to a situation in which one had an "intellectual aristocracy, practically atheistic in faith, yet molding the policy of the nations" (*Christian Work in Latin America* 1917, 1:84, 157).

The delegates spelled out the specific ways in which Protestantism could create and sustain the progress of Latin America. A major focus of this thinking dealt with the political effects of Protestantism and its role as the moral and spiritual basis for democratic societies. Protestantism was seen to be the "home and the propelling force of true democracy" (*Christian Work in Latin America* 1917, 1:273), and the gospel was the "most potent, democratizing influence known among men." The gospel exalted

> the worth and dignity of the individual till he comes to have self-respect, and to demand that respect from others. At the same time it makes him his brother's keeper. It enforces such a spirit of consideration of justice and of kindness that by it men can live together in peaceful communities, governing themselves (*Christian Work in Latin America* 1917, 1:294).

The political philosophy emphasising the moral and spiritual implications of Protestantism stressed the material effects of the mission efforts. Missionaries and governments "are working for the same great fundamental objectives, the spread of education, the suppression of disease and crime, the eradication of the causes of moral corruption and of the breakdown of character; also the safeguarding of the rights of the people to the peaceful pursuit of industry and happiness (*Christian Work in Latin America* 1917, 2:300). According to the delegates, Protestantism had a vast experience in social work, and it could supplement state efforts in education and social services even as it inculcated the moral qualities through its educational efforts that were so important for a flourishing society (ibid., 1:292–93, 505).

The moral, material, and educational emphases of Protestantism were expected to lead to the structuring of a sustainable democratic society through the creation of middle classes:

> An outstanding claim on Christianity in every country is that of the depressed classes for evangelization, for education and for training into their just place in the national and social order. A major contribution of vital religion must always be greatly to accelerate the formation and growth of the middle classes (*Christian Work in Latin America* 1917, 1:194).

Industrial and agricultural education of the Indians and the poor would not only turn them into "quiet and orderly citizens," but it would also "help to bridge the chasm between the rich and the poor by building up an intelligent middle class that would ultimately become the chief factor in the social structure" (*Christian Work in Latin America* 1917, 1:96, 484).

To their credit, delegates were self-critical in their assessment of powerful actors and interests from their own country, the United States, and some of the missionaries felt a special responsibility for the problems associated with commerce and industrial revolution. Representatives of foreign capital, the delegates said, had adopted "sordid commercial standards," including the giving of bribes, and had profited from "industrial injustice" stemming from "undisguised materialism":

> Undoubtedly, the chief impact now being made from abroad upon that civilization is commercial and industrial – an influence that will be highly accentuated during the period immediately ahead. At its best this movement frankly represents materialism. It is accompanied by other grave perils to moral and spiritual life (*Christian Work in Latin America* 1917, 1:154, 192).

As a consequence, the "duty of Christians is to abate the attendant evils" of the increasing influence of international commerce on Latin America and to "cleanse political life of graft, industrial life of cruelty, commercial life of dishonesty, and all social relations of vice and depravity" (*Christian Work in Latin America* 1917, 1:75–76, 282).

In addition, Protestantism made a special claim to be able to provide guidance on the myriad issues that accompanied this process of social change, including housing, sanitation, class consciousness, socialism, syndicalism, anarchism, rights, duties, and opportunities. Prevention of social ills was seen to be particularly important, especially those connected with overcrowding and tenement housing in the cities, and child labour. As summarised by one delegate:

> The changes which [the Industrial Revolution] inevitably works have taught Great Britain and the United States some costly and valuable lessons. It is to be hoped that Latin Americans, by avoiding mistakes made in other lands, may make a far greater success in dealing with these rising social problems (*Christian Work in Latin America* 1917, 1:286, 289, 283).

This holistic approach dominated the work of the mainline missions in Latin America for the next half-century. Led by the CCLA and working for the most part in a collaborative manner, the mission boards increased their work in education, health, and agriculture, all in the context of the evangelistic endeavour. They created a journal to foster discussion among the intellectual class over religion and social change; established schools, universities, hospitals, and agricultural programmes; developed new educational approaches; planted churches and developed Sunday school curricula; opened seminaries, publishing houses, and radio stations; carried out mass evangelistic campaigns; and promoted the development of the student Christian movement and national federations and councils of churches as a way to "latinize" or "nationalize" the missionary endeavour (see the CCLA's *Latin America News Letter* and the Foreign Missions Conference reports).

Holism Lost: Social Science, Professionalisation, and Polarisation

By the end of the 1950s the CCLA and the mainline Protestant missions were operating in an environment that was increasingly filled with specialised organisations, many of which they themselves had created in conjunction with their counterparts in Europe. The humanitarian needs that shook the world during WWI and WWII had spawned the creation and networking of a host of Protestant relief organisations founded by denominations and state churches in the United States and Europe, and these NGOs soon turned their attention to relief and development work in Latin America.

The new "discipline" of community development in the 1950s, which drew heavily on techniques developed by missionaries and others engaged in social change, launched the era of professionalisation in the development field (Holdcroft 1978; Voth and Brewster 1989; Blair 1985). The rapidly developing "science" of development economics, focusing on theories of stages of growth emphasising the importance of the agricultural sector and infrastructure, cemented a faith in social science that permeated the international community. The labelling of the 1960s as the development decade was just one manifestation of the emerging confidence that the new theories, techniques, and developmental approaches, none of which included "spiritual variables," would soon make poverty a thing of the past (Rostow 1960 and 1971; Packenham 1973; Korten 1990).

As faith-based organisations like Church World Service, created in 1946 by the same boards that had formed the CCLA, responded to emergencies in Latin America and began to shift their focus to community development work, the pull of the technical approach was strong. Specialised relief and development organisations already had a natural tendency to overlook spiritual variables in their search for solutions, for they had been specifically created to respond to immediate material needs and problems with material solutions, not spiritual ones. As they settled into the longer-term work against poverty, they maintained this aspiritual focus to problem solving. Poverty had become a technical problem to be dealt with using social science methods and tools, and the increasingly professionalised development context exacerbated tendencies.

The reliance on social science by new specialised and increasingly professional Christian organisations was matched and even surpassed by the Latin American Protestant leaders associated with the CCLA, many of whom came out of the Student Christian Movement, which had received extensive support from the CCLA. A series of seminars on rapid social change sponsored by the World Council of Churches in the late 1950s and early 1960s provided the space in which Protestant theologians, in collaboration with Catholic counterparts, created a new theology that focused on the liberation of oppressed sectors of society (Neely 1977; Abrecht 1993; Smith 1991). This Latin American theology, or liberation theology, as it came to be known, while developing new insights about the role of sin in social structures, did away with the focus on evangelisation and individual values as crucial elements for successful social change. Rather, it advocated the creation of broad-based alliances with other secular and religious actors who shared the interpretive framework of class struggle to press for ways of restructuring society.[5]

The increasingly polarised mission environment in Latin America also drove some to separate evangelism from social change. Mission efforts by the conservative churches that focused almost exclusively on evangelism were expanding, and by the mid-1900s the majority of missionaries and half of the Protestants in Latin America represented this theological tradition (Strachan 1957, 6–9; Bastian 1986, 136). They were also deeply suspicious and mistrustful of those linked to the CCLA, not only because of their emphasis on social work, but also because of their increasing collaboration with the post–Vatican II Catholic church. Churches affiliated with conservative mission groups began to take over the federations and councils of churches, dismantle social programmes, and create their own parallel regional associations focusing on evangelism (NCC 1974). The climate of mutual mistrust and the creation of separate structures put pressure on those advocating a holistic approach to the gospel to choose sides, leading to a polarisation that endures today.

From One Approach to Another

Meanwhile, in secular development circles the optimism of the 1950s soon dissipated. By the early 1960s there was disillusionment with the lack of results. The strategy of community development was abandoned by government agencies, which began instead to concentrate on the provision of technical assistance, infrastructure, and the promotion of the Green Revolution (Holdcroft 1978).

As the technical approach also appeared to fail in the battle against poverty, attention shifted by the end of the 1960s to analyses of the power structures within societies. Entrenchment of landed elites, the lack of participation at the community level in decision-making (project planning and project ownership), government corruption and inefficiency, and lack of democratic structures and independent judicial systems were some of the major factors identified as impediments to successful development. These impediments, in turn, justified a new succession of development strategies of basic needs in the early 1970s, integrated rural development in the late 1970s, structural adjustment programmes in the 1980s, the emphasis on private investment and privatisation in the 1990s, and the present focus on governance and civil society (for strategies prior to 1970, see Pastor 1980 and Packenham 1973).

The emphasis on domestic structures was complemented by increased attention given to the structures of the international economic order. The impact of colonial relationships in producing under-development, the continued dependency of developing economies on developed countries, the lack of access to markets by the developing countries, the mounting foreign debt situation, the imposition of free-market policies by the international financial institutions, the power of multinational businesses, and the use of force by major powers to maintain their privileged positions led to calls for increases in foreign assistance, increases in export quotas, the forgiveness of debt, and changes in the terms of the "partnership" relations between the donor and recipient nations (see Evans 1979; see also the Reality of Aid and Jubilee 2000 websites).

As the official agencies abandoned the community development approach in the late 1950s, NGOs affiliated with the ecumenical movement, like Church World Service, did not, for their expertise and scope of action lay at the community level. Nevertheless, Church World Service became concerned about the technical problems it encountered in its development work by the end of the 1960s, as infrastructure it had helped build in the communities such as latrines, water projects, and roads deteriorated due to a lack of maintenance (Brown 1992).

At the same time, ecumenical agencies were increasingly forced to come to terms with the political aspects to development. The US invasion of the Dominican Republic in 1965 and the rise of repressive regimes in Latin America over the next several years led the CCLA and Latin American mainline Protestant leaders to challenge Church World Service to respond in some way (NCC 1974, 8; *Latin America News Letter #63* 1965). The increasing use of structural analyses of the 1960s and the struggle of the liberation movements against colonialism and authoritarian governments all over the world during this time led the ecumenical movement to call into question both the power exercised by Northern churches and service agencies in the ecumenical movement vis-à-vis their Southern counterparts and also the role each should play in missions and development.

These political and technical/resource challenges led Church World Service and other leading agencies in the ecumenical circles to change their perception of their role in development and their community development methods in a number of ways. Responding to the call to do more in the North, Church World Service established in 1974 a joint Office on Development Policy in Washington, D.C., with Lutheran World Relief; a year or so later it expanded this office to be responsible for development education in the United States (Stenning 1996, 70, 78). Both of these steps were geared towards educating the population in the United States about the political causes of poverty in the South, including the culpability of the United States, and to build a network of informed people for pressuring the government and multilateral agencies to adopt policies that would benefit the most vulnerable.

The English-language publication of Paulo Freire's *Pedagogy of the Oppressed* in 1970 had a profound influence on ecumenical development NGOs and the community-development methods they used in the South (for its effect on Oxfam, see Black 1992, 187–92). Freire's method, which became known as popular education, allowed development NGOs to address both "technical/resource" and "political" problems at the local level. Freire's emphasis on education for political change gave NGOs two ways to conceptualise community organisation and participation in the decision-making processes. First, popular education could strengthen local organisational capacity to build and maintain the community infrastructure needed for development. The key was giving the community "ownership" of the process. Second, raising political awareness at the community level, or conscientisation, held the promise of creating grassroots movements that would challenge the status quo and lead to structural change. In this way Freire's writings undertook a structural analysis of society that identified politics and power at all levels as the main barriers to development and presented a solution to this problem: the empowerment of the people at the local level.

The focus on politics also moved development NGOs to support and work with a wider range of actors. As repression in Latin America increased in the 1970s and 1980s, Protestant NGOs in Europe began to reach out and fund peasant, labour, and human rights organisations that were seen as key bulwarks against authoritarian governments.[6] Coupled with a new understanding of global interdependence, many NGOs began to stress the importance of creating a dense web of linkages and capacity building for social movements at the national, regional, and international levels.

This new approach to development included both direct and indirect support for revolutionary movements. In Central America, European agencies gave tacit and at times direct support to the guerrilla movements, in part as a counterweight to the support given by the United States to the repressive regimes (Biekart 1999, chap. 5). Church World Service, which by this time had merged with the CCLA in an attempt to put mission and service on the same page, took a similar approach in Central America by supporting church groups sympathetic to revolutionary struggles.

The 1990s brought a new set of changes. The negotiated settlements to the civil conflicts in Central America made possible by the fall of the Soviet Union, the collapse of the leftist struggle for power in Latin America, the spread of neo-liberal market policies, the weakening of labour and *campesino* movements, and an increasing emphasis on decentralisation and local municipal authorities created a new political and economic environment in which social movements believed that they could achieve better developmental results by engaging the national authorities through lobbying and advocacy. While maintaining the importance of mobilising constituencies for mass protests, the locus of the political project began to shift to the development of capacity to propose concrete policy alternatives and methods for getting these into national legislation. The increased attention given to strengthening the capacity of development, human rights, and research NGOs came at the expense of peasant and labour organisations. The new focus also came about at the local level as community organisations were taught to design projects and take them to the municipal authorities, thereby making government more responsive to the needs of its people.[7]

These newly christened civil society organisations have now come to be seen as the cornerstone of democracy building and development. As Kees Biekart states in an insightful review of private aid agencies and civil society building, "Civil society building strategies of private aid agencies aim to actively incorporate marginalized sectors into civil society and try to further democratization by increasing the leverage of civil society *vis-à-vis* the state. . . . This type of civil society building essentially aims to strengthen *political society*" (Biekart 1999, 97).

CASE STUDIES

The above history of the interaction between general development theory and the development of the Protestant church in Latin America is intended to provide a background for understanding the present focus on civil society building and the involvement of religious actors in these efforts. I now turn to two case studies to look more closely at faith-based organizations and the complexities they face in social change efforts that involve bolstering civil society.

The Christian Commission for Development

The first case study is that of the Christian Commission for Development (CCD), a Southern faith-based NGO working in Honduras since the early 1980s in integrated community development and theological education.[8] CCD's motto comes from the first half of Galatians 6:10: Therefore as we have opportunity, let us do good to all people. Recognised as one of the leading Southern NGOs in Honduras, and indeed as one of the most effective in the worldwide ecumenical network, CCD's origins were deeply influenced by mission efforts outlined above and by the history of polarisation between Protestant churches in Latin America.

CCD's origins lie in an organisation called the Evangelical Committee for National Development (CEDEN), an agency founded after Hurricane Fifi in 1975 by the conservative Honduran churches to administer aid received from ecumenical and evangelical circles. In the early 1980s CEDEN became deeply involved in administering Salvadoran refugee camps in Honduras, and its member churches were upset by what they perceived to be a sympathy by CCD's leadership for the El Salvadoran guerrilla movement. This conflict led to the ousting of the director of CEDEN and several of her staff, prompting the resignation of thirty people in protest. Twelve of these people, including the director, formed the Christian Commission for Development and most European and US ecumenical funding agencies shifted their funding from CEDEN to CCD over the next few years because CCD was more in line with their own progressive approach to social change. CEDEN ceased to exist in the late 1990s.

Over the next few years CCD began working in four different regions in Honduras promoting integrated community development programmes in agriculture, health, small productive projects, and literacy. At the same time, CCD worked with Protestant pastors and Catholic delegates of the Word (lay pastors) in theological education and social concerns, activities it kept separate from its development work. By 1997 CCD was working in over 100 communities in six regions of Honduras, and though it was theologically aware, it avoided any direct connection with evangelistic activities, in part because of the difficulties this would present for its collaboration with the Catholic church. CCD staff come from both Protestant and Catholic backgrounds, and all participate in weekly Bible studies as part of their work. Top-level staff receive theological training at the Protestant seminary in Honduras, and CCD is primarily viewed as a nondenominational, ecumenical, Protestant organisation.

A review of CCD's community development methods from 1982 to the present sheds an interesting light on the history and precursors of the current focus on civil society's role in development. During the past two decades, CCD has gone through three distinct stages, moving from an initial apolitical approach to development to an approach that integrates political concepts much more thoroughly.

At the core of CCD's methodology is a strategy to promote local organisations and strengthen community groups and movements. In the 1980s, the organisation of community groups was seen primarily as a way to ensure the ownership and sustainability of its integrated community development projects. CCD's projects in health, agriculture, literacy, and commerce were carried out through men's, women's, and community-wide groups, as well as through production co-operatives that CCD had either helped form or strengthen. Education was a key component of CCD's community development approach. Group leaders were trained in specific skills, and the groups as a whole received training in organisational management. The educational method employed was the popular education approach drawn from the work of Paulo Freire and was based on the concept of using local knowledge to strengthen problem-solving and critical-thinking skills, including a consideration of the barriers faced by the *campesinos* in their daily lives.

While there was an informal acknowledgement that the organisation of groups in the repressive setting in Honduras in the 1980s might lead local groups to make more demands on government and possibly challenge local structures of power, CCD never made the political side of development a part of its overt goal. This was despite much pressure by its European funders to link its programmes with those of the combative peasant movements of the country. As a result, the political side of the organisation was never clearly spelled out, formally or informally, and it remained at a level of generality. While one of the regular seminars it held with its community groups covered an assessment of the "national reality," CCD shied away from leading the *campesinos* to political conclusions, leaving it to them to make their own decisions in terms of affiliation with peasant or other movements.

With the decline of repression in Honduras in the early 1990s, CCD slowly shifted its development strategy to a more overtly political approach. By 1997, building on its earlier work, it asked the communities to carry out self-analyses of their organisational make-up, to identify the top priorities for development, and then to engage in a full-blown process at the village level to elect candidates to carry out CCD-supported development projects. CCD was thus aiming to train people to engage in civic processes by electing their own authorities, thereby creating a nonpartisan rural movement that would engage local and regional government authorities (see Hoksbergen and Espinoza 1997, 52 n.37).

Since 1999, CCD has adopted a strategy geared towards helping the community groups link to development opportunities presented by a decentralisation process that has left the municipal authorities with increased power. Incorporating advocacy material produced primarily by the Washington Office in Latin America that lays out simple strategies for lobbying local and national governments on specific issues, CCD's strategy now consists of getting community groups to present their development proposals to the municipal development committees and to press for municipal approval. At the same time, it continues with its basic work in promoting health, agriculture, literacy, and economic projects.

While CCD is most known in international development circles for its community development work, it has also carried out extensive work in the area of religious education. It has developed an extension programme in theological education and spearheaded the opening up of a Protestant seminary in Honduras affiliated with the prestigious evangelical Latin American Biblical University. One of the main goals for the theological education programme is to promote social programmes and social awareness among conservative Pentecostal churches and to chip away at the bitter rivalries that exist between Protestants and Catholics. It has formed groups of Protestant pastors in rural and urban areas of Honduras to discuss the social aspects of the gospel and promoted exchanges between them and delegates of the Word of the Catholic church, with whom CCD continues to work closely. Even though CCD keeps its development and pastoral work separate, rural pastors and delegates of the Word have played key leadership roles in the formation of the community development groups.

CCD's rootedness in faith has led it to play a leading role in building civil society in two unique ways. First, it is one of the few, if not the only, organisation in Central America working with both conservative Protestant pastors and Catholic delegates of the Word with the objective of building relationships between them. The basis of this work lies in an appeal to become engaged in social issues. In this work CCD is planting the seeds of the creation of a potentially powerful community. If Catholic lay leaders and Protestant pastors are able to form such a community of religious leaders from historically hostile camps brought together around social concerns, it will be something very new and powerful in terms of influence on community and national life.

The second unique focus of civil society building in which CCD has been engaged has been the attempt spurred by Church World Service to create a new model of relationships between the Northern and Southern ecumenical NGOs. Inspired by long-standing discussions on partnerships in several World Council of Churches conferences (see Taylor 1995), the Latin America and Caribbean Office of Church World Service (LACO) in 1986 began what came to be known as the São Paulo process. This process was designed to include its Southern partners in the highest level of decision-making and to create greater networking and exchanges of ideas and information among the Southern partners themselves regarding their work and relationships (Bronkema 1996). After achieving a great degree of success, the São Paulo process came to an abrupt end in 2000 when a restructuring of Church World Service led to the elimination of its geographically based units, including LACO. CCD has now taken the lead in trying to re-create a space for US/Latin America and Caribbean ecumenical community building among entities involved in mission efforts.

The Alternative Community Trade Network (COMAL)

The second case study is of the Alternative Community Trade Network (COMAL) in Honduras.[9] COMAL's members have close ties with the Catholic church, and the network came into being with the assistance of the American Friends Service Committee (AFSC), a Northern faith-based (Quaker) NGO with a vast array of human rights, economic justice, and development programmes all over the world.

In 1992, as Central America was recovering from a period of civil wars and economic stagnation, the food-security situation of small farmers in Honduras was in a tenuous state. Pushed and pulled by structural adjustment programmes, the Honduran government reduced state support to the country's small-farmer sector. Largely dependent on high prices charged by intermediaries for consumption goods, credit, and agricultural inputs, and on low prices offered for their crops, the *campesinos* in the rural and isolated regions of Honduras were further buffeted by increasing inflation rates and a steadily declining local currency. In a country where small farmers produce more than half of the basic grains for internal consumption, the difficulty in making ends meet led to substantial drops in the production of basic grains in the country as a whole, further increasing prices and creating scarcity of beans and maize, staple foodstuffs in the rural areas.

Undercut by legislation passed by the government in Honduras in the early 1990s that rescinded a law allowing *campesinos* to take over idle lands, and by national leaders who had succumbed to the temptations of power and money, the campesino movement in Honduras lost much of its legitimacy and effectiveness. Still, many local *campesino* groups remained, in large part led by delegates of the Word who maintained close ties with the Catholic church and were driven by their faith and *campesino* identity to continue their struggle for social change. With the help of the church, several of these women's, small farmer, and artisan groups began to open community stores as a way to make ends meet.

In 1992 AFSC sent two Central America field representatives to Honduras with a mission: talk with the *campesino* sector to find out what kinds of new and innovative solutions might exist in the face of this drastically changed economic and political environment for small farmers. Over the next three years the AFSC representatives spearheaded the creation of a novel network among the *campesino* organisations of Honduras dedicated to creating marketing channels for consumption and production that reached into the poor and isolated sections of the country.

Under the legal umbrella of the AFSC, COMAL was founded in 1995 and has grown significantly since then. Purchasing basic goods in bulk from factories, COMAL now distributes goods to 450 community stores run by the member organisations, while at the same time buying the production of small farmers in these communities and marketing it either in the community stores or on the national market. COMAL's member organisations manage the regional warehouses and distribution systems in addition to the stores, while the national staff handles the systems set up for purchasing items in bulk and distributing them to the 38 regional warehouses. A sophisticated education programme geared towards developing and maintaining the local capacity to administer the stores and distribution centres has been put into place. A market information system providing weekly updates on market prices around the country is another important strategic element in COMAL's operations, allowing it to take advantage of the best deals.

Reaching more than 14,000 families through 35 member organisations in 14 of Honduras's 18 departments, COMAL has already had a tremendous impact. By providing products at lower prices than those charged by the intermediaries, and by purchasing harvests at prices higher than those offered by the intermediaries, COMAL's stores have made a significant contribution to raising family incomes. In addition, the effect goes far beyond the items sold in the community stores. Due to the presence of COMAL, intermediaries and other retail establishments have been forced to lower the prices they set for other consumers and to increase the prices they offer producers. In effect, COMAL has been able to influence prices in favour of small consumers and producers far beyond its own network.

COMAL has also developed innovative *campesino* businesses, such as organic brown sugar factories, drawing on agricultural knowledge and skills from *campesinos* and indigenous peoples from Honduras and other countries. In addition to providing greater profit margins for rural farmers, COMAL is creating jobs in the rural areas. The fact that COMAL has established itself as a large purchasing and retail enterprise in the country also gives it the leverage needed to speak with strength on matters of government policy affecting food security and economic development measures, a role it is just beginning to play. Finally, COMAL has branched out to help create and strengthen similar efforts in other Central and South American countries, and it has helped bolster the formation of a network of community trade organisations in Latin America.

COMAL's success and rapid growth is due to several factors, especially its emphasis on the education of its member organisations in accounting, marketing, and administration, and the formation of a strong management team. This local management has been complemented by complete local ownership by the *campesino* organisations. A strong board of directors elected by the member organisations, a policy of hiring *campesinos*, and an apprentice programme for *campesinos* that has allowed them to fill high-level staff spots ensures that COMAL will remain a member-owned and managed organisation.

Perhaps the most important factor, however, has been the emphasis by COMAL on the principles and values established from the beginning as the guiding force behind this project. The COMAL network is cemented by a focus on values that make it more than just a successful business that has improved the material livelihood of rural Hondurans. Working on the basis of nine principles developed by the member organisations, the COMAL network comes together around the importance of fair prices and weights; economic transparency; justice; respect for all persons and equality of rights; honesty; respect for life and nature; and solidarity. The past experience of the *campesinos* with corrupt leaders is a powerful reminder of the importance of keeping the values and principles at the heart of COMAL. Another important check and balance is the strong presence of delegates of the Word on COMAL's board of directors, helping to provide a spiritual basis for these values and to keep them at the core of the organisation. The opening words of Auristela Argueta, a delegate of the Word and president of the board of directors of COMAL, in her speech on 16 June 2000 as COMAL officially received its legal status from a government representative, are indicative of this source of strength: "Most of all, I want to thank God . . . "

Conclusions

We began with two questions having to do with, first, with the relationship between civil society and development, and second, with the potential unique contribution by Christian development NGOs to development strategies, including civil society building. From the history and case studies reviewed above, I am drawn to four main conclusions in response to those initial questions:

1. The current focus on civil society as a development strategy, far from being a passing fad, is a step in the evolution of development strategies and techniques that are based on increasing awareness of the political nature of development and are applied to changing global and national conditions.

The history of development, supplemented and detailed by the case studies, shows that some key NGOs did not jump from one development fad to another. Rather, they built on important lessons learned from each previous strategy. As the context in which they operated changed, and their understanding of development became more complex, they reoriented their methods.

The concept of civil society and its relationship to development is just the latest step in this constantly evolving process of the conceptualisation of society and development strategies based on increasing awareness of the political nature of development in changing global and national conditions. In this context, civil society is seen as a wide range of non-government entities that can be mobilised to advise and pressure the government to take steps towards creating a better society. In particular, CCD's work in civil society building is a natural extension of the work begun by Protestant missions to Latin America over 100 years ago. CCD is engaging in a series of actions designed to increase the power and input of local organisations vis-à-vis the government, including conducting advocacy training and linking organisations with powerful international actors.[10]

2. The effectiveness of development strategies focusing on civil society is highly dependent on elements of previous development strategies and techniques that emphasise basic needs and capacity building.

There is at present a debate over the effectiveness and worth of the development endeavour as a whole. I believe there are worthwhile reasons for supporting development activities. It is also my opinion that social science will provide us with insights to help us both correct the problems of past development approaches and foster and create new approaches that will get us closer to our goal of more just societies. While there may be passing fads in development, change may also represent progress in both understanding and practice.

In effect, the crucial question is whether the present focus on civil society represents an advance in the effectiveness of approaches to social change. In short, will a focus on civil society building bring about results that past development approaches were unable to achieve? And if so, what are the best practices for engaging in civil society building?

A close look at the above case studies and history of development shows that rather than being an advance over past development approaches in the sense that it supersedes them, civil-society building is an approach that is complementary and that to a large degree depends on their continuation. There are two main reasons for this claim. First, the ultimate success of any development approach depends on the creation of the capacity of communities to be full participants in their own development. Second, and intimately related to the first, the creation of capacity in communities to be full participants relies on processes of organisation and social mobilisation that, in turn, rely on developmental approaches that stress attention to immediate or short-term material benefits.

If civil society building is successful in gaining the space to negotiate with the government and to channel resources to needy communities, one of the main challenges will be how to ensure that local communities actually have input into policy and the capacity to implement and manage their community's development. The creation of local technical and political capacity is exactly what CCD and other NGOs engaged in empowerment approaches have been doing for the last 20 years.

For successful organisation to take place, the problems and difficulties of motivation must be addressed. People living day to day more likely than not will become involved in social change efforts only if they can see a clear and direct correlation with how their own short-term material situation will improve. CCD's strategy of using material projects to promote the organisation of community groups, and at the same time using the organisations to ensure the effective implementation and sustainability of its material projects in health, agriculture, and economic activities, is based on this reality. In fact, CCD ran into trouble in the mid-1990s when in its pursuit of a more political approach, it down-played the material side of its projects. It had to revise its strategy when a significant number of communities began to show a lack of interest in participating in CCD activities. The latest community strategy of strengthening the capacity to research and produce proposals to be channelled through the municipal authorities is another step in the development of organisational capacity around the motivating factor of material benefits.

In summary, while it is certainly true that there is much work to be done in successfully developing civil society by focusing on training in advocacy, lobbying, policy research, and development of transnational linkages, this strategy needs to be complemented by a continued focus on basic needs projects. Moreover, basic organisational work at the community level creates more opportunities for mobilising people to provide leverage for the high-level advocacy efforts and lends greater legitimacy and accountability to the whole process. Finally, the myriad organisational and educational efforts at the community level also produce leaders who become key actors in policy level negotiations with the government. Thus, there are a number of ways agencies can build civil society (Biekart 1999, 96–101).

In the final analysis, there seems to be a division of labour in development circles. Those working at the community level in apparently apolitical development projects are, intentionally or not, creating a base on which those more interested in the structural questions can build. Beyond the importance of being aware of the political context in which one is operating, to say nothing of the cultural and social contexts, this points to the importance of linkages and potential co-ordination of work with other actors.[11] While it is true that some agencies have the resources to work at all levels at the same time, most do not. This calls, therefore, for organisations to be aware of the political context in which they work and to seek opportunities to collaborate with those doing advocacy work if they cannot do it themselves. The cues, of course, must be taken from the community, for ultimately it is their lives that are at stake.

3. Development strategies as a whole, including those focusing on civil society, are deeply flawed in terms of their effectiveness due to their blindness to the implications of human sinfulness, their faith-like reliance on social science and techniques designed to produce intended outcomes, and their concomitant disregard for the spiritual side of the human person.

A Christian perspective on development and civil society needs to place our development strategies on the analytical block of Scripture, just as we should let our interpretation of Scripture be challenged and enriched by social theory (see Myers 1999, chap. 1). We know from Scripture and experience that human beings are sinful by nature, are unable to see the whole truth, and lack the capacity to control ultimate outcomes. If we look at typical development strategies in this light, it becomes immediately clear that they contain deep flaws. There is a huge emphasis on the structural but no emphasis on the personal. Worldly conditions are highlighted but not spiritual ones. Such an imbalance, or, to use other terms, this lack of a holistic approach to development is a problem not only for effectiveness in development, but also for the fundamental purpose of social change as Christians should understand it.

The Implications of the Sinful Nature of Humans

Missionaries to Latin America from the mainline churches through the 1960s, despite all the cultural baggage they carried, had a holistic approach to mission that was both personal and structural. They believed that conversion to Christ would lead to changes in society, and they preached to the leaders of the societies the relevance of Christianity for the creation of just societies. They emphasised the crucial role that values and principles played in this endeavour based on their interpretation of social problems as stemming from sinful human nature.

There are hints that the broad community of people and organisations involved in development and social change both in the South and the North is beginning to return to a philosophy that incorporates the fundamental importance of values and principles in society. The increasing talk about the need to change the political culture of societies in a way that enshrines values such as transparency, honesty, and accountability is in this way encouraging. Still, this new outlook tends to focus on structures and leaders and is limited in its preaching to the importance of values and principles in people at all levels to create effective and long-lasting change in how societies are managed and governed. The problems of corruption, malfeasance, and abuse of power are not present only among the powerful. They run rampant through civil society organisations as well. As long as the issue of personal sin and its role in building up structures remains unacknowledged and unexplored, the effectiveness and sustainability of development programs, including the building of civil society, will be severely limited.

The Implications of Faith-Like Reliance on Social Science and Techniques

There is a tendency today to hold an implicit, if not explicit, belief in the power of social science to make development approaches more effective. But such a reliance on science leads many times to overconfidence in our ability to bring about intended outcomes, an attitude of arrogance and imperialism, and a flawed view of the ultimate goals of development, and causes us to overlook important methods to achieve those goals.

A major danger in placing one's faith in a scientific approach is that it can lead a person to "play God." Science is based on an analysis of the world that begins and ends with humans and the environment, and one of its fundamental tenets is that the physical world and human behaviour are caused by a variety of identifiable and manipulable variables. By manipulating these variables one can control both the physical environment as well as what people think and do. Development practitioners in the late 1950s and early 1960s were convinced that economics and other social sciences had given them the tools with which to eliminate poverty.

Their faith in the scientific approach led to spoken and unspoken arrogance that permeated their relationships with those for whom they were working. The resulting predilection to impose projects, policies, and strategies, from the management of whole economies to local community development, is still alive and well today in both overt and subtle forms.

To some degree the confidence and arrogance in social science has been tempered over the years by the increased awareness and appreciation of the importance of indigenous knowledge and the complexity of human interaction. This moderation has been brought about by the repeated failures of social-change planners to achieve intended outcomes and by the negative unintended consequences of well-meaning development programmes. New scientific discoveries showing the enormous complexity of the natural world and new analytical tools such as chaos theory have also contributed to moderating confidence in the ability to control results. But the belief remains strong that it is just a matter of time before humans come to understand this world fully through their science. There is thus an ongoing tendency to leave God out of the picture, maintaining our faith in human capacity to solve problems with our own methods. Yet Christians know that finite humans can see only a part of the truth and that only God is able to control what ultimately will happen. Because of our inability to see the full truth, and because of our sinful nature, we will always be unable to solve all social problems through social science, a reality that helps illuminate the meaning of Jesus' declaration that "you always have the poor with you" (Matt. 26:11).

A practical problem with an overreliance on science is that it limits the inclusion of spiritual components in our definition of the goals and methods in social change. Development strategies are primarily geared towards the goal of solving material poverty. Civil society building strategies are now seen by some as a means to that end. While the more recent quality-of-life debates go beyond material poverty by positing individual freedom and choice as fundamental elements of a good life, there is still something sorely missing: the centrality of spirituality in giving our lives purpose and fulfilment.

The absence of spirituality in discussions of quality of life in development circles is far from coincidental, for the scientific approach to social change rules God out as an explanatory variable and places humans at the centre of the universe. The human need for a relationship with God is generally out of bounds. Scripture teaches, however, that life without a relationship with God is impoverished and incomplete, and development strategies that do not take this into account are fundamentally flawed.

The confidence in social science and the inherent accompanying tendency of setting aside the spiritual elements of life also lead to the minimising of a central method called for by Scripture: prayer. The Bible is clear that we are to ask God to bring about things we desire and that God hears and answers our prayers, although not as we would like at times. In the preparations for the first Latin America missions conference in Panama in 1916, the CCLA placed great emphasis on calling on the congregations of the involved denominations to pray for the endeavour. Yet over time, as the scientific approach gained more and more sway, belief in the central importance of prayer to the success of worldly work has diminished or been lost. Social change efforts that do not incorporate an emphasis on prayer are also fundamentally flawed.

4. Christian development NGOs should base their development approaches on firm biblical foundations, adopt community building as an end in and of itself, promote a focus on principles and values rooted in obedience to Christ, and engage in development evangelism.

Social science tools, as gifts from God, have great power to make this world a better place. Nevertheless, they contain elements that inherently push God aside and marginalise or eliminate the spiritual side of the world. The reliance of secular and Christian NGOs alike on a scientific approach to development has led them to the point of adopting development strategies that are indistinguishable in terms of their elements and guiding principles.

For Christian development NGOs to make a unique and faithful contribution to development, they must be clear on the foundations for understanding and engaging in social change and on what these imply for their actions. Among these foundations, I believe, are at least the following:

• The sinful nature of humankind
• The inability of humankind fully to control outcomes
• The centrality of spirituality in human life
• The need for people to obey Christ's teachings and to believe in him

From these firm, biblical foundations,[12] there are at least three specific courses of action in which Christian development NGOs can and should take the lead in development in general and civil society building in particular:

• Build community as an end in and of itself
• Preach and model obedience to Christ
• Engage in development evangelism

Community Building

The focus on civil society building, and on other development activities should have as an end in and of itself the building of community. The centrality of spirituality in quality of life means that relationships with God and with fellow human beings are at the core of the purpose of our existence and should be at the core of our focus of social change efforts. The focus on building community holds deep implications for the way we go about engaging in social change. It cautions against arrogance, against the improper wielding of power in relationships, and for love, mercy, and grace in our dealings with each other. It also argues for relationship building with our partners in both the North and South and for a long-term commitment to the communities with whom we work (cf. Myers 1999, 50).

The focus on building community also holds implications for how we measure success in development. One interesting example of such thinking is the 1979 document produced by Church World Service entitled the "Nature of Church World Service." In this theological justification for its development activities, Church World Service declares that the fundamental purpose of its actions is to create community and that the material aspects of its activities are important, but secondary. Nevertheless, it did not spell out the implications of this focus for its community development methods, civil society building, or creation of networks. It is important for Christian development NGOs to take a close look at how they could improve their work by placing community building at the centre of their focus.

Principles and Values
The second specific course of action through which Christian development NGOs can make a distinct contribution is to promote a focus on principles and values as a main part of the development agenda. Christian development NGOs should proclaim the importance of obedience to Christ to effective development work. The sinful nature of humankind means that promoting lives and actions guided by the principles and values laid forth by Christ is essential for promoting more just societies. This is applicable both in the North and in the South, to all people in all roles and at all levels.

Looking at it this way brings up the question of the appropriateness of expressing one's faith in the public sphere. The Christian faith integrates the components of obedience and salvation, which in some ways correspond to the scriptural commands to engage in social work and evangelism. Obedience to Christ involves guiding one's life and relationships with others by a set of principles and values that can be translated into secular terms and which in fact are at the root of many Western values. The functional effect of giving principles and values a central role in development strategies, promoting these in training and projects, would not necessarily raise particular problems of transcendence. The greatest difficulty may be in how these values and principles are expressed cross-culturally.[13]

The example of COMAL in placing principles and values at the centre of development and civil society building is thus a helpful illustration, and its success so far is encouraging, although it is still at an early stage. Questions remain about how the principles and values can best be transmitted and institutionalised in the network as new members join and old staff leave. The priority COMAL attaches to placing principles and values at its core points to how this second course of action is intimately linked to the first: the principles and values are a source of community identity, in this case *campesino* identity, and as such are crucial to the building of community.

Development Evangelism
While the translation of the obedience component of Christianity addresses the lack of balance between the personal and the structural in development programmes, it does not deal directly either with the spiritual part of people or the proclamation of the salvific message. Clearly, evangelism should be part and parcel of the outreach of Christian NGOs (see Bradshaw 1993). This is the third specific course of action, and it builds on the other two.

Taking a page from the method of friendship evangelism, which calls for establishing relationships as the basis for opening up opportunities for presenting the gospel, Christian NGOs should engage in what might be called development evangelism. If Christian NGOs take up promoting the core necessity of personal values and principles in development, promote them functionally in their development programmes, and combine them with the building of community at local, national, and international levels, the door will likely open for a deeper presentation of the gospel. If Christian NGOs take the lead in addressing the rest of the development community in these terms, and model such values successfully in their programmes, then the discussion in the broad practitioner community may eventually turn to a consideration of what really gives sustenance and sustainability to personal, community, national, and international development.

NOTES

[1] For the meaning and use of the term *development,* which has received much deliberation in print, see Bryant L. Myers, *Walking with the Poor: Principles and Practices of Transformational Development* (Maryknoll, N.Y. Orbis Books, 1999), esp. chap. 4; and David Bronkema, David Lumsdaine, and Rodger A. Payne, "Foster Just and Sustainable Development," in *Just Peacemaking: Ten Practices for Abolishing War,* ed. G. Stassen (Cleveland: Pilgrim Press, 1998). As a summary definition herein I use *development* as a term that encompasses material, political, cultural, and spiritual change for the better at the individual, local, national, and international levels. It is a process that is inherently "political," even if it is not recognised as such by those engaging in it, in the sense of bringing about changes in power at all levels.

[2] For a good idea of the sophistication of these actors by that time, see Committee on Society, Development, and Peace, *In Search of a Theology of Development: Papers from a Consultation on Theology and Development held by Sodepax in Cartigny, Switzerland, November, 1969* (Geneva: Committee on Society, Development, and Peace, 1969). For an excellent historical summary of the debates carried on in the circles affiliated with the World Council of Churches, see Michael Taylor, *Not Angels But Agencies: The Ecumenical Response to Poverty – A Primer* (Geneva: World Council of Churches, 1995). The "evangelical" branch of Protestantism got a later start, but produced very useful material in the 1990s (see especially Myers, *Walking with the Poor.*

[3] For our purposes, *Christian development NGOs* are defined as those organisations that draw their inspiration from the Christian faith and church, and reflect that inspiration at the very least in their rhetoric. For a detailed consideration of this issue, see Thomas H. Jeavons, *Identifying Characteristics of "Religious" Organizations: An Exploratory Proposal,* Program on Non-Profit Organizations and Institution for Social and Policy Studies Working Paper no. 197 and ISPS Working Paper no. 2197 (New Haven, Conn.: Program on Non-Profit Organizations and Institution for Social and Policy Studies, 1993).

[4] While this was a point of tension in mission efforts, categorised by William Hutchison as differences over "civilizing" and "evangelizing," there were many other tensions in Protestant circles during these years (William R. Hutchison, *Errand to the World: American Protestant Thought and Foreign Missions* [Chicago: University of Chicago Press, 1987]). Probably the strongest one revolved around "scientific" challenges to the authority of the Bible through the theory of evolution, questioning the scientific accuracy, and therefore the literal truth, of Scripture. For the fierce battles fought over this issue, see George M. Marsden,

Fundamentalism and American Culture: The Shaping of Twentieth-Century Evangelicalism: 1870–1925 (Oxford: Oxford University Press, 1980), esp. 171–84.

⁵ For a conservative view of how the World Council of Churches developed a theology of "New Mission" that did away with the importance of evangelism, see Harvey T. Hoekstra, *The World Council of Churches and the Demise of Evangelism* (Wheaton, Ill.: Tyndale House, 1979); and Roger E. Hedlund, *Roots of the Great Debate in Missions* (Madras: Evangelical Literature Service, 1981). Liberation Theology played a large role in this, according to the authors.

⁶ Church World Service was more limited in its direct outreach to these new social movements because its mandate only allowed it to work through churches and church groups. This was a source of great frustration to some within the organization (see Lowell Brown, director of Sub-Unit #2 of Church World Service. Interview by author [1992]).

⁷ The drastically changing contextual changes spurred those heavily involved in popular education into a process of rethinking the methods, approaches, concepts and role of Popular Education in social change. The proceedings from a series of workshops gathering together the cutting-edge intellectuals involved in this endeavour give a good summary of the issues with which they were wrestling (*Construyendo Pedagogía Popular: Encuentro de Experiencias Pedagógicas* [Mexico City: American Friends Service Committee and Servicio, 1997]; *Educación Popular en la América Latina: Tendencias y Desafíos*, Seminario Latino-Americano y Caribeño de Educación Popular, Olinda-Brasil [Recife: Escola de Formação Quilombo dos Palmares, 1999]; *Educación Popular y alternativas políticas en América Latin,*. vol. 1 (Havana: Editorial Caminos, 1999]).

⁸ This section is drawn from my personal experience in working with CCD from 1983 to 1985, and from my dissertation research notes from a four-month stretch of participant observation with CCD in 1997.

⁹ This section draws on my present work as programme co-ordinator for the Latin America and Caribbean Region of the American Friends Service Committee (AFSC), with special responsibility for co-ordination of programmes in Central America. Some of this material is taken from unpublished outreach pieces co-written with Dick Erstad, director of AFSC's Latin America and Caribbean Region.

¹⁰ In a sense, civil society is an alternative strategy for social change to the leftist agenda. Yet it is not the only alternative: witness the rise of more authoritarian forms of government in Latin America, such as in Peru or Venezuela. These other alternative forms, especially that of Hugo Chavez in Venezuela, present particular problems for those NGOs committed to democracy, especially when the autocrats have substantial popular support.

¹¹ I'm using "political," "social," and "cultural" here in a way that seems to separate them, but that is not my intention. In reality, they are all linked together, in large part because they all deal with issues of power. For useful theoretical considerations on this issue, see Nicholas B. Dirks, Geoff Eley, and Sherry B. Ortner, "Introduction," in *Culture/Power/History: A Reader in Contemporary Social Theory*, ed. N. Dirks, G. Eley, and S. Ortner (Princeton, N.J.: Princeton University Press, 1994).

¹² Myers offers a set of principles and practices of faith-based development, which he calls "transformational development." The foundations and the courses of action that I set out here have some of the same elements, although they differ substantially from Myers's in part because they are geared towards the development community as a whole, and not just the programmes in the field (cf. Myers, *Walking with the Poor*).

¹³ For good insights into the importance of the translation of the Bible as a way to allow each culture to bring a new refreshing richness to the interpretation of Scripture and

accompanying values, see Lamin Sanneh, *Translating the Message: The Missionary Impact on Culture* (Maryknoll, N.Y.: Orbis Books, 1991).

REFERENCES

Abrecht, Paul. 1993. "The Development of Ecumenical Social Thought and Action." In *A History of the Ecumenical Movement, 1517–1968*. vol. 2., edited by R. Rouse, S. Neill, and H. Fey. Geneva: World Council of Churches.

Bastian, Jean Pierre. 1986. *Breve Historia del Protestantismo en América Latina*. Mexico: Casa Unida de Publicaciones, S.A.

Biekart, Kees. 1999. *The Politics of Civil Society Building: European Private Aid Agencies and Democratic Transitions in Central America*. Utrecht and Amsterdam: International Books and Transnational Institute.

Black, Maggie. 1992. *A Cause for Our Times – Oxfam: The First 50 Years*. Oxford: Oxford University Press.

Blair, Harry W. 1985. "Reorienting Development Administration." *Journal of Development Studies* 23/4: 449–57.

Bradshaw, Bruce. 1993. *Bridging the Gap: Development, Evangelism and Shalom*. Monrovia, Calif.: MARC.

Bronkema, David. 1996. *The São Paulo Process: North-South Donor-Recipient Relationships, Power, and Identity Among Christian Development NGOs*. Program on Non-Profit Organizations Working Paper no. 230. New Haven, Conn.: Program on Non-Profit Organizations.

Brown, Lowell. 1992. Director of Sub-Unit #2 of Church World Service. Interview by author (January 1993).

Christian Work in Latin America. 1917. Vols. 1–3. New York: The Missionary Education Movement.

Comaroff, Jean and John. 1991. *Of Revelation and Revolution: Christianity, Colonialism, and Consciousness in South Africa*. Chicago: University of Chicago Press.

Curti, Merle. 1963. *American Philanthropy Abroad: A History*. New Brunswick, N.J.: Rutgers University Press.

Deiros, Pablo Alberto. 1992. *Historia del cristianismo en America Latina*. Buenos Aires: Fraternidad Teologica Latinoamericana.

Evans, Peter, 1979. *Dependent Development: The Alliance of Multinational, State, and Local Capital in Brazil*. Princeton, N.J.: Princeton University Press.

Firth, Raymond. 1981. "Engagement and Detachment: Reflections on Applying Social Anthropology to Social Affairs." *Human Organization* 40/3: 193–201.

Foreign Missions Conference of North America. 1940. *Report of the Forty Seventh Annual Meeting of the Conference of Foreign Mission Boards in Canada and the United States*. New York: Foreign Missions Conference of North America.

Freire, Paulo. 1970. *Pedagogy of the Oppressed*. Trans. Myra Bergman Ramos. New York: Seabury.

Hall, Peter Dobkin. 1992. *Inventing the Nonprofit Sector, and Other Essays on Philanthropy, Voluntarism, and Nonprofit Organizations*. Baltimore, Md.: The Johns Hopkins University Press.

Hatch, Nathan O. 1990. *The Democratization of American Religion*. New Haven, Conn.: Yale University Press.

Hoksbergen, Roland, and Noemi R. Espinoza Madrid. 1997. "The Evangelical Church and the Development of Neoliberal Society: A Study of the Role of the Evangelical Church and Its NGOs in Guatemala and Honduras." *The Journal of Developing Areas* 32/1 (fall): 35–52.

Holdcroft, Lane E. 1978. *The Rise and Fall of Community Development in Developing Countries, 1950–1965: A Critical Analysis and an Annotated Bibliography*. MSU Rural Development Paper no. 2. East Lansing, Mich.: Dept. of Agricultural Economics, Michigan State University.

Hopkins, Charles Howard. 1940. *The Rise of the Social Gospel in American Protestantism 1865–1915*. New Haven, Conn.: Yale University Press.

Hutchison, William R. 1987. *Errand to the World: American Protestant Thought and Foreign Missions*. Chicago: University of Chicago Press.

James, Estelle. 1987. "The Nonprofit Sector in Comparative Perspective." In *The Nonprofit Sector*, edited by W. W. Powell. New Haven, Conn.: Yale University Press.

Jeavons, Thomas H. 1993. *Identifying Characteristics of "Religious" Organizations: An Exploratory Proposal*. Program on Non-Profit Organizations and Institution for Social and Policy Studies Working Paper no. 197 and ISPS Working Paper no. 2197. New Haven, Conn.: Program on Non-Profit Organizations and Institution for Social and Policy Studies.

————. 1994. *When the Bottom Line Is Faithfulness: Management of Christian Service Organizations*. Bloomington, Ind.: Indiana University Press.

Korten, David C. 1990. *Getting to the Twenty-first Century: Voluntary Action and the Global Agenda*. West Hartford, Conn.: Kumarian Press.

Latin American News Letter #51. 1956. New York: Committee on Cooperation in Latin America.

Latin American News Letter #63. 1965. New York: Committee on Cooperation in Latin America.

May, Henry F. 1949. *Protestant Churches and Industrial America*. New York: Harper & Brothers Publishers.

Myers, Bryant L. 1999. *Walking with the Poor: Principles and Practices of Transformational Development*. Maryknoll, N.Y. Orbis Books.

NCC (National Council of Churches). 1974. *Justice, Liberation, and Human Fulfillment in Latin America*. Draft mimeo of NCC statement.

Neely, Alan. 1977. "Protestant Antecedents of the Latin American Theology of Liberation." Ph.D. diss., American University. Ann Arbor, Mich.: Xerox University Microfilms.

Packenham, Robert A. 1973. *Liberal America and the Third World: Political Development Ideas in Foreign Aid and Social Science*. Princeton, N.J.: Princeton University Press.

Pastor, Robert A. 1980. *Congress and the Politics of U.S. Foreign Economic Policy 1929–1976*. Berkeley and Los Angeles: University of California Press.

Rostow, Walt W. 1960. *The Stages of Economic Growth: A Non-Communist Manifesto*. New York: Cambridge University Press.

————. 1971. *Politics and the Stages of Growth*. London: Cambridge University Press.

Smith, Christian. 1991. *The Emergency of Liberation Theology: Radical Religion and Social Movement Theory*. Chicago: Chicago University Press.

Stenning, Ronald E. 1996. *Church World Service: Fifty Years of Help and Hope*. New York: Friendship Press.

Strachan, Kenneth. 1957. *The Missionary Movement of the Non-Historical Groups in Latin America*. Study Conference on the "Message of the Evangelical Church in Latin

America," Buck Hill Falls, Pennsylvania. New York: Committee on Cooperation in Latin America.

Taylor, Michael. 1995. *Not Angels But Agencies: The Ecumenical Response to Poverty – A Primer*. Geneva: World Council of Churches.

Voth, Donald E., and Marcie Brewster. 1989. "An Overview of International Community Development." In *Community Development in Perspective*, edited by J. A. Christenson and J. W. Robinson. Ames, Iowa: Iowa State University Press.

12

POTENTIAL AND PITFALLS CONFRONTING CHRISTIAN NGOS IN THE WORLD OF MICROFINANCE

Koenraad Verhagen

INTRODUCTION: CIVIL SOCIETY ORGANISATIONS ENTERING THE FINANCIAL MARKET TO SERVE THE POOR

The new ideology of privatisation and liberalisation is rolling like a wave over the world (liberation through liberalisation). Foreign currency controls have been lifted in most developing countries. The new economic climate of deregulation offers new challenges and opportunities for private local and foreign financial institutions to deliver financial services to all sections of the population, including the poor, without undue government interference. As a result, many organisations within the NGO community in the South and the North have added microfinance to their agenda.

Microfinance is the provision of financial services, especially savings and credit, to resource poor households and their very small enterprises, called micro-enterprises.[1] Multilateral and bilateral aid organisations have become so enthusiastic about this new field of development co-operation that they have started interacting directly with NGOs in the South to fund their programmes. The result is a remarkable alliance between government institutions (the state) and NGOs (civil society) with the common view to promote the development of financial markets to serve the poor. Governmental actors have also given impetus to setting up new special funds and financing organisations at national or international levels to act as "wholesalers" on the microfinance money market for private microfinance "retailers," known as microfinance institutions (MFIs).

Microfinance is business. It is a financial system regulated by the market forces of supply and demand. The many NGOs that have entered this market work for

The author would like to acknowledge the many, valuable, sometimes extensive comments he has received on an earlier draft of the paper, especially from Larry Hendriks of Hendriks & Associates, Frank Bakx of the Rabobank, Elli Bosch of IC Consult and Wim Kluft, and from field and headquarters staff of CRS.

profit to cover their costs, including capital costs. The justification for profit-seeking is threefold: (1) poor people need financial services; (2) conventional financial institutions do not offer them; and (3) by covering costs NGOs can ensure the permanence of those services. Thus, traditional civil society actors transform themselves into market players to serve that niche in the market where the potential clientele is not served well or not served at all.

Some of these private microfinance actors are faith-based organisations. They aim at contributing to the transformation of the human being and society in a direction consistent with their fundamental religious beliefs and convictions. They share with other organisations a commitment to induce positive change from economic, social, political, and cultural points of view. They differ in that they regard spiritual development as an important element of change and see spirituality as a pervasive, God-given driving force for all human action, to be practised in all spheres of human life, including financial and related business transactions.

How does a faith-based orientation affect the implementation of microfinance projects? First, we review the dominant patterns of thinking on which microfinance theory and practice are based, the industry's key actors, and recent trends. Though faith-based organisations have not been the industry trend setters, Christian organisations such as Catholic Relief Services, World Relief, World Vision, Opportunity International, and many others are doing important work in microfinance. Then we consider how Christian values and "principled practices (Wilson 2000) from one Christian tradition, the Roman Catholic tradition, can influence faith-based organisations to witness and "make a difference" in the crowded field of national and international players.

This is not the first time in economic history that civic engagement and action have given rise to the establishment of new economic institutions that have become powerful players in the market. For example, co-operative organisations, which count 750 million members worldwide, typically emerged from civil associations. In the financial sector co-operative institutions are known as savings-and-credit co-operatives or credit unions, and about a hundred million people are members (Genberg 1999). Some credit unions are large, while others operate on the microfinance market with an average loan size below US$100.[2] There is thus some overlap between the microfinance sector and the co-operative financial sector. Financial co-operatives, however, have tended to focus more on low-income salaried workers and (male) farmers, while most new microfinance actors target women, have a more outspoken poverty focus, and concentrate on the informal economy.

THE MICROFINANCE PLAYING FIELD: DEVELOPMENT PHILOSOPHY AND KEY ACTORS

Philosophy

In the past, many credit programmes initiated by government or civil society organisations were unsustainable because they emphasised poverty reduction and minimised the importance of realising a profit. At present, the new actors, as well as some of the old ones, claim to operate so as to pursue the double objective of serving the poor and achieving the financial sustainability of their organisations. Currently, MFIs work on the basis of a largely common set of assumptions that characterise mainstream thinking in microfinance. These assumptions, listed below, can be found in the brochures and policy documents of international (donor) and implementing agencies:

1. Most of the poor have untapped entrepreneurial qualities of self-development. Through access to credit (sometimes as little as US$50) at a reasonable rate of interest, they can start up or expand their business, free themselves from poverty, and participate in a free-market economy.
2. The promotion of self-employment through micro-enterprise is the most effective way to accomplish broad-based economic development and poverty alleviation.[3]
3. The poor are creditworthy and "bankable." MFIs can cover their costs and be sustainable if they are well managed, apply an appropriate credit technology, and enlarge their portfolio by scaling up their activities.
4. To optimise MFI performance and social impact, micro-credit delivery should focus on women. They constitute the majority of the poor, repay their loans much more reliably than men, and manage money in a more responsible way.
5. Replication of best practices is the most effective way to achieve success and expand outreach. Among these, the Grameen Bank model is outstanding; it reaches over 2.5 million poor people in Bangladesh.
6. The market for micro-credit in developing countries can be estimated at 500 million poor people, but the number of poor people with access to micro-credit is probably between 12.5 million (CGAP 2000, 2) and 23.5 million (MCS 2000, 7). Whatever the correct number, the need clearly justifies the undertaking of a Microcredit Campaign, a "nine-year fulfilment campaign" started in February 1997 through the Microcredit Summit held in Washington D.C., with an outreach target of 100 million clients by the year 2005 (for updated information, see the microcredit.org website).
7. This ambitious target cannot be achieved without a substantial increase in donor financing to capitalise the loan portfolios of local MFIs.
8. Such donor funding will eventually be replaced by local MFIs accessing national or international money and capital markets, resulting in the full integration of the microfinance sector into national and international financial markets. A level of local competition beneficial to low-income borrowers is expected to result.[4]

The above is a highly schematised representation of mainstream thinking, but presenting it in this way can help us understand reservations expressed by critics or opponents, some of whom, like MicroSave Africa, are working to give it a different orientation. Other critics believe that financial-services delivery simply does not attack the root causes of poverty.

Reservations and criticisms of microfinance can be summarised as follows:

- Microfinance has a high potential for further growth and expansion, but it is not the unique or necessarily most effective response to the multifaceted problem of poverty eradication.
- Not all poor people have the ability or ambition to become self-employed micro-entrepreneurs.
- Even for those who have that ability, credit alone is not sufficient to overcome other impediments such as the "imperfect" markets in which the poor have to sell their goods and services and the quick saturation of these markets resulting from too many micro-entrepreneurs selling the same goods and services.
- Not all micro-entrepreneurs need credit. Reducing their vulnerability and increasing their security of life are first priorities for most of the poor. Donor-supported MFIs have focused on lending and neglected other financial products poor households need, such as access to savings and insurance facilities.
- The greatest innovation microfinance has brought about in the field of banking practice and development action is the delivery of credit directly to poor women, a focus that tends to overlook the fact that most micro-entrepreneurial activities are family undertakings. Irresponsible behaviour in money and social matters on the part of men cannot be solved by targeting women and excluding men.
- Replication of best practices, especially when sanctioned by donor money, carries the danger of imposing models not adjusted to local cultures (for example, Grameen Bank replications in Africa).
- Microfinance programmes tend to ignore existing informal knowledge and financial management systems. Poor and low-income people have not waited for development organisations to set up their own savings and credit systems and clubs: member-managed rotating savings and credit associations (ROSCAs) and third-person-managed accumulating savings and credit associations (ASCAs).
- Fund-raising campaigns in the North and disbursement pressure of donors undermine the development of more autonomous financial systems that thrive on the mobilisation of local resources.
- A financial-sustainability orientation causes many MFIs to move away from the poor as their preferred clientele. They tend to start providing bigger loans closer to the low-income section of the population instead of deepening their outreach to include the most needy.
- Micro-credit is not a panacea for poverty. Unfortunately, there is a tendency in the media and promotional literature to present micro-enterprise and micro-credit as a substitute for broad-based social development.[5]

A major philosophical pitfall of the microfinance approach to development, stemming from the current appeal of the neo-liberal orientation, is its suggestion that all poor people can break out of "the vicious circle of poverty" by their own efforts as micro-entrepreneurs. According to this view, overcoming poverty thus becomes the responsibility of the individual person or family, and by being given "access to credit" for investment, poor people are offered the opportunity to strengthen their place in the market; increase their income; and be in a position to buy food and pay school fees, medical bills, and so on. Credit and the (informal) market, in a "free economy" can thus solve the poverty problem. The state is left to concentrate on law and order and is not faulted if poverty persists. The poor have only themselves to blame. Such thinking leads readily to a denial of the responsibility on the part of governments to secure access to basic social services like health, education, and food for *all* its citizens, even those who cannot pay for them.

In the discourse of some agencies and actors access to credit for poor women is often presented as a tool of empowerment, but this is a dangerous suggestion because it raises expectations beyond what mere access to credit can achieve. A much broader range of educational and supporting activities is needed to change the position of poor women in their economic, social, and cultural setting (Krauss, Joussen, and Verhagen 2001). Credit is known to be used for a variety of purposes within the household and can even have the effect of consolidating inequalities if women have little or no control over the use of money. The process of empowerment is so fundamental that it cannot be reduced to a process of development of individual entrepreneurship and the economic dimensions of life.

Key Actors in the South

The poor, especially female, non-farm micro-entrepreneurs, are now considered to be "bankable." They have shown the ability to repay relatively small loans of between US$50 to US$500, which they have used as working or investment capital for their small, family-based enterprises. They are also able to pay relatively high or very high interest rates on these loans (effective interest rates, between 20 per cent and 90 per cent, calculated on an annual basis), which allows the MFI to cover costs of lending. The spectacular expansion of some of these programmes and high repayment rates have caused many traditional NGOs and donor agencies to turn their attention to this field. Successful technologies of credit delivery and repayment have been documented and subsequently propagated for replication as best practices (Grameen Bank, Banco Sol, and others). As a result, the number of organisations providing microfinance facilities to the poor has also grown substantially in almost every developing country, mainly through traditional NGOs and social movements setting up special units for credit delivery or transforming themselves into MFIs. The Consultative Group to Assist the Poorest (CGAP) estimates their number at 10,000. The Microcredit Campaign reports that of the 23.5 million people reached by the 1,065 institutions and special programmes reporting to the campaign, 13.8 million can be qualified as "poorest," defined as belonging to the poorest half of the population living below the poverty line. Of these 13.8 million, over 10 million are women (MCS 2000).

In places where microfinance has gained momentum, practitioners report strong competition among microfinance service providers who target largely the same low-income clientele. Independent observers agree that competition will make most of the donor-dependent financial NGOs disappear within the next ten years. Only a few strong ones, having achieved a high degree of financial self-sufficiency, are likely to survive.

As in the conventional banking industry, competition also elicits new forms of co-operation. MFIs have formed networks at national, regional, and international levels. Some networks have set up special funds to act as "bridges" between the international donor community and MFIs, with the intention of gradually replacing donor funding by commercial funding. Examples are Acción's Bridge Fund, PROFUND, the Grameen Trust, and Women's World Banking (Wisniwski 1998).

In most countries conventional commercial banks have shown little interest in that segment of the market that serves low-income people and has been the exclusive domain of informal moneylenders, savings collectors, informal savings and credit groups, conventional savings and credit co-operatives, and development organisations. In Latin America, however, this has started to change as many traditional retail-banking institutions have introduced high interest micro-loans. Robert Christen (2000) expects them to become the biggest players in microfinance in Latin America and likely to outperform MFIs that have their origin in the NGOs sector, the most important of whom are members of the Acción Network (the biggest MFI network of Latin American MFIs). Whether this will evolve into co-operation or competition between conventional banks and financial NGOs is not yet clear.

Civil Society Actors in the South Partnering with Intergovernmental and Governmental Donors of the North

Many leading intergovernmental and governmental international aid organisations have considerably expanded their support in the microfinance field. Among donors, they have become the main players, carrying more weight and disbursing larger sums than Northern NGOs and private foundations.[6]

The leading players in the South, referred to as practitioners, are institutions that have generally emerged from the NGO sector. These best practice MFIs have set up a global association, the MicroFinance Network, which has close connections with leading donor institutions. Standards for the industry are being developed and determined through the interaction among the above groups of players, among which the World Bank-initiated CGAP Secretariat plays an important catalytic and co-ordinating role.

This public/private alliance is not unique to the microfinance sector. It is an expression of a more general trend of government-controlled aid agencies seeking alliances with civil society actors in the North and the South. At least three factors have facilitated the move toward public-private alliances: (1) the inefficiency of government-implemented programmes in the South; (2) disbursement pressures of aid agencies in the North; and (3) agency policies of decentralisation that give more space for decision-making to regional offices and embassies.

Some European-based NGOs have given important financial support to MFIs in the South in the start-up phase, but they have had to give way to multilateral and bilateral institutions that have greater funds at their disposal.[7] The same applies to US-based and Canada-based NGOs, some of which are also important players in both funding and programme implementation.[8]

Organisations like CGAP, the Best Practice Program of the United States Agency for International Development (USAID), the German GTZ, and the British Department for International Development identify innovative and best practice programmes, issue awards, and develop training material and programmes. As government agencies they also see it as their specific role to assist local governments and central banks in the development and introduction of convenient regulatory mechanisms and to remove inappropriate, obsolete legal obstacles and regulations. They thus promote an enabling environment for the microfinance industry.

Northern NGOs provide similar support to their partners in the South through funding and organising technical assistance and training workshops, but with less impact. Moreover, many of them are also heavily dependent on funding from bilateral or multilateral organisations through the mechanism of co-financing. It is interesting to note how the pervasive power of market forces has changed the culture of international aid. In the microfinance sector government-controlled institutions in the North have become the most staunch supporters of market-based approaches. They are followed by many civil society actors in the North and the South who traditionally were hostile to, or very suspicious of, the market as a regulatory mechanism for sustainable development.

All-important players seem to agree that governments in the South should no longer engage directly into the provision of financial services to low-income people. Instead, governments should leave this to private initiatives and concentrate on establishing a regulatory climate that ensures fair competition among microfinance service providers, for example, by requiring transparency of interest rates charged to borrowers.

TRENDS IN THE MICROFINANCE INDUSTRY

Several recent trends in microfinance are directly relevant to the discussion of the practice of faith-based microfinance programmes.

Savings: A Better Deal than Credit?

Many credit-led programmes, targeted at the poor, have started poverty-lending operations without asking themselves or their potential clients what kind of financial service poor people value most. Practice has shown that where poor people have a choice, the demand for savings accounts is much greater than for loan accounts. Telling examples are the experiences of large MFIs like the Bank Rakyat Indonesia – Unit Desa System, Indonesia, the rural Kenya Savings and Credit

Co-operatives, and Self-Employed Womens' Association (SEWA), Hyderabad, India. "They [poor people, especially women] are desperate to get their small savings out of the house, at a safe and accessible place" (Acción 1999). It is somewhat ironic that while most poor people seem to have a higher demand for savings services than credit services, development organisations have emphasised the latter.[9]

Savings are important to the poor for several reasons, among which are consumption smoothing, purchase of consumer durables (especially housing), social and religious purposes, education of children, ill health, disability, predictable seasonal variations in cash flow, unpredictable natural catastrophes, and economic activities (small investments and working capital). Many poor people prefer to save because they are afraid to get into debt. Still, savings are often not enough to cover needed or desired expenditures, making access to credit at reasonable terms an important service.

Following a period of sometimes bitter debate in the microfinance sector between protagonists of savings-led and credit-led approaches, there is now broad agreement in the industry that poor people need both savings *and* loan facilities, and that they are best served by flexible programmes that respond to their specific family and individual financial needs. Microfinance is increasingly seen as a form of personal banking. The poor are best served if financial services help them manage their (little) money in an optimal fashion by serving them with the right type of financial products at the right time and place.

The service emphasised so far by the microfinance industry has been lending for income-generating activities because it responded best to prevailing perceptions of how to overcome poverty. But this perspective, without necessarily being wrong, is based on a too narrow perception of poor people's demand for financial services, and it is gradually changing.

The Dark Side of Micro-credit: People in Debt

In international microfinance discussions there was initially a certain abuse of language suggesting that the MFI lending programmes were reaching out to the "poorest of the poor." It gradually became clear in the 1990s that credit programmes, even those with a very specific poverty focus, had great difficulty in reaching the bottom 50 per cent of the poor (David Hulme in Harper 2000; Morduch 1999). Moreover, it also became known that the poorer the client the greater the likelihood that credit would do more harm than good (Harper 2000, 2).

It has taken some time for the microfinance industry to realise that credit services and multiplication of MFIs can lead to over-indebtedness for clients who borrow from several lenders (Acción 1999, 87). The idea that poor people repay their loans from additional income has also turned out to be a myth. A 1999 study by the Bangladesh Rural Advancement Committee showed that the poor often repay their loans primarily from family income. The main explanatory factors for high repayment rates turn out to be the promise of a new, bigger loan together with pressure from loan officers and peers. The debt burdens contribute to tension, conflict, violence, and even suicide (Rahman 1999).

One of the major conclusions of the June 2000 North South Dialogue Workshop in Bad Honnaf was that MFIs tend to be so much preoccupied by their own financial sustainability that they give little attention to the sustainability of the livelihood of their indebted clients. Credit-led MFIs assume that their clients want to continue borrowing and that the size of the loans they require will increase. Thanks to the loan, the borrower's micro-enterprise will expand, giving rise to a growing demand for affordable credit. Those who stop borrowing are looked upon as "drop outs" (see MicroSave Africa publications for 1998 and 1999, available online). The author's personal observation of MFI practice in Tanzania and Kenya in March 2000 was that MFIs, through credit shops and similar devices, actually induce potential savers to become borrowers. They do not promote financial self-reliance of their clients or of groups. Even accessing personal, compulsory savings after full repayment of the loan is administratively complicated, because the institutions want to keep them as collateral for future loans.

While there is growing awareness of the negative sides of debt as "credit that has got out of hand" (ECLOF/Oikocredit 2000), the overall effect on the living standards of the millions of poor people reached by MFI services is still regarded as positive.

Growing Recognition of the Importance of Non-financial Services

Microfinance was "discovered" as a development instrument in the late 1980s, because some NGO development workers had found that something essential was missing in the package of services the poor require. From the numerous impact evaluations made since then, as well as direct observations of practitioners, it has become clear that financial services provision is a necessary but not sufficient condition for substantial poverty reduction. Two types of additional services are needed:

- Non-financial *social* services, such as basic education, technical training, health, and housing.
- Non-financial *economic* services, such as appropriate marketing channels for the goods and services produced.

Local NGOs are encouraged by their financiers (donors) not to mix financial and non-financial services, and to concentrate exclusively on the former with a view to achieving full financial self-sufficiency. While this is probably the correct strategy for institutional development, it also leads to a growing gap in service levels. For many poor, access to financial services has become relatively easy, while access to badly needed non-financial services has become more difficult. Due to the growing number of NGOs that have gone into banking, especially credit delivery, the supply of non-financial services by non-banking NGOs is diminishing or lagging behind. Yet both types of services are indispensable for the poor to overcome their poverty.

CATHOLIC SOCIAL TEACHING
AS A FRAME OF REFERENCE

In development circles, programme and project objectives and performance criteria and indicators are normally expressed in secular terms. In contemporary Europe, for example, faith-based development organisations have to be careful about emphasising their Christianity and convictions as a basis for selection of overseas partners, or for definition of criteria for project appraisal and evaluation. Explicit faith-inspired criteria and religious language may arouse suspicions of religious bias, a hidden "missionary" agenda, and unprofessional behaviour in relations with partners. Stressing religious identity and church affiliation is particularly delicate when many of the organisation's financial resources originate in governmental or intergovernmental (European Union) sources. Even to obtain private donations, a church connection no longer pays. Church communities in Europe, the traditional source of funds for faith-based development organisations, are aging, and church attendance is declining rapidly. For effective fund-raising, modern media and marketing techniques have to be used to reach a public that is not particularly church-minded.[10]

There is competition among development organisations in the North for access to funds from public authorities (especially official bilateral aid) and from private sources (donations or cheap loans, the so-called charity market). Similarly, there is competition among those in the South in their quest for development funding, defense of territory, and enlargement of outreach to new target groups or geographical areas. There is enormous performance pressure in this kind of arena, and there is little time to reflect on how to integrate and consistently apply a religious message. Performance criteria are set by the industry, and, like everyone else, committed Christians have to adjust if they do not want to be labelled amateurish or charitable rather than professional development practitioners.[11] A no-nonsense mentality prevails. Without demonstrable and measurable impact, the development activity cannot be regarded as having delivered "value for money" and is likely to be discontinued.

In microfinance discussions reference is sometimes made to Islamic banking as a form of financing in which the provider of funds does not charge interest on loans but has to cover its costs from administrative fees or profit sharing (see, for example, Zahid Elahi 2000). Others speak openly of ethical banking. The expression Christian banking, on the other hand, is nonexistent; if an organisation were to use such a term, it would fall under the suspicion of being fundamentalist in its thinking and intentions.

In spite of this somewhat hostile environment, however, especially in Europe, integrity demands that Christians evaluate their development ideas and practices on the basis of Christian principles. Thus I will summarise some key principles from Catholic social teaching and use them to assess and evaluate the microfinance strategy of development.[12]

A Preferential Option for the Poor

This principle is a call to make a fundamental option for the poor that extends to all who are deprived of fundamental economic, political, cultural, religious, or personal rights (Dwyer and Montgomery 1999, 755–59). The notion is solidly rooted in the Old and the New Testament. It was a central theme of the Latin American bishops' conferences in Medellín (1968) and Puebla (1979) and of the liberation theology that emerged in Latin America during the 1960s. As a principle for action it has been cautiously accepted by the Vatican administration under the condition that it is understood neither as an exclusion of the non-poor nor an invitation to class struggle in the Marxist sense.

In micro-credit discourse "access to credit" is often put forward as a right. When taking into account the latest insights into the nature of financial services the poor require, it seems fair to say that access to financial services, including savings, credit, and perhaps insurance, is a basic economic right, since it enables poor people in a vulnerable position to manage risk and optimise the use of the few monetary resources they have for production or consumption purposes.

The preferential option for the poor has several implications for microfinance work, including the following:

Give Special, But Not Exclusive, Attention to Women

Out of the 1.3 billion people living on less than US$1 a day, 900 million are women. They are known to play a central role in managing the household economy, and there is a high frequency of single parent, female-headed households. Many agencies have opted for an exclusive or almost exclusive focus on women for social reasons (as an antidote against discrimination and oppression) and/or for pragmatic reasons (women have a better repayment ethic and are more receptive to peer pressure). The focus on women, however, leaves unresolved the often irresponsible behaviour of men in money and social matters, a societal issue causing suffering for both sexes.

In dealing with the delicate matter of group formation, one can take guidance from the informal sector, where savings and credit groups are flourishing, especially among women. It is now widely accepted that women should have the right and freedom to set up their own savings and credit groups, but it is not up to providers to push them in either direction: women only or mixed groups.

Prioritise Savings over Credit Facilities

In critical situations (illness, poor harvest, and so on) having small monetary reserves can forestall the need to sell or mortgage the few assets the poor have. "Faulty perceptions about the poor have led to faulty policy strategies and financial products" (Zeller and Sharma 2000, 1). That is, the myth that poor people are unable to save or to pay for insurance has led development organisations to neglect the demand for appropriate savings and insurance products.

Use Cross-subsidisation to Include the Poor

The option for the poor does not imply that the not-so-poor or even the lower middle class should be barred from co-operative membership or excluded from microfinance services. There are good economic and social reasons for including them. Servicing the not-so-poor is relatively cheap, while servicing the poor and the poorest is relatively expensive. To achieve financial sustainability, then, the MFI can apply a strategy of "cross-subsidisation." This means that the poorest are serviced below cost; their financial transactions are partly subsidised from the surpluses realised on savings or credit transactions with the not-so-poor or lower-middle-class clients. This policy draws also on the principle of solidarity, because the same rate of interest on both loans and savings is applied to clients regardless of their economic status, and regardless of the fact that financial losses are incurred in dealings with the poorest.

Apply Market-based Pricing Where Possible

One of the basic principles in the microfinance industry is market-based pricing. Christians might fear that such a principle counters any faith-based purposes, but the use of the market mechanism to regulate supply and demand is not in itself wrong, for it normally allows the provider of goods and services to cover its costs and ensure the permanence of the institution (*Centesimus annus,* nos. 19, 34). Serving clients/members over the long term is honouring a promise and an expectation, which make sustainability of the organisation a moral issue. This is even more true when low-income people have deposited their savings with the MFI. A market orientation is not by definition a merciless application of commercial principles. It means that the MFI makes a serious effort to explore the market in order to identify the categories of the poor it wants to serve and the type of financial services they demand. Subsequently, it designs and tests its products. When some products are priced below costs for social reasons, the MFI should determine in advance from which earnings it can cover that loss.

Link with Other Institutions for Access to Non-financial Services

Financial services alone are not enough to solve the problem of poverty. This does not suggest, however, that faith-based MFIs should necessarily enlarge their service package to include other economic, social, and educational services. Professional, low-cost delivery of financial services is difficult to achieve without a high degree of specialisation, so it is important for MFIs to stay focused on this important area of work among the poor. Still, the preferential option for the poor principle entails the duty for the MFI to facilitate links with other institutions that can deliver important additional services.

Subsidiarity

Just as it is gravely wrong to take from individuals what they can accomplish by their own initiative and industry and give it to the community, so also it is an injustice and at the same time a grave evil and disturbance of right order to assign to a greater or higher association what lesser and subordinate organizations can do (*Quadragesimo anno*, no. 79).

A Preference for Member-owned, Member-controlled Institutions

The principle of subsidiarity is both relevant and compelling for the development of the microfinance sector. Essentially, it means encouraging and allowing people to help themselves. The higher-level institution is conceived as a service institution to the lower-level institution, and the higher-level institution does not appropriate or maintain powers, responsibilities, or tasks that the lower-level one is capable of assuming.

Acceptance of this principle for the development of microfinance systems implies the recognition that people have the capacity, or can acquire the capacity, to govern themselves, develop their own rules and regulations, and set up and run their own financial institutions. Suffocating this self-help potential through top-down interventions in local communities is an example of what the encyclical sees as a "disturbance of right order." In the practice of microfinance, however, there is a tendency to impose standardised models of service delivery simply because they have worked well elsewhere. Local communities are confronted with a "take it or leave it" offer from the MFI and have insufficient opportunity to appropriate and own the process. Putting the principle of subsidiarity into practice means searching for an optimal devolution of powers to the lower level. It easily leads to a preference for member-owned, member-controlled types of structures over more directive approaches, as applied by some financial NGOs.

A Preference for Growth Strategies that Avoid Subordination of the Lower Level to the Higher Level

In reviewing the significance of the subsidiarity principle for microfinance practice, it is helpful to distinguish the different levels, starting with the lowest level (most local) at which financial transactions take place:

- household or family level
- group level (the savings and credit group)
- MFI
- national-level institutions performing financial wholesale functions
- institutions operating at the international level

The higher level supports the lower level. The lower level cannot grow without this support, while the higher level cannot operate, and has no reason for existence, without the lower level; they are interdependent. What one often sees in practice, however, are relationships of dependence and subordination of the lower level to the higher level. The higher level defines unilaterally the rules and regulations, and the lower level is expected to comply. Among the common types of dependence that form are the following:

- Dependence of the household on the lending institution as a result of an MFI policy that tries to secure the permanence of its own organisation by aggressively encouraging clients to take repeat loans. Such a practice may turn access to credit into lasting indebtedness.
- Dependence of the group on its supporting MFI when the group is discouraged from creating its own source of lending capital from the pool of savings, reserves, and/or shares of its members. The group is thus forced to continue borrowing from the MFI. (Though the MFI may require group savings, the purpose of those saving is to guarantee loan repayment.)[13]
- Dependence of the MFI itself may emerge if its affiliated international donor or a government bank offers cheap loans or grants to the MFI. The "cheap money" may come directly from a donor agency or a national fund established with donor support, performing a subsidised wholesale function for its MFI clients. This facility acts as a disincentive for resource mobilisation at the lower levels of the system. Such practices must be carefully reviewed and relationships among the levels should provide ample opportunity for growth and development at the lower levels.

A Preference for the Development of Domestic Financial Markets

Some development agencies in the North are actively searching in the South for lending opportunities, but they are confronted with the limited absorption capacity of Southern MFIs. Like the MFIs in the South, Northern agencies have adopted a business orientation and aim at achieving self-sufficiency of their own institution by becoming independent from aid money. On the emerging international microfinance market, they operate as lending institutions. One must keep in mind, however, that in order to achieve self-sufficiency at each level, the end user (the poor borrower) must bear the administrative costs of the upper levels of the system. It is questionable whether this is the right direction for the development of financial systems destined to serve the poor, for it stands in the way of Southern organisations becoming the architects of their own systems and financiers of their own development.

Some institutions have been set up at regional levels covering several countries or a continent, for example, PROFUND for Latin America (based in Costa Rica) and AFRICAP operating from Dakar. These were established with donor support on the premise that the MFIs in the South need to be capitalised by external financing and that commercial funds cannot be found and mobilised locally in sufficient manner for rapid institutional growth.

From a subsidiarity point of view, priority should be given to the development of domestic markets rather than international markets. This does not mean that any form of external financial resource input directed from the higher to the lower level is inherently wrong. External financing and support can be well justified when conceived and provided as a form of "bridge financing" that gives time and the opportunity to the lower level to build up its own asset and capital base.

Community

Catholic social thought "expresses the idea that authentic human life is lived in community" (CRS 1997, 4). People have been created as social beings. When community is understood in a generic sense, different levels of community life come into view: the nuclear family, the extended family, the rural or urban neighbourhood (village or city quarter), the broader national community, and the international community. Communities have the responsibility to secure the well-being of all their members. Solidarity with, and inclusion of, those community members who are economically or socially weak is the touchstone for the moral quality and social performance of a community institution. In development circles *community* is generally understood as a particular locality, such as a village or a city quarter, where citizens reside and share a broad range of common characteristics.

Applied to microfinance, the principle of community leads one to ask how the MFI and its methods of operation affect the interactions and relations within households and the local community. In other words, how does microfinance foster (or break down) the social capital of the primary social units to which a person belongs? (The relationship of the microfinance strategy to social capital and community formation is illustrated well in Chapter 13 herein.)

A Preference for Community-based, Member-owned Organisations

A preference for community-based, self-managed institutions is the reasonable choice for a development organisation that wants to contribute towards strengthening the social fabric of villages or urban-based communities. Apart from access to financial services, member-owned financial institutions can provide other benefits such as fostering relationships among members and encouraging co-operation. A small, community-based MFI, such as a village bank, can act as the financial nerve centre of a community and provide a participatory organisational framework for addressing issues like the involvement of the marginalised sections of the community, the type of financial services to promote, and the link with non-financial services to be provided by other institutions.

Family and Group Membership

The community principle, in its broader sense, pleads in favour of opening up membership to entire families and groups in addition to individual membership. In some co-operatives and village-banking programmes in East and West Africa, this option already exists. True, it complicates the voting system, but it is more in line with the local culture and creates additional space for people's preferences and participation.

The Community Approach and/or Flexibility

A community development approach for structuring the microfinance sector at the grassroots level sounds beautiful, but it is not always feasible or even desirable given the tensions and differences in status and power that may exist among residents of the same locality. Such local realities may call for setting up gender-specific small savings and credit groups or for limiting membership to people in a similar economic or social position. Gender-specific or occupation-specific groups can become visible expressions of hope and self-confidence of marginalised groups. As such, they are part of the social capital of a community in transformation, and they may be a step on the way to a fuller and more inclusive realisation of community.

Dignity and Equality of the Human Person

> All of humanity has been created in the image of God. . . . Each person has a basic dignity that comes not from any action on our own part but because of our very creation. Each individual is a person worthy of dignity and respect (CRS 1997, 2).

Self-respect Through Microfinance

One of the common laments of low-income people in developing countries is the lack of respect they encounter in commercial banks. They are attended in an off-hand manner and confronted with procedures and papers they do not understand and that are not explained to them.

In response to the treatment the poor receive at commercial banks, microfinance works to give new dignity to people who have long been regarded as not "bankable" and not able to pay for bank services. Women, for example, were once regarded as less bankable and creditworthy than men, though the opposite has proven to be true in practice. Financial NGOs, on the other hand, build self-esteem and dignity by telling themselves and their sponsors that microfinance is not charity. Borrowers are treated as valued clients. They pay a market-based price or close to it, and they get a service for it.

In spite of their market orientation, however, MFIs must also prepare for the possibility of default. When the poor are unable to pay back their loans, feelings of shame, loss of dignity, and loss of respect often result. The respectful yet effective treatment of defaulters is a constant challenge to each MFI.

Increased self-respect is also felt by people who, through self-imposed discipline, have been able to put aside some of their small earnings in the form of savings. Savings not only give a sense of security but also of achievement and self-esteem.

Well-informed Users Whose Choices Are Respected

Another aspect of dignity is respect for the people's choices. Many programmes are still characterised by degrading paternalistic overtones regarding the use of the loan. MFIs are increasingly recognising that exercising this kind of control is virtually impossible due to the fungibility of money in a household economy. From a human dignity point of view, the practice of supervised credit should also be rejected. If lenders have no trust in borrowers' honesty or repayment capacity, they should not lend; if lenders trust borrowers, there is no need to impose the type of conditionality that characterises supervised credit programmes. Those conditions and concurrent control operations are humiliating and have also proven to be ineffective. Providing users with good information so that they can make well-informed decisions and responsible choices is part of the MFI's responsibilities.

Solidarity

[Solidarity] . . . is above all a question of interdependence, sensed as a system determining relationships in the contemporary world in its economic, cultural, political and religious elements, and accepted as a moral category. . . . This then is not a feeling of vague compassion or shallow distress at the misfortunes of so many people, both near and far. On the contrary it is a firm and persevering determination to commit oneself to the common good; that is to say to the good of all and of each individual because we are all really responsible for all (*Sollicitudo rei socialis*, no. 38).

The message for the microfinance sector is that solidarity must be practised as a virtue in the way microfinance promoters or providers set their objectives, choose target groups, determine their strategies, and act in the field. Promoting MFIs or setting up new ones is not just about the delivery of financial services. It is also about shaping human relationships. Solidarity implies a commitment to the common good.

Solidarity Groups

In the microfinance sector we see the widespread practice of group lending and of MFIs working with "solidarity" groups. By participating in a group, mutual responsibility is required for repayment of debt to the MFI as well as for the maintenance of savings discipline, often an obligatory corollary of the credit service. Some observers are critical of this group approach, typically forced upon people by the MFI to ensure repayment, because borrowers themselves seem to prefer a more individualised approach. Here the pitfall is that the language of "solidarity" masks another reality that is not the people's choice but is instead part of a strategy chosen by the more powerful MFI.

Underpaying Staff

At the MFI level "solidarity" is sometimes enforced by pressuring staff members to accept not only harsh working conditions but also considerably lower salaries than they could earn in conventional banking. The pitfall here is the exploitation of social commitment of staff who pay the price of their commitment and solidarity with the poor by underpayment and poor secondary work conditions (no pension fund, no adequate health insurance, and so on). Such pressures motivate staff to leave the organisation, and sometimes the microfinance sector, to look for greener pastures elsewhere. Church-connected institutions in the South have a special reputation for poor labour conditions. But these practices are not necessary. If the microfinance-sector principle of market-based pricing of products is well applied, the efficiently run MFI should be able to pay decent salaries to staff without exploiting the target group.

Co-operation or Competition?

"Catholic teaching on solidarity has been primarily pastoral" (Dwyer and Montgomery 1994, 910). Referring to *Sollicitudo rei socialis*, Matthew Lamb says, "Solidarity . . . is not just a vague feeling of compassion. . . . It must be practised between individuals, professionals, classes, communities and nations" (in Dwyer and Montgomery 1994, 909). In development circles *solidarity* has been used primarily in a political sense of promoting "solidarity among the poor" and "with the poor." It is used much more rarely when speaking of development organisations that have the common objective of serving the poor. Yet any practitioner of microfinance can give examples from field experience of how the lack of co-operation among organisations at local, national, and international levels is causing considerable waste of scarce human and financial resources. Because of sectarian religious zeal, competition among faith-based organisations of different denominations can be particularly fierce and destructive, going completely against the biblical vision of an alternative society based on co-operation and solidarity. On the other hand, a co-operative spirit needs to be balanced with a reasonable sense of competition required by the market.

The danger is that perceived organisational interests, competition, and a profit orientation can prevent the exchange of lessons learned by organisations. Consequently, co-ordination is often minimal, and the poor who could gain from greater proficiency of MFIs and streamlining of interventions are not as well served as they could be.

In situations where co-operation could be beneficial to the quality of service and expansion of the sector, lack of co-operation due to organisational rivalry, misunderstandings, and prejudice betrays the principles of solidarity and responsible stewardship.

Common Good and Stewardship

Act locally, think globally expresses very well the essence of the principle of the common good as it applies to the microfinance industry.

The common good principle asks for the use of a broad perspective in the design of development activities. In microfinance, local action should be viewed in connection with larger social structures that shape the economic and social life of a community, a region, or a nation. Through international funding there are also connections with money transfers at a global level.

Microfinance Promotion from a Broad, Financial-System Perspective

Promoting the common good means that the design of microfinance programmes and institutions should take into account what other organisations are already doing in the communities under consideration. The ultimate goal is not the sustainability of a single institution but of an entire financial system that serves the poor and supports them in their self-development.

Implementation of the principle of common good may require microfinance providers or promoters to advocate at national levels for legal provisions and regulations that do not hinder but instead facilitate microfinance initiatives and innovations. A typical example is the removal of government-dictated interest ceilings that aim to protect borrowers against usury but in fact facilitate the operations of informal lenders who have no public accountability.

A self-sustaining and sustainable microfinance sector is part of the common good of a society. Where microfinance systems are well advanced, as in Bangladesh, Indonesia, and some West Africa countries, they are precious national assets, even if they have not finally solved the problem of persistent poverty.

Stewardship "at its foundation, is based on the principle of responsibility and is intrinsically linked to the common good. . . . We are called to respect and justly share the resources in a way that provides for the needs of all" (CRS 1997, 10).

In the 1990s there was a revival of the notion of stewardship (see LWF, 1994). This principle calls for the implementation of cost-effective and socially effective strategies and methods of work. Responsible stewardship brings professionalism and commitment together, not as opposites, but as complementary requirements for serving the poor.

MFI Managers as Stewards

Stewardship in the Christian sense, and *good governance,* a term often used in the civil society discussion, are closely related. In the microfinance sector, stewards are entrusted with management of the human and financial resources of an MFI organisation, with the custody of the people's savings deposited with the MFI, and with the issuance of loans in a responsible and fair manner. Managers, of course, do not work in isolation, so the principle is also relevant to board members and other MFI staff. The moral obligation to act professionally is even more compelling when the MFI administers poor people's savings.

At a personal level stewardship "presupposes one has a deep personal spirituality. . . . Stewards do not function on some island, making decisions and plans in isolation" (Dwyer and Montgomery 1994, 921). Stewardship leads to a value-sensitive, participatory style of management.

Protecting the Value of Small Savings Against Inflation

In recent years many monographs and manuals have been written, especially in the United States, that are geared towards improving MFI efficiency. To my knowledge, however, no manuals have been written that deal with how to protect the value of deposits of small savers against inflation. With easy access to international money markets, stable foreign currencies, and hedging instruments, there are certainly possibilities to do so. International and regional funds serving the microfinance sector already exist, such as the Acción Bridge Fund and PROFUND, but these funds have concentrated on facilitating access to international capital, not to products that protect the value of people's savings. The principle of steward-ship should motivate development organisations to take up this challenge.

CONSEQUENCES FOR FAITH-BASED DEVELOPMENT ORGANISATIONS IN THE NORTH

Putting together the general principles of microfinance with the principles of Catholic social teaching leads to some difficult choices for faith-based develop-ment organisations in the North.

First, there is the basic strategic choice: Should we be engaged in the "busi-ness" of microbanking or stay out of it? Once the decision to engage has been taken, other strategic and tactical choices must be made about how to operate from a Christian perspective and how to become trend setters rather than trend follow-ers. I would like to suggest two principles to guide choices and actions that are consistent with the principles of Catholic social teaching:

1. Aim at added value when operating in a field with many other professional actors; and
2. Make use of the comparative advantages of church-linked organisations while minimising comparative weaknesses.

Catholic and other Christian organisations are not immune to influence by their environments, and many Northern organisations have undergone a process of secularisation. This is partly due to the fact that it is not always obvious what value they can add or what comparative advantages they have as faith-based organisations.

Enter the Arena of Microfinance?

Christian development organisations are already involved in many important areas of development work: human rights, education, social development, agricul-ture, health, food, nutrition, and more. Is microfinance a high enough priority for Christian organisations to focus more attention there? A group of international microfinance experts say: "The poorest of the poor don't need debt. They need food, medicines, employment and skills training. Then they can make use of microfinance" (Acción 1999, 46). Indeed, the very destitute, the street children, the neglected elderly, and the mentally or physically disabled are not served at all by microfinance.

On the Development Finance electronic mailing list (hosted by Ohio State Uni-versity), the most widely known ongoing virtual conference for people working in the microfinance sector, this question was raised: Is their any proof that the dollar, pound, krone, or euro spent on microfinance is better spent than the one spent on health, education, water and sanitation? No such proof was presented. Compara-tive impact analysis between sectors either does not exist or suffers from method-ological flaws. At the same time, there remains a broad consensus that it is very difficult for poor people to overcome poverty without access to sustainable financial services.

A Christian Model?

Theoretically, one can design a model of an MFI that perfectly matches the principles of Catholic social teaching. Whether it can also find embodiment in the real life of a market economy however, is doubtful. But creating the perfect microfinance model is not the role of Catholic social teaching. Instead, it should provide orientations that can serve as a framework for reflection, analysis, and evaluation. Even then, extreme caution should be exercised in labelling one approach more "Christian" or "Catholic" than another on the basis of its closeness, in concept or practice, to the value orientations embodied in the official social teaching of a church.

Some Donor Guidelines

Whether a development organisation should enter (or withdraw from) the field of microfinance has no universal answer. The following considerations may be helpful, however, to guide Northern NGOs trying to determine their role in the world of microfinance.

- Donor organisations should be aware that "there is already too much donor money floating into microfinance" (Acción 1999, 62).
- "If donors want to help they should be subsidizing the learning curve [of the MFI]" by focusing on institutional development (Acción 1999, 55).
- Donors should take care not to disturb the development of financial markets in the South with cheap lending, grants, or subsidies.
- Northern NGOs should be demand-led institutions, implying that they should provide equity, loans, guarantees, or grants as appropriate, and give special attention to equity.
- Grant-making organisations should work in alliance with organisations that have the mandate and skills to act as investors or bankers. The latter provide loans and guarantees, and the grant-making organisation the subsidies, as and when appropriate.
- Good practices in the South (not necessarily the "best") should be disseminated freely, because the sector is best served by a variety of approaches.
- "They [donors] should get out of the funding of loan portfolios" (Acción 1999, 59). Money for capitalising loan portfolios of the MFIs should be generated by mobilisation of domestic resources, including lending from local banks.

"Added Value" and "Comparative Advantages" as Principles to Guide Choice and Action

How to Add Value to the System

Adding value can be achieved by not copying and repeating the orientation and bias of most international, bilateral, and non-governmental funding agencies that tend to direct their financial support to microfinance providers that distribute short-term loans for micro-enterprise development in urban or rural urbanised, commercial centres. Adding value can be achieved by international organisations that are willing

- to support, in the long term, local organisations that have accepted the challenge to develop financial services in the more remote/poorer areas not yet served by existing MFIs .
- to support savings-led rather than credit-led approaches that are also connected with micro-insurance services.[14]
- to support innovative practices that seek to establish a link between financial services and sustainable development in health and education sectors.
- to support, through technical assistance and subsidies, computerisation of accounts and development of management information systems (gains in efficiency reduce the costs of transactions with the poor).
- to give special attention to partners that have chosen to be promoters rather than providers of financial services. Promoters assist the poor in setting up their own savings and credit systems and/or accompany the poor in their choice and planning of economic activities.

Another way to add value is by focusing not on microfinance, but rather on small-enterprise finance. The microfinance hype has meant that less attention has been given to the technical and financial needs of small entrepreneurs (5 to 20 employees) who are able to generate employment for people who are poor but do not have the abilities or interest to be self-employed.

Church Linked: An Advantage?

A Lutheran World Relief publication says that "churches or church-related institutions are usually not particularly business minded. Business requires a different type of management, a different philosophy, a different approach altogether" (LWF 1994, 78). Realistically, the drive for covering organisational costs is not a high priority in churches. Repayment of loans thus seems particularly problematic. A microfinance expert expressed this as follows "The minute it smells, even smells, of the church, people don't pay you back" (Acción 1999). The following is a schematic overview of the strengths and weaknesses of church or church-related institutions in the South engaged in microfinance and often the privileged partners of faith-based organisations in the North:[15]

Strengths	Weaknesses
• Present in poor areas	• Inward looking
• Trusted (good for savings-led approaches)	• Poor financial management and accounting
• Concerned about social performance	• Too little attention to financial performance; reluctant to charge cost-covering interest rates
• Perceive human development holistically	
• Committed staff	• Low gender awareness
	• Professional staff underpaid

A FINAL REFLECTION ON TEMPTATIONS AND PITFALLS

I have argued that microfinance systems and institutions can be sustainable, while serving the low-income sections of the population, including the poorest, and operating in a manner consistent with the principles of Catholic social teaching.

In the analysis of what organisations could or should be doing, one must recognise that development aid institutions in the North and many of their partners in the South, faith-based or not, are not driven only by development objectives. They also have their own organisational objectives and targets to achieve in terms of income and expenditure, funds to be raised, and disbursements to be made. They have to secure their own survival in a highly competitive atmosphere. The transfer of funds from the North to the South to enable microfinance to serve the credit needs of the poor also serves the organisational objectives of local MFIs and their international supporters.[16] While international financial support is definitely needed to build up a viable microfinance sector, there is a major pitfall: international support may undermine a strategy that seeks to optimise the use of local financial and human resources available in the communities and the countries of the South. Temptations for organisations in the North include the relative ease with which funds for "access to credit for the poorest" can be raised in the North from the public, or, under the existing co-financing facilities, from multilateral or bilateral aid programmes. The North-South flow of funds may thus, under the banner of "solidarity," create a chain dependence of organisations in the South on funding by organisations in the North, a phenomenon well known from other sectors of development aid.

NOTES

[1] Micro-enterprises are enterprises run by one or two persons belonging to a resource-poor household. Micro-enterprise is a form of self-employment. Unlike a small enterprise, a micro-enterprise has no more than one to two employees, and household and enterprise are financially integrated. There is, however, no universally accepted definition of micro-enterprise; some specialists identify firms with fewer than five employees, and others fewer than ten employees, as micro-enterprises.

[2] For example, the Sri Lanka SANASA movement serving 725,000 members with an average loan size of US$90 (Microcredit Summit 1997) and the Indian SEWA with 130,000 women members, average loan size US$53 (Annette Krauss, Birgit Joussen, and Koenraad Verhagen, *Finanzsystementwicklung – Spar- und Kredit institutionen für die Armen* [Bonn: North-South Dialogue 2001, publication forthcoming]).

[3] *Poverty alleviation* or *reduction* is the term preferred by most of the well-established development organisations, instead of *poverty eradication,* a concept promoted by radical NGOs that advocate fundamental changes in the current economic order.

[4] Commercialisation and competition have become the key words in the international microfinance discussion. The Bolivian situation is referred to as a case of healthy competition among credit providers. In Bolivia (mostly) urban-based micro- and small entrepre-

neurs now can choose from several providers. The rate of interest is one of the factors they take into account.

[5] In October 1998 a veteran in microfinance, Katherine McKee, the new director of USAID's Office of Microenterprise Development, declared: "We are becoming increasingly aware that for most MFIs, only a small percentage of clients qualify as truly poor. As a result – we both donors and practitioners have become dishonest and irresponsible in our claims about who micro-credit serves and can benefit most, and casual about our use of 'poorest of the poor' language" (*Nexus* 42 [1999]; *Nexus* is a publication of the Small Enterprise Education and Promotion Network [SEEP]).

[6] Important bilateral players are USAID, the German GTZ, the British Department for International Development (formerly ODA), and the French AFC. The most important multilateral institutions are World Bank, United Nations Development Programme (UNDP)/ United Nations Capital Development Fund (UNCDF), International Fund for Agricultural Development (IFAD, Rome), Inter-American Development Bank (IDB, Washington D.C), African Development Bank, the European Union, and CGAP. CGAP is a group of the most important donor agencies. Initiated by the World Bank, it brings together the most important multilateral and bilateral agencies in this field. NGOs in the South, too, have formed regional networks and may take over the lead in the years to come.

[7] In international microfinance promotion a new category of financial institutions has come up in Europe called social investors, private institutions that do not provide grants but use other financing instruments like loans and guarantee schemes or become direct shareholders. Oikocredit (formerly Ecumenical Development Co-operative Society [EDCS]) in the Netherlands is one of the pioneers in the provision of loans. Many European social investors are grouped in the Brussels-based network INAISE (International Association of Investors in the Social Economy) with over 30 members. Microfinance has also attracted the attention of some European universities and development institutes: in France, IRAM (Institut de Recherche Agronomique, Paris) and CIRAD (Centre de Coopération Internationale en Recherche Agronomique pour le Développement, Montpellier); in Germany, the Universities of Hohenheim, Köln, and Frankfurt; in the UK, the University of Manchester and Brigham Young University; and in the Netherlands, Wageningen University.

[8] Relative heavyweights in the field are US-based and Canada-based NGOs that specialise in a specific form of lending called village banking and are members of the SEEP network (such as Care, Catholic Relief Services, Foundation for International Community Assistance (FINCA), Freedom from Hunger, World Vision, Opportunity International, Desjardins). Some of them implement their own programmes through regional or country offices based in the South, others by working together with local partners. In the North American hemisphere we find the headquarters of the most important multilateral players, including the World Bank, IDB and UNDP/UNCDF, and it is also home to USAID, the most important bilateral donor. Some important think tanks of international reputation, like the Development Finance Group (Ohio State University), the consultant firm DAI, Inc. (Development Alternatives), and the universities of Boulder and New Hampshire for training, are also located in the United States.

[9] For a review of seven best practices in savings mobilisation in Asia, Africa, and Latin America from the private and public sector, see A. Hannig, *Mobilizing Microsavings: The Millenium Challenge in Microfinance* (Eschborn, Germany: GTZ, 1999). This strategic paper, issued just before the 1999 Microcredit Summit meeting in Abidjan, argues that savings mobilisation can be organised in a cost-effective way and is an important ingredient in any

284 • Koenraad Verhagen

strategy aiming at MFI financial sustainability and balanced financial systems development. It is one of the many GTZ publications on savings mobilisation.

[10] In March 2001 the Belgian Catholic weekly *Tertio* (no. 59) published in Dutch an
article by Johan van der Vloet entitled "Christianity Is More than Ethics," a critique on the
way progressive Catholic organisations present themselves to the public and their relative
silence about their Catholic roots and source of inspiration. It sparked off a virulent debate
on the way faith-based organisations should interact with their church constituency and
manifest themselves in the larger society. See also the reactions in *Tertio* 62 (Antwerp: CU
Tertio Millennio).

[11] Catholic Relief Services is the only Catholic organisation in the North that, to the
author's knowledge, has made a serious effort to derive policy principles from Catholic
social thought for microfinance practice. These principles are: (1) serve the poorest clients;
(2) link loans to savings; (3) use solidarity guarantees; (4) practise participatory management; (5) invest in scale and self-sufficiency; and (6) plan for permanence (see Kim Wilson,
Principled Practices in Microfinance, CRS Microfinance Unit [Baltimore, Md.: Catholic
Relief Services, 2000]).

[12] Perhaps the most comprehensive book on Catholic social teaching is the *New Dictionary of Catholic Social Thought,* ed. Judith A. Dwyer and E. L. Montgomery (Collegeville,
Minn.: The Liturgical Press, 1994). Catholic social thought is a wider concept than Catholic
social teaching, but as a frame of reference for this discussion, I have limited myself to the
official teaching of the Catholic church as laid down in official church documents.

[13] Among US-based agencies involved in village banking, there is a discussion on whether
prominence should be given to the development of the self-managed internal account capitalised by the members' savings or to the external account capitalised by the MFI. The
dilemma is this: How can the higher-level institution financially survive if the lower-level
group becomes financially autonomous?

[14] In recent years a broad consensus seems to have emerged that savings and credit
services deserve equal attention, but that the combination of savings collection and lending
by one and the same institution asks for an even higher degree of professionalism and moral
integrity than just credit delivery.

[15] When the author presented these strengths and weaknesses to a group of practitioners
mainly working in Africa, there was broad endorsement for the weaknesses but reservations
concerning the supposed strengths.

[16] This transfer was estimated at US$1.4 billion for 1995–98 for international and bilat-
eral government organisations only (CGAP *Report 1999* [Washington D.C.: World Bank,
CGAP Secretariat, 1999]).

REFERENCES

Acción. 1999. "Microfinance: Conversations with Experts." Washington D.C.: Acción In-
ternational/Calmeadow.
CGAP (Consultative Group to Assist the Poorest). 1999. *Report 1999.* Washington D.C.:
World Bank, CGAP Secretariat.
———. 2000. *Report 2000.* Washington D.C.: World Bank, CGAP Secretariat.
Christen, Robert P. 2000. *Commercialisation and Mission Drift: The transformation of
Microfinance in Latin America.* Washington D.C.: World Bank, CGAP Secretariat.
CRS (Catholic Relief Services). 1997. *Main Principles of Catholic Social Thought.* Balti-
more, Md.: Catholic Relief Services.

Dwyer, Judith A., and E. L.Montgomery, eds. 1994. *The New Dictionary of Catholic Social Thought*. Collegeville, Minn.: The Liturgical Press.

ECLOF (Ecumenical Church Loan Fund)/Oikocredit. 2000. "'Signs of Hope': Jubilee 2000 and Credit to the Poor." Seminar invitation brochure.

Genberg, B. 1999. "Savings and Credit Co-operatives in a Changing World." International Co-operative Alliance Discussion Paper. Geneva: ICA.

Harper, Malcolm, ed. 2000. *Small Enterprise Development* 11/1 (March). London: Intermediate Technology Publications.

Krauss, Annette, Birgit Joussen, and Koenraad Verhagen. 2001. *Finanzsystementwicklung – Spar- und Kredit institutionen für die Armen*. Bonn: North-South Dialogue 2001. Publication forthcoming.

LWF (Lutheran World Federation). 1994. *Stewardship and Accountability to God*. Geneva: Lutheran World Federation.

MCS (Microcredit Summit). 2000. "Empowering Women with Microcredit." *Microcredit Summit Campaign Report 2000*. Edited and compiled by Lise Adams et al. Washington D.C. Available on a number of websites.

Morduch Jonathan. 1999. "The Microfinance Promise." *Journal of Economic Literature* 37: 1569–1614.

Nexus. 1999. No. 42. *Nexus* is a publication of the Small Enterprise Education and Promotion Network (SEEP).

Rahman, Aminur. 1999. "Micro-credit Initiatives for Equitable and Sustainable Development: Who Pays?" *World Development* 27: 67– 82. Great Britain: Elsevier Science Ltd.

Wilson, Kim. 2000. *Principled Practices in Microfinance*. CRS Microfinance Unit. Baltimore, Md.: Catholic Relief Services.

Wisniwski, Sylvia. 1998. *Microfinance – Multinationals: Netzwerke und Geberinitiativen in Überblick*. Eschborn, Germany: GTZ.

Zahid Elahi, Muhammad. 2000. "Islamic Modes of Financing." Conference and workshop report presented in Peshawar, Pakistan. Association for Creation of Employment (ACE), November.

Zeller, Manfred, and Manohar Sharma. 2000. "The Demand for Financial Services by the Poor." Policy Brief no.1. Washington D.C.: International Food Policy Research Institute (IFPRI).

13

FAITH, COMMUNITY, AND DEVELOPMENT

A Christian Approach to Poverty Reduction in the Third World

Rebecca Samuel Shah

> *Development which is not only economic must be measured and oriented according to the reality and vocation of man seen in his totality, namely, according to his interior dimension. . . . In trying to achieve true development we must never lose sight of that dimension which is in the specific nature of man, who has been created by God in his image and likeness (cf. Gen 1:26). It is a bodily and a spiritual nature, symbolised in the second creation account by two elements: the earth, from which God forms man's body, and the breath of life which he breathes into man's nostrils (cf. Gen 2:7).*
>
> —JOHN PAUL II, *SOLLICITUDO REI SOCIALIS*, NO. 29

The Bridge Foundation (TBF), a faith-based micro-enterprise development organisation has had an impact in India. What is unique about TBF is that while it provides economic opportunities for the poor, as one would expect, it also contributes to the enhancement of non-material values such as the creation of social capital and the formation of community. This impact is in large part due to the Christian character of TBF and the deep spiritual values that pervade its work. The effectiveness of TBF is thus measured by much more than the simple fact that the incomes of the poor are rising, or even that active and vocal civil society groups are being formed. Instead, by actively emphasising the role of faith, TBF is contributing to a dramatic spiritual transformation of individuals and communities, a

I owe special thanks to Eddie Swamynadan, director of The Bridge Foundation (TBF) of Bangalore, India, for helping me to carry out the field work that is the empirical basis of the chapter, and to the staff of TBF. I would also like to acknowledge the assistance of Vinay Samuel and Timothy Samuel Shah. The views I express in this paper are not necessarily those of the World Bank.

transformation consistent with what Pope John Paul II has called "true development."

To highlight TBF's faith-based approach to development, its work and its impact can be compared with the development models that have guided the World Bank. These models include the traditional growth-led model of development that dominated development thinking and practice for many years after World War II, as well as the more recent model of development that envisions a greater role for civil society and broadens the economic approach to include considerations of individual freedoms and capacities. This model has been heavily influenced by the work of Nobel Prize winning economist Amartya Sen. Drawing especially on the work of Alasdair MacIntyre, I argue that both of these models fall short in light of Christian understandings of individuals and communities.

DEVELOPMENT AND CIVIL SOCIETY

In all its forms, civil society is probably the largest single factor in development. If not in its monetary contribution, then certainly in its human contribution.

—JOHN WOLFENSON, WORLD BANK

For much of the post-war period, development policy has emphasised per capita income as the primary measure of human welfare. This notion of human welfare evolved out of a growth-led model of development that has dominated development policy and practice since the mid-twentieth century. Based partly on the success of the Marshall Plan, it assumes that abundant financial resources and prudent fiscal regulations are sufficient to lift societies out of economic and social deprivation. Proponents of the model attest to the validity of this approach by citing the spectacular successes of Europe and Japan in the post-war period.

Established initially to meet the need for post-war economic reconstruction in Europe and Japan, the World Bank and the International Monetary Fund (IMF) soon thereafter assumed responsibility to address poverty in the developing world and have served as bankers to the world's poorest nations ever since. The bank's ongoing mandate is to provide loans for "sectoral" development, such as the provision of health care, basic education, and infrastructure. In addition to providing loans for development projects, the World Bank has also contributed research and ideas about development policy, trained public policy-makers, financed reform, and expanded public services.[1]

With respect to the world's developing nations, foreign aid administered over the last fifty years by multilateral organisations such as the World Bank has ranged from being highly effective, as in the case of the Republic of Korea in the 1960s (the country went from economic crisis to rapid development),[2] to unmitigated failure, as in the case of Zaire (decades of financial assistance had no impact on the country except to make Zaire's Mobuto Sese Seko one of the richest men in the world). While the post-war period has witnessed greater progress in poverty alleviation than any other period in human history, more than one billion people continue to live in abject poverty on less than US$1 a day. More than 60 per cent of the developing world lacks basic services such as clean water, sanitation, education, electricity, and health care. Along with those who vigorously protested outside World Bank and IMF headquarters in Washington, D.C., in the spring of 2000, one cannot help but wonder whether the bank could be more effective. Such protests, along with internal reflections on the checkered history of the resource-focused growth-led model of development, have led the World Bank to seek fresh answers to the pressing question: How can development assistance be more effective in reducing global poverty? (this is the focal concern of Dollar and Pritchett 1998). Bank management and staff are aware that with increasing globalisation and greater market freedom around the world, this question has profound urgency (see de Soto 2000).

Globalisation and increasing free trade raise critical issues, especially in regard to their direct consequences for the poor. The liberalisation of highly volatile capital flows can foster boom-bust cycles that have a devastating effect on the already weak economies of the South. Furthermore, poor economies are unable to participate fully in globalisation because they lack the requisite supporting institutions and policies. In 1997 poor nations contributed 0.4 per cent to international trade, down by half from 1980. The World Bank understands that globalisation, with its promise of economic and cultural openness among countries, as well as shared prosperity, nevertheless brings enormous risks for the poorest and most vulnerable. To facilitate the transition to the global economy and to prevent the poorest from being left behind, it is clear that effort must be made to give them access to training and affordable credit.

In search of a more inclusive, transparent, and sustainable model of economic development, the World Bank has been led to rethink its fundamental approach. Since the late 1980s the bank has moved away from a top-down, technocratic approach to development and towards a more participatory approach that focuses instead on partnering with project beneficiaries and especially with civil society (see Drèze and Sen 1989). Civil society is now recognised as an important partner in the formulation and implementation of a country's national development strategy. Ownership of World Bank projects is now understood to go beyond the government to include key stakeholders such as the independent associations, groups, and NGOs that constitute civil society.

The World Bank has come to realise that civil society contributes to the achievement of development outcomes by enhancing the bank's ability to target and engage the poor and other socially vulnerable groups more effectively in its projects. A 1998 World Bank publication, *Assessing Aid,* argues that citizens' voices add a strong, independent, positive influence to the performance of bank-financed government projects. To the extent that societies enjoy greater civil liberty, and citizens take advantage of this liberty to make their voices (including voices of dissent) heard, there is a positive and statistically significant affect on the economic rate of return (ERR) on bank projects.[3] The fact that projects with an active civil society component produce a higher ERR suggests that civil society is a powerful force for improving government performance in human development, especially in "highly distorted environments" where the government generally fails to provide supportive policies and effective services (Dollar and Pritchett 1998, 25). Particularly in countries with low government capacity, civil society is a critical player in pressuring the government to improve service provision or, in the worst cases, to take responsibility for service provision itself. An active civil society enables the bank not only to target more sharply focused poverty-alleviation initiatives, but also to achieve a better return on its investment. It is therefore not surprising to see the significantly increased involvement of civil society organisations (CSOs) in bank projects over the last few years. According to the bank, the involvement of CSOs in bank-funded projects increased from 28 per cent in 1993 to 60 per cent in 1998 (Aparicio 1999, 2).

DEVELOPMENT AS FREEDOM: RETHINKING THE THEORY AND PRACTICE OF DEVELOPMENT

The participatory approach to development recently adopted by the World Bank is based in part on the seminal theoretical work of Nobel Prize–winning economist and moral philosopher Amartya K. Sen, who was presidential fellow at the World Bank in 1996. Sen's 1999 book *Development as Freedom,* hailed as a key resource for development practitioners, arose out of lectures he gave at the World Bank.

According to Sen, development, properly understood, enables the poor to "lead the kind of lives they value and have reason to value." Poverty is not merely a shortage of income but also an inadequacy of "capabilities" that deprives the poor of the freedom to live as they wish. Poverty alleviation, therefore, must involve more than increasing the ability of the poor to earn higher incomes, a goal that would have been the sole concern of the growth-led model of development. Poverty alleviation must now also include the expansion of basic capabilities and basic freedoms of the poor. Therefore, an assessment of the state of any country's development should take into account the deprivation or provision of the basic freedoms of the poor. For Sen, the role of freedom is both "constitutive" and "instrumental" – that is, it is not only a crucial part of the process of development, but also the leading end of development (Sen 1999, 3–11).

Sen criticises economists for focusing too much on "income inequality," which he believes leads them to neglect other important inequalities or inequities such as unemployment, lack of health care, and lack of education. By concentrating on income inequality over other types of inequality, economists overlook the fundamental issue of the provision of basic capabilities and freedoms, such as the freedom to experience a longer life without succumbing to premature mortality. A striking illustration of this point is offered by the life expectancies of African Americans. Demographic data show that African American males have lower life expectancies than people in much poorer countries, like China and India. Key factors contributing to this are violence and crime. Life expectancies of African American women are likewise lower than those of women in the relatively poor state of Kerala, India (Sen 1999, 21–24). Sen's freedom-based approach to development evaluates progress not just in terms of income generation but also assesses whether basic freedoms, such as the freedom to live a longer life, are enhanced.

Sen's view usefully critiques the traditional growth-centred model of development. Many of his observations are no surprise to those who hold holistic views of development. But a Christian approach would go even further than Sen does in appreciating the breadth of the holism required for a complete understanding of development. Consider Pope John Paul II's vision of development, articulated in his 1987 encyclical *Sollicitudo rei socialis (On Social Concern)*, from which the opening epigraph to this paper is drawn. In a way similar to Sen's, though on radically different foundations, the pope recognised that the fundamental role of development is not to achieve material surfeit but to liberate humanity:

> Development which is merely economic is incapable of setting man free; on the contrary, it will end by enslaving him further. Development that does not include the *cultural, transcendent and religious dimensions* of man and society, to the extent that it does not recognize the existence of such dimensions and does not endeavor to direct its goals and priorities toward the same, is even *less* conducive to authentic liberation. Human beings are totally free only when they are completely *themselves*, in the fullness of their rights and duties. The same can be said about society as a whole (*Sollicitudo rei socialis*, no. 46, emphasis added).

A concrete example of holistic and authentic development in action can be helpful. The following discussion is based on an empirical study conducted in South India in September-October 2000 of a successful, faith-based microfinance organisation, The Bridge Foundation.

Case Study: TBF

In 1984, when most development institutions, including the World Bank, were sceptical about the potential of microfinance to reduce poverty significantly, TBF established a microfinance or micro-credit programme for the enterprising poor in two major cities in South India, Bangalore and Madras. Founded by Indian Christian activists and business people, TBF embodied an active and integrally Christian approach to poverty reduction premised on the agency as well as the inherent dignity and spiritual nature of the poor.

Modelling its programme after the traditional savings and credit systems established by the poor themselves, TBF offered affordable loans that were intended to be an alternative to the exploitative traditional banking systems that virtually enslaved the poor. The microfinance movement, of which TBF was a forerunner, targeted that segment (about 10 per cent) of the poor that demonstrated substantial enterprise abilities and offered affordable loans with no requirements for collateral. TBF focuses also on providing the poor with an opportunity to create wealth by providing circulating capital. In addition to providing credit at reasonable interest rates and opportunities for saving, TBF provides the poor with access to business advice that enables them to acquire critical business skills and escape poverty. TBF offers loans (*not* grants or charitable donations). These loans must be paid back, with interest, within a fairly short period of time. Loans range from one thousand to ten thousand rupees (approximately US$50–US$500) and are given at a 10 per cent interest rate for twelve months. During 1999, TBF achieved a nearly 100 per cent loan repayment rate, even though TBF is a trust and cannot take legal action against defaulters. Clients therefore are not legally bound to repay their loans.

A distinctive feature of TBF is its reliance on *sangams*, or self-help groups. Sangams are small communities of clients who assume a shared liability for paying one another's loans. These groups are predominantly female and may include as many as 25 members. In areas where sangams do not already exist, TBF actively encourages clients to form them. It is the prerogative of existing members to choose new members. Evaluations of loan programmes demonstrate that female-dominated sangams have lower default rates than those dominated by males. Female clients are among the most successful, repaying loans significantly faster than their male counterparts. Female clients are also more likely to qualify for a second loan. Nearly 90 per cent of female clients are married (or have been married) and have children. but it is not uncommon for these women to be the sole breadwinners in their families or to be single parents raising small children.

To assess the character and depth of development occurring in communities where TBF works, TBF loan officers conducted 25 interviews with female clients. These women ranged in age from 18 to 45 and lived in three linguistically and culturally distinct regions of South India: Bangalore, in the state of Karnataka; Trichy, in the state of Tamil Nadu; and Hyderabad, in the state of Andhra Pradesh. All interviewees were successful, loan-repaying clients. Loan officers conducted semi-structured interviews in all three locations and assured interviewees that their responses would in no way affect their standing with TBF.

Interviewees were asked the following open-ended questions: (1) Why did you want to pay back your loan on time? (2) What is the most important result of being involved in a sangam? (3) If TBF had not come into your community, would things be any different? Typical responses were simple, forceful, and clear, exhibiting self-assuredness and confidence, traits not typically associated with the poor, especially the female poor.

FOR THE WELL-BEING OF THE OTHER

What motivated these women to repay their loans on time? Interviewers expected the women to say that they repaid their loans on time for fear of being blacklisted and denied future opportunities to qualify for another loan on better terms. Contrary to expectations, however, virtually every interviewee responded that she did not want her *fellow sangam members* to suffer and to lose *their* chance for another loan. One might have expected the women who had successfully re-paid their loans to be more self-interested, especially because TBF has a policy of providing larger loans to successful loan-repaying clients. All the women inter-viewed had successful micro-businesses that they planned to expand.

Their commitment to each other is a strong indication of the powerful ties that bind the sangam members together, and which clearly go beyond fiduciary links and mutual financial responsibilities. The strength of their mutual commitment is all the more remarkable given that sangams are constituted by voluntary choice rather than natural (particularly caste-based or religious) affinity.

Bearing One Another's Burdens

> *Once, I was selling seasonal goods and was unable to make the loan repayments, but I did not lose my loan because other members contributed from their profits and paid my monthly instalment.*
>
> —Gowri, TBF client

One of the salient themes emerging from the interviews was the importance of social unity or community. More than 50 per cent of the respondents talked about how important it is to work together and to have the security and strength of the group behind them.

In contrast with the views of TBF clients, the typical secular belief is that pov-erty and deprivation are profoundly isolating. When one is in abject need, this theory goes, one tends to focus first on oneself. Think of Hobbes's state of nature: "The life of man is *solitary,* poore, nasty, brutish, and short" (Tuck 1996, emphasis added). But from evidence gathered in these interviews, it does not have to be this way.

Human Beings Not Just Business Partners

> *When my sister was getting married, I had to raise 2,000 rupees, without which the marriage could not have taken place. The sangam members donated this money, and the wedding took place as planned.*
>
> —Jaya, TBF client

The concern sangam members had for one another's welfare went far beyond income. More than half the respondents related incidents when sangam members stepped in to assist them in meeting not only their economic needs but also their family and religious obligations. The incident Jaya related, in which sangam mem-bers pitched in to cover the costs of her sister's wedding, is but one example.

The larger and particularly spiritual significance of TBF's sangams is well cap-tured by the words of Pope Paul VI in his 1967 encyclical *Populorum progressio*

(On the Development of Peoples), which was the predecessor and inspiration of John Paul II's 1987 *Sollicitudo rei socialis:*

> Increased possession is not the ultimate goal of nations nor of individuals. All growth is ambivalent. It is essential if man is to develop as a man, but in a way it imprisons man if he considers it the supreme good, and it restricts his vision. Then we see hearts harden and minds close, and men no longer gather together in friendship but out of self-interest, which soon leads to oppositions and disunity. The exclusive pursuit of possessions thus becomes an obstacle to individual fulfillment and to man's true greatness. Both for nations and for individual men, avarice is the most evident form of moral underdevelopment (*Populorum progressio*, no. 19).

There is broad economic significance to the fact that sangam relationships exhibit a minimum of "avarice" and instead offer strong evidence of mutual generosity: such relationships help create the environment necessary for a properly functioning market. As Alasdair MacIntyre observes: "Market relationships can only be sustained by being embedded in certain types of local nonmarket relationships, relationships of uncalculated giving and receiving, if they are to contribute to overall flourishing, rather than, as they so often in fact do, undermine and corrupt communal ties" (MacIntyre 1999, 117). Rather than markets corrupting morals, sangam relationships have at least the potential to create a dynamic in which morals of generosity and mutual support facilitate healthy markets that favour human flourishing.

Hope, Human Capital, and Spiritual Capital

> *If it were not for TBF, a coolie worker like myself could never have an opportunity to start her own business. I now have enough money to feed and clothe my children. I can even send them to school.*
>
> —Prema, TBF client

The 1999 research of M. B. Neace on entrepreneurs in emerging economies reveals that human capital in the form of the entrepreneurial attributes of ambition, determination, and hope is critically important for business success and economic development. According to Neace, these qualities are a feature of human capital that is crucial to entrepreneurship and small business development (Neace 1999).

As crucial as these qualities are, faith-based NGOs see the qualities that make up what one might call spiritual capital as equally important (Samuel 2000). One might even argue that there is some overlap between entrepreneurial attributes and spiritual capital – the virtue of hope. In the promotion of development, hope may be the most crucial component of spiritual capital. Prema testified that she is now capable of doing things that affect her future for the better. Now that the "impossibility" of starting her own business has become possible, other things in Prema's life seem possible also.

By offering, or at least stimulating, hope, faith-based agencies enable the poor to challenge rather than succumb to the reality of the present, however hopeless it may seem, and plan for a better future. With hope, the poor are no longer bound to the inevitability of poverty and deprivation and can actively look for opportunities to invest their resources and time in the present with a firm expectation of progress in the future. With hope, the poor can be confident that the cost of investing their time and effort in the present will be rewarded by a future in which their own choices can affect their well-being.

Even if Prema is unable to realise a profit immediately, TBF's willingness to "bank with the unbankable" generates hope, optimism and a sense of confidence that she is valuable and has as much dignity as any other human being, rich or poor. The hope that TBF engenders is due in no small part to the clear yet non-coercive Christian witness of TBF staff members. The hope they share is based not only on the material world, but also on the knowledge and understanding of the empowering work of Jesus Christ through the Holy Spirit, who gives hope for the present and the future. This great and specifically Christian hope encourages them not only to go forth confidently and change the course of their own lives but also to give of themselves in order to transform the wider community. It is one thing to feel confident for oneself, and quite another to translate that confidence into self-giving for the sake of others.[4] Any assessment of the impact of faith-based development provided by NGOs should take into consideration their ability to provide the poor not only with opportunities to alleviate material need but also to instill clients with a hope and confidence concerning both the present and future.

FAITH-BASED MICRO-ENTERPRISE DEVELOPMENT AND CIVIL SOCIETY

In the previous section the roles of civil society and TBF's Christian character were implicit. I would now like to draw out those connections more explicitly by addressing the following questions: First, how do our broad theory of development and TBF's experience relate to civil society? And second, what is the distinctive contribution of Christian faith to the approach to development exemplified by TBF?

Definitions of civil society have disproportionately been framed by Western history and institutions,[5] and the focus of these definitions has been more political than economic. This has also been true in the recently revived interest in civil society, for it arose in large part because of the collapse of communism in Eastern Europe and the Soviet empire. In a country such as India, however, building civil society in the slums and shanty towns of Bangalore and Madras must focus first of all on the reality of poverty, even though politics and political reform may be important for long-term development.

In the formation of sangams, an emerging civil society group, it is interesting to note that all 25 respondents mentioned that TBF enables them to avoid the exorbitant interest rates of moneylenders by providing loans at a lower interest rate. More than half added that their ability to earn a living and support their families changed the way in which they were viewed by the community and local authorities. By focusing on and addressing economic need, microfinance programmes provide the poor with the means to gain economic security and independence from loan sharks and exploitative economic arrangements. This, in turn, makes it possible for them to have an independent influence on their communities and make their own contribution to civil society.

Involvement in community life has both political and economic aspects. Amartya Sen defines poverty as the deprivation of basic capabilities rather than merely having a low income. Some critics of Sen's freedom-based approach to poverty alleviation misunderstand Sen to mean that income enhancement is not necessary in order to address poverty. To argue this, however, would be both unrealistic and unreasonable. Sen's perspective does not deny the importance of income as one of the major causes of poverty, but rather states that "sometimes the lack of substantive freedoms relates directly to economic poverty" (Sen 1999, 4). Yet his argument does not explicitly deploy the crucial idea that for the poor to have the capability and therefore the freedom to lead the kind of lives they value and have reason to value, some level of economic independence is necessary so that they are not merely pawns of a wealthy creditor. TBF directly addresses the inadequacies of the state and the market economy by giving the poor an opportunity to achieve greater economic independence and thus have the substantive freedom to lead the lives they value.

Furthermore, the means by which TBF restores economic entitlements of the poor through affordable loans managed by sangams is critically important in developing intermediary networks of trust in which the poor have a strong sense of ownership and participation. Sangams create social capital that is associational, interpersonal, and organisational. The social capital thus nurtured by TBF is essential to removing the sense of powerlessness and helplessness the poor sometimes feel as individuals. It is also essential to the creation of a strong civil society. In a context of abject poverty such as in India, where the absence of robust local political institutions and enforceable government regulations often yield a volatile and unaccountable business environment, the profound need for a fund of mutual trust and goodwill that reduces mutual exploitation is met at least in part by social capital. MacIntyre's point about the need to embed market relationships in local nonmarket relationships of uncalculated giving and receiving is all the more crucial in this context, and Neace's research on civil society and micro-businesses in Eastern Europe confirms the importance of civil society among the poor for the success of micro-businesses (Neace 1999).

In assessing the state of North American community Robert Putnam dichotomizes two types of social capital; "bonding" and "bridging" (Putnam 2000, see esp. chap. 4). In the Indian context, however, such a stark dichotomy is inappropriate, for the sangams create both bonding *and* bridging social capital; they create tightly knit social bonds and communities *among* the poor while at the same time building bridges *across* divides of caste and creed. To that extent, sangams conquer what John Hall calls the "final enemy" of civil society:

> A final enemy of civil society is cultural. The desire to balance the state and to respect individualism is not inscribed in the historic process, an acorn somehow ready in every culture to turn into an oak tree. The emphasis on caste in Indian civilization emphatically condemns people to a status order (Hall 1995, Introduction).

It is noteworthy that Hall's main example of a cultural barrier to civil society is the Indian caste system. It is against this cultural barrier that sangams work so impressively by empowering the poor regardless of caste or creedal background and by creating religiously inclusive grassroots communities.

In the last decade many previously "closed economies" have opened up in hopes of enjoying the merits of the market. Proponents of the market point to the ability of competitive markets to achieve higher levels of efficiency than can centralised systems. Yet what market advocates often fail to mention, or take account of, is that market systems do not function well unless based on social capital: trust, mutual responsibility, truthfulness, and co-operation. Micro-enterprise programmes help produce such public goods that are crucial for ongoing development in an open economy. In the communities where TBF works, sangams help create an environment of mutual reliance, trust, and co-operation, thus strengthening social capital in the sangams themselves as well as in the broader communities in which the sangams are located.

The remarkable experiences of sangam members demonstrate that the kind of civil society created by faith-based organisations is based ultimately on truths to which the Christian faith bears clear witness. We have a self-giving God who created us with dignity as well as a propensity to give of ourselves for the sake of the full flourishing of others.

The kind of civil society created by faith-based organisations is rooted in the principles of Christian faith that Adam Ferguson, for example, an intellectual leader of the eighteenth-century Scottish Enlightenment, articulated. Ferguson's reflections strike at the heart of the Hobbesian individualism that is sometimes thought to be the foundation of both the modern liberal state (and its civil society) and the modern market economy:

> [Ferguson] rooted civil society in "love of mankind," a quality that was dramatically different from the commercial interest some thinkers were placing at the center of human organization. "Affection, and force of mind, which are the band and strength of communities, were the inspiration of God, and original attributes in the nature of man," [Ferguson] asserted. . . . It was clear to him that people form societies for reasons broader than mere survival (Ehrenberg 1999, 91).

CONCLUSION:
DEVELOPMENT AS THE DEVELOPMENT OF FAITH AND COMMUNITY

TBF's approach to poverty reduction is rooted in the truths of Christian faith. Indeed, these truths, such as the holistic nature of the person, the critical importance of hope, and the moral and spiritual excellence of self-giving, pervade the TBF approach.

It might reasonably be inferred from the foregoing discussion that faith is understood and practised differently in non-Western faith-based NGOs than it is in Western faith-based NGOs. In the latter, faith tends to be just one element that defines and directs work with the poor, and for some it is likely to occupy the background rather than the foreground of this work, one cause of which is the secularising pressure associated with competing for government funding. These organisations sometimes struggle to reconcile their faith traditions with the increasingly a-religious and pluralistic environment in which they compete for donors. Other faith-based organisations in the West downplay their Christian identity or avoid talking about their Christian beliefs altogether for fear of being considered exclusive or cultural-imperialist. Still others fear that because of their beliefs they are in danger of being associated with an anti-cultural, Western, and implicitly superior view of the world.

On the other hand, faith is to local faith-based NGOs such as TBF what freedom is to Sen, not only instrumentally significant but also intrinsically important. Faith pervades the outlook, understanding, and practice of TBF. Faith becomes the crucial means of achieving true or authentic development. Such NGOs harness and build faith in order to transform both the economic and spiritual lives of individuals and communities.

TBF conceives of faith as intrinsically significant to development. The distinctiveness of TBF's approach to development vis-à-vis the characteristically Western approach can perhaps best be seen by drawing out the contrast with the secular development framework of Amartya Sen. Sen's conception of development begins with the individual and ends with the individual – specifically the ideal of the autonomous individual. Development, in his view, is the process of enhancing the "real freedoms" and thereby the capabilities of *individuals* to choose to live the kind of lives they value and have reason to value. Sen's approach includes both the process of *removing* "unfreedoms" from the lives of individuals – unfreedoms such as social deprivation, tyranny, and political limitations – and the provision of *opportunities* for individuals to increase their personal and social circumstances. The latter has a constitutive role and the former an instrumental role in fostering development. An assessment of the success of development is confined to an assessment of the freedom experienced by individuals *as* individuals and not, for example, as members of families, religious groups, or self-help communities such as sangams.

Martha Nussbaum largely concurs with Sen's capabilities approach and suggests that true development for Indian women is coextensive with the expansion of their autonomy as individuals. Her analysis mentions women's obligations to family and faith only as actual and potential barriers to development. In other words, family and faith do not appear at all on the positive side of Nussbaum's ledger. They are conspicuously absent from her list of central human functional capabilities, even though she developed this list partly based on conversation with Indian women like the ones we interviewed for our study (Nussbaum 2000; see also Nussbaum and Sen 1993).

Sen's and Nussbaum's secular understanding of what makes an individual's life free and valuable privileges individualist virtues of independence and self-reliance. The beneficiaries of TBF, however, understand that vulnerability and dependence are central to the human condition. The sangam members we interviewed gladly acknowledged, and described in detail, their mutual dependence, and their dependence on the work of TBF. TBF's work is rooted in the Christian belief that human beings are not only incapable of being self-sufficient but ought not to seek to be self-sufficient. This belief, in turn, is consistent with the notion that we need God's grace to transform our proud self-reliance into brotherly love and our weaknesses into strengths (cf. 2 Cor 12:7–10; Rom 15:1–3). TBF even encourages its clients to use whatever economic independence they are able to achieve for the benefit of the sangams and larger communities of which they are a part.

In contrast to Sen's and Nussbaum's ethic of individual autonomy, TBF fosters through its sangams an ethic of giving and receiving. The character of such an ethic, and how it depends on community for its full realisation, is well described by Alasdair MacIntyre. According to MacIntyre, it is only in a type of community he calls a "network of giving and receiving" that people can develop virtues appropriate to the human condition, a condition marked much more by dependence and vulnerability, and much less by independence and autonomy, than most Western moral philosophers have cared to recognise. MacIntyre's description of networks of giving and receiving, and how they teach essential virtues, readily recalls the sangams TBF promotes in its micro-enterprise development work among South India's poor (MacIntyre 1999).

One of the most important implications of MacIntyre's account is that networks of giving and receiving, including sangams, are more than self-seeking affiliations, even though they do benefit their members as individuals. Rather, they are networks of relationships in which

> each of us achieves our good only if and insofar as others make our good their good by helping us through periods of disability to become ourselves the kind of human being – through acquisition and exercise of the virtues – who makes the good of others her or his good, and this not because we have calculated that, only if we help others, will they help us, in some trading of advantage for advantage.

MacIntyre continues:

To participate in this network of relationships of giving and receiving . . . , I have to understand that what I am called upon to give may be quite disproportionate to what I have received and that those to whom I am called upon to give may well be those from whom I shall receive nothing. And I also have to understand that the care that I give to others has to be in an important way unconditional, since the measure of what is required of me is determined in key part, even if not only, by their needs (MacIntyre 1999, 108).

As in MacIntyre's network of giving and receiving, it is critical to emphasise that what any sangam member contributes to the sangam may in fact be disproportionate to what she has received or will receive. This may be especially true when another sangam member experiences a particularly serious need, such as a disability that requires the sangam to provide an unusually high level of support.

On the other hand, to say that sangams are not self-seeking and that sangam members may and often do give beyond what they receive is not to imply the false alternative that they are purely altruistic or that their members' behaviour is purely altruistic. The behaviour of the sangam members we observed transcends simple altruism or egoism precisely because the sangam approximates the function of a true network of giving and receiving. Again, this point is aptly made by MacIntyre:

Adam Smith's contrast between self-interested market behavior on the one hand and altruistic benevolent behavior on the other, obscures from view just those types of activity in which the goods to be achieved are neither mine-rather-than-others' nor others'-rather-than-mine, but instead are goods that can only be mine insofar as they are also those of others, that are genuinely common goods, as the goods of networks of giving and receiving are (MacIntyre 1999, 119).

The goods of financial, moral, and relational support that sangams share and distribute are not, for example, Gowri's-rather-than-Jaya's or Jaya's-rather-than-Gowri's, but readily and equally available to any and all sangam members as they have need. The goods of the sangam are "genuinely common goods."

With MacIntyre's account of networks of giving and receiving in mind, the contrast between TBF's faith and community-based approach and Sen's and Nussbaum's secularist-individualist approach to development is all the more apparent. In particular, it is clear that they yield completely different evaluations of the role that family and faith communities play in development. According to the secular view of development promoted by Sen and Nussbaum, there could hardly be a greater source of "unfreedom" for individuals than the obligations that attend familial and religious communities (obligations that are constitutive of identity and transcend choice) or the binding obligations that result from the need and dependence of one's fellow sangam members. The Sen-Nussbaum conception of development will be quick to point out that family, faith, and sangam obligations will inevitably and directly conflict with what we otherwise have reason to value and will greatly and unexpectedly limit our freedom. It is clear, however, that our overall flourishing as complete human beings requires fulfilling these obligations, for only by doing so can we enjoy the common goods of family, faith, and community. Indeed, the deep value in family, faith, and communities of giving and receiving consists in the fact that we are not so much autonomous choosers as graciously and mysteriously chosen. In relation to these common granted goals, at least partly independently of our own choosing, we become objects of love who are called on to love in return even when we may seem valueless or have little to offer. The value of such communities, in so far as they are genuine networks of giving and receiving, consists further in the fact that they teach us to be more than self-interested individuals. They teach us also to be unconditional givers as well as humble receivers.

The Christian foundations of TBF enable it to realise the good that both comes from, and is a part of, faith and community. Even secular institutions like the World Bank note that the self-reported definitions of well-being given by the poor themselves again and again give prominence to faith, family, and community affiliations (see Narayan-Parker 1997; idem 2000a; idem 2000b). TBF, however, understands that these affiliations have a value that is both instrumental and constitutive. Indeed, by encouraging faith and strengthening community as an integral part of its development work, TBF helps give the poor a deeper understanding that faith and community are ultimately divine gifts for the true development of "man seen in his totality" (*Sollicitudo rei socialis*, no. 29).

NOTES

[1] The World Bank provides developing countries with two main types of loans: IDA (International Development Assistance) loans and IBRD (International Bank of Reconstruction and Development) loans. The former are low-interest loans payable over a long period (40+ years in some cases). To qualify for IDA loans, countries must have a per capita income below US$400.

[2] Effectiveness is defined here as the positive impact of World Bank aid on economic growth in real gross domestic product (GDP) per capita. It is based on research that shows that a robust effect on growth of World Bank aid depends on sound economic management (see Craig Burnside and David Dollar, "Aid, Policies, and Growth" [Washington, D.C.: World Bank, 1997]). Where there is sound economic management, cross-country studies show that assistance amounting to 1 per cent of GDP translates into a sustained increase in economic growth of 0.5 per cent. During its involvement with the World Bank, Korea adopted sound policies of inflation control, budget surplus creation, and a liberal trade policy, which, World Bank research shows, helped Korea achieve a good return on World Bank assistance. See also the recent discussion of estimating the effect of aid on economic growth in Appendix 1 of David Dollar and Lant Pritchett, *Assessing Aid: What Works, What Doesn't, and Why,* a World Bank Policy Research Report (New York: Oxford University Press/World Bank, 1998), 121–25.

[3] Economic rates of return (ERR) are a useful means of evaluating the performance of governments in implementing public World Bank–funded projects. "Since the World Bank applies the same project and implementation procedures across all countries, the *differences*

across countries in returns are an indication of how effective the government is in implementing public projects" (Dollar and Pritchett, *Accessing Aid*, 135).

[4] Indeed, from a secular viewpoint, hope and self-confidence are virtually identical. This is strikingly evident in Hobbes, for example, who defines hope as "*confidence* of our selves" (Richard Tuck, ed., *Hobbes: Leviathan* [Cambridge: Cambridge University Press, 1996], part I, chap. VI).

[5] While insightful, Charles Taylor's historical and theoretical analysis of the concept of civil society in "Modes of Civil Society" is a good example of the overwhelming Western bias of most such analyses (*Public Culture* 3/1 [1990]: 95–118). For an effort to correct this bias, see Chris Hann and Elizabeth Dunn, eds., *Civil Society: Challenging Western Models* (London: Routledge, 1996).

REFERENCES

Aparicio, Teresa, et al. 1999 (fall). *Thinking Out Loud: Innovative Case Studies on Participatory Instruments*. Washington, D.C.: World Bank. Online at the World Bank website.

De Soto, Hernando. 2000. *The Mystery of Capital: Why Capitalism Triumphs in the West and Fails Everywhere Else*. New York: Basic Books.

Dollar, David, and Lant Pritchett. 1998. *Accessing Aid: What Works, What Doesn't, and Why*. A World Bank Policy Research Report. Washington, D.C.: World Bank/Oxford University Press. Online at the World Bank website.

Drèze, Jean, and Amartya Sen. 1989. *Hunger and Public Action*. Oxford: Clarendon Press.

Ehrenberg, John. 1999. *Civil Society: The Critical History of an Idea*. New York: New York University Press.

Hall, John A., ed. 1995. *Civil Society: Theory, History, Comparison*. Cambridge, UK: Polity Press.

John Paul II. 1987. *On Social Concern: Encyclical Letter* Sollicitudo Rei Socialis *of the Supreme Pontiff John Paul II*. Boston: St. Paul Books and Media.

MacIntyre, Alasdair. 1999. *Dependent Rational Animals: Why Human Beings Need the Virtues*. The Paul Carus Lecture Series. Chicago: Open Court.

Narayan-Parker, Deepa. 1997. *Voices of the Poor: Poverty and Social Capital in Tanzania*. Washington, D.C.: World Bank.

———. 2000a. *Can Anyone Hear Us? Voices of the Poor*. New York: Oxford University Press/World Bank.

———. 2000b. *Crying Out for Change: Voices of the Poor*. New York: Oxford University Press/World Bank.

Neace, M. B. 1999. "Entrepreneurs in Emerging Economies: Creating Trust, Social Capital, and Civil Society." *Annals of the American Academy of Political and Social Science* 565: 148–61.

Nussbaum, Martha Craven. 2000. *Women and Human Development: The Capabilities Approach*. The John Robert Seeley lectures. Cambridge: Cambridge University Press.

Nussbaum, Martha C., and Amartya Sen, eds. 1993. *The Quality of Life*. Oxford: Clarendon Press.

Paul VI. 1967. *On the Development of Peoples: Encyclical Letter* Populorum Progressio *of His Holiness Paul VI*. Washington, D.C.: United States Catholic Conference.

Putnam, Robert D. 2000. *Bowling Alone: The Collapse and Revival of American Community*. New York: Simon and Schuster.

Samuel, Vinay K. 2000. "Theology and Development." Paper presented at the Oxford Centre for Mission Studies, Oxford, United Kingdom, May.

Sen, Amartya K. 1999. *Development as Freedom*. New York: Alfred A. Knopf.

Tuck, Richard, ed. 1996. *Hobbes: Leviathan*. Cambridge: Cambridge University Press.

14

STRENGTHENING CIVIL SOCIETY
FOR RURAL DEVELOPMENT

An Analysis of Social Capital Formation
by a Christian NGO Programme in Bolivia

Terrence L. Jantzi and Vernon E. Jantzi

Civil society, with its myriad forms of formal and informal non-governmental civic association, can serve as an instrument for citizen organisation to meet needs not addressed by governmental or business structures. One important facet that contributes to a functional civil society is the social capital available within a society. Social capital has generally been defined as "the features of social organization, such as networks, norms, and values which facilitate coordination and cooperation for mutual benefit" (Flora 1998, 2; Putnam 1993b, 1). Although the exact definition of civil society can vary from theorist to theorist, the role of social capital within these definitions remains relatively unchanging. Social capital is the agent that determines the ease of citizen mobilisation and organisation. Social capital may be seen as the facilitating agent that allows for the rapid construction of civic organisations.

This definition of social capital assumes that the presence of strong social capital is always a positive influence. Some social theorists have attempted to argue that too much social capital in a community or region may be detrimental (Schulman and Anderson 1999; Brown, Xu, and Toth 1998; Wall, Ferrazi, and Schryer 1998; Woolcock 1998), but these criticisms are usually based on incomplete definitions of social capital (Jantzi 2000). Within the theoretical definition presented below, high levels of social capital in a community or region will increase the responsiveness of civil society to address unmet needs. A functional civil society cannot exist in areas of low social capital because efforts at mobilisation or organisation will meet with resistance and failure. Consequently, understanding how to strengthen regional or community social capital is an important component in the building of a functional civil society (Duncan 1996; Butler Flora 1995; Putnam 1995).

Social capital is socially constructed. It is the product of the social interactions, social networks, norms, and values in a region or community (Flora 1998; Woolcock

1998). Consequently, factors that impinge on the social lives and interactions of citizens will perforce have an effect on social capital, even if social capital is not intentionally targeted. NGOs focused on international or community development provide an example of social forces with unintentional effects on social capital. Most non-governmental development organisations tend to emphasise technical, economic, or political development efforts and do not formally articulate strengthening social capital as part of their mission. Nevertheless, because these initiatives are carried out within the social arena, they will affect social capital in the course of implementing project objectives through the distortion or creation of social networks, the changing of values or norms, or the construction of new forms of interaction and leadership structures.

The relationship between social capital and NGO projects can also be seen as iterative and reciprocal. NGO programmes can influence social capital through their presence in the social arena. At the same time, the levels of social capital present in a community or region can enhance the effectiveness of NGO natural resource, economic, social, or political development programmes, because social capital increases the ease of citizen mobilisation and collective co-operation (Jantzi 2000; Butler Flora 1995).

It is important to explore the relationship between NGO programmes, particularly Christian NGOs, and social capital within a community, region, or society. We first develop a theoretical framework for defining social capital, then a theoretical framework for how NGOs may influence social capital. Third, we apply this framework to a case study of a specific Christian NGO programme. And finally, we summarise the results of the case study and reflect on the implications for Christian NGO programming.

A Theoretical Framework for Social Capital

> *Social capital, while not all things to all people, is many things to many people. A dramatic restriction of what one might mean must precede any attempt to estimate either social capital or its effect.*
>
> —Deepa Narayan and Lant Pritchett, "Cents and Sociability"

Defining Social Capital

Robert Putnam describes four types of capital inherent in all communities: natural resource, infrastructural, human, and social capital. Natural resource capital consists of the natural resource base upon which the community rests. He defines infrastructural capital as the physical infrastructure that exists in a community, for example, roads, factories, and schools. Human capital consists of the collection of skills and experiences possessed by individuals in the community. A community's social capital exists as the sum of the network of relationships embedded within a community and the shared norms and values that facilitate co-operative action (Putnam 1993a). Our working definition for *social capital* is this:

*Civil society is the features of social organisation (social and associational rela-
tionship networks, norms, and values) that facilitate collective analysis and collective mobilisation to address issues within the environmental, economic, or political spheres and which create an environment that allows for the preservation of
potential to address future issues.*

Social and Associational Networks

Numerous writers have stressed the contribution that dense and overlapping
social networks make to a community's social capital (Narayan and Pritchett 1999;
Flora 1998; Putnam 1995; Coleman 1990). These networks can consist of either
the formal associational networks found in civic groups (for example, Narayan
and Pritchett 1999; Bebbington 1998) or the informal social networks present in
any community or region (Falk and Harrison 1998; Green 1998; O'Brien, Raedeke,
and Hassinger 1998). Both types of networks are important for social capital. These
networks allow for the flow of information throughout a community, allow for
exchanges to occur, and provide a matrix within which to carry out community
analysis, discussion, and consensus building.

Still, the mere existence of social networks does not imply a high level of social
capital. The quality of the networks (that is, the structures and norms inherent in
the networks) reflect different types of social capital. Robert Putnam classifies a
community's social capital as horizontal, hierarchical, or nonexistent based on the
type of social networks present in the community. He contends that social networks that are dense, overlapping, promote egalitarian exchanges, and consist of
both horizontal (within similar social classes or within a community) and vertical
(between social classes or to external sources) connections will give rise to *horizontal social capital.* Horizontal social capital is considered a positive factor in
community development. In contrast, Putnam's *hierarchical social capital* is found
in social structures that contain strong vertical networks between classes but weak
or nonexistent horizontal networks. Patron-client relationships or communities that
depend upon a single industry typically exemplify hierarchical social capital. All
social connections and exchanges run vertically between the patron and the clients. Horizontal connections between networks are discouraged as they may expose clients to resources beyond the influence of the patrons. This type of social
structure is prevalent in areas of persistent poverty.

Nonexistent social capital results from extreme isolation and the absence of
any social networks. Communities with nonexistent social networks are
characterised by high rates of transition, high levels of crime and delinquency, and
low trust. Such communities often substitute other forms of capital for security,
such as private guards, fenced neighbourhoods, and elaborate security systems.

Within our current framework, these multiple definitions are collapsed into two
categories. Strong social capital is considered to be present when there are both
horizontal and vertical social networks that are dense, overlapping, and encourage
diverse egalitarian exchanges (Putnam's definition of horizontal social capital).
Strong social capital promotes community mobilisation and organisation. Weak

social capital consists either of the presence of vertical networks without horizontal networks (hierarchical social capital) or the absence of any social networks (nonexistent social capital). Weak social capital inhibits community mobilisation and organisation.

One factor that influences social capital is the presence of power differentials (see Wilson 1999; McKnight 1995). Loci of increased power can act to form vertical relationships among groups or individuals, leading to the formation of hierarchical social capital. Ricardo Vergara cites the relationships formed around NGO programmes as one venue where power differentials can drive the formation of hierarchical social capital. He argues that many NGOs create power differentials and vertical networks when they enter a community. He differentiates between *citizen* and *beneficiary* NGO relationships. When NGOs focus on a community's strengths, *citizen* quality relationships occur that help community members relate to the NGO from a position of strength as citizens who require forms of accountability or reciprocal obligation from the institution. In contrast, when NGOs focus on a community's weaknesses, participants relate to NGOs as *beneficiaries*. Community members form relationships with the NGO personnel from a position of weakness. Consequently, norms of reciprocity or accountability are generally absent (Vergara 1994).

Norms and Values

Social capital does not consist solely of the network structures in a community but also includes the set of norms embedded within these social relationships. These norms will influence the quality of the social capital present in a community or region. This set of norms includes trust (Fukuyama 1995), reciprocity (Putnam 1993), accountability (Vergara 1994), inclusiveness (Flora 1998), symbolic diversity (Butler Flora 1997), and broad resource definition (Butler Flora 1995).

Trust

Most theorists consider trust to be one of the most important norms for social capital. In the absence of high levels of trust, efficient collective collaboration and mobilisation is unlikely to occur. To put it colloquially, if people do not trust one another in a community, they aren't going to be willing to work together to achieve a common goal or meet a common need.

Reciprocity and Accountability

The concept of reciprocity in social capital originated within the theoretical framework of economic exchange theorists who contended that individuals engage in exchanges for mutual benefit (Wall, Ferrazzi, and Schryer 1998). Later, theorists developed the concept of generalised reciprocity, where exchanges do not occur directly between individuals, but rather individual contributions are invested in improving the general community environment from which all benefit (for example, Putnam 1995, Flora 1998). Butler Flora uses the example of a well-established Western farmer writing a check to help a struggling new farmer. His only request is that someday the newcomer will help someone else. The established farmer has made an investment in community social capital rather than direct remuneration (Butler Flora 1995, 6).

Theoretical discussions of reciprocity tend to emphasise the material nature of exchange – the direct or indirect transfer of goods or services – but also important is the concept of reciprocal social obligations or *accountability*. Community or group norms define members' relationships with one another. The importance of one-way and two-way relationships (reciprocal and nonreciprocal interactions) lies not only in the direct and indirect material exchanges, but also in the obligations and expectations embedded in these roles. When individuals or groups are mutually accountable and perform their roles in a transparent manner, social capital is strengthened and community development improves (Glaeser 1999; Fukuyama 1995). When parties or individuals within a group are not accountable to the larger group or do not operate transparently, abuse of power, corruption, lack of trust, and the reallocation of resources to benefit a small group at the expense of the greater community are likely to occur. This explains why vertical networks contribute to low social capital. Vertical relationships typified by patron-client relationships are based on power differentials. These essentially one-way relationships benefit a small group (the patron) at the expense of the larger group (the clients).

Inclusiveness

Norms of inclusiveness encourage the presence of a greater number of viewpoints, experiences, and skills in the community decision-making matrix. An inclusive community intentionally embraces marginalised elements within the group. Greater inclusion allows for more perspectives to be integrated into discussions and can foster greater creativity in problem solving.

For example, within the Christian church some denominations are ethnically as well as theologically based. Mennonites have traditionally had ethnic roots in Swiss-German or Dutch ethnic backgrounds. A Mennonite church that contained high levels of inclusiveness would welcome non-ethnic believers into its congregation and encourage a diverse ethnic representation among its leadership. A Mennonite church that contained low levels of inclusiveness may tolerate the presence of non-ethnic believers in its congregation but might be reluctant to allow such persons to become involved in the decision-making or leadership structures of the church.

Symbolic Diversity

Cornelia Butler Flora defines *symbolic diversity* as an appreciation among community members of different meaning sets (Butler Flora 1995, 9). This implies an acceptance of diverse viewpoints and an acceptance of controversy (Gardner 1996). In a community with high symbolic diversity, community members can disagree but still respect one another. Citizens make the distinction between *different from* and *better than*.

An example of the presence of symbolic diversity within the Christian church is interdenominational co-operation and ecumenical initiatives. These efforts require the acceptance of a range of religious beliefs other than one's own (a Calvinist college inviting Mennonite, Catholic, and evangelical theorists to a Calvinist-sponsored conference is an example of high symbolic diversity). Interdenominational conflicts or tensions that divide communities along denominational or religious lines are the result of low symbolic diversity. Low symbolic diversity inhibits broad social network formation and consequently reduces social capital.

Broad Resource Definition

This component is linked to the concept of reciprocity. Reciprocity reflects egalitarian exchanges of either material goods and services, or mutual accountability in social obligations that exist between relationships. To have a broad base of egalitarian exchange, however, there must first exist a broad definition of valuable resources worthy of exchange. If valued resources are defined narrowly (for example, as financial resources), then fewer members of the community will be able to participate in reciprocal exchanges. If resources are defined more broadly and include a variety of different features (financial resources, local history knowledge, folklore, spiritual resources, and so on), then more members of the community can participate in egalitarian reciprocal relationships by drawing on diverse features recognised as valuable contributions (Ritchey 1996; Butler Flora 1995). In other words, if many talents are valued, more people will feel they have value in the community. For example, older people in a community could be seen as a financial drain because they cannot contribute to the economic or productive life of the community (narrow resource definition), while in a context of broad resource definition, they may be seen as valued for their storytelling ability or as a fount of folklore or local history. Communities with high social capital value a diverse array of talents and contributions that individuals can make. Communities with low social capital place a value on a narrow range of talents or arenas, such as only those things that contribute to economic growth or material production. Narrowly defining valued resources forces individuals into exchanges across unequal power, which leads to the construction of Putnam's hierarchical social capital.

Social Capital and Collective Analysis and Mobilisation

A community dominated by a single patron or a small elite may be seen as an example of efficient mobilisation if the community always acts without question upon any decision instigated by the patron. Such a community will have only a limited number of interests and stakeholders represented in the decision-making process, and the decisions made and implemented may not necessarily serve the whole community's best interests. Furthermore, a decision-making structure that represents only a small elite will, of necessity, contain a limited number of viewpoints, experiences, and skills to draw on for analysis and problem solving. On the other hand, relationships and structures that encourage broad stakeholder participation will have a greater probability of developing creative solutions that benefit the whole community. Some components of social capital important for facilitating collective analysis and mobilisation are dense and overlapping networks, norms of inclusiveness, and norms of symbolic diversity.

One component often overlooked in discussions of social capital is the potential of social capital to help a community address future issues. An example from biodiversity conservation provides a metaphor for the importance of maintaining potential within a group to address future circumstances. Proponents who support biodiversity conservation often argue that the diverse genetic potential that exists in biological diversity can serve as a resource for adapting to new conditions if global systems should change. The greater the diversity, the more likely it is that there might be a species that can adapt to the new conditions (see, for example, Reaka-Kudla, Wilson, and Wilson 1997; Soule 1989; Wilson and Frances 1988).

This analogy is useful for understanding the importance of norms and values that encourage the preservation of diverse viewpoints (for example, broad resource definition and symbolic diversity). The more diverse and varied the perspectives in a community, the more likely there will exist resources within the community to confront unanticipated problems. Thus, norms or values that foster an environment of multiple perspectives, rotating leadership roles, and inclusiveness help maintain diverse gifts, skills, or perspectives in the community. These skills, although they may not seem important to solving a current issue, may become important for meeting future needs. Norms that encourage dispersed capacity among all group members also preserve potential for addressing future issues. Albert Hirschman's analysis of the creation and transformation of social energy reflects this principle (see Hirschman 1983). Opportunities for leadership enhance an individual's capacity. Even when the organisations or structures that gave rise to these leadership opportunities disappear, the potential built by this influence remains in the community for addressing future issues.

A comparison between a hypothetical patron or elite-dominated community with one that has a dispersed leadership and norms of rotating and multiple leadership roles provides a good example of this feature of social capital. A patron-dominated group cannot incorporate diverse perspectives into the decision making structure as well as a dispersed or democratic group. Thus, a patron-dominated group cannot contain as much potential for creative problem-solving in its decision-making system. In addition, although a patron-dominated system may mobilise much faster than a community that requires the input of multiple perspectives, the two systems differ with regards to their potential to address future issues. In a patron-dominated group, the community's potential to organise to meet future needs will be severely weakened if the dominant person or group is removed from the community (through emigration or death, for example). In contrast, in a community that contains norms encouraging multiple leadership roles or rotating leadership, a greater proportion of the community will have had opportunity to engage in leadership activities, analysis, or facilitation. As a result, if one or two members leave, the community's ability to mobilise will still remain relatively high.

The value of social capital norms (for example, symbolic diversity, inclusiveness, broad resource definition, or rotating leadership norms) should not be judged solely on the strength of a community's ability to mobilise to address a current issue. It is also important to examine how the norms or values inherent in a community might preserve potential in the community to address future issues.

Definition Summary

Based on the above descriptions, we can develop a list of indicators or components necessary for analyzing a community's social capital. Each individual indicator is a necessary but not sufficient component of strong social capital.

- dense and overlapping social networks
- flexible and permeable boundaries in organisational structures and social responsibility
- norms of trust
- norms of reciprocity
- norms of broad resource definition
- norms of symbolic diversity
- norms of inclusiveness
- horizontal (two-way) relationships
- "citizen" quality relationships across organisational levels
- norms of participatory decision-making and analysis
- norms and values contributing to a quality-of-life framework which emphasises balancing the spheres of interest (environmental, economic, political, social)

Factors that strengthen or weaken these different components in a community or group influence a community's social capital. By developing a framework of analysis for NGO programmes, we can begin to understand how specific NGO programmes may influence a community's social capital, even if the goals of the NGO programme are not implicitly directed at these aspects.

NGOs and Social Capital – A Theoretical Perspective

Most NGOs do not specifically emphasise strengthening social capital as a goal of their work. Nevertheless, the presence of an NGO programme in a community or region will have some influence on the nature of the social relationships, the norms, and the values in the community as an inadvertent byproduct of the principal programme priorities (Wall, Ferrazzi, and Sschryer 1998). Although many researchers cite the importance of social capital for community development, there has been relatively little analysis of how a specific NGO presence may influence the social capital levels in a community or region. Given the social capital theory discussed earlier, we can infer that a programme can positively influence social capital levels if structures or programmes promote information flow throughout a community, reduce power differentials, and build dispersed capacity. How these components relate to social capital formation and NGO programmes will be explored in greater detail in the following sections.

Social Networks and Trust

NGOs are not faceless entities that interact in some amorphous form with a community or group. NGO programme plans are implemented through the actions and interactions of specific individuals (such as development officials, extension officers, or government representatives). The levels of trust embedded in the social relationships among these specific individuals and individuals in the communities or population influence the degree of receptivity to the programme. Putnam's study in Italy suggests that local governments were more effective in northern Italy because government officials were more closely integrated into broad social networks (Putnam 1993a). Joshua Winchell noted that the more socially integrated extension workers are in a community, the more likely farmers will trust the extensionists and be willing to work with them (Winchell 1996). His findings imply that not only must the extensionists be known in the community, they must also be trusted and respected. Alberto Mutti describes individuals or institutions that have high levels of trust invested in them as "trust diffusers" (Mutti 1998). These trust diffusers are important for mediating community-government interactions and mobilising community members to engage in collective action. For NGO development workers, establishing trust and integrating into broad social networks can help increase social capital reserves in a community or region by expanding networks and increasing trust.

Power Differentials and the Quality of Relationships

Although social network integration is necessary, it is not sufficient for tapping into the social capital reserves of a community or target population. The quality of these networks will also affect social capital reserves (Butler Flora 1995). Power differentials embedded in the relationships between development personnel and community or target populations can inhibit trust formation, limit the potential for reciprocal exchanges, and create one-way relationships leading to vertical or hierarchical social capital (Duncan 1996; Matthews 1996; Eyben and Ladbury 1995). Although he does not use social capital vocabulary, Robert Chambers's critique of the professionalism and professional development programmes emphasises the problems inherent in low social-network integration and high power differentials (Chambers 1993). NGO programmes that emphasise community strengths can develop *citizen* relationships that reduce power differentials between NGOs and communities (Vergara 1994). In contrast, when NGO programmes emphasise community weaknesses, *beneficiary* relationships develop that increase power differentials and promote vertical network formation.

Informal Interaction

Research in social or community learning has begun to validate the importance of informal interpersonal interactions in promoting community learning, reflection, and analysis (Falk and Harrison 1998; Green 1998). Interestingly, most professional development programmes attempt to create learning through formal interactions (such as workshops, seminars, or trainings), and in the process minimise the role of informal interactions in their programme structures. While there is a role for formal structures in community learning, this emphasis on the short-term and formal involvement underestimates the role that informal interactions and long-term interactions can play in social learning (Falk and Harrison 1998; Frankfort-Nachmias and Palen 1993; Booth and Owen 1985).

Summary

The value of the social network integration of the change agent, the role of informal interactions, and community learning and trust-building are not necessarily new concepts within the fields of development, and they are generally assumed to be important for increasing the effectiveness of technology transfer. Interpreting these principles through the lens of social capital theory, however, suggests that these aspects may have implications that reach beyond simple technology adoption. An NGO programme that negatively affects the social capital levels in a community or region can depress the potential of the region or community to build a strong civil society. NGO programmes may thus need to be evaluated not only in terms of whether they have accomplished their goals related to technology transfer or economic development, but also in terms of whether they have positively or negatively affected a community's or region's social capital and subsequent civil society.

For example, power differentials structured into development programmes can lead to the creation of hierarchical social capital. In an analysis of community-based conservation programmes around the world, Katrina Brandon pointed out that when large, powerful outside organisations became involved in community conservation programmes, these programmes almost invariably failed. One contributing factor to this failure was the negative effect that the power differentials embedded in these large, external organisations had on community or regional social dynamics and subsequent social capital (Brandon 1998).

Ironically, this leads to the possibility that NGO projects labelled successes on narrow sets of criteria may actually reduce social capital and thereby depress community or regional potential. For example, an evangelical NGO may enter a community in Latin America and implement an economic development project. The project may be an economic success in the sense of increasing economic production in the community, but if the NGO chooses to work only with members of a specific church, tensions among the various churches in the community may increase. If so, then the economic growth might come at the expense of increased interdenominational tension or conflict. Conversely, NGO projects labelled failures may actually enhance community development potential if their presence creates higher levels of healthy social capital in a region. For example, an NGO project aimed at wildlife conservation or preventing deforestation through environmental education may not succeed in its objectives to stem deforestation. But if in the course of the project farmers from a variety of different communities establish social networks, these new networks may be the source of some form of future mobilisation. By increasing the range of social networks in a region, NGO efforts may strengthen the regional social capital, even if they fail in their immediate goal.

The MCC Yapacani Regional Development Programme

Overview

The Mennonite Central Committee (MCC) is the relief, development, and service arm of the Mennonite and Brethren-in-Christ Churches of the United States and Canada. MCC has approximately 1,400 workers based in 57 countries. Founded in 1917 as a means to provide relief to Mennonites facing famine and war in the Ukraine, MCC's programmes now cover a wide range of arenas from disaster relief and material-aid programmes to international development programmes in education, health, agriculture, peace and justice, relief, and job creation. As a church-based organisation, MCC's mission statement is motivated by Christian values. Mennonites believe that the Bible calls Christians to serve people who are in need. Consistent with its faith-based values, most of MCC's programmes are centred in material relief or economic development activities.

MCC Bolivia – Programme History

MCC's Bolivia programme is one of its largest country programmes, comprising 60 to 70 expatriate and national personnel. The headquarters for MCC Bolivia is located in Santa Cruz, the principal city of the eastern lowlands.

Prior to the mid-1990s, MCC Bolivia's rural development policy emphasised the establishment of integrated development programmes centred in zones of spontaneous colonisation in the eastern tropical lowlands of Bolivia. Since 1952, landless farmers from the Bolivian highlands had been migrating to the relatively under-developed eastern lowlands in search of land and opportunity not available to them in the crowded highlands. Beginning in the 1960s, MCC worked in different colonisation zones to provide agricultural, health, and educational assistance to these groups of struggling and extremely isolated farmers.

Traditionally, the MCC Bolivia rural development programme placed in each zone a small team of MCC workers, including an on-site co-ordinator and an interdisciplinary team, which might vary in size from five to forty people. In addition to supervising the interdisciplinary co-ordination among specialties, the regional co-ordinator elaborated the programmatic philosophy, provided logistical and emotional support to the MCC staff in the zone, and represented MCC at various institutional or formal events. MCC's programmes were based on a transfer-of-technology paradigm in which members of the MCC team were considered extensionists and promoters who trained farmers and community members in appropriate health, education, or agricultural practices. Individual MCC team members typically lived in a specific rural community and usually focused their work on a few surrounding communities. In addition to their community work, the volunteers attempted to co-ordinate their work as a team to address cross-discipline issues throughout the zone.

For most of its history, MCC Bolivia did not have an articulated goal of improving community social capital. MCC Bolivia programmes emphasised increasing economic production through technical development in agriculture, health, or education. Still, MCC's work informally acknowledged the key role that social network integration, reducing power differentials, and reciprocal relationships can play in strengthening communities and improving community development efforts. New MCC workers would often be told that relationships would be the most important part of their work or encouraged to take time to get to know the people, their neighbours, the community. "Take part in community events. Visit people. All these things will be important parts of your work." Therefore, even though the main emphasis of MCC's programmes revolved around economic development, certain aspects of the informal organisational philosophy had positive implications for strengthening social capital. The tension between the articulated economic development goals and the informal relational goals and subsequent effect on social capital is particularly evident within the subject of our case study – The Yapacani Integrated Development Programme.

The MCC Yapacani Integrated Rural Development Programme

Location and History of Yapacani

The Yapacani colonisation zone is located about 120 kilometres northwest of the city of Santa Cruz and has been a relatively isolated region due to the barrier posed by the broad and winding Yapacani River, located on the eastern border of the colonisation zone. The construction of a one-kilometre bridge over the Yapacani River in 1968 allowed increased access to the zone. Since the early 1970s the zone's population steadily and rapidly increased and in 1999 was estimated at approximately 40,000 people. Nearly 10,000 families lived in 122 rural communities scattered throughout the 8,000 square kilometres of the zone plus the principal town of Yapacani (population 10,000). The zone consists primarily of a tropical rainforest ecozone. Although there is some topographical variation, the zone mainly comprises low-lying periodic wetlands and swamps. Its principal products are rice and cattle. For a period of 10 years, from 1990 to 1999, MCC sponsored an integrated development programme in the Yapacani zone. In 1999, for a variety of reasons, MCC discontinued the programme.

MCC Yapacani Programme Description and History

In 1989 MCC received an invitation from the Yapacani colonisation zone's rural governing body, *la Central de Colonizadores,* to send agricultural and rural development workers to the Yapacani zone under its auspices. MCC exploratory trips suggested that the subcentral of Cascabel, located in the northern section of the Yapacani zone, might be a suitable place for an MCC integrated development programme. The northern section was the least accessible and least developed part of the Yapacani zone. The swamps, mosquitos, and relatively unproductive soils had discouraged earlier colonisation settlements, and this section of the colonisation zone was settled only when more accessible and fertile lands had already been colonised. Communities in the northern zone were generally less than 10 years old.

In addition to running a traditional extension and rural development programme in the northern section of the Yapacani zone, MCC also envisioned promoting institutional strengthening with a local health and agriculture NGO called Educacion, Salud, y Agricultura (ESA). ESA trained promoters in agriculture and health issues and conducted community workshops throughout the zone. In 1990, ESA was organisationally weak and struggling to find funding, and the original MCC Yapacani team began to collaborate with ESA. The hope was that ESA would become stronger and MCC would gain legitimacy by working through a local NGO.

Consequently, the MCC Yapacani programme contained two distinct features. One feature consisted of a traditional MCC extension and rural development programme based in the northern section of the Yapacani zone where programme personnel were placed in local communities and carried out community development activities centred in agriculture, health, and education. The second feature consisted of institutional strengthening and regional focus. MCC personnel involved in this aspect were based in the town of Yapacani and collaborated with local institutions such as ESA, the hospital, or *la Central* and promoted institutional strengthening both at the level of the Yapacani institutions and at the level of the widespread community organisations.

Volunteers engaged in the institutional strengthening component lived in the central town, attended numerous inter-institutional meetings with other development professionals, and travelled to many communities across the colonisation zone. Primary emphasis was given to formal interactions – meetings with other professionals and workshops in communities. In contrast, the community-based extension personnel lived in rural communities and tended to focus their efforts around that single community plus a small number of neighbouring communities.

The Yapacani team remained relatively small. Throughout the 10-year period of MCC involvement in the Yapacani programme, the MCC team comprised an average of four to six workers who lived either in the main town and worked at a zone-wide level or who lived in rural communities and worked at a local level.

Social Capital and the MCC Yapacani Programme: A Synopsis

Programme structures and assumptions have important implications for social capital development. The transfer-of-technology and growth-with-equity programmatic assumptions used by MCC Bolivia have been criticised by researchers for not addressing structural or political inequities and for the power differentials often created by these types of programmes and subsequent distortions of community dynamics (see Chambers 1993). Nevertheless, MCC's programmes typically enjoyed considerable support by both community members and other organisations. It was not necessarily the soundness of the MCC extension programmes that contributed to this perception of success, however, but the positive effects the programmes had on community social capital. Although social capital strengthening was not an objective of the MCC programmes, the traditional programme structures, such as an emphasis on MCC personnel living in rural communities, placed volunteers in positions where they could influence the formation of social capital. These programme structures strengthened social capital by contributing to the creation of successful and trusted initiatives. On the other hand, as a complex and highly dynamic programme, the MCC Yapacani programme had other elements and structures that inhibited social capital development.

Elements that Enhanced Community Social Capital

According to our framework, programmatic elements that strengthen social capital are those that reduce power differentials between NGO personnel and community members, that promote diverse, overlapping horizontal networks, and that build dispersed capacity within the community. Within the MCC Yapacani programme, these elements included low resource availability, placing volunteers in communities, the practice of personal and programme values that emphasised power devolution (for example, servanthood values from their faith-based perspective or a simple living ethic), shared collaborative activities, and emphasis on relationships. Ecumenical appreciation by volunteers and acceptance of long-term, informal interactions present in communities also strengthened social network overlap and thus enhanced community social capital reserves.

Low Budget and Minimal Programme Resources

Economic wealth and status are one source of power. MCC generally operated with an extremely low budget. Programmes usually allocated enough for the personal maintenance of programme personnel, but with few, if any, additional resources for programme infrastructure or funding projects. This emphasis on low resource availability made MCC personnel based in communities doing extension more dependent on their neighbours for carrying out programme activities. This, in turn, encouraged reciprocal exchanges and reduced power differentials between the volunteers and the community. The MCC personnel were not the only ones who had something to give, for the community members also had something to offer MCC personnel. The low resources also encouraged more creative approaches to problem solving that drew on social capital reserves for successful implementation. This enhanced the social capital reserves in communities and demonstrated the value of collective mobilisation or co-operative networks.

Placing Personnel in Communities

Assigning MCC workers to live in communities placed them in relationally dense contexts. The opportunity for forming relationships and for deep integration into rural social networks was much greater for community-based MCC workers than for volunteers placed in the large town who made only periodic visits to communities. Volunteer integration into the community social networks facilitated network expansion and allowed for the volunteer perspectives and insights to be integrated into the community decision-making matrix. Placing volunteers in communities also reduced power differentials between the community members and the MCC staff. Living as neighbours provided an equality status to volunteers that helped off-set MCC's professional power, allowing horizontal relationships to form.

Values

MCC workers often possessed personal values or attitudes that intentionally sought to reduce power differentials between themselves and community members. For example, as a Mennonite faith-based organisation, MCC recruits place a high priority on service and servanthood. As a consequence, MCC personnel in Bolivia often intentionally sought to place themselves in positions of relatively low power in community dynamics; rather than coming with an attitude of "we are here to teach you," they came with an attitude of "we are here to serve you." This value stance had the effect of helping to promote horizontal relationships between MCC workers and community members by reducing the inherent power that MCC personnel brought to the context as relatively highly educated, United States or Canadian citizens. The reduced power differentials made it easier to form horizontal relationships with community members, particularly the more marginal and silenced elements in the community.

Egalitarian Involvements

MCC workers usually brought a facilitative or participatory ethos to their community level involvements. A former country director once commented that "relationships are built through shared activities," meaning that volunteers should work collaboratively with community members. Volunteers thus worked alongside farmers harvesting their crops, clearing the land, or helping out with community projects such as clearing boundary lines or repairing school buildings. By working side by side with community members in shared activities rather than as supervisors or trainers, volunteers reduced power differentials between themselves and community members and helped promote the creation of horizontal networks with the community members. The egalitarian involvements also helped create greater trust between community members and MCC workers. During community interviews, farmers often stated how much they valued the fact that volunteers would work alongside them and go out of their way to relate to people collaboratively.

Norms that Emphasised the Importance of Relationships

MCC, as an institution, placed a priority on the importance of relationship formation in its programme strategies. Volunteers were encouraged to seek out opportunities to build personal relationships as part of their work. This validation of relationship building (or social network integration) meant that volunteers were free to invest time and energy into activities that promoted increased social network integration. Still, even though this validation was present within MCC as an institution, it is important to note that relationship building was never formally incorporated into the planning and outcome evaluations of the MCC programme. (This has implications later in the chapter when we analyse factors that contributed to the weakening of social capital.)

Ecumenical Approaches

MCC volunteers were faith-based workers. As such, they naturally participated in the communities' religious life, which is of course an integral component of community life (Salamon 1989; Wuthnow 1994; Beyer 1992). The volunteers' willingness to participate in community spiritual life gave them greater credibility with community members and increased their acceptance among the people.

Religious differences can also be a divisive force within communities or societies (see, for example, Dunn and Morgan 1991; Perez-Agote 1986; Vellenga 1983). The two principal religious institutions represented in Yapacani communities were the Catholic and evangelical churches. These two church bodies have had a long history of conflict throughout Latin America, and it is relatively rare for evangelical and Catholic social networks to overlap in rural communities (Jantzi et al. 1999; Jantzi 1995). This dynamic was evident in the Yapacani communities where MCC worked (Hertzler 1995). In the interest of working with all the community members and not appearing to take sides with one group or the other, MCC personnel living in communities usually adopted an ecumenical approach and supported both denominations through attendance and participation in activities sponsored by both churches. They also carried out community-wide activities, both secular and religious, that incorporated both church bodies. These ecumenical practices encouraged the creation of overlapping networks in communities that crossed these religious boundaries, fostered increased tolerance among members of the different churches, and strengthened the norm of inclusiveness. These factors in turn helped increase the ease of community mobilisation and organisation to address community-wide issues.

Informal and Long-term Interactions Versus the Legitimisation of Presence

Placing volunteers in communities and emphasising the importance of personal relationships helped volunteers integrate into the informal and long-term community networks where much of the collective learning occurs, and this integration helped facilitate enhanced community reflection and analysis of issues. However, although the MCC volunteers were placed in communities, they legitimised their presence by depicting themselves as development professionals (rather than church workers for example). This particular strategy for legitimising their presence forced certain decisions and strategies on volunteers that led to outcomes which also weakened social capital.

Elements that Inhibited Community Social Capital

While there were elements within the MCC programme that strengthened social capital, other elements were also present that limited social capital formation in communities. Elements within the MCC programme that reduced social capital levels were ones that reinforced power differentials and inhibited volunteer integration into community social networks.

High Resource Availability: The Donor Project

Although the community-level aspect of the Yapacani programme emphasised low resource availability, the regional focus and the strategy of legitimising MCC personnel as development professionals simultaneously encouraged structures that drew on assumptions of high resource availability. These assumptions increased power differentials and inhibited healthy social capital formation. One example of this dynamic is the emphasis on donor financing for projects.

Many NGOs in Bolivia had created a specialised industry in writing projects in the name of rural and urban communities to be funded by international donors (Bebbington 1997). However, much of this funding was used for the maintenance of the NGOs themselves (salaries, vehicles, travel expenses, and so forth). Consequently, many communities in the Yapacani zone were suspicious of the goals of these NGOs. They suspected that these organisations did not necessarily have the best interests of the communities at heart but were more interested in maintaining their own organisations through these funds.

Persistent corruption in Bolivia created an environment of suspicion and distrust surrounding any type of money or resource allocation. Rural colonist communities were highly suspicious of anyone and any institution that controlled money destined for others (Hertzler 1995). They believed these institutions or individuals must, of necessity, be stealing or embezzling available funds. This suspicion made it difficult for communities and some NGOs to work together when large amounts of financial or material resources were at stake.

The MCC personnel in the Yapacani programme reasoned that communities needed to take charge of their own development rather than rely on these NGOs of whom they were suspicious. According to the MCC workers at the time, this meant that communities should be able to write and submit their own projects for foreign funding. The argument was that this would make the communities less dependent on NGOs.

This contention was challenged, however, when project proposals written by (usually semi-literate) community farmers had to be given to MCC workers for revision. MCC workers then presented the revised proposals to international donors for financing. Consequently, communities were still dependent on an NGO in the project donor process. The fact that MCC now served as the link between the community proposals and the international financiers meant that community suspicion about corruption devolved onto MCC personnel. Many of the projects took a long time to receive funding, and MCC Yapacani faced some credibility problems when community members started demanding money they felt had been promised to them through MCC workshops.

Although the rationale for this project emphasis had been to allow communities access to the donor resources, MCC still essentially acted as the sole communicating body between the communities and the donors. The fact that the programme required MCC to act as a "gatekeeper" for access to international donor funds unintentionally created vertical networks between community members and Yapacani MCC workers reminiscent of Duncan's (1996) vertical social capital networks found in zones of persistent poverty (Duncan 1996). In addition, because MCC personnel had placed themselves in a position of gatekeeper to funds, communities occasionally suspected that the MCC workers were embezzling or misappropriating "their" (the community members') funds. This suspicion often eroded the levels of trust that MCC personnel had been able to establish with rural community members.

Zone-wide Coverage

Although one feature in the MCC programme placed volunteers in rural communities, the programme also contained a more region-focused component that placed personnel in the central town to operate on a zone-wide level. The three or four volunteers living in the main town were expected to cover a zone of 10,000 families, which meant that they were not able to integrate very well into any single community social network. Communities did not get to know the volunteers when their efforts were at a zone-wide level and consequently did not trust them as much.

Overemphasis on Formal Workshops

Due to the emphasis on zone-wide coverage in one part of its programme, MCC involvement in many communities was limited to infrequent, high-intensity workshops with little or no interaction outside of these programmed workshops. Although the workshops did have a positive impact in some communities, the high-intensity format divorced from the informal, longer-term follow up meant that the workshops did not necessarily contribute to strengthening the local social capital available in communities as much as they might have.

Interchangeability of Personnel

Even though the MCC in Yapacani informally acknowledged the value of relationships and a relational approach in its programmes, the fact that it was never formalised and that MCC personnel often legitimised their presence through depicting themselves as development professionals meant that there existed an underlying assumption within the programme that personnel were inherently interchangeable. Consequently, in some areas of the programme a series of short-term personnel were used interchangeably to continue a process or programme. These frequent transitions in MCC personnel inhibited relationship formation, trust building, and social network integration, which in turn minimised the potential of the MCC workers to engage in social capital strengthening.

Rural Population Transience

The MCC programmes also faced problems due to the constant turnover of people in Yapacani rural communities. "It is difficult to do community development when the community won't sit still to be developed," quipped one volunteer in a quarterly report. One of the inherent assumptions in the community development programmes in MCC Yapacani was that the people with whom MCC would be working would be the same individuals over a long time span. The institutional strengthening approaches taken by MCC also assumed that the institutional personnel would remain relatively constant during this period of accompaniment.

Both of these stability assumptions, at the community level and at the institutional level, were inconsistent with the reality of the Yapacani colonisation zone. For example, the MCC health worker who was to work in collaboration with the hospital continually expressed frustration in her reports that every year she had to begin working again with a new set of personnel due to Ministry of Health policies which rotated hospital personnel on a yearly basis. Just as she was forming a level of trust and a working relationship with the rural training staff, the annual rotations would occur and she would have to start all over working with new people who brought their own assumptions and agendas.

The rural communities were not immune to this dynamic. Colonisation zones experience frequent rural population transience. High community turnover affected MCC's attempts to build relationships in communities. MCC worked in one northern zone community where over half of the community farms changed hands during a two-year period. From a social capital perspective, it is difficult to form relationships and build trust in communities that are undergoing rapid turnover. Although volunteers were able to form relationships with specific individuals and integrate themselves into community social networks, the high levels of transience in the communities made these tasks more difficult. High population transience also leads to weaker social networks in the community and inhibits social capital (Butler Flora 1995; Freudenberg and Jones 1991), implying that communities experiencing higher transience would contain lower social capital reserves and thus make it more difficult to efficiently utilise other forms of capital development.

Quince and Challavito: A Tale of Two Communities

Social capital issues can be highlighted by comparing the MCC experience in two rural Yapacani communities. Quince de Agosto and Challavito are neighbouring communities in the northern section of the Yapacani zone. They have been settled for roughly the same length of time and have similar natural resources and economic capital. MCC worked in both communities for at least six years. However, the two communities demonstrated radically different responses to MCC programmes.

MCC programmes carried out in Challavito yielded encouraging results. The community took the initiative to design, develop, and implement several community-based projects. In contrast, Quince de Agosto was an extremely problematic experience for MCC workers. In 1996 tensions and frustration between MCC workers and community members reached the point that MCC made a decision to discontinue its work there. This is particularly interesting because the Quince de Agosto leaders were among the first to lobby MCC to set up a rural development programme in the Yapacani colonisation zone. Reports from early volunteers in the zone contained many positive references to the potential of Quince de Agosto. Challavito at the time was thought to have less potential. Why this difference between two similar, neighbouring communities? Contributing factors can be divided into two parts: (1) community characteristics, and (2) subtle differences in MCC's programmatic presence. Both affected social capital potential in the communities.

Community Characteristics

The two communities possessed very different levels of social capital; this was reflected in their demographic and social structures. Quince was a relatively large colonisation community of 80 families who represented a wide range of economic levels and social status. A strong, authoritarian leader dominated the community. Other members had few opportunities to participate in leadership roles, and there were weak norms related to rotating or dispersed leadership structures. Based upon the social capital analysis presented earlier, these characteristics would indicate a fairly low level of community social capital.

Challavito was a smaller community of about 35 families. The community was much more homogenous in terms of economic levels and social status. While community homogeneity is not an indicator in and of itself of strong social capital, a homogenous community is more likely to have overlapping horizontal networks that facilitate information flow. In addition, there was a tradition within the community of diverse leadership and strong norms related to rotating leadership roles. These factors contributed to higher levels of social capital in the community. MCC workers noted that it was much easier to work in Challavito than in Quince. Challavito community members demonstrated greater creative analysis during community workshops and were more likely to take advantage of the available MCC technical resources.

Differences in MCC Programming

Although MCC had similar programmes in each community, outcomes were influenced by several significant differences in social capital pertaining to MCC's different mode of operation in each community. One of these factors was the relative continuity of the MCC personnel in each community and their integration into the social networks in the communities. MCC placed volunteers in both Quince and Challavito for the first six years of the Yapacani programme. However, the quality of the volunteer presence in each community differed significantly. In Quince, a succession of short-term volunteers lived in the community for periods of several months to one year. Eight different MCC workers worked in the community over a six-year period. The quantity of volunteers and the relatively short periods involved meant that it was difficult for trust to build between the community and the specific MCC workers, making it difficult for volunteers to integrate into the social networks of the community. In addition, the two volunteers who did live in the community for relatively longer periods (between two and three years) focused primarily on zone-wide work. They spent most of their time visiting communities throughout the entire Yapacani zone and relatively little time in Quince itself. As a result, even though they were living in the community for longer periods, their continued absences made it difficult to sustain adequate follow-up in Quince and spend time informally interacting with the community members. Nor could they take the time to create the high levels of trust or social network integration necessary for social capital formation.

In contrast to the situation in Quince, Challavito had a much more stable and long-term MCC personnel presence. Two MCC workers lived in succession in the community for three years each. The longer time frames allowed for greater trust and social integration to build. In addition, both three-year volunteers made a conscious decision to focus their work on Challavito. Therefore, although they did visit other communities in the region, they were much more involved in community life. The time spent in Challavito allowed for greater social network integration, more thorough follow-up of programmes, and greater trust to form. Consequently, the volunteers in Challavito functioned in a manner that was most consistent with strengthening community social capital. They integrated into the social networks of the community, they interacted informally with the community members outside of the planned programme activities, and they built greater levels of trust and co-operation between themselves and community members.

Summary

Social capital enhancement has a multiplier effect on the impact of other forms of development. Much of MCC's reputation for success originated from the soundness of its agricultural, health, and education programmes, but more important, from the unintentional social capital strengthening that occurred due to the assumptions that shaped its programme structures (Kreider and Goosen 1988) – this in spite of the fact that the social capital sphere was not formally acknowledged in MCC Bolivia's programme plans. Consequently, MCC Bolivia found itself in the ironic position where workers' efforts to become more professional in its rural development programmes (working at a zone-wide level and presenting themselves as development professionals rather than church workers) led to the creation of programme structures which inhibited social capital strengthening. Yet the social capital strengthening aspect of MCC's work had contributed to MCC's reputation for success in the first place.

The mixture of programme approaches within the overall Yapacani programme created an environment where some elements in the Yapacani programme helped strengthen social capital while other elements inhibited social capital development. The elements that strengthened community social capital were those that reduced power differentials between MCC personnel and community members, encouraged the formation of horizontal relationships, built high levels of trust, and encouraged the formation of norms of reciprocity. These elements included:

- low resource availability;
- relationally dense contexts for volunteer placement;
- values or norms possessed by the volunteers that sought to devolve power or lessen power differentials;
- egalitarian or collaborative involvement in community affairs;
- norms that emphasised the importance of relationships;

• informal and long-term interactions in communities; and
• ecumenical relationships.

Elements that inhibited community social capital reinforced power differentials, created vertical patron-client networks, and inhibited the formation of trust or relationships between the MCC personnel and the communities. These elements included:

• assumptions of high resource availability (for example, the donor-project emphasis);
• a zone-wide orientation that inhibited social integration into local networks;
• an overemphasis on infrequent, formal interactions in programming;
• frequent MCC personnel transitions; and
• frequent turnover in institutional or community membership.

The single factor that most influenced social capital formation was the dynamic of the power differentials between MCC personnel and community members. By dint of who they were, where they were coming from, and the resources they represented, MCC personnel possessed considerable power relative to the communities where they worked. Those aspects of the programme structure that sought to reduce power differentials between MCC workers and community members increased social network integration and the formation of horizontal networks based in trust and reciprocity. This consequently served to increase healthy forms of community social capital. Those aspects of the programme that maintained or reinforced power differentials often served to set up vertical patron-client relationships and subsequently limited community social capital development.

IMPLICATIONS FOR CHRISTIAN NGOS

The principles distilled from the theoretical development of social capital and its application to the MCC Bolivia case study provides some important insights for other Christian NGOs. These insights can be applied to different NGOs in the form of four questions:

Do Programme Values Emphasise Service and Minimising of Power Differentials?

Reducing power differentials as much as possible between NGO personnel and community members (or other institutions) is important for creating horizontal relationships, trust, and social network integration. A Christian NGO that emphasises service and servanthood from a position of relative powerlessness will be more effective at reducing power differentials than an NGO that maintains its power or uses it in such ways that vertical relationships are created between the NGO and the local communities.

Does the NGO Operate with Assumptions of Resource Abundance or Scarcity?

Para-church mission organisations frequently need to use development and mission models that emphasise results for which the organisation can take credit in order to continue to generate financial resources. Hence they are frequently trapped in a situation in which they have to spend money in order to continue to generate income. This makes it very difficult to function as a resource scarce organisation. It also means that the programmes carried out will disproportionately reflect programme-wide goals and objectives and high levels of specialisation in what they do best in order to deliver the goods and make a difference. These features militate against social capital creation. A more social capital friendly approach generally means that the organisation has to be willing to risk that its supporting constituency will not understand or share the perspective from which it works thus putting in jeopardy its long-term survival.

Ecumenical Orientation

Religious organisations are frequently caught in the religious/ethnic/social po-larities that exist in communities. Unless organisations make special efforts, they will likely heighten community divisions rather than ameliorate them. If NGOs are to contribute to the strengthening of civil society, they must actively work to bridge religious and social differences in communities and regions. This appears to be a basic condition for social capital creation.

The Creation of New Leadership Opportunities

Most NGOs and mission organisations do create new positions for leadership because the focus on religious or social change usually includes the institutionalisation of new organisations, whether development related (such as health, education, or water committees) or church related (such as pastor, youth worker, or evangelist). Albert Hirschman contends that even when these efforts are not successful and the local organisations disappear or people leave them, indi-viduals do gain some leadership or group experience that can be used later in a variety of community contexts as they work at future problems (Hirschman 1983).

This case study suggests that Christian NGOs can indeed play an important role in strengthening civil society through enhancing community or regional so-cial capital. The religious orientation implies that Christian NGOs can have some voice or some legitimacy in addressing religious tensions or divisions in commu-nities. The values and norms that Christian workers bring with them can also give rise to stances that seek to promote service and servanthood and thus unintention-ally reduce the power differentials that might exist between the NGO personnel and local communities.

However, it is important to note that Christian NGOs only have the potential to play a role in strengthening social capital (and consequently civil society) when their stances are consistent with the criteria described in this paper. Unfortunately, many Christian NGOs may operate in ways that strengthen power differentials, reduce social network integration, or heighten divisions between groups in communities. Thus, it is important for each Christian NGO to analyse its programme structures not only in light of its stated programme goals, but also in terms of how these structures might be inadvertently contributing to social capital creation or destruction. When Christian NGO programmes maintain unhealthy types of structures or norms, they may, in spite of their best intentions, end up weakening regional social capital, inhibiting the formation of civil society, and consequently, undermining the prospects for development.

REFERENCES

Bebbington, Anthony. 1997. "New States, New NGOs? Crises and Transitions Among Rural Development NGOs in the Andean Region." *World Development* 25/11: 1755–65.

———. 1998. "Sustaining the Andes: Social Capital and Policies for Rural Regeneration in Bolivia. *Mountain Research and Development* 18/2: 173–81.

Beyer, Peter. 1992. "The Global Environment as a Religious Issue: A Sociological Analysis." *Religion* 22/1: 1–19.

Booth, Norman, and Edward Owen. 1985. "The Relevance of Formal and Informal Networks for Community Development: Lessons Learned from Three Cases. *Research in Rural Sociological Development* 2: 159–72.

Brandon, Katrina. 1998. *Parks in Peril: People, Politics and Protected Areas*. Washington, D.C.: Island Press.

Brown, R. B., X. Xu, and J. F. Toth. 1998. "Lifestyle Options and Economic Strategies: Subsistence Activities in the Mississippi Delta." *Rural Sociology* 63/4: 599–623.

Butler Flora, Cornelia. 1995. "Social Capital and Sustainability: Agriculture and Communities in the Great Plains and the Corn Belt." *Research in Rural Sociology and Development: A Research Annual* 6.

———. 1997. Building social capital: The Importance of entrepreneurial social development. *Rural Development News* 21/2: 1–3.

Chambers, Robert. 1993. *Challenging the Professions: Frontiers for Rural Development*. London: Intermediate Technology Publications.

Coleman, James. 1990. *Foundations of Social Theory*. Cambridge, Mass.: Harvard University Press.

Duncan, Cynthia. 1996. "Understanding Persistent Poverty: Social Class Context in Rural Communities." *Rural Sociology* 61/1: 103–24.

Dunn, Seamus, and Valerie Morgan. 1991. "The Social Context of Education in Northern Ireland." *European Journal of Education* 26/2: 179–90.

Eyben, Ruben, and Sharon Ladbury. 1995. "Popular Participation in Aid-assisted Projects: Why More in Theory than Practice?" In *Power and Participatory Development*, edited by N. Nelson and S. Wright, 192–201. London: Intermediate Technology Publications.

Falk, Ian, and Lesley Harrison. 1998. "Community Learning and Social Capital: 'Just Having a Little Chat.'" *Journal of Vocational Education and Training* 50/4: 609–27.

Flora, Jan. 1998. "Social Capital and Communities of Place." *Rural Sociology* 63/4: 481–506.

Frankfort-Nachmias, Chavam and John P. Palen. 1993. "Neighborhood Revitalization and the Community Question." *Journal of the Community Development Society* 24/1: 1–14.

Freudenburg, William R., and Robert Emmett Jones. 1991. "Criminal Behavior and Rapid Community Growth: Examining the Evidence." *Rural Sociology* 56/4: 619–45.

Fukuyama, Francis. 1995. *Trust: The Social Virtues and The Creation of Prosperity*. New York: The Free Press.

Gardner, John. 1996. "Building Community." *Community Education Journal* 23/3: 6–9.

Glaeser, Edward. 1999. *What Is Social Capital? The Determinants of Trust and Trustworthiness*. Cambridge, Mass.: National Bureau of Economic Research.

Green, Sebastian. 1998. "Community Practice: Opportunities for Community Building." *Maatskaplike Werk* 34/4: 362–69. First published in *Social Work* 34 (1989).

Hertzler, Douglas. 1995. "Settlers' Communities in the Bolivian Lowlands: Local Organizations, National Networks, and U.S. Intervention." Master's thesis, University of Iowa, Iowa City, Iowa.

Hirschman, Albert. 1983. "The Principle of Conservation and Mutation of Social Energy." *Grassroots Development* 7/2: 3–9.

Jantzi, Terrence. 1995. "Factors Influencing Forest Patch Conservation and Conservation Orientations Among Small-scale Landholders in Costa Rica." Master's thesis, Cornell University, Ithaca, New York.

———. 2000. "Local Program Theories and Social Capital: A Case Study of a Non-Governmental Organization in Eastern Bolivia." Ph.D. diss., Cornell University, Ithaca, New York.

Jantzi, Terrence, John Schelhas, and James Lassoie. 1999. "Environmental Values and Forest Patch Conservation in a Rural Costa Rican Community." *Agriculture and Human Values* 16/1: 29–39.

Kreider, Robert, and Rachel Goosen. 1988. *Hungry, Thirsty, a Stranger: The MCC Experience*. Scottdale, Pa.: Herald Press.

McKnight, John. 1995. *The Careless Society: Community and Its Counterfeits*. New York: Basic Books.

Mutti, Alberto. 1998. "Trust Diffusors." *Rassegna Italiana di Sociologia* 39/4: 533–49.

Narayan, Deepa, and Lant Pritchett. 1999. Cents and Sociability: Household Income and Social Capital in Rural Tanzania." *Economic Development and Cultural Change* 47/4: 871–97.

O'Brien, David J., Andrew Raedeke, and Edward W. Hassinger. 1998. "The Social Networks of Leaders in More or Less Viable Communities Six Years Later: A Research Note." *Rural Sociology* 63/1: 109–27.

Perez-Agote, Alfonso. 1986. "The Role of Religion in the Definition of a Symbolic Conflict." *Social Compass* 33/4: 419–35.

Putnam, Robert D. 1993a. *Making Democracy Work: Civic Traditions in Modern Italy*. Princeton, N.J.: University Press.

———. 1993b. "The Prosperous Community: Social Capital and Public Life. *American Prospect* 13: 35–42.

———. 1995. "Bowling Alone: America's Declining Social Capital." *Journal of Democracy* 6/1: 65–78.

Reaka-Kudla, Marjorie L., Don Wilson, and Edward Osborne Wilson, eds. 1997. *Biodiversity II: Understanding and Protecting Our Biological Resources*. Washington, D.C.: Joseph Henry Press.

Ritchey, Vance Marion. 1996. "Social Capital, Sustainability and Working Democracy: New Yardsticks." *Grassroots Development* 20/1: 2–9.

Salamon, Sonya. 1989. "What Makes Rural Communities Tick? *Rural Development Perspectives* 5/3: 19–24.

Schulman, Michael D., and Cynthia Anderson. 1999. "The Dark Side of the Force: A Case Study of Restructuring and Social Capital. *Rural Sociology* 64/3: 351–73.

Soule, Michael E. 1989. "Conservation Biology in the Twenty-first Century: Summary and Outlook." In *Conservation for the Twenty-first Century,* edited by D. Western and M. C. Pearl, chap. 1. New York: Oxford University Press.

Vellenga, Dorothy. 1983. "Racial and Ethnic Conflict in a Christian Missionary Community: Jamaican and Swiss-German Missionaries in the Basel Mission in the Gold Coast in the Mid-Nineteenth Century." *Studies in Third World Societies* 26: 201–45.

Vergara, Ricardo. 1994. "NGOs: Help or Hindrance for Community Development in Latin America?" *Community Development Journal* 29/4: 322–28.

Wall, Ellen, Gabriele Ferrazzi, and Frans Schryer. 1998. "Getting the Goods on Social Capital. *Rural Sociology* 63/2: 300–322.

Wilson, Arthur L. 1999. "Creating Identities of Dependency: Adult Education as a Knowledge-Power Regime." *International Journal of Lifelong Education* 18/2: 85–93.

Wilson, Edward, and Peter Frances. 1988. *Biodiversity.* Washington, D.C.: National Academy Press.

Winchel, Joshua. 1996. "The Influence of Change Agent Image on the Adoption of Conservation Practices in Western New York." Master's thesis, Cornell University, Ithaca, New York.

Woolcock, Michael. 1998. Social Capital and Economic Development: Toward a Theoretical Synthesis and Policy Framework." *Theory and Society* 27: 151–208.

Wuthnow, Robert. 1994. *Sharing the Journey: Support Groups and America's New Quest for Community.* New York: The Free Press.

15

MCC in the Land
of the "Ascending Dragon"

How Should Foreigners Promote Civil Society in Today's Vietnam?

Kenneth Martens Friesen

The ancient name for the city of Hanoi is Thang Long, the ascending dragon. Today, the whole of Vietnam is commonly known in Southeast Asia as the ascending dragon because of its growing assertiveness in the economic and political affairs of the region. Expectations for development in Vietnam run high, and many see in Vietnam the potential to become the next East Asian "miracle" economy. To what extent has civil society played a role in Vietnam's development? More particularly, what role might the Mennonite Central Committee (MCC), a Christian international NGO, play in the both the formation of civil society and in Vietnam's overall development? A case study of MCC's work in Vietnam demonstrates that effective social and economic development can take place even in the context of an authoritarian state in which civil society institutions play a relatively minor role. Moreover, though international NGOs like MCC should work to enhance the role of civil society as a long-run strategy, it may be more important in the short run for them to concentrate on relating effectively with government institutions.

The issues raised here are important because of the way civil society is often being portrayed these days as the new saviour of third-world nations. James Wolfensohn, president of the World Bank, stated in 1999 that "in all its forms, civil society is probably the largest single factor in development, if not in its monetary contribution, then certainly in its human contribution and its experience and history." Similarly, Alan AtKisson argues that "civil society makes a transformation to sustainability possible, because it is the place where many of humanity's best traits come forth, most strongly and most reliably" (AtKisson 1997, 289). In this view civil society is seen as the champion of human destiny, a force that challenges and confronts the transgressions of ineffective or heavy-handed states and best embodies humanity's desire for freedom and democracy.

329

Such platitudes raise many questions about the role civil society can and should play in the developing world today. Is the civil society model transferable across cultures and political systems? Can development occur only if civil society is present and vibrant? What kind of strategy should Christian organisations such as MCC take when civil society institutions, including religious ones, are severely restricted or co-opted by the state? Sometimes, as in the case of Vietnam, such questions can be quite specific. For example, how should MCC relate to the local church when the local church itself falls under the tight control of the state? These are questions the case study explores.

For the purposes of this analysis, civil society is understood as "the array of people's organizations, voluntary associations, clubs, self-help groups, religious bodies, representative organs, NGOs (non-governmental organizations), foundations and social movements which may be formal or informal in nature, and which are not part of government or political parties, and are not established to make profits for their owners" (Fowler 1997, 8). This understanding of civil society is shared by much of the international NGO community, perhaps in part because the roles of their institutions are highlighted and given prominence.

For Fowler, this definition of civil society fits well with a certain view of overall development, also shared by the international NGO community. Development is understood to be intrinsically participatory, empowering, and socially transformative in nature. Rather than being a simple process of linear growth, with known objectives being achieved through the injection of a series of well-tested inputs, development is instead seen to be a creative, dynamic, and multifaceted process of human and social change (Fowler 1996). It is no surprise, then, that civil society, with its underlying principles of community participation, transparency, accountability, and co-operation, would be seen as highly correlated with this broad view of development.

Such a high view of civil society somewhat naturally leads us to pit civil society over and against the state, seeing them as competing and antagonistic actors. Though Fowler himself does not presuppose it, such a polarisation between civil society and the state is often taken for granted. Philip Oxhorn, for example, describes civil society as collectively being able to "resist subordination" to the state and to "demand inclusion" into national political structures (Oxhorn 1995, 252–53). The state is thus viewed as a force determined to crush popular expression. Civil society, on the other hand, is seen as dedicated to enhancing and enabling virtues like freedom and democracy. Civil society actors and actions are idealised, while the state is vilified. Civil society positions are portrayed in the media as pure and untainted by self-interest in their noble efforts to achieve radical reform of corrupt governments.

Antonio Gramsci's ideas on civil society have supported this simplistic view. Gramsci argued that civil society is a public space where ideas can be translated into action. Writing in the context of fascist Italy in the 1930s, Gramsci held that though civil society is a public space, it is hardly a neutral space. Instead, civil society is often dominated by the state itself, which uses its coercive powers to dominate the direction of public opinion and therefore political and social life. In doing so, the state attempts to develop a hegemonic influence over society through a combination of coercion and consent. Gramsci argues that in order to resist the state's powerful control over society, civil society is a sphere where oppressed social groups, led by the working class and other progressive elements of society, can organise their opposition and form an alternative hegemony (Forgacs 1988).

Many of Gramsci's ideas were adopted by political dissidents in Eastern Europe prior to the end of the communist governments' era in those states. Social movements from the 1980s Solidarity movement in Poland to the August 2000 Peoples Revolt in Yugoslavia seem well explained by Gramsci. In the Third World, the 1986 People Power movement in the Philippines and the 1999 Reformisi movement in Indonesia seem also to fit this scheme. A Gramscian perspective argues that a regime falls when its leaders no longer can contain an alternative and competing ideology and power bloc. It is the role of progressive opponents to the regime to develop and nurture that alternative ideology.

Does the case of Vietnam also fit this mould? Some dissidents who left Vietnam seem to think so. They point out that the present regime uses its coercive power to persuade people to support its cause even as it quashes dissenting views. These same dissidents also seem to be leveraging their power base in an attempt to build up a civil society capable of producing an alternative philosophical and theoretical understanding of society within Vietnam. In doing so, it is hoped that enough resistance can be built towards the present regime to eventually re-compose it.

Dissidents and human rights groups in the West argue that civil society is seriously lacking in Vietnam, largely because the Vietnamese government tightly regulates domestic and international press, religion, and individual freedoms. Independent organisations are generally not tolerated if they exhibit interest in reforming the political system. Amnesty International reported that in 1999 there were at least 56 prisoners of conscience and possible prisoners of conscience held throughout the year. The United States Department of State reported that in 1999 several Protestant church leaders were arrested, and serious restrictions were enforced on Catholics, Cao Dai, Buddhist, and other religious traditions in Vietnam. No significant debate is tolerated over the political future of the country, and serious consequences often befall those who attempt to expand the influence of alternative political or social institutions.

With the general lack of individual freedoms in Vietnam today, it seems clear that civil society, as defined by Fowler, plays virtually no role in Vietnam's development. It is essential, however, to take a closer look at how Vietnamese society and institutions function. In the real world the division between the state and civil society is rarely so stark or unambiguous. In the case of Vietnam, equating the Vietnamese government and its many state-run institutions with the embodiment of malevolence and as the archenemy of civil society is at best problematic. It is certainly true that under the leadership of the Vietnamese Communist Party, the government in the north of Vietnam has had significant control over civic affairs for the past 45 years, and in the south since the country was reunified in 1975. But it is the way in which the government operates, and especially the role that state-directed institutions played in the development process, that must be better understood in order to realise the nature of civil involvement in Vietnam and the way in which a Christian NGO like MCC has responded within that context.

AN ALTERNATIVE PERSPECTIVE OF THE STATE AND CIVIL SOCIETY IN VIETNAM

Two noted long-term researchers of Vietnam, Adam Fforde and Douglas Porter, argue that while Western conceptions of civil society are useful, civil society cannot be seen as something entirely separate from the state in Vietnam. The reality of Vietnamese society, they say, is that civil society traditionally was, and still remains, "the way in which people within various structures used their position(s) to do things that they thought would benefit their or other communities" (Fforde and Porter 1994, 24). Fowler's description of civil society, on the other hand, assumes a strong demarcation between the state and civil society, a common assumption among definitions that emerge in the West. Vietnamese have long understood their relationship to the state differently. In the pre-colonial days each person was ultimately subject to the emperor, and the village structure was part of this hierarchical system (Truong Ngoc Nguyen 1994, 2). There was little sense that any societal structures could exist outside those established by the king.

Western concepts of freedom and independence introduced by the French during their rule in Vietnam were not applied by Vietnamese at a personal level but rather on a national one. Vietnamese organisations that formed in opposition to the French in the early part of the twentieth century were largely movements that sought increased sovereignty and national independence from France rather than personal freedoms. The Vietnamese Communist Party organised northern rural Vietnamese society in the 1940s to further the goal of independence from the French and national unification, not to pursue individual freedoms as defined by the West.

As part of that liberation process, the Vietnam Fatherland Front was established by the Communist Party to organise different sectors of society to support the revolution: Peasants' Union, Farmers' Association, General Confederation of Trade Unions, Women's Union, and Youth Union all were created to mobilise significant sectors of society for the war effort (Truong Ngoc Nguyen 1994, 4). Each of these various unions, also known as mass organisations, continued after the reunification of the country in 1975 under the umbrella of the Vietnamese Fatherland Front. Their initial role was to mobilise the general population to support government policies and programmes and, secondarily, to provide basic welfare services.

Though such tight government links may not fit the Western definition of civil society, these links are not seen as a breech of civil society norms by Vietnamese scholars. There is, rather, a tendency within Vietnamese academic circles to equate organisations like the Women's Union and others under the Vietnam Fatherland Front as institutions of civil society, including defining them as NGOs.

For example, Nguyen Van Thanh, executive vice president of Vietnam's Union of Friendship Organization, noted in a 1996 speech at an international development forum: "Now in Vietnam at the central level we have 160 national NGOs. At the provincial we have some 600 NGOs. At the grassroots level the number is difficult to know – thousands and thousands. It may compare to the Philippines and India where there are thousands and thousands of people's organizations" (Thanh Van Nguyen 1996). For Thanh little distinction is made between local NGOs in the Philippines and India and the various unions inside Vietnam; both support development initiatives and carry forth policies promoted by the government.

Noted Vietnamese scholar Professor Nguyen Ngoc Truong similarly exemplifies this vague differentiation made between the state and civil society. Professor Truong writes about "grassroots organisations" that sprang up in rural and urban Vietnam following economic reforms in 1986. Professor Truong notes that the ascendancy of "Huong uoc" (villages rules) resulted in "the appearance of a growing number of groups and popular organizations working for economic, family clan, religious or professional association purposes in the rural areas" (Truong Ngoc Nguyen 1994, 8). These grassroots organisations "contribute to the development of a necessary ethical environment, of the caring behaviors and of the appreciation of national identity and culture and the endeavors for the happiness of all the people" (ibid., 9). Hundreds of organisations at the local level and tens of thousands of non-formal ones operating at the city, village, or commune have been set up since 1986, according to Professor Truong (ibid., 12). These include associations that promote activities in the areas of science and technology, literary and fine arts, humanitarian work, sports and gymnastics, culture, and peace and friendship. At first glance one might assume that such associations fit standard Western definitions of civil society, but, without hesitation or a sense of irony, Professor Truong makes it clear that the associations he is referring to are closely linked with the Vietnam Fatherland Front and hence are implicitly connected with the state:

> While studying the emergence of new mass organizations in Vietnam in the recent years, it will be a mistake if we only emphasize their absolute independence or their private nature or confront them with the ruling Party and the State. . . . Millions of demobilized soldiers, tens of thousands of active or retired public servants and CPV members in or out of local Party organizations and other mass organizations working under the framework of the Vietnam Fatherland Front, constitute the backbone of all political, cultural and social activities at the grass-root level (Nguyen 1994, 18).

The state must, Professor Truong notes,

> take punitive measures against the abuse of charity, humanitarian or other public interest groups by individuals or collectives, to prevent extremist, divisive, illegal activity, or superstitious practices by groups or organizations judged dangerous to the public interest, social order and security. The

society lends support to the State in ensuring law and order (Nguyen 1994, 18).

The state and civil society, though technically independent from each other, according to Professor Truong (ibid., 19), represent two of the three troika (the other being the market) "pulling Vietnam along the transitional path towards the goal of modernization and industrialization."[1]

Given this close-knit relationship, international NGOs represent something entirely outside the state, likely even opposed to the state. Because all "legitimate" development occurs somehow in relation to the unions, being connected to these or other quasi-state institutions means everything. The idea of a foreign "non-government" organisation therefore raised many suspicions in the minds of Vietnamese leaders in the north after 1975. Nguyen Quang Tao, president of the Vietnamese Union of Friendship Organizations, recalled in 1995 at "Strategies for Engagement: Twenty Years' Experience; Goals to the Year 2000," a major forum of international NGOs in Indochina, that many Vietnamese government officials reasoned that if a foreign development organisation was "non-governmental," then it was not part of the state and was therefore "anti-government." In a country where being connected with the state is so important, it should be no surprise that independent organisations are viewed with suspicion.

It is important to note, however, that in the Vietnamese context it was not the communist ideology alone that created the desire to unify Vietnamese society under the leadership of the state. Traditional Confucian ideology, already deeply ingrained in the psyche of the Vietnamese through over 1,000 years of domination by China earlier in the millennium, enabled a form of authoritarian leadership without effective checks and balances to be established in Vietnam. This legacy of Confucian ideology is a powerful motivator in the Vietnamese consciousness, and it plays a major role in explaining the dynamic relationship between the state and people's organisations in Vietnam today.

MASS ORGANISATIONS IN VIETNAM

The various mass organisations or unions established under the auspices of the Vietnamese Fatherland Front became important bridges between national government policies and local support for those policies throughout the Vietnam Communist government era (1954–present in the north, 1975–present in the south). It is therefore important to understand the nature of these unions in order to further realise the structure of civil society in Vietnam and to assess international NGOs' responses, including MCC's, to these structures. The various unions are all large, having memberships sometimes numbering in the tens of millions. They operate under the umbrella of the Vietnamese Communist Party and are vertically integrated alongside the government structure; that is, there are representatives of the various unions at the national, provincial, district, commune (group of villages), and hamlet (village) levels, reflecting the political organisation of society. The plans of the unions at the national and provincial levels are integrated with state development plans. Operating expenditures for staff and supplies have been traditionally paid by the state, but increased commitment to reducing state budgets since economic reforms in 1986 have resulted in providing only for minimal operating and project expenses.

The government policy of reducing funding to mass organisations is one reason for the interest in partnering with international NGOs. In addition, as the central government reduces payments to the mass organisations, especially at the district and commune levels, they have become more independent of government supervised policy direction and have been more open to developing their own goals and objectives. Many international NGOs in the 1990s began to work with the Women's Union at the district level when they realised that the Women's Union already had a well-established presence on the ground and had moved away from primarily mobilising peasants in the war effort to supporting socio-economic development activities throughout the country.

Like local NGOs in many other developing countries, the primary purpose of the Women's Union is developmental; its mission aimed at "taking care of and protecting women's and children's rights and benefits and making favorable conditions for women in development." The Women's Union accomplishes this mission through (1) providing programmes to improve knowledge in literacy and agricultural production; (2) generating income through Grameen-style women's savings' groups; (3) maternal and child health care and responsible parenthood; (4) strengthening the Women's Union through capacity building; and (5) researching women's issues in order to improve the legal framework for women (Cuc Kim Nguyen 1997).

These five objectives could be the same as those of many international NGOs and traditional local NGOs working in various parts of the world. The question of whether Christian international NGOs should partner with a government-directed institution like the Women's Union or should instead attempt to create alternative, more "independent" structures in this authoritarian state, is a most important one. A case study of the MCC and its history of development work in Vietnam may shed some light on this question.

MCC and Civil Society in Vietnam

MCC's work in Vietnam began in 1954 when it began assisting refugees who had fled from the North during the French pull-out in Vietnam. As the American military presence in Vietnam increased during the 1960s, MCC contributed voluntary personnel and financial assistance to help those who were suffering as a result of the conflict. MCC also became increasingly vocal in its opposition to the war. In 1975, following the unification of the country by the North Vietnamese army, MCC's programme in the south and central parts of the country closed, and all MCC volunteers eventually left the reunified country.[2] MCC's efforts in Southeast Asia then turned towards externally displaced refugees, and MCC's Thailand programme office began working intensively with Cambodian, Laotian, and Vietnamese refugees who had fled extremely difficult political and economic situations in the years following 1975.

MCC remained committed, however, to be programmatically connected with Vietnam and its people. As a result, in 1981 MCC set up its Vietnam programme office in Bangkok, Thailand and, with a country representative based there, began a new chapter and a new style of working in Vietnam. This working style was quite atypical, given MCC's natural aversion to high-level, government-directed development programmes. The MCC country representative, Louise Buhler, made regular trips to Vietnam but met mostly with Vietnamese officials rather than ordinary peasants. Through regular trips into the country, Buhler began to develop significant relationships with these officials. These ongoing country visits in the 1980s and discussions with Vietnamese government officials were, however, instrumental in giving MCC greater flexibility when it eventually set up its development programme in Vietnam. The relationship was valuable as a means to help myopic Vietnamese officials understand the world around them.

Buhler discovered there was little conception by most Vietnamese government officials that organisations existed outside Vietnam independent of the state. She was repeatedly questioned about her connections with the Canadian government (she was a Canadian citizen). They could hardly believe her when she stated that the Canadian government did not know (or even care) that she was working in Vietnam under the auspices of an international development agency (Buhler 2000). For the Vietnamese officials who were escorting her on her regular visits to Vietnam, the concept of foreign NGOs working in Vietnam, outside state control, was unfamiliar to their mental constructs.

It was through these visits that some officials began to understand how foreign NGOs operated. The US-led embargo against Vietnam through the 1980s was instrumental in making Vietnam a virtual pariah state among many Western nations. Buhler reported that officials she met with were starved for information from the outside world, and she viewed her role in part as interpreting that Western world to Vietnamese officials (Buhler 2000). It was the trust-building presence of Buhler as a representative of a North American international NGO, and those of a handful of other like-minded faith based organisations including the American Friends Service Committee and Church World Service, that was the source of much of Vietnam's news of the outside world, including examples of alternative social organising.

Largely because of MCC's small but consistent efforts at building trust with government officials through the 1980s, MCC was granted permission to establish a representative's office in Hanoi in 1990. MCC was the first North American international NGO, and one of three Western international NGOs, to be given such a permit. Considering the atheistic orientation of Vietnam's Communist regime, it is interesting to note that two of the three agencies that received permission to have a representative's office in Vietnam at this time were Christian-based organisations.[3] In an ironic twist, the Vietnamese government endorsed these Christian international NGOs in part because they felt they could be trusted as actors independent of US or European government foreign policy.

The establishment of a Hanoi-based office in 1990 enabled MCC country representatives somewhat greater access to ordinary Vietnamese society, but there remained, at least initially, a great deal of control over their lives. Although MCC representatives were initially allowed to live only in government-sanctioned hotels, they were watched at all times by assigned shadows, their phones were tapped, and their visits with Vietnamese people were strictly monitored. A Foreign Ministry employee was assigned by the government to work for MCC as a translator and liaison officer. As such, a highlight during the first representative's three-year tour of duty was the permission granted to sleep overnight in a village outside of Ho Chi Minh City (Reedy 2000). The government in 1990 was very fearful of outside influences and remained committed to the idea of firm control over most social and economic processes.

Things changed quickly in Vietnam in the early 1990s. MCC's presence in the first few years of this decade changed from being one of the few international NGOs, and fewer openly Christian ones, to a position of relative insignificance in a rapidly expanding pool of foreign development organisations working in Vietnam (including several other overt, and some covert, Christian international NGOs). From the virtual absence of international NGOs in Vietnam in 1990, by 1995 there were 160 (Etherton 1995).

The most significant reason for this rapid increase in international NGOs was the new economic policy that the Vietnamese government was pursuing. In 1986 and again in 1989 the Vietnamese Communist Party Congress declared the need for dramatic economic changes. These included calls for increased domestic and international private investment in the economy, decentralisation of economic decision-making power, and decreased government responsibility for the economy. The *doi moi* (economic renovation) policy, enacted in stages beginning in 1986, enabled international NGOs to work more easily in Vietnam. In spite of the government's general lack of understanding of the international NGO world, the government permitted more international NGOs into the country with the hope that these agencies would provide much needed capital and training for poor Vietnamese. This opening attracted many international NGOs that were eager to work in a country where the gross domestic product in the early 1990s was one of the lowest in the world, and where health, education, and social services were beginning to deteriorate as the government slowly decreased its involvement in those areas.

A Two-Pronged Approach to Enhancing Civil Society

As a result of a general openness and lessening of restrictions in Vietnam during the late 1980s and early 1990s, MCC was able to begin working with lower levels of Vietnam's government and with more "genuine" civil society partners in its development programmes. In the 1980s virtually all the financial assistance MCC gave in Vietnam was directed to a provincial level authority or to a central ministry institution. In such cases, projects were proposed by government bodies to MCC, and MCC was asked to assist financially. MCC could do relatively little to help design, implement, monitor, or evaluate the aid that was given, and no North American volunteers were allowed to be present to work with local groups. This was not the kind of community development that MCC was known for in many other countries around the world.

Throughout the 1990s, however, the focus of MCC's work increasingly shifted towards lower levels of Vietnamese society. MCC national staff enjoyed increasing personal contact with farmers and other villagers involved in MCC training and development activities. Though many obstacles were present, MCC was able to push to work with and to benefit directly the people at the lowest economic and social strata of Vietnamese society.

MCC has maintained a two-pronged focus to its development work in Vietnam. On the one hand, MCC workers have long recognised the validity, integrity, and importance of government-related institutions for carrying out development work in Vietnam. MCC has recognised district- or commune-level people's committees (akin to county or township governments), or party-connected institutions under the Vietnam Fatherland Front, especially the Vietnam Women's Union, as valid and appropriate organisations with which to work in order to promote sustainable development and civil society in Vietnam. On the other hand, it has encouraged and nurtured indigenous institutions that more closely reflect Western notions of civil society in Vietnam. Both of these "prongs" are discussed below.

Reforming Existing Structures

MCC's work with government-related institutions began to shift in the early 1990s because of increased opportunities to work at the grassroots. A needs assessment survey done in 1992 revealed a great need for rural credit and savings programmes in poor districts surrounding Hanoi. By this time it was acceptable to hire Vietnamese to carry out a rural development programme initiated by an international NGO, so MCC hired a Vietnamese programme officer to initiate a rural credit and saving programme in Tam Dao district of Vinh Phu (now Vinh Phuc) province, northwest of Hanoi. In consultation with Vietnamese government officials, MCC chose this district because of its high rates of poverty, lack of access to credit, and general lack of government programmes.

In 1992 there was never a question as to who would be MCC's local development partner, as there was a complete absence of local independent NGOs in northern Vietnam. The option of trying to work with an independent NGO to implement a credit and savings programme in a local district was unthinkable. Likewise, the option of helping foster the creation of a local independent NGO was fraught with difficulties, the chief one being the lack of legal status that such an NGO would have. So MCC worked with district or commune government officials (People's Committee members) to help implement the credit and savings programmes and other development work.

The MCC credit and savings programme ran for several years in Tam Dao district. Some communes in the district became mired in financial problems, due in part to local corruption and in part to the government's policy of subsidising interest rates below a sustainable rate (McCrae and McCrae 1998). This credit and savings component was eventually turned over to the Vietnamese Bank for Agriculture, while the MCC programme evolved into a much broader rural development programme that focused on components of health, nutrition, agriculture, and capacity building. Yet through all the changes, the ties with mass organisations remained strong.

As the rural development work of MCC grew over the years, MCC turned increasingly to representatives of one of the mass organisations, most often the Women's Union, as a partner in its development programmes. This approach was quite different from the ones MCC employed in most other countries, where it seeks out church agencies or local NGOs to form partnerships. In Vietnam, however, district and commune Women's Union officials were in many communities the de facto development co-ordinators for their communities. They often put in long hours for very low wages to ensure that a health or nutrition programme was successfully carried out in a local commune. Many international development organisations have found that local chapters of the Women's Union, though burdened with much bureaucracy and a slow learning curve, are the groups most concerned about the health and welfare of their community. Their established presence in virtually every district and commune in Vietnam also make it possible to replicate effective development programmes throughout a wider geographic area and affecting greater numbers of poor people.

Still, one of the main drawbacks of the Women's Union has been its highly bureaucratic and hence ineffectual approach to carrying out development programmes. For many years the heavy top-down approach to development meant that local chapters of the Women's Union and other local government-directed agencies simply administered decrees given to them from above. The programmes implemented were not necessarily ones local communities requested or needed.

In response to the heavy bureaucracy traditionally involved in the Women's Union, capacity building has become a focus of much of MCC's work in recent years. MCC's Vietnamese rural development staff works closely with a programme management committee (often made up of local officials and mass organisation representatives) to build up the district or commune development programme and enable the local committee to "own" the projects that it chooses to design and implement. In addition, funding is made available for development training in capacity building, conducted either in the field or in Hanoi, to ensure that development concepts are well understood.

A key objective of training is for local officials to gain greater awareness of the development process, including how to appraise, design, implement, monitor, and evaluate development work. Following the training, these community leaders, though most often government officials, return to their village having been made aware of a vision of development that stresses principles of community participation, transparency, accountability, and co-operation.

These are precisely the principles that form the basis of Fowler's description of a civil society. Thus, as MCC perceives it in Vietnam, promoting sound development policies may well prove to be the best setting for increasing the "space" for civil society in Vietnam. The principles stressed in capacity-building training run counter to the hierarchical, authoritative, and often hidden agenda of the historically authoritative Vietnamese state. As increasing numbers of local officials begin to inculcate the values taught in capacity-building training, it is likely that demands for change higher up in the system will increase.

Thus, ironically, embryonic forms of civil society in Vietnam may have the greatest chance of occurring through these government-directed institutions. Though intimately tied with the state at district, commune, and higher levels, the Women's Union and other unions have a great deal of independence in thought and action, a continuation of traditional Vietnamese philosophy that "the rule of the king stops at the entrance of the village." MCC personnel have found that in general it is at the district or commune level that officials are most excited about the possibilities for carrying out bottom-up development policies that stress the need for farmers and the community as a whole to participate in all steps of the decision-making process. MCC's traditional strength of working at the grassroots of society is seemingly finally paying off, as villagers and the officials are genuinely interested in co-operating to achieve goals in rural development.

Encouraging Alternative Structures

But the focus of MCC has not been only on government-directed institutions like the Women's Union. MCC volunteers and national staff have also worked closely at enhancing the development of more "genuine" civil society structures in Vietnam. Many of these initiatives have been small and unobtrusive in order to encourage these institutions to survive in Vietnam without depending on the influence of foreigners, while at the same time avoiding any undue attention. Some of the initiatives have been in co-operation with other like-minded international NGOs, but the results have been mixed. In some cases supporting the creation of alternative structures in the realm of Western conceptions of civil society has seemed genuinely worthwhile, while in other cases it seems to have been an exercise in frustration.

As far as this writer is aware, there has never been an extended discussion within MCC Vietnam about the relative merit of encouraging these alternative institutions versus attempting to "reform" the existing government-related institutions. The one document that alludes to such a discussion is the 1996 Vietnam Program Guidelines, which states that

> Vietnam, though economically poor, has well-developed social structures, a strong cultural identity, and good basic infrastructure in health and education. We believe that providing some water for the many seeds already planted can bring great improvements to the lives of people here (McCrae 1996).

The purpose behind encouraging alternative institutions, therefore, is not necessarily directly related to the goal of promoting the philosophically loaded notion of civil society. Rather, a major philosophical and theological priority for MCC throughout its worldwide programmes is people-to-people contact. MCC sends volunteers to enhance mutual understanding and dialogue between people throughout the developing world and North America. In Vietnam, attempts by MCC to get to the grassroots can be seen more as a means to enhance mutual understanding and dialogue than any overt attempt to promote civil society.

In the process of "watering the many seeds," MCC Vietnam has striven in several of its programmes to work with institutions outside the direct state apparatus. For example, one area MCC has seen as appropriate to encourage alternative institutions is the field of handicraft design and marketing. The sale of handicrafts, especially those of the more than 50 ethnic minorities that live in Vietnam, is an important source of income for many poor people in Vietnam. MCC Vietnam, both within its own structures and through MCC's sister organisation Ten Thousand Villages (previously known as Self Help Crafts) has supported the creation and development of several local Vietnamese handicraft organisations in northern and southern Vietnam.[4]

In the south MCC has had a connection supporting Mai Handicrafts in Ho Chi Minh City since 1991. Mai Handicraft was begun by two Vietnamese social workers in 1990 as a means to provide income for women who were able to create handicraft goods. Much of the focus of Mai Handicrafts has been with women from ethnic minority backgrounds, who are among the poorest in Vietnamese society, but who also have extremely colourful embroidery traditions. MCC workers in the early 1990s encouraged Mai Handicrafts by connecting the group with fair trade organisations that help bring handicraft goods from around the world to the North American market. MCC North American volunteers placed in Vietnam have regularly consulted with Mai Handicraft staff on issues of design and marketing and have aided their entry into the international market.

In northern Vietnam MCC has had a long-standing relationship with Craftlink, another craft development and marketing organisation. Craftlink was formed in the early 1990s by a small group of international NGOs, including MCC, to address the needs of poor rural women in Vietnam. In some ways similar to Mai Handicraft in the south, Craftlink is a small local NGO that works both to develop the skills of handicraft producers and to market their products to local tourists, a growing Vietnamese middle class, and to foreigners through export markets. An MCC volunteer has served on the steering committee since its inception, and MCC volunteers have worked at enhancing skills of the Craftlink staff and handicraft producer groups in financial management, marketing, and design. One method of skill development is travelling, including exposure trips to other countries in Southeast Asia, and working for a year at the Ten Thousand Villages headquarters in North America.

Neither Craftlink nor Mai Handicraft is a particularly large organisation. Both directly employ fewer than 10 persons and have relatively modest sales. In part they are small out of necessity, for as nonprofit, independent organisations, they operate outside the normal structures in Vietnam and are in a grey area of legality.

They are thus reluctant to raise their profile lest some government body decide they should not be allowed to continue to operate. Yet their very existence in Vietnam is testament to the fact that alternative structures are both presently viable and are a beacon of what might be.

Besides its handicraft programme, MCC has encouraged the development of local NGOs in Vietnam through its rural development programme. One of the most obvious examples is through the training of development programme staff. MCC has a strong commitment to build the management capacity of development programme staff, who may then use their training either to continue work at MCC or another international NGO, or, as in the case of Dang Ngoc Quang, to leave MCC and create a local Vietnamese NGO. Mr. Quang was hired as a programme officer by MCC in 1992 to head its burgeoning credit and savings programme. After two years of experience with MCC, during which time he gained development management training and experience, Quang left MCC. In part because of the experience and training gained while working with MCC, Quang was able to begin the Rural Development Services Center (RDSC). Under Quang's leadership, RDSC expanded into a full-fledged local independent NGO, implementing research, training, and development work in several districts in northern and central Vietnam. RDSC's funding now comes primarily from international organisations that channel money through this local NGO to develop, implement, and help monitor development projects.

RDSC was considered one of the first local NGOs in northern Vietnam. MCC's assistance in training Quang in community development and management principles was essential to the creation of RDSC. Its existence remains somewhat of an anomaly, however, as the number of true local NGOs in northern Vietnam remains very low. A workshop held in September 1998 brought together only five Vietnamese-run organisations in the north that could be considered local rural development NGOs (Interchurch Organization 1998).

Compared to many international NGOs, RDSC's impact is not terribly significant. Unlike Care or World Vision, both of whose Vietnam budgets are in the millions, RDSC operates on a relative shoestring and has programmes in only a few districts. RDSC's value, therefore, is more in the fact that it, like Craftlink and Mai Handicraft, exists as an alternative structure in a country that has yet to embrace this kind of option.

The fact remains that the government actively discourages the development of local NGOs, preferring that international NGOs carry out the majority of local development efforts in the country. At a meeting of international NGOs in 1999, the director of the government agency that oversees the work of all international NGOs in Vietnam stated outright that the government of Vietnam does not support the development of local NGOs (Phan 1999). This statement was a reminder to some that the government is in no hurry for international NGOs to "indiginise" their operations and leave Vietnam with an externally funded but locally staffed and directed operation. The government of Vietnam remains firmly committed to the premise that strong leadership in economic and political affairs requires a single voice. Allowing numerous local NGOs and other institutions of civil society to flourish would jeopardise the government's ability to maintain this authority.

Even so, many international NGOs, including MCC, are training their own Vietnamese staff in radically new ways. International NGO staff certainly see the obvious incongruity between the new approach and that demonstrated in daily life by the government. While most programme officers are not able to go out and begin their own local NGO, as Mr. Quang did, their training in the values of transparency, decision-making, participation, and bottom-up development is having a strong impact on what is taught and practised in their own development work.

RELATING TO THE CHURCH IN VIETNAM

In many places throughout Africa, the Middle East, and Latin America, MCC works closely with the church or church-related groups which are considered to be its key partners. Church partners help define what MCC's role should be in the country and help to foster the people-to-people contact that MCC attempts to nurture.

In Vietnam there has been far less opportunity for the church to play an active role in development activities, and hence for MCC to consider a close relationship with it. Under Vietnam's communist leadership, the church has often felt the bitter winds of oppression due to continuing government animosity toward the Catholic and Protestant churches. This attitude stems from the church's former support for the colonial French and American-backed Vietnamese administrations, but is due also to the government's lack of tolerance for institutions outside its control. To control the independence of the church, the government sanctioned "official" Catholic and Protestant churches,[5] which meant that if one wanted to legally practise one's faith, one was obliged to do it within the context of one of these official institutions.

Religious belief, though officially permitted by the constitution, has, over the past 25 years, been actively discouraged. This has been true in the official churches but especially in unofficial religious groups, including unsanctioned Buddhist and Christian groups. Within Christianity, minority ethnic populations have been especially attracted to evangelical Protestant missions, with the result that, according to some estimates, at least two-thirds of the 700,000 Protestants in Vietnam are from ethnic minorities (United States Department of State 2000).

The official Catholic and Protestant churches in Vietnam are restricted in their proselytising and training activities, but they are legally permitted to worship, and their day-to-day actions are not as closely monitored as are those of the unofficial churches. The degree to which the official church has been co-opted by the state is largely a matter of interpretation; those on the outside often have a much more critical view of the official church than do those on the inside, who may complain about the restrictions, but who are also grateful they are able to worship more or less freely.

Some Christian international NGOs have taken an aggressive stance toward working with the church and with nonbelievers in Vietnam. They see their development work in Vietnam as secondary to the mission of evangelism and find whatever possible means to encourage Vietnamese to hear and believe in the gospel. Several of these Christian international NGOs have had great difficulties working in Vietnam because the government does not trust their motives. The government has made it clear that while religious freedom is tolerated in Vietnam, "importing" religion from outside is not. While the government is increasingly turning a blind eye to Vietnamese citizens having unofficial church involvement, it is very wary of allowing foreign influence into the religious sphere.[6]

MCC in Vietnam sees one of its primary missions as building bridges of reconciliation between the peoples of Vietnam and North America. As a result, it has generally attempted to support official church groups rather than actively supporting unofficial ones. Similar to its relationship with government-directed organisations, MCC has a two-pronged approach in relating to the church in Vietnam. There has been a consistent and positive relationship with the Catholic Committee for Solidarity, an official, government-approved church body whose mandate is to promote various social and development causes that enhance the welfare of the people of Vietnam. Over the past decade MCC has sponsored a variety of development projects, scholarships, and workshops through the Catholic Committee. MCC also sponsored a key person in the Catholic Committee to attend a three-month course in conflict resolution in England in the early 1990s. The long-term relationship that has developed with him as a result has proven to be a valuable entryway into the life of the Church in Vietnam.

MCC has also had meaningful contact with churches outside the official realm in Vietnam. The primary contact has been through the Vietnamese Mennonite Church. This body began in southern Vietnam as a result of Mennonite missionaries working in the 1950s and 1960s. When the South Vietnamese government fell in 1975, the Vietnamese Mennonite Church was not given official status by the new regime, bringing to an end its life as an official body. The group, however, survived difficult times in the late 1970s and 1980s, with members scattered about, worshipping in various Protestant congregations. In the 1990s the group renewed efforts to bring its members together again. It has petitioned the government to allow it to become a recognised Protestant church, though it has received no indication that this will be granted.

MCC has been able to support the church informally through focusing on its social welfare efforts. On several occasions members of the congregation have banded together to help provide emergency assistance to victims in the often flood-besieged central and southern coastal provinces. Mennonite church members have on several occasions gathered several thousand dollars of relief supplies, supplemented by contributions from MCC, and, through good contacts with a variety of government officials in several provinces, provided quick assistance to victims of flooding. The good works done by the Vietnamese Mennonites do not go unnoticed, and the hope is that their continued efforts at helping provide assistance to those in need will eventually help the government realise that they are a legitimate church group that deserves recognition in its own right.

REFLECTIONS ON BUILDING CIVIL SOCIETY
FROM A CHRISTIAN INTERNATIONAL NGO IN VIETNAM

In the context of post-war Vietnam, an independent civil society (as defined in the West), has not been allowed by the government to flourish. Instead, the government has fostered the development of state-directed mass organisations, which have functioned largely as a means to implement many of the state's development activities. Though not fitting within the confines of traditional Western definitions of civil society, these mass organisations have enabled economic and social development to take place in Vietnam. The mass organisations, especially the Women's Union, have also been a vital link for international NGOs coming into Vietnam. They have facilitated disbursement of resources and knowledge into rural areas in Vietnam in a way that would have been extremely difficult without their presence.

I believe the case of Vietnam suggests that the concept of civil society is not as unambiguous or one-dimensional as some would suggest. MCC has learned that fostering civil society in Vietnam (though MCC has rarely consciously thought of fostering it) may occur best in a very roundabout way and with unexpected partners. Working within the government-controlled system, MCC has provided resources and training that build the capacity of local government and mass organisation officials to think more creatively and independently. Though it may not be obvious to all at first, local officials may well turn out to form the basis of a new way of thinking about the development process and, in so doing, about the relationship of these local organisations to the state.

MCC has also learned that these changes take place slowly and only through a great deal of time. Effective development work for MCC in Vietnam took years to nurture and came at the expense of traditional operational modes. MCC gave up some of its traditional modes of operation for the sake of another important principle: establishing and maintaining long-term relationships that were ignored or rejected by other international NGOs, including Christian international NGOs, because of US political priorities. The willingness to maintain a relationship with Vietnam after the war and through the 1980s, in spite of its unpopularity in North America, enabled MCC to establish a permanent presence in Vietnam soon after the loosening of restrictions in the late 1980s. It also has enabled MCC to be more creative with its development programme in the following years, including beginning to work with local NGOs more removed from the government. It may be that a commitment by Christian international NGOs to being present in difficult or dangerous situations is a more powerful and more appropriate expression of faithfulness than efforts to replicate Western models of civil society.

MCC's work with capacity building of local Vietnamese NGOs suggests that now may not be the time to push for the creation of local institutions that resemble Western notions of civil society. The extreme difficulty these local NGOs have had in finding a niche in Vietnamese society makes it questionable whether this is the most effective way to promote social and economic development in Vietnam today.

MCC has acknowledged that in the case of Vietnam, it has been at least as effective to enhance civil society values within the established structures as it is to promote the creation of alternative structures. Though this is a conclusion that runs counter to the philosophy of some large foreign donors and aid programmes in Vietnam, it is nevertheless an analysis that should be taken seriously.

Building civil society in post-war Vietnam has not been quick, nor easy, nor unambiguous. The power of the state and its influence in daily life permeate Vietnamese society. MCC's commitment to building relationships rather than simply promoting the latest Western development concept has made it take seriously Vietnam's own history and traditions, and to then try to work in a manner appropriate to the Vietnamese context. MCC hopes that as it does so it can continue to wrestle with what it means to be faithful and to affect positive change in the land of the ascending dragon.

NOTES

[1] Professor Truong's image of the troika of government, economics, and civil society curiously resembles Senator Bill Bradley's image of civil society as part of a three-legged stool composed of government, market, and civil society.

[2] Four MCC volunteers stayed in Vietnam following the collapse of the South Vietnamese regime as a symbolic gesture to the North that MCC did not take sides in the war but rather was present to help with the needs of the Vietnamese people. The story of the four MCC volunteers is chronicled in Earl Martin's 1978 book *Reaching the Other Side* (New York: Crown Publishers).

[3] CIDSE (International Cooperation for Development and Solidarity), a coalition of European Catholic development agencies, also had commitments in Vietnam stemming back to 1978, when it began delivering relief aid to Vietnam, while Oxfam Great Britain was permitted to establish its office in Hanoi at the same time as MCC.

[4] Even these local organisations have their government connections. In order to gain legal status in Vietnam, these nonprofit institutions must be registered. In order to register, they must somehow fall under the umbrella of a government-related association. So Mai Handicrafts in Ho Chi Minh City, for example, gains its registration status under the National Psychology Association.

[5] This was not only true of Christianity, which makes up only 7 per cent of the population, but also Buddhism, which claims up to 50 per cent of Vietnamese as followers, and other smaller groups including the Cao Dai and Muslim.

[6] Much of this concern dates back to when many Protestant groups and the Catholic church sided with the southern forces during the war. The difficulties that some Christian international NGOs face working in Vietnam is generally in sharp contrast to the several international NGOs that were permitted to establish offices in Vietnam in the early 1990s. These international NGOs, including MCC, American Friends Service Committee, CIDSE, and Church World Service, were all known to the Vietnamese government for many years prior to being permitted to open offices in Hanoi. In the case of MCC and AFSC, it was largely because these two organisations had clearly maintained a neutral stance during the American war and had continued relating to the government and the people of Vietnam after the war that their early re-entry into Vietnam and their cordial relationship with the government continue today.

REFERENCES

Amnesty International. *Annual Report on Viet Nam.* 1999. Accessed 13 June 2000 at the Amnesty International website.

AtKisson, Alan. 1997. "Why Civil Society Will Save the World." In *Beyond Prince and Merchant: Citizen Participation and the Rise of Civil Society,* edited. by J. Burbridge, 285–92. New York: Pact Publications.

Buhler, Louise. 2000. "Mennonite Central Committee Country Representative, 1981–1987." Interview by author, Hanoi, Vietnam, 15 March.

Etherton, Mary, ed. 1995. *Vietnam NGO Directory 1995–1996.* Hanoi: NGO Resource Centre.

Fforde, Adam, and Doug Porter. 1994. "Public Goods, the State, Civil Society, and Development Assistance in Vietnam: Opportunities and Prospects." Paper presented at 1994 Vietnam Update Conference: Doi Moi, The State and Civil Society, 10–11 November, in Canberra, Australia.

Forgacs, David, ed. 1988. *A Gramsci Reader: Selected Writings 1916–1935.* London: Lawrence and Wishart.

Fowler, Alan. 1996. "Assessing NGO Performance: Difficulties, Dilemmas, and a Way Ahead." In *Beyond the Magic Bullet: NGO Performance and Accountability in the Post-cold War World*, edited by M. Edwards and D. Hulme. West Hartford, Conn.: Kumarian Press.

———. 1997. *Striking a Balance: A Guide to Enhancing the Effectiveness of Non-Governmental Organizations in International Development.* Sterling, Va.: Earthscan.

Interchurch Organization for Development Cooperation. 1998. "Workshop Report on Coordination and Cooperation Among Local NGOs." Hanoi, Vietnam. September.

McCrae, Bruce. 1996. "MCC Vietnam Program Guidelines." Hanoi, Vietnam. February.

McCrae, Bruce, and Betsy Headrick McCrae. 1998. "Not a Dot-to-Dot Operation." *Common Place* (July).

Nguyen, Cuc Kim. 1997. "The Women's Union in Vietnam." Speech given at Indochina Forum, July, Washington, D.C. Cuc Kim Nguyen is director, International Relations Department, Vietnam Women's Union.

Nguyen, Quang Tao. 1995. Speech given at Sixth National NGO Forum on Indochina, June, in New York. Quang is president of the Vietnamese Union of Friendship Organizations.

Nguyen, Thanh Van. 1996. Non Profit Sector in Vietnam. Unpublished paper, Hanoi, Vietnam.

Nguyen, Truong Ngoc. 1994. "Grassroot Organizations in Rural and Urban Vietnam During Market Reform: An Overview of their Emergence and Relationship to the State." Paper presented at the 1994 Vietnam Update Conference: Doi Moi, The State and Civil Society, 10–11 November, in Canberra, Australia.

Oxhorn, Philip. 1995. "From Controlled Inclusion to Coerced Marginalization: The Struggle for Civil Society in Latin American." In *Civil Society: Theory, History and Comparison*, edited by J. Hall, 250–77. Cambridge: Polity Press.

Phan, Trong Thai. 1999. Speech given at Meeting with International Non-government Organization, September, Hanoi, Vietnam. Phan Thai Trong is director of the People's Aid Coordinating Committee.

Reedy, Stan. 2000. "Reminiscences from the Early Days." E-mail correspondence with author, 22 March.

United States Department of State (Bureau of Democracy, Human Rights, and Labor). 1999. *1999 Country Reports on Human Rights Practices*. Accessed at the state department website on 13 June 2000.

——— 2000. *2000 Annual Report on International Religious Freedom*. 5 September.

Wolfensohn, James. 1999. "A Proposal for a Broader Approach to Partnership and the Management of the Development Process." Washington, D.C.: World Bank.

16

WESTERN NGO SUPPORT OF GRASSROOTS CHRISTIAN ORGANISATIONS IN RUSSIA

Kathleen Braden and Heather Eggen

Western observers might perceive that the newly independent states born after the 1991 breakup of the USSR are in dire need of the development of civil society, especially in light of the life circumstances of ordinary citizens. Evidence suggests that the standard of living has not improved for most citizens; the gulf between the very wealthy and the impoverished has grown ever larger; life expectancy has declined; diseases long thought conquered, such as tuberculosis, have made a new appearance; prison conditions are deplorable; orphans live in poor circumstances; the health of the natural environment is worse than under the former Soviet regime; and political and economic life is riddled with corruption.

Into this dismal scene the advent of philanthropic organisations that can provide some respite for post-Soviet society is very welcome, and both Christian and secular NGOs have taken up the mantle of social assistance. While this involvement of civil society is good news, there are some constraints that may inhibit the efficacy of Christian organisations to promote the growth of civil society in Russia. It is not necessarily lack of commitment, resources, or objectives that are the barriers to effective citizen engagement to meet these needs, but rather the very nature of culture and definitions of civil society itself.

The goal of many Protestant and Catholic groups which have turned their attention to Russia is not only to plant seeds for the growth of the Christian gospel message, but also to contribute to a democratisation process and to strengthen civil society. The challenges facing these Christian groups are considerable. Among the most important of these challenges is whether Westerners can really understand these goals from the inside out, for it is not clear that we even speak the same language as our counterparts in the newly independent states in determining what we mean by civil society and its relation to God's plan for human salvation.

POST-SOVIET RUSSIA AND THE ATTEMPT TO CONSTRUCT A NEW SOCIETY

The breakup of the former USSR brought with it hope that democratisation, progress toward an open society, respect for human rights, and a nascent market system would emerge in its wake. Instead, Russia has come to experience an economic and political system in the strong grip of corruption and organised crime. The Interior Ministry of Russia estimates that there are between 5,000 and 9,000 criminal organisations operating in the country (O'Neal 2000; CSCE 1999; Dempsey and Lukas 1999). Because the government is not yet effective at protecting people from racketeering, extortion, and homicide, the private security business is booming. Oleg Kharkhordin refers to this phenomenon as the "absent monopoly of legitimate violence," as shadow governments compete with the actual government and usurp the state sphere of action. As a result, Russia has a weak state and a most *un*civil society (Kharkhordin 1998).

Yet for the average citizen the distinction between shadow and legitimate governments may be hard to make. A complex maze of laws, tax rules, regulations, permits, and bureaucracies (that pre-date the Bolshevik revolution and were continued by the Soviet regimes) has been reinvigorated since 1991, providing significant new opportunity for bribery. Even the charities themselves may be suspect:

> Not that post-communist charities are spotless. Too many are dodgy. Some, such as some army veterans' groups and sports clubs, have been covers for criminal gangs. Other state-backed bodies have been crony-ridden and ineffective – except as ways to evade taxes and customs duties on imports such as alcohol (*The Economist* 1998; see also Tismaneanu 1995).

In the face of such a predatory economic and political system, Western groups looking to assist Russia or nudge it along the path towards democracy and capitalism may be tempted to throw up their hands in despair and look for a culprit. The sense of triumph and opportunity that dominated Western attitudes toward Russia at the end of the Cold War has given way to confusion, despair, and the search for an explanation. *Why* did civil society, markets, and an uncorrupted political system not emerge once the chains of the CPSU (Community Party of the Soviet Union) were thrown off?

Multinational firms have been particularly disappointed with the high cost of doing business in Russia caused by the endemic corruption and heightened security requirements. In searching for explanations, many Western sources have been quick to link the need to build a moral-based society where business is safe to grow with the damage done by more than 70 years of communism, concluding that it *must* be the same totalitarian mindset the West has countered for so long that continues to bedevil us now. The names of US government inquiries called to find an explanation to the dilemma illustrate the Western bias inherent in attempting to analyse the former USSR: the Committee on Safety and Cooperation in Europe sponsored a briefing in February of 1999 entitled "Civil Society, Democracy, and Markets in East Central Europe and the NIS: Problems and Perspectives." An article in a Western business journal had a paragraph expressing a typical response to the post-Soviet disappointment of the West:

Clearly, this insular and cruel past has taken a huge toll upon Russian society. Devoid of democratic traditions and of the basic elements of civil society, Russia is left with attitudes and habits that will be difficult to change. The appeal of Marxism was its promise to fuse the "moral" and the "scientific" facets of society into a "perfectly unified human community." Cynicism, distrust, lack of initiative, antipathy toward market activities and individualism, dependence on strong authorities, passivity, hopelessness, suspicion toward the West, and moral and ethical confusion are all behavioral and attitudinal qualities engendered over these long years of autocratic rule (Taylor, Kazakov, and Thompson 1997).

In short, post–Cold War Russia has not lived up to the promise of post–World War II Japan and Germany. The average person's lack of respect for contract law and the absence of entrepreneurial spirit (although former party officials who quickly seized newly privatised national industrial resources were quite entrepreneurial) were understood to be the result of the failure to develop civil society under the Soviet regime. But maybe these explanations are too easy and too self-serving. Could there be another, deeper explanation for why Western solutions and institutions do not seem to work very well in Russia, an explanation based on cultural differences and on the differences in Orthodox and Western traditions of Christianity?

CIVIL SOCIETY AND CHRISTIAN NGOs IN RUSSIA

The historic relationship between Marxist Russia and the Christian church was fraught with tension and mistrust. In terms of social action the Soviet government promulgated a law in 1929 forbidding the Orthodox church from operating charities. This prohibition continued in effect until the Gorbachev regime loosened restrictions on religion with the 1990 Law on Freedom of Conscience and Law on Public Associations (texts available online). As a result, the number of charities skyrocketed and more than 60,000 charities now operate in Russia. Many of them are run by Orthodox, Protestant, or Catholic churches, with strong financial and personnel support from Western Christians.

In a flush of excitement after the breakup of the USSR, grassroots organisations also multiplied rapidly. NGOs associated with environmental causes were the first out of the starting blocks once impediments to their existence were eliminated. The Center for Civil Society International (CCSI) in Seattle, Washington, published a 1996 guide (followed by a similar one for Central Asia in 1999) and noted that while independent organisations had never been completely stamped out during the Soviet period, their activities had been greatly restructured: "Obliterated by 1937, the volunteer urge in Russia reappeared like Lazarus in the 1960s, a mere quarter century later" (Ruffin, McCarter, and Upjohn 1996, xi). In the mid-1990s University of Washington student Catriona Logan, with support from CCSI, travelled to Russia and published her master's thesis on NGOs in four cities, finding

1,200 NGOs registered in Novosibirsk; 2,000 in Ekaterinberg; 800 in Krasnodar; and 200 in Pskov (Logan 1998). Inside Russia, Daniel Granin urged the rediscovery of philanthropy (Granin 1987). Granin himself was approached by the Gorbachev government to help centrally organise the new rapidly forming groups, but he declined, believing that small-scale and personal NGOs worked most effectively.

Western-based Christian organisations began to increase support for NGOs within Russia, and many of the grassroots organisations that emerged during the 1980s had church-based members (White 1993). But with every group that distributed the gospels or provided charitable aid, it seemed that the alienation of Russians increased because of how these groups worked. Western evangelical organisations, mistrustful of the Russian Orthodox Church and its relationship with the Soviet government in the past, called for a society in which religious pluralism could be made secure. While from a Western perspective this appeal for freedom was consistent with democratic ideas, it was seen by Russians to be an insult to the Orthodox church. It thus triggered a backlash, resulting in the passing of the 1997 Law on Religious Organizations that placed restrictions on designated "non-native" church groups.[1] Larry Uzzell, of the Keston Institute in England, which has long tracked religious liberty issues in Russia, testified on 14 January 1997 before the Commission on Security and Cooperation in Europe (hearings on religious freedom in Russia):

> I think that Protestants, and especially American Protestants, have a lot to answer for in the way that they have poisoned the waters of religious dialogue in Russia. Many Protestants have gone over to Russia as if they were going to New Guinea, as if they were going into a land that had never heard the Gospel preached before, that did not have its own Christian history. They have done so without studying Orthodoxy. Sometimes I run into American Protestant missionaries who have never even read the text of the Orthodox liturgy or who have never set foot in an Orthodox Church before going to Russia. It's understandable that Russians react with great annoyance to that phenomenon.

The 1997 law passed by the Russian Duma guaranteed rights for religious organisations while maintaining Russia as a secular state (that is, not declaring the Russian Orthodox Church as a state religion). On the other hand, it also declared in the preamble that Orthodoxy, Islam, Judaism, and Buddhism deserve special recognition as traditional religions practised in Russia, with Orthodoxy described as "the inalienable part of the Russian historical, spiritual, and cultural heritage." Other denominations or faiths were not given equality of religious association in Russian law and, unlike Orthodox associations, must complete a registration process, particularly if they are foreign based, *unless* they can show they have operated within Russia for at least 15 years. Religious groups that operated in Russia before the passage of the law need to re-register annually. If a group fails to register or meet the requirements of the 1997 law, it is prohibited from carrying out many activities in the sphere of civil society, including working in schools, hospitals, nursing homes, or publishing materials (CSCE 1998, 24).[2]

Evidence suggests that the impact of the 1997 law has varied. By December 1999 only half of the groups affected by the law had registered; President Vladimir Putin therefore extended the deadline for another year. Several Pentecostal groups in Yakutia were banned under the federal law, and in Voronezh, 13 local religious organisations were taken to court (although some are in the process of being re-registered after pressure from the federal Ministry of Justice). In a 16 September 2000 editorial against the new law, *The New York Times* noted:

> This year in the Russian town of Kostroma, a panel of university professors, local government officials, a psychiatrist, a psychologist and a lawyer met to ponder whether two local Pentecostal churches should be legally registered. After watching a video of church services, the group concluded that the church leaders used ''psychological manipulation.'' The two churches were not allowed to register, and court proceedings are beginning to ban them. If this happens, their members would be able to meet in a home to pray, but they will be second-class religious citizens. Their community will not be able to distribute literature, rent or own a building, invite foreigners to preach or carry out other activities integral to religious freedom.

Meanwhile, the work of Western-based Christian NGOs in Russia to assist in building civil society through charitable social aid may yet prove useful. International Orthodox Christian Charities has been one vehicle by which both American food aid and aid through the US government Fund for Democracy have been distributed in Russia. Since 1992 this NGO has sent more than US$30 million for aid to projects throughout Russia, channelling this aid through the 100 Orthodox church archdioceses in the country (8,000 parishes). Other evangelical NGOs, many of which are associated with church creation, education, or Bible distribution, are diverse in both size and mission. For example, according to a 3 November 2000 broadcast (in Russian) by the Association of Christian Broadcasting, the Christian Life Church in Krasnoyarsk opened a rehabilitation centre called Trust and Triumph for drug addicts in 1998 and now has served more than 400 addicts.

To attempt to understand the character and impact of civil society organisations in Russia, the authors sent questionnaires in Russian and English to more than thirty Christian NGOs. Only six organisations responded, but their responses illustrate the variations in size of operation and the range of activities. The survey found that the impact of the 1997 law was not a major issue. Most respondents highlighted the special role of Christian NGOs in terms of focus, goals, and influence on society through reconciliation and forgiveness. One organisational representative noted:

> Every week we see examples of this as family members become reconciled to each other through our church and social service ministries. Through the ministry of the nine congregations that we have in this region, we have been

354 • Kathleen Braden and Heather Eggen

privileged to be part of God's plan of reconciling people to him. We have also been able to participate in minority groups and organisations becoming "reconciled." For example, our social services complex in St Petersburg successfully and harmoniously holds programmes for "client groups" as different as alcoholics, Leningrad siege survivors, people with no home, children from families in crisis, youth groups, former prisoners, people who are HIV-positive, and drug addicts. This includes both Christian and non-Christian self-help groups. When we began our thinking and planning . . . [there was] so much prejudice, fear and scape-goating linked to people associated with these groups that we were confidently warned that our goal was impossible to achieve. This negative attitude was strongly reinforced by the heads of the institute which surround our building and whose courtyard we share. They even threatened to use force to prevent clients from coming into their yard so that they could have access to our building. But within weeks of opening in August 1997 we had successfully demonstrated that all the fears were groundless, and we now have hundreds of people each day co-operating in their use of the building and in joint training events and shared networks. The institute has not only become "reconciled," but now actively helps us in our task.

This group's success may in part be due to its willingness to take an "insider's" view of Christian charitable work in Russia. This report also gives evidence of how various factors, such as restrictive laws, the potential for Russian backlash, and the presence of corruption, suggest that Christian organisations hoping to assist Russia in the move toward civil society have a daunting task before them. The full realisation of potential to assist Russia may come with a recognition that the very foundations of Christian thought and civil societal structures we take for granted in the West may not automatically transfer to the situation in Russia. We turn therefore to examine the foundations of civil society within the various streams of Christian traditions to suggest which one may be best suited to post-Soviet Russia.

THREE BRANCHES OF CHRISTIANITY AND CIVIL SOCIETY: WHICH ONE FITS MODERN RUSSIA?

There have been many and varied scholarly views about the role of the early church in political life. Some scholars suggest that the Christian church should reject the notion of being involved in matters of state (see, for example, Arendt 1958 and Ehrenberg 1999). Others argue that the foundational principles of civil society and political organisation can be traced back to basic beliefs of religious groups. In an examination of how Christians contribute to building community and civil society, Weaver, Mahurin, and Isaac write that "religious thought has contributed to the basic ideas concerning the importance of the individual (a foundation of the human rights movement) and the power of citizenry to improve their lives (the basis of civil society)" (Weaver, Mahurin, and Isaac 1998, 127). They go on to note that these foundations are especially evident in the Western practice of Judaism and Christianity, where the idea that all people stand in equality before their Lord and creator evolved into the notion of democratic tradition and practice. Most important for our consideration of Russia, they note the central part played by the view of progress in Greek thought as well as in Western religions: "The vision of progress became embodied in the persona of the Messiah – a hope for a better future." This hope extended beyond strictly religious issues: "People began to think of getting forward, of being able to see hope ahead, and of working for a better future – not in the hereafter, but now. Thus, the secular vision of a better life is rooted in the most basic values of religion" (ibid., 128).

Any reticence the early church may have had to take an active role in political life was dramatically altered during the Reformation. Luther argued that each Christian had a duty to accept involvement in worldly affairs and that action as well as prayer would glorify God. John Calvin also emphasised the legitimate Christian calling to life in the public sphere of this world.

Did the ethic of Protestant involvement with civil society extend far enough eastward in Europe to have an impact on Russian Orthodox Christianity? Oleg Kharkhordin considers this question and combines in his work the classifications of Charles Taylor and Adam Seligman to define the outlook of Lutheranism/Calvinism. He describes this outlook as the "L-stream civil society of the Anglo-American liberal tradition" (L after John Locke), in which civil society is a "set of associations . . . that mediates relations between the individual and the strong state and defends the former from the encroachments of the latter" (Kharkhordin 1998).

A second Western approach is the M-stream variety of civil society (M after Montesquieu), which takes for granted the pre-existence of a strong, centralised state. In this context the role of civil society is to mediate between the individual and the state (Kharkhordin 1998). Kharkhordin, working from Seligman's analysis, calls this the Catholic tradition of civil society. M-stream theories originated in Southern Europe, a predominantly Catholic area, where congregations faced strong political entities already in place. In these regions secular powers maintained worldly order while the church cared for the spiritual realm. Kharkhordin suggests that M-stream theorists based their ideology on the ethical role of the Christian congregation in this world, with the church as "the last barrier against absolutism."

M-stream civil society came to Russia by way of Eastern European movements, but this fundamentally Catholic vision does not take the cultural and religious differences of Russia into account. Therefore, Kharkhordin maintains, neither L-stream nor M-stream civil society played out in Christianity can provide a full portrait of Russian thinking and history. To understand why, we must turn to an understanding of Orthodox Christian tradition.

The Orthodox view of society described by Kharkhordin is illustrated by an excerpt from *The Brothers Karamazov*:

Every earthly state should be, in the end, completely transformed into the Church and should become nothing else but a Church, rejecting every purpose incongruous with the aims of the Church. . . . The Church is not to be transformed into the State. That is Rome and its dream. That is the third temptation of the devil. On the contrary, the State is transformed into the

Church, will ascend and become a Church over the whole world – which is
... the glorious destiny ordained for the Orthodox Church. The star will
arise in the east!

Kharkhordin describes this as "the radical denial of evil through the deification of
man and through the reconstruction of the world on church principles." The three
central correctional practices of the church are to denounce sin, to admonish into
righteousness, and "if the sinner does not listen to admonitions – to excommuni-
cate" (Kharkhordin 1998).

The Orthodox vision of civil society "may be seen as advocating non-militaris-
tic and civilized life," like the Protestant version, as well as serving to "defend
individuals from state encroachments on their liberties and educate them in virtue," as in the Catholic view. More deeply, however, "the Orthodox version of civil
society would strive to completely supplant the secular state and its use of the
means of violence by bringing church means of influence to regulate all terrains of
human life" (Kharkhordin 1998). When traditional Russian Orthodox ideas on
charity are closely examined, one is led to better understand Russian views on
charity and building civil society. Contrary to common contemporary perceptions,
recent publications by Lindenmeyr, Kharkhordin, and White reveal that deep-set
attitudes toward the civil sphere of charity may not have been eliminated by the 70
years of communism. One might even ask whether Enlightenment notions of the
role of the church in civil society had even begun to permeate Russian consciousness prior to the Bolshevik Revolution (see Lindenmeyr 1990; idem 1996;
Kharkhordin 1998, White 1993).

For example, the Russian word for *charity, miloserdiye*, suggests also the word
mercy and an inner quality rather than a charitable *action*. Lindenmeyr and
Kharkhordin both contend that we must understand the Russian Orthodox Church
traditional (pre-eighteenth century) ideas of salvation and charity to appreciate
how much they still influence Russian attitudes. Charity, in the sense of giving, is
an individual act that must be spontaneous, anonymous, and born out of genuine
love. A good example of this concept is in Leo Tolstoi's short story "Martin
Avdeitch," in which the hero finds true joy and meaning in life (and an encounter
with Jesus Christ) when he engages in a spontaneous act of giving. In Russian
thinking the poor man and the rich man are locked together in an eternal dance of
mutual salvation – the beggar is fed by the rich man and the rich man is saved by
the beggar's prayer. This tradition is evidenced today by the number of people
outside Russian churches asking for alms.

In contrast, the idea that churches undertake charitable activity as *social* acts
that may *improve* society is more rooted in Western European Enlightenment notions and the Reformation than in Russian tradition. Only with the advent of some
European notions such as the Mason movement in eighteenth- and nineteenth-
century Russia did the focus of churches shift somewhat to "good deeds." Otherwise, traditional Orthodox values hold that human society is not perfectible. The
shift from traditional peasant society to the incipient industrialisation that occurred

in Russia during the late nineteenth century reinforced the notion that people were obliged through a civil society sphere (including the church) to assist others through forming *organisations*.

The interplay between the Orthodox church and the state, however, may be far different in the Russian perception than are church-state relations in the minds of North European Protestants or Southern European Catholics. The idea that it is not the role of the church to counter the state in its actions or to supplement a minimal role by a state system, but rather that the state system itself should *evolve* into a system based on Christian principles is one found, for example, in the views of nineteenth-century Russian writers such as Dostoevsky and Tolstoi (Kharkhordin 1998). The ills of the world are ultimately to be transformed not by the secular actions of people, but by the holy actions of the church.

WHAT DOES THE CASE OF RUSSIA OFFER TO OUR UNDERSTANDING AND PROMOTION OF CIVIL SOCIETY?

We have suggested above that the initial sweep of Western optimism about change in Russia might have been premature. Perhaps, however, the key to effective action by foreign Christian NGOs is understanding Russian cultural and faith concepts from an insider's viewpoint and accepting that Russian Orthodoxy presents its own brand of interpretation, separate from those of European Christian traditions. If it is true that the Orthodox notion of Christian faith and civil society is still having an impact on Russian thinking, even against the backdrop of a corrupt state, organised crime, and a reaction against "foreign" religious influences, what might Western Christian NGOs do to improve our understanding of Russia and our ability to engage Russian society constructively?

To begin with, we need to make an important shift in our own attitudes with respect to the links among civil society, faith, and democratic ideals. The re-emergence of *nationalism* in Russia, associated with political ideology and law on religion, has been somewhat of a mystery to Westerners who wish to nudge Russia toward sustainable development, an improved material situation, and political and religious freedoms enjoyed in the West.

But do concepts such as civil society and democracy "translate" similarly into Russian culture? Marcia Weigle has provided some valuable insights for Western Christian supporters of Russia's nascent NGO movement. She notes that the current crisis of values in Russian society may be linked to an aborted process moving Russia into the period of Enlightenment and liberalism that had earlier swept across Europe. Weigle asks whether modernisation and Westernisation go hand-in-hand for today's Russia: "Russian and non-Russian analysts agree that if Russia's post-communist experiment is to be successful, it must develop deep roots in social bases of support and in values orientations that act as the foundation for political and economic institutions and processes" (Weigle 2000, 419).

One reason Russia may be adrift in determining how to cope with civil society is the native perception of a liberalism that seems inherently materialistic, individualistic, and based on reason (rationality) and the perfectibility of human society. Could it be that the remnants of pre-communist liberalism were embedded only in a small percentage of an urban elite in late nineteenth-century Russia, and that this set of values has not filtered down to other groups or moved from the few industrial cities to the countryside?

Weigle suggests that the sixteenth-century Russian notion of *sobornost,* or sense of the collective, born out of early councils (related to words meaning ecumenical councils, the cathedral, and "gathering" in Russian), still reflects an important societal goal. Such deep-rooted sentiment for collective identity is *not* to be confused with the communist-socialist ideology of the collective imposed by Western European Marxist ideology early in the twentieth century. The notion of *sobornost,* rather, argues that goodness may be defined for society in what is the good for all, rather than the Western liberal notion that the individual, when not inhibited by too intrusive a state system, will act in rational self-interest along with other individuals for the good of the civil sphere. Weigle suggests that in Russian consciousness the supremacy of the community over the individual very much formulates the notion of a collective search for salvation. At first glance this argument seems at odds with (1) the corrupt and predatory nature of contemporary Russian society that inhibits the development of civil society and material progress; and (2) the idea expressed earlier that charity is an act of individual character, not group action.

But the presence of a *sobornost* perception does suggest an avenue of support for Christian NGOs more in keeping with indigenous values and the Orthodox church. Although citizens take part in an inherently *un*civil system, they are tied together in a common bond by being both victims of, and participants in, the system. As church groups move increasingly into the Enlightenment notion of charity that crept into Russia in the eighteenth and nineteenth centuries, the motivation of individual humility, spontaneity, and love must be cherished. But Christian NGOs should resist a desire for public recognition or credit for their achievements in social action. The Western-based links of civil society, "market" economics, and democratic values that seem to have pushed Russian democracy into expressions of nationalism and exclusion may also be dangerous bedfellows for Christian NGOs that hope to assist Russia.

Finally, there is an irony in the cross-purpose views of individualism and collective action juxtaposed by Western and Russian ideas of civil society. Westerners see in Russia a society of selfish and corrupt individualism and simplistically assume it has been imposed on the national psyche by 70 years of communism. We cannot understand clearly why Russia is hesitant to move into the world of civilised global society. From the Russian viewpoint, what is imported as civic action, goodness, and progress for society may be embedded in an underlying individual and personalised path to salvation that is anathema to pre-nineteenth-century Orthodox Christian consciousness. Christians immersed in Calvinist or Catholic understandings of civil society may want to ask themselves with humility which tradition truly advances the collective sphere of human interaction for the common good. How far can human civil agency advance the holy work of God? As we look for answers to this question, we might ask not only how Christian NGOs are advancing civil society, but also whether we need to be open to different understandings of civil society. The case of Russia may prove useful in examining this last question.

NOTES

[1] See, for example, various discussions of the work of CoMission and evangelical activity in Russia: Joe Woodward, "Pre-Evangelizing Mother Russia," *Alberta Report* 22/49 (20 November 1995): 34–35; Perry Glanzer, "Teaching Christian Ethics in Russian Public Schools: The Testing of Russia's Church-State Boundaries," *Journal of Church and State* 41/2 (spring 1999): 285–306; Peter Deyneka and Anita Deyneka, "Evangelical Foreign Missionaries in Russia," *International Bulletin of Missionary Research* 22/2 (April 1998): 56–62; Geoff Ellis and Wesley Jones, *Russian Evangelical Awakenings* (Abilene, Tex.: ACU Press, 1996); Beverly Nickles, "Ready to Stand on Their Own?" *Christianity Today* (13 November 2000): 36.

[2] For a discussion of Russian perception of cult activity that influenced the passage of the law, see Marat Shterin and James Richardson, "Effects of the Western Anti-Cult Movement on Development of Laws Concerning Religion in Post-Communist Russia," *Journal of Church and State* 42/2 (spring 2000): 247–72. One example of the interplay between mainstream Christian organisations operating in Russia and the emergence of new sects is the website of the Public Relations Center in Moscow, which is funded by the Reverend Sun Myung-Moon church but proclaims its focus to be nondenominational. The website collects and distributes *all* news stories about persecution of any religious group within the borders of the former USSR.

REFERENCES

CSCE (Committee on Security and Cooperation in Europe). 1998. Status of the Russian Religious Law. 12 February briefing, Washington D.C.

———. 1999. Commission on Security and Cooperation in Europe. Hearing before the United States Congress. 21 July.

Dempsey, Gary T., and Aaron Lukas. 1999. "Is Russia Controlled by Organized Crime?" *USA Today Magazine* 127/2648 (May): 32–34.

Economist, The. 1998. "Russian Love in a Cold Climate." 15 August.

Kharkhordin, Oleg. 1998. "Civil Society and Orthodox Christianity." *Europe-Asia Studies* (September).

Lindenmeyr, Adele. 1990. "The Ethos of Charity in Imperial Russia." *Journal of Social History* 23/4 (Summer): 679–94.

———. 1996. *Poverty Is Not A Vice: Charity, Society, and the State in Imperial Russia.* Princeton, N.J.: Princeton University Press.

Logan, Catriona. 1998. "Civil Society Development in Russia's Regions: A Survey of Local NGOs." Master's thesis, International Studies, University of Washington.

O'Neal, Scott. 2000. "Russian Organized Crime." *FBI Law Enforcement Bulletin* 69/5 (May): 1–5.

Ruffin, Holt, Joan McCarter, and Richard Upjohn. 1996. *The Post-Soviet Handbook: A Guide to Grassroots Organizations and Internet Resources in the Newly Independent States*. Seattle: Center for Civil Society International.

Taylor, Thomas, Alexander Kazakov, and C. Michael Thompson. 1997. "Business Ethics and Civil Society in Russia." *International Studies of Management and Organization* 27/1 (spring).

Tismaneanu, Vladimir, ed. 1995. *Political Culture and Civil Society in Russia and the New States of Eurasia*. Armonk, N.Y.: M. E. Sharpe.

Weaver, Robert T., Ronald P. Mahurin, and Donald J. Isaac. 1998. "Community Building: A Key to Civil Society." In *Civil Society: A Foundation for Sustainable Economic Development*, edited by M. Rose and L. Ewert, 121–32. Mercy Corps International: CCCU Publications. August.

Weigle, Marcia A. 2000. *Russia's Liberal Project: State-Society Relations in the transition from Communism*. University Park, Pa.: The Pennsylvania State University Press.

White, Anne. 1993. "Charity, Self-Help, and Politics in Russia, 1985–91." *Europe-Asia Studies* 45/5.

Other Publications from World Vision

COMPLEX HUMANITARIAN EMERGENCIES
Lessons from Practitioners
Mark Janz & Joann Slead, editors
In this volume, experienced practitioners address the question of how we can respond appropriately to CHEs by linking conceptual and theoretical thinking to practical application at the grassroots level.

288 pp.
2000
Y-007
$24.95

DEVELOPMENT DILEMMAS
NGO Challenges and Ambiguities
Alan Whaites, editor
What role should humanitarian aid workers play in influencing international policymaking? NGOs have a growing obligation to speak up about micro and macro issues that keep the poor poor and contribute to tragic suffering among millions with few legal or social protections.

288 pp.
2002
Y-022
$29.95

GLOBAL CONTEXT FOR ACTION 2001
Bryant L. Myers with Don Brandt and Alan Whaites
Originally intended for an internal audience, this World Vision piece provides a strategic and incisive perspective on the issues facing many NGOs. By honestly presenting one organization's perspective on proactively responding to a shifting global paradigm, Myers, Brandt and Whaites share knowledge on organizational strengths, weaknesses and knowledge.

31 pp.
2001
X-006
$6.95

MASTERS OF THEIR OWN DEVELOPMENT
PRSPs and the Prospects for the Poor
Edited by Alan Whaites
Introduction by Ann Pettifor
"This report by my colleagues from World Vision has outlined many of the problems that have been encountered with PRSPs since 1999. Their analysis is all the more interesting because World Vision has tried to support the idea of PRSPs from the start. It is clear from their research that even those who have stood by PRSPs are finding the experience increasingly frustrating."
—*Ann Pettifor, from the introduction*

137 pp.
2001
X-013
$6.95

GOD OF THE EMPTY-HANDED
Poverty, Power and the Kingdom of God
Jayakumar Christian
The author explores the relationship of poverty to powerlessness by masterfully integrating anthropology, sociology, politics and theology. Avoiding easy answers, he offers a new paradigm that can shape our responses to the poor and provide a workable framework for grassroots practitioners.

224 pp.
1999
Y-003
$21.95

1-800-777-7752 • www.worldvisionresources.com
marcpubs@wvi.org • 626-301-7720 ph • 626-301-7789 fax

World Vision

Other Publications from World Vision

148 pp.
2000
S-022
$14.95

WORLD VISION SECURITY MANUAL
Safety Awareness for Aid Workers
Charles Rogers and Brian Sytsma, editors
Global trends and recent events signal the growing vulnerability of international aid workers and missionaries. Filling the void for safety manuals, this pocket-sized book is designed to help create a complete personnel safety policy.

144 pp.
1999
O-010
$13.95

CALLOUSED HANDS, COURAGEOUS SOULS
Holistic Spirituality of Development and Mission
Robert J. Suderman
Begins to articulate the nature of Christian spirituality in mission and development. Helps us make sure our lives and work are seen as Christian and discernible from other spiritualities in the marketplace of values.

192 pp.
1999
Y-002
$16.95

WORKING WITH THE POOR
New Insights and Learnings from Development Practitioners
Bryant L. Myers, editor
Development practitioners from around the world struggle to overcome the Western assumption that the physical and spiritual realms are separate and distinct from one another in answering the question, *How do Christian practitioners express authentically holistic transformational development?*

112 pp
2002
FO-34
$12.95

GOD'S STEWARDS
The Role of Christians in Creation Care
Don Brandt, editor
Foreword by Eugene H. Peterson
Written as a call to positive action for Christians, it asks that traditional beliefs be re-examined and that the importance of sustainable development be recognized through thorough understanding of how God tells us to care for His creation. It is also a primer for understanding the Christian perspective on this timely issue.

288 pp.
1999
Y-008
$21.95

WALKING WITH THE POOR
Principles and Practices of Transformational Development
Bryant L. Myers
Drawing on theological and biblical resources, secular development theory and work done by Christians among the poor, Myers develops a theoretical framework for transformational development and provides cutting-edge tools for those working alongside the poor.

1-800-777-7752 • www.worldvisionresources.com
marcpubs@wvi.org • 626-301-7720 ph • 626-301-7789 fax